Edited by

GRAHAM LOCK and DAVID MURRAY

THRIVING ON A RIFF
Jazz & Blues Influences
in African American Literature and Film

OXFORD
UNIVERSITY PRESS

2009

OXFORD
UNIVERSITY PRESS

Oxford University Press, Inc., publishes works that further
Oxford University's objective of excellence
in research, scholarship, and education.

Oxford   New York
Auckland   Cape Town   Dar es Salaam   Hong Kong   Karachi
Kuala Lumpur   Madrid   Melbourne   Mexico City   Nairobi
New Delhi   Shanghai   Taipei   Toronto

With offices in
Argentina   Austria   Brazil   Chile   Czech Republic   France   Greece
Guatemala   Hungary   Italy   Japan   Poland   Portugal   Singapore
South Korea   Switzerland   Thailand   Turkey   Ukraine   Vietnam

Library of Congress Cataloging-in-Publication Data
Thriving on a riff : jazz and blues influences in African American literature
and film / edited by Graham Lock and David Murray.
p.   cm.
Includes bibliographical references and index.
ISBN 978-0-19-533702-0; 978-0-19-533709-9 (pbk.)
1. American literature—African American authors—History and criticism.
2. American literature—20th century—History and criticism.
3. Music and literature—History—20th century.
4. Motion pictures and music—United States.
5. African Americans—Intellectual life—20th century.
6. Blues (Music) in literature.   7. Blues (Music) in motion pictures.
8. Jazz in literature.   9. Jazz in motion pictures.   10. Music and literature.
I. Lock, Graham, 1948–   II. Murray, David.
PS153.N5T465 2008
810.9'3578—dc22   2007049329

Recorded audio tracks (marked in text with ⬤)
are available online at http://www.oup.com/us/thrivingonariff.
Access with username Music5 and password Book1745.

1 3 5 7 9 8 6 4 2

Printed in China
on acid-free paper

In memory of Julius Hemphill

Acknowledgments

This book, and its companion volume *The Hearing Eye*, initially took shape as part of a research project, to which we gave the rather grandiose title *Criss Cross: Confluence and Influence in Twentieth-Century African American Music, Visual Art, and Literature*. The project was funded by the Arts and Humanities Research Council of Great Britain and housed in the School of American and Canadian Studies at Nottingham University, and to them we are greatly indebted. Indeed, many of the book's chapters began life as papers presented at the Criss Cross conferences we hosted at Nottingham in 2003 and 2004: thanks are due to our keynote speakers, panelists, chairs, and all other participants for their contributions (which in 2004 included a poetry reading by Michael S. Harper); to the AHRC, the British Academy, and the University of Nottingham Research Committee for additional conference funding; and to everyone who provided administrative, artistic, technical, and other essential assistance, especially David A. Bailey, Sally Britten, Sheila Jones, Ali Norcott, Horace Ové, Shona Powell, Ellen Salway, Byron Wallen, John Walsh, and Jim Waters from Nottingham Castle Museum.

The School of American and Canadian Studies offered both financial backing and a supportive intellectual home for the project and for our subsequent work on the books. We are grateful to our colleagues, notably Ian Brookes and Richard King, for their advice and encouragement, and to the school's ever-efficient office staff for their help over the years. We have also benefited from the aid of other Nottingham colleagues, in particular Mervyn Cooke (Music), as well as the conceptual swingers of the campus Jazz Listening and Reading Group.

We were fortunate to have backing for our project from Anthony Braxton, Bill Dixon, and Nathaniel Mackey; their endorsement in the initial stages proved crucial. We also wish to thank the following people for their valuable input: Jayne Cortez and Michael S. Harper for graciously consenting to interviews and to the inclusion of their poems; Paul Beatty and Nathaniel Mackey for allowing us to quote extracts from their work; our contributors, especially John Gennari for letting us adapt an extract from his *Blowin' Hot and Cool*, and Krin Gabbard and Steven C. Tracy for their generosity with time and expertise; Norm Hirschy, our exemplary editor at Oxford, for his guidance, patience, and unfailing good humor; the anonymous readers whose comments on the original manuscript have, we hope, helped to make this a better book; and Paul Austerlitz, Jayne Cortez, Michael S. Harper, Nathaniel Mackey, Steven C. Tracy, Gillian Atkinson of Document Records, and Lindsay Hill of the Spoken Engine Co. for permitting us to include examples of their recordings on the *Thriving on a Riff* Web site. (There is more about the Web site in the postscript to the introduction.)

Readers will already have noticed the striking painting reproduced on the cover of the paperback edition. We are honored and delighted that Joe Overstreet agreed to let us use this work, *Second Line II*, a canvas from his 1988 *Storyville Series*, which explores the birth of jazz in New Orleans during the early years of the last century. The term *second line* refers, of course, to those people who, drawn by the music, danced along behind the parading bands—an apt visual analogy for the way in which the music has attracted so many American poets, novelists, filmmakers, and visual artists. (There is more about the *Storyville Series* in *The Hearing Eye*, which includes an interview with Joe Overstreet.)

Finally, GL, as chief editor and roving researcher, wishes to add a few personal acknowledgments: "I'd like to say a special thank you to Marilyn Crispell, Bill Dixon, and Kevin Norton for their hospitality when I was in the United States; to Tony Aitman at Black Voices, Leo Feigin at Leo Records, Karen Pitchford at Sanctuary, Brian Priestley, and Paul Wilson at the British Library Sound Archive for providing information and recordings; and—with a Miles Davis trumpet fanfare—to Ian Brookes, Jack Collier, Nicole Dalle, Jeff Eaman, Roz Laurie, Stephen C. Middleton, Chrissie Murray, Dave Murray, Susie Roth, Victor Schonfield, Chris Trent, Diane Wallace, Nick White, and Val Wilmer for all kinds of support through some tough times in recent years, when the kindness of friends and the solace of music have been my lifelines, together with the hope of seeing *Eye* and *Riff* into print. I am deeply grateful to everyone who has made this possible."

Contents

Contributors

Bertram D. Ashe is Associate Professor of English and American Studies at the University of Richmond, in Virginia. He has published *From Within the Frame: Storytelling in African-American Fiction* (Routledge), as well as essays on black hair, jazz, and post-soul black culture in the anthology *Signifyin(g), Sanctifyin' and Slam Dunking*, ed. Gena Dagel Capone (University of Massachusetts Press) and the journals *Race, Gender and Class*, *Columbia*, and *African American Review*. He is at work on a book on post-soul black literature, as well as a memoir titled *Twisted: The Dreadlock Chronicles*.

Ian Brookes is a Special Lecturer in American Culture in the School of American and Canadian Studies at the University of Nottingham. While his research interests include musical performance in American film, he is currently working on a study of the World War II veteran in post-war American film narratives.

David Butler lectures in Screen Studies at the University of Manchester. He is the author of *Jazz Noir: Listening to Music from "Phantom Lady" to "The Last Seduction"* (Praeger) and has ongoing research interests in the use of music and portrayal of the fantastic in film and television. Current and recent projects include *The Cairn*, a speech and sound collaboration with the musician-composer John Surman, and a study of fantasy film, to be published by Wallflower Press.

Mervyn Cooke is Professor of Music at the University of Nottingham. He edited (with David Horn) *The Cambridge Companion to Jazz* and has authored two illustrated histories of jazz for Thames and Hudson/The Abbeville Press; he also contributed a chapter on modern jazz to *The Cambridge History of Twentieth-Century Music*. His other research interests are the music of Benjamin Britten, on which he has published several books, and film music; his *History of Film*

Music has recently been published by Cambridge University Press and he is currently editing a Hollywood film-music reader for Oxford University Press.

Krin Gabbard is Professor of Comparative Literary and Cultural Studies at the State University of New York at Stony Brook. He is the author of *Hotter Than That: The Trumpet, Jazz, and American Culture* (Faber and Faber); *Black Magic: White Hollywood and African American Culture* (Rutgers University Press) and *Jammin' at the Margins: Jazz and the American Cinema* (University of Chicago Press); the co-author of *Psychiatry and the Cinema* (American Psychiatric Press); and the editor of *Jazz among the Discourses* and *Representing Jazz* (both Duke University Press).

John Gennari is Associate Professor of English and Director of the U.S. Ethnic Studies Program at the University of Vermont. He is the author of *Blowin' Hot and Cool: Jazz and Its Critics* (University of Chicago Press), winner of the 2007 John G. Cawelti Award for the Best Book in American Cultural Studies, and winner of a 2007 ASCAP-Deems Taylor Award for excellence in music criticism. He has authored many articles on jazz and African American culture, Italian American cultural studies, visual culture, film, and sports.

Nick Heffernan teaches American Studies at University College Northampton. He is the author of *Capital, Class and Technology in Contemporary American Culture: Projecting Post-Fordism* (Pluto Press), of articles on American literature, popular culture, and critical theory, and of forthcoming monographs on crime cinema and Don DeLillo.

Michael Jarrett is Professor of English at Penn State University, York Campus. He is the author of *Drifting on a Read: Jazz as a Model for Writing* (SUNY Press) and *Sound Tracks: A Musical ABC* (Temple University Press).

Graham Lock is a freelance writer and editor, with special interests in music and African American culture. From 2001 to 2004 he was a Senior Research Fellow in the School of American and Canadian Studies at Nottingham University, working on the Criss Cross project. His books include *Blutopia: Visions of the Future and Revisions of the Past in the Work of Sun Ra, Duke Ellington, and Anthony Braxton* (Duke University Press), *Chasing the Vibration: Meetings with Creative Musicians* (Stride), and *Forces in Motion: Anthony Braxton and the Meta-reality* *of Creative Music* (Quartet). He is the author of numerous articles and liner notes and is co-editor, with David Murray, of *The Hearing Eye: Jazz & Blues Influences in African American Visual Art* (Oxford University Press).

David Murray is Professor of American Studies at the University of Nottingham and was director of the Criss Cross research project. He has published widely on American Indians, including *Indian Giving: Economies of Power in Early Indian-White Exchanges* (University of Massachusetts Press) and *Forked Tongues: Speech, Writing and Representation in North American Indian Texts* (Indiana University Press), as well as on American poetry and cultural studies. His latest book is *Matter, Magic, and Spirit: Representing Indian and African American Belief* (University of Pennsylvania Press). He is also co-editor, with Graham Lock, of *The Hearing Eye: Jazz & Blues Influences in African American Visual Art* (Oxford University Press).

Steven C. Tracy is Professor of Afro-American Studies at the University of Massachusetts at Amherst. He is author of *Langston Hughes and the Blues* (University of Illinois Press), *Going to Cincinnati: A History of the Blues in the Queen City* (University of Illinois Press), and *A Brush with the Blues: 26 Portraits* (Rep House LLC); editor of *Write Me a Few of Your Lines: A Blues Reader* (University of Massachusetts Press), *A Historical Guide to Langston Hughes* and *A Historical Guide to Ralph Ellison* (both Oxford University Press); and general co-editor of *The Collected Works of Langston Hughes* (University of Missouri Press). He has also published numerous articles and liner notes dealing with American and African American literature and culture. His latest book, as co-editor with John Edgar Tidwell, is *After Winter: Selected Writings on the Art and Life of Sterling Brown*, to be published by Oxford University Press. A blues singer and harmonica player, he has recorded with his own band, Steve Tracy and the Crawling Kingsnakes, as well as with Pigmeat Jarrett, Big Joe Duskin, Albert Washington, and the Cincinnati Symphony Orchestra.

Corin Willis is a Lecturer in Screen Studies at Liverpool John Moores University. He has published a chapter entitled "Meaning and Value in *The Jazz Singer* (1927)" in *Style and Meaning: Studies in the Close Analysis of Film*, ed. Doug Pye and John Gibbs (Manchester University Press). He is currently working on a book on blackface and the stereotyping of African Americans in early sound film.

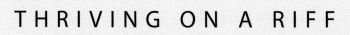

THRIVING ON A RIFF

Introduction:
You've Got to Be Jazzistic

Thriving on a Riff is a contribution to the growing body of work on jazz, blues, and their multiple influences in other forms of African American and American culture. The provisional term for this relatively new area of discourse is jazz studies, although there may be a case for Sun Ra's tongue-in-cheek neologism "jazzisticology," which (considered etymologically) appears to mean the study of the "jazzistic," in other words, that which aspires, or pertains, to being like, about, or in the style of, jazz.[1] While jazzisticology seems unlikely to catch on, it does have the advantage of marking a distinction between the study of jazz itself (in a nuts-and-bolts musicological sense) and the study of things that are jazz related. *Thriving on a Riff* belongs to the latter category and sharpens its focus further to examine two of the many cultural forms affected by African American music: literature and film.

While that music has become hugely popular and influential far beyond the communities that produced it, its role within African American culture has been especially profound. Numerous black writers have confirmed this: from James Baldwin's bald assertion, "It is only in his music . . . that the Negro in America has been able to tell his story," to Bob Kaufman's more poetic coinage:

> Dirt of a world covers me
> My secret heart
> Beating to unheard jazz.[2]

This recognition of the music's crucial importance, both to African American culture and beyond, can be traced back to W. E. B. Du Bois, who referred in *The Souls of Black Folk* to the gifts that Africans had brought to America, notably "a gift of story and song—soft, stirring melody in an ill-harmonized and unmelodious land."[3] That gift was tempered by the tribulations of slavery and segregation, which served to channel African Americans' creative energies toward music, if only because they were long denied access to most other forms of cultural expression. While Du Bois believed the spirituals represented the artistic apotheosis of that gift, it was later black secular musics such as ragtime, blues, and jazz that transformed American culture—and perhaps less through "soft melody" than by their rhythmic vitality, rooted in the everyday activities of work and dance and in sync with the developing industrial technologies of railroad and automobile. To find your way in America, Fats Waller advised, just use rhythm as your compass.[4]

It was in the Harlem Renaissance of the 1920s and '30s that jazz and blues began to make a major impact in African American literature. The musics themselves, as well as their wider cultural influences, were largely deplored by senior figures like Du Bois, who regarded them as, at best, raw material that needed to be "elevated" into art forms more akin to European classical models, as had happened with the spirituals.[5] However, blues records were selling in the tens of thousands to black audiences, and the younger generation of writers were not only enthusiasts of the music but willing to argue for its cultural significance too. The poet Langston Hughes, disdaining black middle-class assimilation to European notions of artistic refinement, declared: "Let the blare of Negro jazz bands and the bellowing voice of Bessie Smith singing the Blues penetrate the closed ears of the colored neo-intellectuals until they listen and perhaps understand."[6] And Sterling Brown, in his poem "Strong Men," not only made clear black music's role as a survival tool, a means by which African Americans were able to resist successive phases of American racial oppression, he also stressed that the music was a continuum, with spirituals, work songs, and blues each serving the same social function and grounded in the same vernacular: "Walk togedder, chillen / Dontcha git weary . . . Ain't no hammah in dis lan' / Strikes lak mine, bebby / Strikes lak mine."[7] In resisting the "elevating" tendencies of Du Bois, Brown was reaffirming the integrity of a black music tradition that generational and class conflict had threatened to break in two.[8] And, of course, by quoting lines from the songs in his poem, Brown was making claims too for the lyrics' formal status as poetry, as Hughes had also done in many of his 1920s poems.[9]

Brown and Hughes were among the first poets to incorporate blues form, techniques, and diction (plus what Brown called "blues feeling") into their work, thereby collapsing distinctions between so-called high and low culture that ultimately derived from Europe. In so doing, their early collections—Hughes's

The Weary Blues (1926) and *Fine Clothes to the Jew* (1927), Brown's *Southern Road* (1932)—initiated a fertile line of cross-genre interplay in African American culture. Later, poets engaged with jazz and blues as subject matter and formal constituent (Wanda Coleman, Frank Marshall Davis, Henry Dumas, Cornelius Eady, Robert Hayden, David Henderson, Ted Joans, Stephen Jonas, Bob Kaufman, Harryette Mullen, Myron O'Higgins, Raymond Patterson, Sterling Plumpp, Melvin Tolson, Sherley Anne Williams, Al Young, Kevin Young); performed their work with musicians (Amiri Baraka, Nikki Giovanni, Michael S. Harper, Langston Hughes, Yusef Komunyakaa, K. Curtis Lyle, Nathaniel Mackey, Amus Mor, Eugene Redmond, Ishmael Reed); and even, in a few cases (Jayne Cortez, Gil Scott-Heron), fronted their own bands.[10]

It is possible to trace a similar lineage in African American fiction, beginning perhaps with the novels and stories of Rudolf Fisher, Langston Hughes, and James Weldon Johnson, moving through post-war novels such as Ann Petry's *The Street*, Herbert Simmons's *Man Walking on Eggshells*, and John A. Williams's *Night Song,* and continuing through a whole gamut of modern fiction by authors such as Amiri Baraka, Paul Beatty, Xam Wilson Cartiér, Leon Forrest, Gayl Jones, Nathaniel Mackey, Clarence Major, Paule Marshall, Albert Murray, J. J. Phillips, Ntozake Shange, and John Edgar Wideman, to name only a sample dozen. This line would also take in many of the most highly acclaimed names in the black fiction canon—James Baldwin, Ralph Ellison, Zora Neale Hurston, Toni Morrison, Ishmael Reed, Alice Walker—all of whose work has been profoundly shaped by their relationship with black music.

Conversely, there are many musicians who have set, or have been inspired by, texts by black authors: Marion Brown and Andrew Hill have composed pieces in response to Jean Toomer's *Cane*; Bill Dixon has dedicated pieces to Henry Dumas, Larry Neal, Allen Polite, and N. H. Pritchard; Taj Mahal has set lyrics by Langston Hughes; Ronald Shannon Jackson has performed poems by Sterling Brown; Max Roach has adapted texts by Bruce Wright. And many musicians are themselves writers and poets, who have set or performed their own texts to music: examples include Duke Ellington, Joseph Jarman, Oliver Lake, George E. Lewis, Charles Mingus, Archie Shepp, Sun Ra, and Cecil Taylor.[11]

Given this wealth of material, perhaps it is not surprising that interest in the criss-crossings of music and literature (and especially the jazz-poetry strand) both preceded the rise of jazz studies and has since provided its major area of focus.[12] It is literary scholars, too, who have produced the most influential theoretical writing to date on the music's presence in African American culture.

Houston A. Baker Jr.'s notions of a blues matrix and of the black discursive strategies he terms "mastery of form" and "deformation of mastery," Henry Louis Gates Jr.'s concept of "Signifyin(g)," and James A. Snead's focus on the uses of repetition have greatly enhanced our understanding of African American cultural dynamics, and all have invoked black music to exemplify and validate their theories.[13]

Such work has helped to promote a more inclusive embrace of African American vernacular forms that had previously received scant attention from the academy. However, critics have also pointed to the dangers inherent in such uses of music in relation to theories that are chiefly grounded in literary texts and the precepts of literary criticism. Peter Townsend, for example, cites Gates's apparent misunderstanding and subsequent misuse of the jazz term *riff*, an error that, he says, has now been repeated so often by other literary scholars that its uses in such commentary "have moved steadily away from its use in jazz performance." The end result of this slippage, he argues, is to render these literary comparisons to jazz utterly meaningless: "'jazz' here is not jazz as a musical culture, but an inadvertent reconstruction of the term in literary-critical discourse."[14] Whether the guilty party here was Gates or his (mis)interpreters,[15] Townsend's general point is surely valid: the academy's long-standing lack of interest in jazz and blues created a hermeneutical vacuum, into which all sorts of scholars are now rushing, some of whom appear to have very little appreciation of the music, its history, or its own canonical (albeit largely journalistic) literature. Indeed, Townsend further criticizes the lack of references to jazz texts and jazz recordings in much literary-critical writing that discusses jazz, and he deplores the tendency of literary theorists to treat jazz as if it were "text."[16] Similar points are made by Charles O. Hartman and by Angela Davis, the latter noting that Baker, in his *Modernism and the Harlem Renaissance*, "tends to relegate music to the status of literary material . . . [and] restricts the Renaissance to the realm of literature."[17] She remarks, too, on the fact that, although Baker has a photograph of Ma Rainey on the cover of his book, he neglects to mention any of her recordings.[18] Still, while such criticisms offer a salutary reminder of the old folk adage "you got to *go* there to *know* there," some valuable theoretical work on black music and black culture has resulted, as scholars have duly repeated, deformed, and Signified on the ideas proposed by Baker, Gates, and Snead.[19]

One area in which this has been happening is the relatively new field of research into the music's relationship to cinema, both black and white. Examples would be Krin Gabbard's "Signifyin(g) the Phallus: Representations of the Jazz Trumpet," Arthur Knight's "'Aping' Hollywood: Deformation and Mastery in *The Duke Is Tops* and *Swing!*," and Richard Dyer's "Is *Car Wash* a Musical?" which uses Snead's work on repetition to propose formal and philosophical distinctions between the black musical and the white musical.[20] Nevertheless, the academic discourse on black music and cinema is not yet as extensive as that on black music and literature.[21] One reason may be that the former relationship has been far more problematic, and on many levels—from the almost total white control of the U.S. film industry since its inception to the fact that, in Krin Gabbard's words, "Most jazz films aren't really about jazz."[22] These problems have perhaps tended to obscure the fact that there have been innumerable instances of music/film cross-genre interactions that certainly invite further consideration. They include the uses of black music by black filmmakers from Oscar Micheaux to Spike Lee; the musics composed or improvised for films by musicians as diverse as Ornette Coleman, Miles Davis, Quincy Jones, and William Grant Still; the (mis)representations of black life and black music in feature films (from *Hearts in Dixie* to *Mo' Better Blues*) and, especially, in feature films that employ musicians in acting roles: examples of the latter include *Black and Tan*, with Duke Ellington; *Cabin in the Sky*, with Louis Armstrong, Duke Ellington, Lena Horne, and Ethel Waters; *Hallelujah!* with Victoria Spivey; *New Orleans*, with Louis Armstrong and Billie Holiday; *'Round Midnight*, with Dexter Gordon; the 1929 *St. Louis Blues*, with Bessie Smith; *Space Is the Place*, with Sun Ra; and *Symphony in Black*, with Duke Ellington and Billie Holiday. Then there are bio-pics (*Bird*, *Lady Sings the Blues*, the 1958 *St. Louis Blues*, with Nat "King" Cole as W. C. Handy); bio-docs (*The Long Night of Lady Day*, *Mingus*, *Ornette: Made in America*); documentaries of events, performances, places, tours (*And This Is Free*, *A Great Day in Harlem*, *Imagine the Sound*, *Jammin' the Blues*, *Jazz on a Summer's Day*, *Last of the Blue Devils*, *Thelonious Monk: Straight, No Chaser*); dozens of cartoons, jukebox "soundies," and promotional shorts; and films that feature either blackface, like *The Jazz Singer*, its sound equivalent (i.e., white music masquerading as black), like *Porgy and Bess*, or both, like *Show Boat*.[23]

The white control of the film industry noted above resulted, of course, in a scarcity of black directors and producers and, perhaps more perniciously, frequent recourse to racial stereotyping in the depiction of black people. Film appearances and performances by African American musicians were often mediated—and distorted—not only by the formal constraints of cinema but also by the expectations and prejudices of white audiences.[24] These audiences, however, might, in turn, find their aesthetic tastes (and racial prejudices) subtly altered by their exposure to the music. This cross-race, cross-genre interplay is an important component of *Thriving on a Riff*. As our subtitle indicates, the book's primary focus is on African American culture; but it is not exclusively so, because we also wished to recognize the music's impact on white filmmakers and white writers. We should make clear, too, that in referring to jazz and blues as black musics, we do not mean to fence them off as racially specific forms, only to acknowledge the historical circumstances from which they emerged and the predominant meanings they accrued as they developed. Finally, our focus on jazz and blues in particular reflects our belief that they were the prevailing musical influences through much of the twentieth century, which is not to deny the importance of, say, funk or gospel, or the current global popularity of rap and hip-hop (or the fact that such genre differentiations are sometimes arbitrary and rarely clear-cut).

The relationship between music and (racial) identity is a theme that runs throughout this collection, linking text and film alike, and our opening two chapters address its complexities with particular reference to performative contexts such as blackface and passing. In placing James Weldon Johnson's *The Autobiography of an Ex-Colored Man* (1912) beside J. J. Phillips's *Mojo Hand* (1966), Nick Heffernan is able to compare two novels, written half a century apart, each of which features an African American protagonist who initially believes himself or herself to be white and then attempts to reconstruct (in Heffernan's words) a "sense of self and racial identity through a prolonged encounter with the aesthetic, cultural, and social meanings of black music." Popular music in the first decade of the twentieth century, when Johnson was working as a songwriter in ragtime and vaudeville, was dominated by the "coon" song, with its vicious racial caricatures; but by the 1920s, and the rise of the New Negro, Johnson must have believed such minstrel imagery had been banished forever. However, as Corin Willis shows in his essay on 1930s Hollywood, the new technologies of cinema gave a further lease on life to the old stereotypes. Willis argues that it was through the redeployment of these stereotypes, particularly in the phenomenon he calls co-presence ("where African American actors and performers were juxtaposed with whites in blackface"), that Hollywood was able to curtail and contain the expressive power of black music.

Following the "Paging the Devil" sequence of chapters on jazz, blues, and literature, to which we will return in a moment, our second special pairing of chapters, which we have dubbed "Until the Real Thing," again takes up the theme of music and identity, this time in the context of autobiographical, biographical, and fictional representations—textual and cinematic—of two of the music's greatest figures: Charlie Parker and Miles Davis. John Gennari's chapter looks at Parker's image as doomed hipster genius and considers the part played in creating this image by Ross Russell, Parker's one-time producer and biographer, and the author of a pulp fiction jazz novel, *The Sound*. Gennari examines how Russell's relationship with Parker not only impinged on his fictional depictions of the jazz world but may have mediated later white portrayals of Parker. If Bird himself had no control over these versions of his life, the same cannot be said of Miles Davis, subject of the following chapter, in which Krin Gabbard explores Miles in autobiographical mode, finding an unexpected link between Davis and Paul Whiteman in their on-screen personas, and traces the difficulties of pinning down what could pass as an authentic identity or even a definitive Miles performance.

Our two longer sequences of chapters, one on jazz, blues, and literature, the other on jazz, blues, and film, offer a guide to the various ways in which music can be present in a range of texts and films. In his close reading of Sterling Brown's 1931 "Strange Legacies," for example, Steven C. Tracy details the poet's uses of black folklore and blues ballad form, specifically accounts of the steel-drivin' John Henry, as he celebrates the continuum of black heroism. The black oral tradition, reshaping itself to greet the twenty-first century, is also examined by Paul Beatty, whose poetry and two novels (*The White Boy Shuffle* and *Tuff*) Bertram Ashe locates in a "post-soul aesthetic" devised by a new generation of writers who have embraced the contradictions of growing up in a "multi-racial mix of cultures." The closing chapter in our literature set can be seen as the latest variation on the classic theme of "body and soul": David Murray teases out Nathaniel Mackey's playful, reflexive interrogations of the notion that black music is a transcendent spiritual force, and he contrasts Mackey's post-structuralist perspective with the more essentialist stance taken by Amiri Baraka.

For a different, frontline, perspective on musical influence in literature, we have also included interviews with two eminent poets, conducted for *Thriving on a Riff* by Graham Lock. The first, with Michael S. Harper, we have placed after Steven Tracy's chapter on Sterling Brown because Harper, who edited Brown's *Collected Poems* and knew him well, begins by talking about Brown's love of African American vernacular culture. He then goes on to discuss his own work's indebtedness to music, notably that of John Coltrane, who continues to be a major inspiration. The second interview is with Jayne Cortez, one of the few poets to lead her own jazz and blues band. She reveals some of the practical and aesthetic issues related to performing with musicians, and talks, too, about her desire to restore the blues to its rightful place in black history, wrenching it back from those who not only steal its forms but even appropriate the voices in which it is sung.

While Hollywood's uses of black music have nearly always been limited and limiting, "Second Balcony Jump," our set of essays on jazz, blues, and film, shows that careful analysis can uncover subtle ways in which individual artists were able to push against the constraints. So Ian Brookes's study of Howard Hawks's *To Have and Have Not* explores how the musical performances in the film, together with the relationships between the key characters, enact surprising forms of democracy and integration that buck the established conventions. Similarly, in their essays on film scoring, David Butler and Mervyn Cooke discuss the confines of Hollywood's racially inflected musical vocabulary, in which jazz was allowed only a tiny and demeaning range of associations. Butler goes on to show how a creative figure such as John Lewis was, on one occasion at least, able to slip these yokes and produce a soundtrack that anticipated more innovative ways of using music in film; Cooke, in looking at scores by Duke Ellington and Elmer Bernstein, takes issue with critics who have dismissed 1950s symphonic jazz and argues that such "crossover" music played a vital, modernizing role in the evolution of the Hollywood score.

The book closes on a new point of departure, a glimpse of how jazzisticology may open up fresh perspectives on artistic criss-cross. Michael Jarrett takes the reader on a train ride through black music history and questions the very nature of influence in a post-literary, post-logic age of electronic culture. If the railroad has been a recurring riff, a resonance, in black music—very audibly so in some of the tracks that Jarrett cites—then the music itself has been a riff, a resource, on which African American and American culture has thrived. Hence our borrowing of Charlie Parker's title. His "Thriving on a Riff" was recorded in 1945 and its out chorus later became another composition, called "Anthropology."[25] Our *Thriving on a Riff* is more jazzisticological than anthropological, although we would certainly concur with Bird's statement, "They teach you there's a boundary line to music. But, man, there's no boundary line to art."[26] We have tried in this collection to elucidate some of the jazz and blues criss-crossings of the other arts, their infiltrations and inspirations, with reference to just a small selection of poetry, fiction, and films. Our hope is that these essays and interviews will enhance appreciation of the texts and films discussed herein and send the reader back to the music with renewed enthusiasm and fresh insight. As Bird and Sun Ra might have agreed, such jazzistic pleasures are a riff on which we all can thrive.

A POSTSCRIPT ON THE *THRIVING ON A RIFF* WEB SITE

One advantage of living in the "post-literary age . . . of electronic culture" noted above is that Oxford University Press has set up the *Thriving on a Riff* Web site, where readers can hear a series of musical and literary performances that will, we hope, enhance their use of the book and provide some enjoyable online listening. (Many of the tracks are downloadable, too.) Details of these recordings—plus an exclusive video—can be found at the end of the relevant chapters, where they are signaled by the Oxford University Press Web site logo. The Web site is password protected, and a password, together with a username, is printed on the copyright page.

While financial, temporal, and copyright constraints have, on occasion, proved insurmountable (no film excerpts, alas), we are absolutely delighted with the material that is available on the Web site and would like to express our gratitude, both to Oxford University Press and to the poets, musicians, and rights holders concerned, for making the virtual a reality.

NOTES

1. It is not clear what meaning Sun Ra ascribed to the word—it is the title of a brief instrumental track on his 1978 LP *The Sound Mirror*—but it is tempting to read into it an appreciative nod to James P. Johnson's sentiment "You've Got to Be Modernistic," together with a passing tilt at the jargonizing tendencies of academic theory. Sun Ra, *The Sound Mirror* (LP; Saturn 19782, 1978). We should note that on our copy of the LP the word is (mis)spelt "jazzisticolgy," but in the authoritative Campbell and Trent Sun Ra discography the spelling is "jazzisticology." Robert L. Campbell and Christopher Trent, *The Earthly Recordings of Sun Ra*, 2nd ed. (Redwood, NY: Cadence Jazz, n.d.), 247, 826.

2. James Baldwin, "Many Thousands Gone," *Notes of a Native Son* (1964; reprint, London: Corgi, 1970), 18; Bob Kaufman, "Tequila Jazz," *Cranial Guitar: Selected Poems by Bob Kaufman*, ed. Gerald Nicosia (Minneapolis: Coffee House Press, 1996), 61.

3. W. E. B. Du Bois, "Of the Sorrow Songs," *The Souls of Black Folk* (1903; reprint, New York: Bantam, 1989), 186.

4. See Fats Waller and Andy Razaf, "Christopher Columbus" (1936). The song is quoted by Joel Dinerstein in his persuasive account of how and why the rhythms of jazz and blues became so influential. See Joel Dinerstein, *Swinging the Machine: Modernity, Technology, and African American Culture between the World Wars* (Amherst: University of Massachusetts Press, 2003).

5. While this belief may have been partly a reaction to the white commodification of jazz and blues as "primitive" and "exotic," a bias toward European cultural values certainly prevented many commentators at the time—and since—from recognizing the significance and the quality of music by Armstrong, Bechet, Ellington, Bessie Smith, and others. See, too, Zora Neale Hurston's comment that the new "glee club" spirituals, whatever their qualities, were "not *Negro* song." Hurston, "Spirituals and Neo-Spirituals," in *Negro: An Anthology*, ed. Nancy Cunard, abridged ed. (New York: Continuum, 2002), 223–25.

6. Langston Hughes, "The Negro Artist and the Racial Mountain" (1926), reprinted in *Keeping Time: Readings in Jazz History*, ed. Robert Walser (New York: Oxford University Press, 1999), 57.

7. Sterling A. Brown, "Strong Men," *The Collected Poems of Sterling A. Brown*, ed. Michael S. Harper (1980; reprint, Evanston, IL: TriQuarterly Books/ Northwestern University Press, 1996), 56–57.

8. Brown was no less critical of the "Tin Pan Alley Manipulators" of black music: see his "Real Mammy Song," in ibid., 171.

9. For more on Brown and music, see Joanne V. Gabbin, *Sterling Brown: Building the Black Aesthetic Tradition* (1985; reprint, Charlottesville: University Press of Virginia, 1994), esp. chapters 5 and 6, and Mark A. Sanders, *Afro-Modernist Aesthetics and the Poetry of Sterling A. Brown* (Athens: University of Georgia Press, 1999), esp. chapters 2 and 3; for more on Hughes and music, see Steven C. Tracy, *Langston Hughes and the Blues* (Urbana: University of Illinois Press, 2001), esp. chapter 3.

10. The names in parentheses are examples, not an exhaustive list. Likewise the following selection of poets and musicians on disc: Amiri Baraka, with David Murray and Steve McCall, *New Music–New Poetry* (LP; India Navigation 1048, 1981); Nikki Giovanni, *The Way I Feel* (Collectables COL 6507, 1995); Michael S. Harper and Paul Austerlitz, *Double Take* (Innova 604, 2004) and *Our Book on Trane: The Yaddo Sessions* (Yaddo 1, 2004); Langston Hughes, with Charles Mingus and Leonard Feather, *The Weary Blues* (1958; Verve 841 660-2, 1990); Yosef Komunyakaa and John Tchicai, *Love Notes from the Madhouse* (8th Harmonic Breakdown 80001, 1988); K. Curtis Lyle with Julius Hemphill, *The Collected Poem for Blind Lemon Jefferson* (1971; Ikef 05, 2002); Nathaniel Mackey, *Strick: Song of the Andoumboulou*

16–25 (Spoken Engine, 1995); Amus Mor, as David Moore, on Muhal Richard Abrams, *Levels and Degrees of Light* (1968; Delmark DD-413, 1991); Eugene Redmond, *"Blood Links and Sacred Places"* (1973; Ikef 01, 2001); Ishmael Reed and Conjure, *Bad Mouth* (American Clavé AMCL 1052/53, 2005), *Conjure: Cab Calloway Stands in for the Moon* (1988; American Clavé AMCL 1015, 1995), and *Conjure: Music for the Texts of Ishmael Reed* (1984; American Clavé AMCL 1006, 1995); Jayne Cortez and the Firespitters, *Borders of Disorderly Time* (Bola Press BLP 2003, 2003), *Cheerful & Optimistic* (Bola Press BP9401, 1994) and *Taking the Blues Back Home* (Harmolodic/Verve 531 918–2, 1996); and Gil Scott-Heron, *The Revolution Will Not Be Televised* (1970–74; RCA ND 86994, 1989). This may also be the place to mention Josh White's 1941 *Southern Exposure: An Album of Jim Crow Blues*, comprising six blues protest lyrics written specifically for him by poet Waring Cuney and initially released with notes by Richard Wright. These tracks are now available (but minus Wright's notes) on Josh White, *Complete Recorded Works 1940–1941 in Chronological Order, Volume 4, 4 June 1940–1941* (Document Records DOCD 5405, 1995).

11. See, for example, Marion Brown, "Karintha," *Geechee Recollections* (LP; Impulse! AS-9252, 1973); Andrew Hill, "Dusk," *Dusk* (Palmetto PM2057, 2000); Bill Dixon, "Essay di Larry Neal," "Ritratti di Allen Polite," "Quadro di Henry Dumas," and "Quadro di N. H. Pritchard," all on *Papyrus—Volume 1* (Soul Note 121308–1, 1999); Taj Mahal, *Mule Bone* (Gramavision GV 79 432–2, 1991); Ronald Shannon Jackson, "Puttin' on Dog" and "Slim in Atlanta," *Puttin' on Dog* (Knitting Factory KCR 3033, 1999); and Max Roach, "It's Christmas Again" and "Christina," *It's Christmas Again* (Soul Note 121153–2, 1994). The George E. Lewis disc features poets Jerome Rothenberg and Quincy Troupe as well as texts by Lewis himself and his father: see George E. Lewis, *Changing with the Times* (New World Records 80434–2, 1993). Other poetry discs by musicians include Oliver Lake, *Matador of 1st & 1st* (Passin' Thru 40709, 1996) and Cecil Taylor, *Chinampas* (Leo CD LR 153, 1991). For more on many of the poets and musicians noted above (and others not listed here) see Aldon Lynn Nielsen, *Black Chant: Languages of African American Postmodernism* (Cambridge: Cambridge University Press, 1997), esp. chapters 4 and 5. For more specifically on Sun Ra, see also Brent Edwards, "The Race for Space: Sun Ra's Poetry," *Hambone 14* (Fall 1998): 177–200; and for more on Cecil Taylor, see also Chris Funkhouser, "Being Matter Ignited: An Interview with Cecil Taylor," *Hambone 12* (Fall 1995): 17–39, and Fred Moten, *In the Break: The Aesthetics of the Black Radical Tradition* (Minneapolis: University of Minnesota Press, 2003), 41–63.

12. Some recent examples include T. J. Anderson III, *Notes to Make the Sounds Come Right: Four Innovators of Jazz Poetry* (Fayetteville: University of Arkansas Press, 2004); Michael Borshuk, *Swinging the Vernacular: Jazz and African American Modernist Literature* (New York: Routledge, 2006); Tony Bolden, *Afro Blue: Improvisations in African American Poetry and Culture* (Urbana: University of Illinois Press, 2004); Nicholas M. Evans, *Writing Jazz: Race, Nationalism, and Modern Culture in the 1920s* (New

York: Garland, 2000); Jürgen E. Grandt, *Kinds of Blue: The Jazz Aesthetic in African American Narrative* (Columbus: Ohio State University Press, 2004); Adam Gussow, *Seems Like Murder Here: Southern Violence and the Blues Tradition* (Chicago: University of Chicago Press, 2002); Michael Jarrett, *Drifting on a Read: Jazz as a Model for Writing* (Albany: State University of New York Press, 1999); Wilfred Raussert, *Negotiating Temporal Difference: Blues, Jazz and Narrativity in African American Culture* (Heidelberg: Universitätsverlag C. Winter, 2000); David Yaffe, *Fascinating Rhythm: Reading Jazz in American Writing* (Princeton, NJ: Princeton University Press, 2006). For details of many earlier publications, see Richard N. Albert, *An Annotated Bibliography of Jazz Fiction and Jazz Fiction Criticism* (Westport, CT: Greenwood, 1996), and Brent Hayes Edwards and John F. Szwed, "A Bibliography of Jazz Poetry Criticism," *Callaloo* 25.1 (2002): 338–46. There have also been a number of influential anthologies, from *Understanding the New Black Poetry: Black Speech and Black Music as Poetic References*, ed. Stephen Henderson (New York: Morrow Quill, 1973) to *Moment's Notice: Jazz in Poetry and Prose*, ed. Art Lange and Nathaniel Mackey (Minneapolis: Coffee House Press, 1993), as well as several valuable jazz- and poetry-related journals such as *Brilliant Corners*, *Hambone*, and *Shuffle Boil*.

13. See Houston A. Baker Jr., *Blues, Ideology, and Afro-American Literature: A Vernacular Theory* (Chicago: University of Chicago Press, 1984) and *Modernism and the Harlem Renaissance* (Chicago: University of Chicago Press, 1987); Henry Louis Gates Jr., *The Signifying Monkey: A Theory of African-American Literary Criticism* (New York: Oxford University Press, 1988); James A. Snead, "Repetition as a Figure of Black Culture," in *Black Literature and Literary Theory*, ed. Henry Louis Gates Jr. (New York: Routledge, 1990), 59–79.

14. Peter Townsend, *Jazz in American Culture* (Edinburgh: University of Edinburgh Press, 2000), 144–45. *Improvisation* is another term that is often misunderstood and misrepresented, both by literary critics and by jazz-inspired poets and novelists themselves. Both Townsend and Jon Panish discuss this problem in relation to Kerouac and the beats, whose appropriation of jazz as an icon of freedom, spontaneity, and individual rebellion led to a romanticization of the jazzman as existential hipster. What this emphasis on individual expression misses is both the sense of community inherent in most jazz performance and an awareness of improvisation as relating to (and signifying on) a tradition. In contrast, as Panish notes, African American writers were more likely to see improvisation "not only [as] a process of creation that emphasizes freedom and spontaneity, but also [as] a culturally specific concept that is ineluctably connected to historical and contemporary social contexts." Jon Panish, *The Color of Jazz: Race and Representation in Postwar American Culture* (Jackson: University Press of Mississippi, 1997), 123.

15. We should perhaps make clear that our own choice of title is not related to this dispute. It is an entirely coincidental reference to Charlie Parker (as we explain below), and not an attempt at Signifyin(g) on Gates, Townsend, or anyone else. Nor do we wish to be drawn into defining *riff* (or *swing* or *jazz*)

ourselves; we suspect that, in the end, it is largely down to a matter of personal listening preferences.

16. Townsend, *Jazz in American Culture*, 178–79.

17. Charles O. Hartman, *Jazz Text: Voice and Improvisation in Poetry, Jazz, and Song* (Princeton, NJ: Princeton University Press, 1991), esp. chapter 3, in which he explores the difficulty of deciding what precisely constitutes text in a jazz context; Angela Y. Davis, *Blues Legacies and Black Feminism* (New York: Vintage, 1999), 149.

18. Davis, *Blues Legacies and Black Feminism*, 149. There is an intriguing echo in all of this of Sterling Brown's reservations about Alain Locke's book on African American music. Brown comments that, while Locke was aware "intellectually" of the importance of jazz and blues, he owned very few recordings and had no real liking or feeling for the music: "he could not hear jazz and he did not see jazz on its own terms." In Charles S. Rowell, "'Let Me Be with Ole Jazzbo': An Interview with Sterling Brown," *Callaloo* 21.4 (1998): 799. Brown, of course, heads a tradition of black poets and fiction writers who have contributed notable essays on the music's importance to black culture. See Sterling A. Brown, *A Son's Return: Selected Essays of Sterling A. Brown*, ed. Mark A. Sanders (Boston: Northeastern University Press, 1996), esp. 207–74. Other examples include Wanda Coleman, "On Theloniousism," in "A Forum on the Prosody of Thelonious Monk," *Caliban* 4 (1988): 67–79; Ralph Ellison, *Living with Music: Ralph Ellison's Jazz Writings*, ed. Robert G. O'Meally (New York: Modern Library, 2001), esp. 3–138; Gayl Jones, *Liberating Voices: Oral Tradition in African American Literature* (1991; reprint, New York: Penguin, 1992); Larry Neal, "The Ethos of the Blues," in *Visions of a Liberated Future: Black Arts Movement Writings*, ed. Michael Schwartz (New York: Thunder's Mouth Press, 1989), 107–17; Sherley Anne Williams, "The Blues Roots of Contemporary Afro-American Poetry" (1979), reprinted in *Write Me a Few of Your Lines: A Blues Reader*, ed. Steven C. Tracy (Amherst: University of Massachusetts Press, 1999), 445–55.

19. One especially interesting example is Vèvè Clark's revision of Baker's "mastery of form" and "deformation of mastery" to include a third possibility, "reformation of form." She cites John Coltrane's 1960 recording of "My Favorite Things" as an instance of someone moving through all three strategies and suggests that the "reformed form" then becomes a point of departure for the next generation of players to master, deform, and reform in turn. See "The Edited Transcript" (of a roundtable discussion), *Lenox Avenue* 1 (1995): 33–34. Two texts that take up aspects of Gates's work on Signifyin(g) and apply them to analyses of black music history and performance practice are Samuel A. Floyd Jr., *The Power of Black Music: Interpreting Its History from Africa to the United States* (New York: Oxford University Press, 1995) and Ingrid Monson, *Saying Something: Jazz Improvisation and Interaction* (Chicago: University of Chicago Press, 1996).

20. See Krin Gabbard, *Jammin' at the Margins: Jazz and the American Cinema* (Chicago: University of Chicago Press, 1996), 138–59; Arthur Knight, *Disintegrating the Musical: Black Performance and American Musical Film* (Durham,

NC: Duke University Press, 2002), 169–94; Richard Dyer, "Is *Car Wash* a Musical?" in *Black American Cinema*, ed. Manthia Diawara (New York: Routledge, 1993), 93–106.

21. For example, as far as we are aware, no one has yet claimed to find evidence of a jazz or blues aesthetic in the work of a black filmmaker, although Arthur Jafa has voiced a desire to make films using what he calls "Black Visual Intonation," a concept he says was inspired by the tone of Aretha Franklin's singing and John Coltrane's playing. "Black Visual Intonation" would, he suggests, comprise a set of cinematic techniques that could produce "the visual equivalencies of vibrato, rhythmic patterns, slurred or bent notes, and other musical effects." Arthur Jafa, "Black Visual Intonation," in *The Jazz Cadence of American Culture*, ed. Robert G. O'Meally (New York: Columbia University Press, 1998), 264–68.

22. Gabbard, *Jammin'*, 1.

23. For further discussion of some of these topics, see, for example, Amiri Baraka, "Spike Lee at the Movies," in Diawara, *Black American Cinema*, 145–53; Donald Bogle, "Louis Armstrong: The Films," in *Louis Armstrong: A Cultural Reader*, ed. Marc H. Miller (Seattle: University of Washington Press, 1994), 147–59; David Butler, *Jazz Noir: Listening to Music from "Phantom Lady" to "The Last Seduction"* (Westport: Praeger, 2002); Thomas Cripps, *Slow Fade to Black: The Negro in American Film, 1900–1942* (New York: Oxford University Press, 1977); Richard Dyer, *White* (London: Routledge, 1997); Krin Gabbard, *Black Magic: White Hollywood and African American Culture* (New Brunswick: Rutgers University Press, 2004); Krin Gabbard, ed., *Representing Jazz* (Durham, NC: Duke University Press, 1995); Arthur Knight, "It Ain't Necessarily So That It Ain't Necessarily So: African American Recordings of *Porgy and Bess* as Film and Cultural Criticism," in *Soundtrack Available: Essays on Film and Popular Music*, ed. Pamela Robertson Wojcik and Arthur Knight (Durham, NC: Duke University Press, 2001), 519–46; Robert Lawson-Peebles, ed., *Approaches to the American Musical* (Exeter: Exeter University Press, 1996); Robert G. O'Meally, "Checking Our Balances: Louis Armstrong, Ralph Ellison, and Betty Boop," in *Uptown Conversation: The New Jazz Studies*, ed. Robert G. O'Meally, Brent Hayes Edwards, and Farah Jasmine Griffin (New York: Columbia University Press, 2004), 278–96; Peter Stanfield, *Body and Soul: Jazz and Blues in American Film, 1927–63* (Urbana: University of Illinois Press, 2005); and Klaus Stratemann, *Duke Ellington: Day by Day and Film by Film* (Copenhagen: Jazz Media, 1992).

24. For example, for their appearances in the 1930 film *Check and Double Check*, Ellington band members Barney Bigard, a Creole, and Juan Tizol, a Puerto Rican, "were forced to put on black makeup so they would appear to be Negro. Racial mixing, even on the bandstand, was opposed by some whites, especially in the South." John Edward Hasse, *Beyond Category: The Life and Genius of Duke Ellington* (New York: Simon & Schuster, 1993), 128–29. Of course, black performance was distorted by white prejudice in other contexts too: see, for instance, Sterling Brown's devastating critique of a live cabaret show in his "Cabaret," *Collected Poems*, 111–13.

25. "Thriving on a Riff" can be found on various compilations of Parker's Savoy recordings; for instance, Charlie Parker, *The Savoy Master Takes* (Vogue VG 660506, 1989).

26. Quoted by Robert Reisner in his *Bird: The Legend of Charlie Parker* (1962; London: Quartet Books, 1974), 27.

WORKS CITED

Recordings

Abrams, Muhal Richard. *Levels and Degrees of Light*. 1968. Reissue, Delmark DD-413, 1991.

Baraka, Amiri, David Murray, and Steve McCall. *New Music–New Poetry*. LP. India Navigation 1048, 1981.

Brown, Marion. *Geechee Recollections*. LP. Impulse! AS-9252, 1973.

Conjure. *Bad Mouth*. American Clavé AMCL 1052/53, 2005.

———. *Cab Calloway Stands in for the Moon*. 1988. Reissue, American Clavé AMCL 1015, 1995.

———. *Music for the Texts of Ishmael Reed*. 1984. Reissue, American Clavé AMCL 1006, 1995.

Cortez, Jayne, and the Firespitters. *Borders of Disorderly Time*. Bola Press BLP 2003, 2003.

———. *Cheerful & Optimistic*. Bola Press BP9401, 1994.

———. *Taking the Blues Back Home*. Harmolodic/Verve 531 918-2, 1996.

Dixon, Bill. *Papyrus—Volume 1*. Soul Note 121308-2, 1999.

Giovanni, Nikki. *The Way I Feel*. Collectables COL 6507, 1995.

Harper, Michael S., and Paul Austerlitz. *Double Take*. Innova 604, 2004.

———. *Our Book on Trane: The Yaddo Sessions*. Yaddo 1, 2004.

Hill, Andrew. *Dusk*. Palmetto PM 2057, 2000.

Hughes, Langston, Charles Mingus, and Leonard Feather. *The Weary Blues*. 1958. Verve 841 660-2, 1990.

Jackson, Ronald Shannon. *Puttin' on Dog*. Knitting Factory KCR 3033, 1999.

Komunyakaa, Yosef, and John Tchicai. *Love Notes from the Madhouse*. 8th Harmonic Breakdown 80001, 1988.

Lake, Oliver. *Matador of 1st & 1st*. Passin' Thru 40709, 1996.

Lewis, George E. *Changing with the Times*. New World Records 80434-2, 1993.

Lyle, K. Curtis, and Julius Hemphill. *The Collected Poem for Blind Lemon Jefferson*. 1971. Reissue, Ikef 05, 2002.

Mackey, Nathaniel. *Strick: Song of the Andoumboulou 16–25*. Spoken Engine, 1995.

Parker, Charlie. *The Savoy Master Takes*. 1944–48. Vogue VG 660506, 1989.

Redmond, Eugene. *"Blood Links and Sacred Places."* 1973. Reissue, Ikef 01, 2001.

Roach, Max. *It's Christmas Again*. Soul Note 121153-2, 1994.

Scott-Heron, Gil. *The Revolution Will Not Be Televised*. 1970–74. RCA ND 86994, 1989.

Sun Ra. *The Sound Mirror*. LP. Saturn 19782, 1978.

Taj Mahal. *Mule Bone*. Gramavision GV 79 432-2, 1991.

Taylor, Cecil. *Chinampas*. Leo CD LR 153, 1991.

White, Josh. *Complete Recorded Works 1940–1941 in Chronological Order, Volume 4, 4 June 1940–1941*. Document Records DOCD 5405, 1995.

Texts

Albert, Richard N. *An Annotated Bibliography of Jazz Fiction and Jazz Fiction Criticism*. Westport, CT: Greenwood, 1996.

Anderson, T. J., III. *Notes to Make the Sounds Come Right: Four Innovators of Jazz Poetry*. Fayetteville: University of Arkansas Press, 2004.

Baker, Houston A., Jr. *Blues, Ideology, and Afro-American Literature: A Vernacular Theory*. Chicago: University of Chicago Press, 1984.

———. *Modernism and the Harlem Renaissance*. Chicago: University of Chicago Press, 1987.

Baldwin, James. *Notes of a Native Son*. 1964. Reprint, London: Corgi, 1970.

Baraka, Amiri. "Spike Lee at the Movies." In Diawara, *Black American Cinema*, 145–53.

Bogle, Donald. "Louis Armstrong: The Films." In *Louis Armstrong; A Cultural Reader*. Ed. Marc H. Miller. Seattle: University of Washington Press, 1994. 147–59.

Bolden, Tony. *Afro Blue: Improvisations in African American Poetry and Culture*. Urbana: University of Illinois Press, 2004.

Borshuk, Michael. *Swinging the Vernacular: Jazz and African American Modernist Literature*. New York: Routledge, 2006.

Brown, Sterling A. *The Collected Poems of Sterling A. Brown*. Ed. Michael S. Harper. 1980. Reprint, Evanston, IL: TriQuarterly Books/Northwestern University Press, 1996.

———. *A Son's Return: Selected Essays of Sterling A. Brown*. Ed. Mark A. Sanders. Boston: Northeastern University Press, 1996.

Butler, David. *Jazz Noir: Listening to Music from "Phantom Lady" to "The Last Seduction."* Westport, CT: Praeger, 2002.

Campbell, Robert L., and Christopher Trent, *The Earthly Recordings of Sun Ra*, 2nd ed. Redwood, NY: Cadence Jazz, n.d.

Coleman, Wanda. "On Theloniousism." *Caliban* 4 (1988): 67–79.

Cripps, Thomas. *Slow Fade to Black: The Negro in American Film, 1900–1942*. New York: Oxford University Press, 1977.

Davis, Angela Y. *Blues Legacies and Black Feminism*. New York: Vintage, 1999.

Diawara, Manthia, ed. *Black American Cinema*. New York: Routledge, 1993.

Dinerstein, Joel. *Swinging the Machine: Modernity, Technology, and African American Culture between the World Wars*. Amherst: University of Massachusetts Press, 2003.

Du Bois, W. E. B. *The Souls of Black Folk*. 1903. Reprint, New York: Bantam, 1989.

Dyer, Richard. "Is *Car Wash* a Musical?" In Diawara, *Black American Cinema*, 93–106.

———. *White*. London: Routledge, 1997.

"The Edited Transcript." *Lenox Avenue* 1 (1995): 5–43.

Edwards, Brent. "The Race for Space: Sun Ra's Poetry." *Hambone 14* (Fall 1998): 177–200.

Edwards, Brent Hayes, and John F. Szwed. "A Bibliography of Jazz Poetry Criticism." *Callaloo* 25.1 (2002): 338–46.

Ellison, Ralph. *The Collected Essays of Ralph Ellison*. Ed. John F. Callahan. New York: Random House, 1995.

———. *Living with Music: Ralph Ellison's Jazz Writings*. Ed. Robert G. O'Meally. New York: Modern Library, 2001.

Evans, Nicholas M. *Writing Jazz: Race, Nationalism, and Modern Culture in the 1920s*. New York: Garland, 2000.

Floyd, Samuel A., Jr. *The Power of Black Music: Interpreting Its History from Africa to the United States*. New York: Oxford University Press, 1995.

Funkhouser, Chris. "Being Matter Ignited: An Interview with Cecil Taylor." *Hambone* 12 (Fall 1995): 17–39.

Gabbard, Krin. *Black Magic: White Hollywood and African American Culture*. New Brunswick, NJ: Rutgers University Press, 2004.

———. *Jammin' at the Margins: Jazz and the American Cinema*. Chicago: University of Chicago Press, 1996.

———, ed. *Representing Jazz*. Durham, NC: Duke University Press, 1995.

Gabbin, Joanne V. *Sterling Brown: Building the Black Aesthetic Tradition*. 1985. Reprint, Charlottesville: University Press of Virginia, 1994.

Gates, Henry Louis, Jr. *The Signifying Monkey: A Theory of African American Literary Criticism*. New York: Oxford University Press, 1988.

Grandt, Jürgen E. *Kinds of Blue: The Jazz Aesthetic in African American Narrative*. Columbus: Ohio State University Press, 2004.

Gussow, Adam. *Seems Like Murder Here: Southern Violence and the Blues Tradition*. Chicago: University of Chicago Press, 2002.

Hartman, Charles O. *Jazz Text: Voice and Improvisation in Poetry, Jazz, and Song*. Princeton, NJ: Princeton University Press, 1991.

Hasse, John Edward. *Beyond Category: The Life and Genius of Duke Ellington*. New York: Simon & Schuster, 1993.

Henderson, Stephen, ed. *Understanding the New Black Poetry: Black Speech and Black Music as Poetic References*. New York: Morrow Quill, 1973.

Hughes, Langston. "The Negro Artist and the Racial Mountain." 1926. Reprinted in *Keeping Time: Readings in Jazz History*. Ed. Robert Walser. New York: Oxford University Press, 1999. 55–57.

Hurston, Zora Neale. "Spirituals and Neo-Spirituals." In *Negro: An Anthology*. Ed. Nancy Cunard. Abridged ed. New York: Continuum, 2002. 223–25.

Jafa, Arthur. "Black Visual Intonation." In O'Meally, *Jazz Cadence of American Culture*, 264–68.

Jarrett, Michael. *Drifting on a Read: Jazz as a Model for Writing*. Albany: State University of New York Press, 1999.

Jones, Gayl. *Liberating Voices: Oral Tradition in African American Literature*. New York: Penguin, 1992.

Kaufman, Bob. *Cranial Guitar: Selected Poems by Bob Kaufman*. Ed. Gerald Nicosia. Minneapolis: Coffee House Press, 1996.

Knight, Arthur. *Disintegrating the Musical: Black Performance and American Musical Film*. Durham, NC: Duke University Press, 2002.

———. "It Ain't Necessarily So That It Ain't Necessarily So: African American Recordings of *Porgy and Bess* as Film and Cultural Criticism." In *Soundtrack Available: Essays on Film and Popular Music*. Ed. Pamela

Robertson Wojcik and Arthur Knight. Durham, NC: Duke University Press, 2001. 519–46.

Lange, Art, and Nathaniel Mackey, eds. *Moment's Notice: Jazz in Poetry and Prose*. Minneapolis: Coffee House Press, 1993.

Lawson-Peebles, Robert, ed. *Approaches to the American Musical*. Exeter: Exeter University Press, 1996.

Monson, Ingrid. *Saying Something: Jazz Improvisation and Interaction*. Chicago: University of Chicago Press, 1996.

Moten, Fred. *In the Break: The Aesthetics of the Black Radical Tradition*. Minneapolis: University of Minnesota Press, 2003.

Neal, Larry. *Visions of a Liberated Future: Black Arts Movement Writings*. Ed. Michael Schwartz. New York: Thunder's Mouth Press, 1989.

Nielsen, Aldon Lynn. *Black Chant: Languages of African American Postmodernism*. Cambridge: Cambridge University Press, 1997.

O'Meally, Robert G. "Checking Our Balances: Louis Armstrong, Ralph Ellison, and Betty Boop." In O'Meally, Edwards, and Griffin, *Uptown Conversation*, 278–96.

———, ed. *The Jazz Cadence of American Culture*. New York: Columbia University Press, 1997.

O'Meally, Robert G., Brent Hayes Edwards, and Farah Jasmine Griffin, eds. *Uptown Conversation: The New Jazz Studies*. New York: Columbia University Press, 2004.

Panish, Jon. *The Color of Jazz: Race and Representation in Postwar American Culture*. Jackson: University Press of Mississippi, 1997.

Raussert, Wilfred. *Negotiating Temporal Difference: Blues, Jazz and Narrativity in African American Culture*. Heidelberg: Universitätsverlag C. Winter, 2000.

Reisner, Robert. *Bird: The Legend of Charlie Parker*. 1962. Reprint, London: Quartet, 1974.

Rowell, Charles H. "'Let Me Be with Ole Jazzbo': An Interview with Sterling Brown." *Callaloo* 21.4 (1998): 789–809.

Sanders, Mark A. *Afro-Modernist Aesthetics and the Poetry of Sterling A. Brown*. Athens: University of Georgia Press, 1999.

Snead, James A. "Repetition as a Figure of Black Culture." In *Black Literature and Literary Theory*. Ed. Henry Louis Gates Jr. New York: Routledge, 1990. 59–79.

Stanfield, Peter. *Body and Soul: Jazz and Blues in American Film, 1927–63*. Urbana: University of Illinois Press, 2005.

Stratemann, Klaus. *Duke Ellington: Day by Day and Film by Film*. Copenhagen: Jazz Media, 1992.

Townsend, Peter. *Jazz in American Culture*. Edinburgh: University of Edinburgh Press, 2000.

Tracy, Steven C. *Langston Hughes and the Blues*. Urbana: University of Illinois Press, 2001.

———, ed. *Write Me a Few of Your Lines: A Blues Reader*. Amherst: University of Massachusetts Press, 1999.

Williams, Sherley Anne. "The Blues Roots of Contemporary Afro-American Poetry." 1979. Reprinted in Tracy, *Write Me a Few of Your Lines*, 445–55.

Yaffe, David. *Fascinating Rhythm: Reading Jazz in American Writing*. Princeton, NJ: Princeton University Press, 2006.

So Black and Blue: Music, Image, Identity

"You Ain't Got to *Be* Black to Be Black": Music, Race Consciousness, and Identity in *The Autobiography of an Ex-Colored Man* and *Mojo Hand*

Nick Heffernan

Though published over fifty years apart, James Weldon Johnson's *The Auto-biography of an Ex-Colored Man* (1912) and J. J. Phillips's *Mojo Hand: An Orphic Tale* (1966) explore in fascinatingly similar fashion the links between black music, race consciousness, and personal identity. Each novel features a light-skinned, middle-class African American protagonist who, up to a crucial and traumatic childhood turning point, believes himself or herself to be white. Thereafter, both protagonists reconstruct their sense of self and racial identity through a prolonged encounter with the aesthetic, cultural, and social meanings of black music. In effect, both engage in a quest to trace black music's root forms backward in time and space, leading to an immersion in the communal life of the rural South where the music's origins lie. Both emerge from this process with a radically altered understanding of who they are and how they relate to the racially polarized culture and politics of America at large.

Despite their similarity in pattern, these quests end very differently. John-son's ex-colored man ultimately renounces both the South and his blackness, living out a spiritually arid life in New York where he passes as a white bour-geois property tycoon. He abandons black music in favor of the Chopin and Beethoven he associates with his wife, whom he describes as "the most daz-zlingly white thing I had ever seen."[1] Phillips's protagonist, Eunice, on the other hand, purges herself of her whiteness through a highly charged sexual union with the phallic bluesman Blacksnake Brown. She bears his child, absorbs and perpetuates his music, and fully assimilates into the collective black folk life of North Carolina. Nonetheless, the questions that each novel explores are identi-cal and are the questions that continue to structure debates about the place and significance of black music in American life today. Is black music the exclusive cultural property of African Americans, or should it be understood as a uni-versal cultural resource? Is it at its most powerful and authentic when closest to its racial, regional, and subcultural origins, or does its irrepressible appeal across the "color line" indicate that it is fundamentally hybrid in form and integrationist in impulse? What credentials must be possessed and what responsibilities assumed by those who would adopt the music for personal expression? And how far can musical innovation and achievement contribute to collective social and political progress for African Americans? The significantly different answers each novel proposes to these questions are to an extent responses to the particular historical and social conditions that prevailed at the moment of their composition, indicating the authors' divergent understandings of the political and ideological priorities facing African Americans in each period.

The Autobiography of an Ex-Colored Man uneasily blends the mildly nationalistic (but never separatist) race pride and the social and cultural assimilationism that animated many of Johnson's fellow leaders of the Harlem Renaissance and the "New Negro" movement. This is a not entirely compatible ideological brew and, as his biographer Eugene Levy points out, Johnson's career can be understood as a prolonged attempt to balance a commitment to black folk culture and racial solidarity on the one hand with an artistic, political, and social outlook shaped by a non-racial cosmopolitanism on the other.[2] Indeed, Johnson's own autobiography makes this fundamental tension clear. Imbued from an early age with "an unconscious race-superiority complex" in favor of black life, and aghast at the "mess the white race has made of civilization," he nonetheless accepted the inevitability of what he called racial amalgamation in America. "Instead of developing them independently to the utmost," he believed, "the Negro will fuse his qualities with those of the other groups in the making of the ultimate American people." This was a vision in which nothing unique to the African American population would remain save "a tint to America's complexion" and "a perceptible permanent wave in America's hair."[3]

The contradictions to which such a vision gives rise are present also in Johnson's fictional autobiography and have led to the book being seen, variously, as an anti-essentialist assertion of the hybridity of racial identity and culture; as a defense of the notion of an authentic and essentially black culture resistant (and superior) to the American mainstream; and as strategically oscillating between these opposing poles in order to destabilize them.[4] At certain points the unnamed narrator's considerable musical talents are presented as a "natural" consequence of the African American "blood" inherited from his quadroon mother. Even as a "white" child he is strangely moved by her renditions of the "old southern songs," expresses "a particular fondness for the black keys" of

Nick Heffernan

the piano, and refuses to be constrained by European musical notation in his piano lessons.[5] Later, his two most profound musical and personal experiences are witnessing the apparently innate improvisational genius of a black ragtime pianist in a New York club (who, we are told, is a "dark man") and hearing the "dark brown" preacher Singing Johnson's moving rendition of the slave songs at an exclusively black camp meeting in rural Georgia.[6]

These episodes suggest not just that the narrator's racial identity, his "blackness," is an essence that is somehow contained in or expressed through specifically African American musical forms, but that this music is in some respects exclusively African American property. His scornful dismissal of those "white imitators and adulterators" who profit from the transcription and publication of black-originated ragtime songs would seem to confirm this.[7] Yet, on the other hand, the novel provides equally powerful evidence for viewing black identity as a thoroughly hybrid, socially constructed matter, and black music as a non-racial, universally shared cultural resource. It is only after he is told that he is in fact black, and embarks on a program of teaching himself how to "be" black, that the narrator's childhood affinity for the piano's black keys blossoms into a properly improvisatory and emotionally expressive, soulful playing style. Ragtime, the music with which he makes his name, derives from European marching songs; and the narrator himself demonstrates how even apparently innate improvisational spontaneity can be learned as he tirelessly imitates the "natural musical instinct" of the New York club's piano genius.[8] Moreover, the aesthetic and personal epiphany provided by the black ragtime pianist is later equaled if not overshadowed by a European musician in Berlin who takes one of the narrator's own ragtime themes and "classicizes" it.[9] Finally, of course, it must be noted that Singing Johnson's variations on the spirituals have the European structure of Christian hymns as their basis.

Here, then, the novel foregrounds what Paul Gilroy calls the "syncretic complexity of black expressive cultures" and demonstrates how racial identity and the cultural materials that underpin it are not essences but are acquired through training, imitation, and adaptation.[10] Indeed, the text draws our attention to the syncretic nature of all—not just black—cultural activity and identities. The narrator moves not only between the white world and the black but also through a striking variety of ethnic, linguistic, regional, class, and cultural communities, all of which he is fascinated by, borrows from, and contributes to. Everywhere this remarkably mobile individual goes he encounters others similarly disregarding lines of social demarcation, mixing and matching styles and influences in everything from music and speech to dress and dance. Embraced by the Cuban laborers in the Jacksonville cigar factory where he works for a spell, he quickly learns Spanish and is elected to the role of reading Cuban newspapers and Spanish novels to his fellow workers. Later, in New York, he frequents with equal ease the low dives of the Tenderloin district and the elevated salons of upper-class bohemia, both of which milieux are marked by varying modes of cross-racial identification and mixing. Among the patrons of the after-hours club where the narrator first hears ragtime music and otherwise immerses himself in the African American subculture of the urban North are many whites who demonstrate a special and not always exploitative or condescending interest in black life and culture.[11] And in the refined circle that revolves around the white millionaire for whom the narrator moonlights as house pianist there is a thirst for ragtime music that culminates one evening in "the whole company involuntarily and unconsciously" breaking into "an impromptu cake-walk."[12]

This is a crucial scene in which Johnson's language deliberately emphasizes that there is nothing willed, studied, or parodic in the white partygoers' embrace of black music and dance. Not only is their cakewalk spontaneous, but it is also an "involuntary" and "unconscious" response to the music and as such is distinct from the self-conscious caricature of African Americans practiced at this time by white (and black) entertainers on the minstrel stage and in the "coon songs" of vaudeville. The scene is a demonstration of the universality of music and movement whose origins might lie in one particular racial and class subculture but whose appeal and appreciation cannot be limited by those origins. But it is more than this. While the partygoers' dance is certainly not a minstrel burlesque, the cakewalk nonetheless carries overtones of racial parody, deriving as it does from African Americans' humorous imitations of the elevated bearing of their white social superiors. Though unaware of the fact, the partygoers are actually engaging in an imitation of a black dance that is itself an imitation of white cultural styles. On one level this reinforces Johnson's larger point about the mutual influencing and borrowing that fundamentally shapes ostensibly separate cultures. On another it complicates questions of cultural ownership and authenticity as our attention is drawn to the multiple processes of often unconscious imitation and imitation-in-return by which cultural forms are mediated. On still another it allows Johnson to make these anti-essentialist points while indulging his self-confessed "race-superiority complex," inasmuch as the scene's full significance will be grasped only by those who understand that the

Nick Heffernan

partygoers are unconsciously colluding in an African American parody of precisely their own white upper-class cultural and social milieu.

In this instance cultural energy is as promiscuous and unclassifiable as sexual desire, the other great force in the novel that constantly subverts the false boundaries of class and color. And the narrator, himself the product of an interracial union and as strongly drawn to white women as they are to him, perfectly embodies the irrepressibly integrationist urge of culture and sex alike. It is therefore entirely appropriate that his lifework should be to produce a marriage of African American vernacular forms and Western classical music of the kind he first accidentally hits upon by ragging Mendelssohn's "Wedding March" and precipitating the millionaire's guests' involuntary cakewalk. Whether this project is motivated by a noble desire to bring credit to his race and further the cause of integration or an opportunistic impulse to exploit a gap in the market, it is nonetheless an entirely consistent extension of everything that the narrator has hitherto felt and experienced.[13] And it exemplifies what appears to be the philosophy of music that structures Johnson's book and is articulated most cogently by the narrator's white millionaire patron: "Music is a universal art; anybody's music belongs to everybody; you can't limit it to race or country."[14]

Why, then, is this projected lifework never realized? Why is the "official" marriage of black and white musics in the American mainstream impossible when promiscuous miscegenation is the unofficial, everyday state of affairs? The narrator abandons his project, along with his black identity and any further involvement with black music, after witnessing a lynching during one of his research field trips to the South. He cites "shame at being identified with a people that could with impunity be treated worse than animals" as the reason for his decision.[15] Other commentators, however, have argued that the failure is more to do with Johnson's unease at the possible dilution and commodification of black culture entailed in the narrator's project of taking subcultural forms into the mainstream.[16] Here the author's own career as a composer of commercial songs with Negro themes becomes relevant. Between 1899 and 1906 Johnson, with his brother Rosamond and another African American musician, Bob Cole, wrote and published numerous ragtime songs and "southern melodies," including two comic operas, some of which were extremely popular and lucrative.[17] Yet Johnson abandoned this career, it has been suggested, because he felt trapped by the demands of mainstream taste. Unwilling to perpetuate the negative racial stereotyping of the "coon songs" so popular at the time and increasingly disillusioned with the banal Tin Pan Alley conventions that were the only viable non-racial alternatives, Johnson became convinced that a productive marriage of black and white musics was impossible within the confines of the culture industry. According to Cristina Ruotolo, this explains the collapse of the ex-colored man's project and the novel's aesthetic and spiritual valorization of those two moments of "pure" and "free" black musical expression in the authentically African American subcultural milieux of the ragtime club and the camp meeting.

It is certainly true that Johnson's own compositions aimed to mark out some middle ground between minstrel stereotypes and the polite, colorless sentimentality of official Broadway fare. He defined this enterprise as "an attempt to bring a higher degree of artistry to Negro songs," and he credited himself and his collaborators with forging a new "style that displaced the old 'coon songs'" and their "crude, raucous, bawdy, often obscene" stereotypes and themes.[18] The sheet music covers of Johnson's compositions provide a visual analogue of his textual strategy as a lyric writer and librettist. Figure 1.1 illustrates the kind of denigrating imagery commonly associated with the ostensibly comic coon song, including those by prominent African American writers and composers such as Paul Laurence Dunbar and, as here, Ernest Hogan. Figures 1.2 and 1.3 show how Cole and the Johnson brothers sought to avoid this kind of racial grotesquerie by emphasizing place over character in their songs (Timbuctoo and Louisiana in these instances) and peddling them to genteel white female performers such as Lillian Russell and Lottie Gilson, who could be pictured in the vignette style characteristic of sheet music for classical and sentimental compositions.[19] Figure 1.4, though, reveals how any small movement away from the sentimental and toward the comic would result in a return of some degree of racial caricature, even if as in this case a photo-vignette of the performer is used instead of the cartoon "darkies" so common elsewhere in coon songs and their derivatives.

Notwithstanding these difficulties, however, there is no evidence to suggest that Johnson judged his own musical efforts to open up a space between caricature and colorlessness a failure. Even if he did—and his autobiography communicates a palpable sense of pride in his achievements as a songwriter—this does not necessarily mean that he thought the project itself impossible or unsound.[20] The novel's enterprise of musical inter-marriage fails, but not because Johnson deems his narrator guilty of exploiting his own people's culture or selling out black subcultural resources to the mainstream. Indeed, the ex-colored man's project echoes not only his creator's own songwriting activities, of which he was proud, but even more directly the serious literary endeavors Johnson undertook in the years after his show business interlude ended. Johnson's

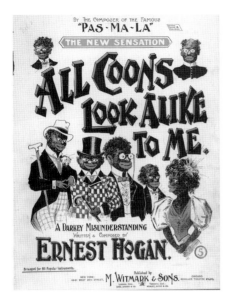

principal literary achievement, in his own eyes as well as those of the American literary establishment of his time, was his series of poems *God's Trombones* (1927). In this volume, in a clear parallel with the ex-colored man's approach to the slave songs and spirituals, Johnson sought "to take the primitive stuff of the old-time Negro sermon," subject it to "art-governed expression," and see it thus "enlarged beyond the circumference of mere race, and given universality." This is to make art out of subcultural resources "in a way similar to that in which a composer makes use of a folk theme in writing a major composition."[21] There is no exploitation, betrayal or selling out here; only a belief in the fundamental compatibility and universal appeal of African American folk materials and Western cultural conventions alike.

It seems more persuasive to suggest, then, that the failure of the ex-colored man's project stems from the fact that he lacks the courage to follow through on his conviction that music, and by extension all cultural activity, is thoroughly hybrid and inherently syncretic. The act of racial violence, the lynching, that the narrator witnesses and that stops him in his tracks demonstrates how culture's inexorable bottom-up logic of miscegenation conflicts with a top-down racist logic of social segregation, just as the millionaire had intimated. For Johnson and other Harlem Renaissance leaders, culture was to be a vehicle for black social advancement, providing a vision of racial integration as more than just black assimilation into the mainstream on white America's terms. But culture's inherent promise of a dynamically and productively mixed or, to use Johnson's own term, amalgamated America—symbolized by the hybrid vitality of the nation's vernacular music—could only be realized if it was accompanied by the acquisition of full civil rights and protection under the law. The program of cultural uplift and integration, then, was inseparable from the political campaign for equality.[22] The ex-colored man's tragedy is that he sees only the former and remains oblivious to the latter. His punishment is that he feels compelled to relinquish his "natural" hybrid identity along with the mongrel music that nourished and expressed it; and he is condemned to a death-in-life not because he chooses white over black, as many commentators have argued, but because he chooses between them at all.[23]

Conspicuous by their absence from the various musical forms encountered and mastered by the ex-colored man are the blues. The ambivalence of many of the Harlem Renaissance's figureheads toward the blues as "primitive stuff," to use Johnson's term for unrefined black folk culture, is well recorded. The blues did not fit the integrationist agenda of cultural respectability as easily as did the spirituals, the folk sermons, and ragtime, with their connections to Christianity and European classical music. Prior to his conversion to Chopin and Beethoven, Johnson's ex-colored man expresses racial pride in these latter forms yet still somewhat apologetically numbers them among "the lower forms of art."[24] However, it was to the blues that African Americans skeptical about the benefits of integration and assimilation turned as relief from what they saw as the pandering to white cultural standards and the bourgeois prejudices of the Negro Renaissance's leaders. Only the music and culture of what Langston Hughes called "the low down folks" could provide proper nourishment for black artists reluctant to conform to the polite standards of "the Nordicized Negro intelligentsia," or indeed for the race as a whole when the dream of integration fell on hard times during the Great Depression.[25]

Hughes was not alone in holding to a conception of the blues as a kind of irreducible substrate for African American collective life. In the poems of *Southern Road* (1932), Sterling Brown drew upon and celebrated the blues as a force that could "Git way inside us, / Keep us strong."[26] Brown sought to maintain a distinction between the "truly folk" blues on the one hand and the "pseudo blues" of Tin Pan Alley on the other. But he conceded that even in the commercialized "cabaret appetizers," as he called them, "a certain kind of isolation—class and racial—remains," an isolation that spoke of a separate African American "underground."[27] Richard Wright, too, himself no apologist for sentimental invocations of black folk life, acknowledged blues culture as a reservoir of collective strength, "a haven of song," for African Americans, particularly those who had made the alienating journey to the industrial North.[28]

Similarly, for Ralph Ellison, the blues were inhabited by an impulse toward "going-under-ground" into a separate and "defensive" African American culture; yet this tendency was counterbalanced by the music's equally powerful outward-looking "will to confront the world" and to "transcend" the conditions of its creation.[29] It was the former quality identified by Ellison, however, that LeRoi Jones/Amiri Baraka developed into a full-blown theory of the music in *Blues People* (1963). The blues, for Baraka, are "a form that is patently non-Western." The music speaks exclusively of "a Negro experience . . . that could not be transferred to a more general significance." As if arguing directly with Ellison's universalist claim in his 1946 essay on Richard Wright and the blues that "The American Negro is a Western type," Baraka declared that "Bessie Smith was not an American." Even Smith's brand of commercial, professionalized, and entertainment-oriented blues "remained outside the mainstream of American thought."[30] Having asserted the music's distance from Western cultural conventions and the American mainstream alike, Baraka argued that The Blues (now capitalized) constituted nothing less than "the racial memory" of African Americans, carrying in aesthetic form "the 'abstract' design of racial character."[31]

Through Baraka the blues became attached to an emergent cultural nationalism that saw the assertion of the essential separateness of black culture from the mainstream as integral to the political and psychological liberation of African Americans: the blues as race essence constituted a bulwark against the inexorably "bleaching" logic of modern American life. It is to this tradition that Jane Phillips's remarkable novel *Mojo Hand: An Orphic Tale* (1966) belongs. In it, the blues are celebrated as the touchstone of African American experience, identity, and authenticity. Importantly, though, they are neither sentimentalized nor neutered as "heritage" as in Congress's declaration of 2003 as the Year of the Blues.[32] Indeed, and significantly for a novel formed in the crucible of the black political and cultural activism of the mid-1960s, the misogynistic elements of the blues are unflinchingly analyzed, and their uneasy fit with any kind of progressive political vision is fully registered.

For the novel's protagonist, Eunice Prideaux, the blues are the key to a reconciliation with blackness after a childhood spent believing she is white and an adolescence spent resenting the assimilationist values of her light-skinned bourgeois parents. On the eve of her cotillion or coming-out into the polite San Francisco colored society of the early 1960s, she discovers an old 78 rpm Race record by Blacksnake Brown that provokes in her the same kind of aesthetic and emotional epiphany experienced by Johnson's ex-colored man through the slave songs and ragtime music. Determined to find and surrender herself to this man and his music, Eunice deserts San Francisco for Raleigh, North Carolina. There she plunges into the communal peasant life of the poor African American masses, from which she has not emerged at the novel's end.

In her pursuit of and surrender to Blacksnake, Eunice is driven by an essentialist understanding of the blues as the wellspring of African American identity. Blacksnake's music is "the source of herself . . . and the others, however much they tried to deny it"; while for Blacksnake, the blues are "his strange statements of essence."[33] This, though, is a powerfully masculine, even misogynistic, essence. As his name suggests, Blacksnake is a version of the "phallic trickster" identified by Houston Baker as a key persona of blues culture;[34] and his intensely sexual music initiates Eunice not into the utopian space of liberated physicality and desire she anticipates on first hearing it, but into a kind of erotic subjugation

Nick Heffernan

that is not far removed from the condition of chattel slavery. Blacksnake defines Eunice as "my exclusive property," while her African American employers at the Raleigh Palace Bar expect her to boost their business by sleeping with the male customers, regarding her as a "newly acquired commodity."[35]

The blues essence is associated with social as well as sexual backwardness. Raleigh's African American community is characterized by "the fact of stagnancy"— a complete lack of interest in political progress or social development; and Eunice accepts her existence there as an "incarceration" that she finds "unbearable."[36] This is emphasized when a white civil rights worker calls on Eunice and Blacksnake, encouraging them to register to vote, to contribute to the advance of their race so that they "may become first class citizens."[37] He is dismissed out of hand, Blacksnake asserting that he does not want "them white folks come messing round here too much" and Eunice claiming that voting "doesn't make any difference."[38] This episode highlights the willed separateness of the blues culture from the American mainstream. Progress, uplift, and integration, whether through politics, culture, or both, Eunice hints, will bleach Blacksnake's world of its distinctiveness, producing a condition in which, she observes, "everybody's going to end up doing the same old things everybody else does."[39] While such impassive anti-modernism guarantees the blues culture's integrity, it also condemns it to the "stagnancy" by which Eunice feels it is defined. It is worth noting here, though, that the novel celebrates rather than critiques the blues for their apparent political and social passivity, despite the fact that Phillips herself was closely involved in the civil rights movement in the early 1960s, traveling from San Francisco to North Carolina where she worked on voter registration campaigns and was imprisoned for civil disobedience. Here *Mojo Hand* stands at a tangent to *The Autobiography of an Ex-Colored Man*. Johnson's protagonist is ultimately condemned to an arid death-in-life for failing to develop a political race consciousness to match his cultural awareness. By contrast, Phillips's characters derive their full-blooded vitality from their willed obliviousness to the political and to questions of social equality for African Americans.

It is possible, though, that in *Mojo Hand* the blues are political, just not in the conventional ways. Blacksnake's world is a defensive refuge from white-defined modernity, a repository of racial distinctiveness and authenticity that counterbalances the "bleaching" effects of integrationist politics and notions of cultural uplift alike. Indeed, for Eunice the blues function as what the narrative defines as a "counterstructure" to the bourgeois "pseudo-rationality" of her assimilationist parents.[40] As such they provide a necessary if not always comfortable education in the brute facts of collective racial existence. As Houston Baker puts it, "the blues offer a phylogenetic recapitulation . . . of species experience. What emerges is not a filled subject, but an anonymous (nameless) voice issuing from the black (w)hole."[41] This perfectly describes the process in which Eunice's bourgeois subjectivity is dismantled through absorption into the collective life of Raleigh's black underclass, a process that is marked by her borrowing and assimilating Blacksnake's blues repertoire. The music operates here in ways already theorized by both Ellison and Baraka. For Ellison the blues are "an autobiographical chronicle of personal catastrophe," and Eunice's blues certainly chronicle such a catastrophe, albeit one that is deliberately sought out and embraced.[42] But they are also an actively wielded weapon whose function is, in Baraka's formula for black music, to "Find the self, then kill it."[43] The absorption of Blacksnake's musicianship and repertoire accompanies the disintegration of the polite, good-girl Eunice—or "You nice" as she is referred to—into the dissolute, drunkenly promiscuous creature who at the novel's climax is animated by a "barbaric germ" to "wander so in frenzy."[44]

This destruction of individuated bourgeois subjectivity in the racial gene pool of the blues, though, can be understood as a necessary prelude to the articulation of a more authentically African American sense of self and beyond that, perhaps, of an expanded social and political agency, as it was in significantly different ways for both Ellison and Baraka. Ellison recognized the "defensive character" and "the impulse toward self-annihilation" in what he called "the pre-individualistic black community," whose principal form of expression was the blues. But this was offset, he argued, by the inherently "pluralistic" nature of both black music and American culture. Thus the blues, and by extension the African American community, could not but engage creatively with the American mainstream—indeed the blues were that mainstream insofar as they constituted "the sound of the American experience."[45] For Baraka, on the other hand, the music's exteriority to the mainstream was its chief characteristic and its chief virtue. The blues were an "ugly reminder" to integrationist blacks "that they had once been outside the walls of the city"; and Baraka concluded *Blues People* by suggesting that only a fool would want in, gesturing toward his role in the establishment of the Black Arts Movement and the increasingly nationalistic perspectives of his subsequent writings on music.[46] In its exploration of the possibilities of the blues for racial self-fashioning, then, *Mojo Hand* is wonderfully representative of its historical moment, one in which African Americans in general and the civil rights movement in particular stood poised between a commitment to an integrationist political vision and an increasingly separatist concern with the politics of cultural identity.

Mojo Hand's assertion of the essentially and exclusively African American nature of the blues is counterbalanced by an equally persuasive, if less obvious, suggestion that the blues and their meanings are anyone's, regardless of race, class, or gender. The novel, like Johnson's before it, shows us a protagonist learning—often awkwardly and ineptly—to become black through imitation and appropriation. Eunice is an interloper in Blacksnake's world, which, even after prolonged immersion in it, remains "a foreign experience" to her.[47] She is regarded as a voyeur, a tourist or a *passe'n blanc* by many in this world; even Blacksnake is never fully persuaded that she is not white.[48] Indeed, Eunice herself cannot decide whether her embrace of the blues culture is "a true act or a posture of defiance" against her light-skinned bourgeois origins.[49] Yet her ultimate acceptance into Raleigh's blues-drenched African American subculture is not conditional upon some irrefutable demonstration of a biological racial essence; it is, rather, an effect of opening herself fully to this world's collective culture and modes of experience, particularly the experiences of sexual enslavement and racist oppression. "Well, you sure as shit is one of us now," Blacksnake tells Eunice after she has been jailed for transgressing the sexual color line on the cops' assumption that she is a white prostitute frequenting the colored section of town to satisfy a taste for "black dick," as they put it.[50] Thus the novel proposes that, as one of Eunice's cell mates declares, "You ain't got to *be* black to be black."[51] Here blackness is an elective identity that can be chosen or decided upon, much as Eunice has consciously and premeditatedly "decided to love" Blacksnake in full knowledge of the suffering and oppression he will inflict on her.[52] But in neither instance is the choice a free one. Both entail payment through the painful acquisition of cultural and experiential credentials; and it is these, rather than any display of racial essence or biological signifiers, which grant Eunice access to the new identity she fashions for herself in Raleigh. For Eunice, blackness must be earned as well as learned.

Like Johnson's novel, *Mojo Hand* plays a double game, at times presenting black music and identity as exclusive racial essences, at others as socially and culturally constructed resources available to all. While its essentialism is often overt, this is deployed as a strategic holding position on the way to a more complex, hybrid, and self-determining mode of subjectivity that has the potential for a more progressive, dynamic, and hopeful political outlook than the blues fatalism of Blacksnake and his subcultural milieu. Eunice ultimately turns away from Blacksnake and the emotionally extreme but stagnant and patriarchal world of his blues. Having achieved mastery of Blacksnake's music, she turns its phallic power against her erstwhile "master," cursing him with a spell (the "mojo hand" of the book's title) that brings about his death at the hands of another jealous lover. Appropriating Blacksnake's guitar, Eunice is now free to move forward as a self-determining subject toward an uncertain but hopeful future. It is not revealed whether this future will involve a renewed engagement with the mainstream or a deeper embedding in black folk life and culture. That is, we are not told whether the reconstructed Eunice will perpetuate Ellison's or Baraka's version of the blues continuum. However, the bluesman's death suggests that his music and the attitudes it embodies are in some respects atavistic if not wholly obsolete. At the novel's end, Eunice returns to Raleigh to live with Blacksnake's mother when she discovers she is carrying his child; but, we are told, "the baby would not have to sing the blues of his father."[53] Though the blues lineage Eunice carries with her is a masculine one—she is pregnant, after all, with Blacksnake's son—she has demonstrated that it is possible for a woman to survive within it and direct it to her own ends. And it is significant that the music she appropriates is not the proto-feminist "classic" women's blues celebrated by scholars such as Daphne Duval Harrison, Hazel Carby, and Angela Davis but the irredeemably phallic and frequently misogynistic tradition of Blind Lemon Jefferson and Robert Johnson.[54] For here again *Mojo Hand* proposes that just as the blues cannot ultimately be defined by race or class, neither can they be fixed in terms of gender. While the novel endorses Langston Hughes's identification of the blues with the specific racial and class culture of the laboring black masses, "the low down folks," it just as powerfully dramatizes their universality in ways that recall the words of Hughes's Oceola Jones when she sings, "How white like you and black like me. . . . How much like a man. . . . And how like a woman. . . . These are the blues. . . . I'm playing."[55]

NOTES

1. James Weldon Johnson, *The Autobiography of an Ex-Colored Man* (New York: Dover, 1995), 93.

2. Eugene Levy, *James Weldon Johnson: Black Leader, Black Voice* (Chicago: University of Chicago Press, 1973).

3. James Weldon Johnson, *Along This Way: The Autobiography of James Weldon Johnson* (1933; reprint New York: Da Capo Press, 2000), 31, 410–12.

4. These positions are represented by, respectively, Eric Sundquist, *The Hammers of Creation: Folk Culture in African American Fiction* (Athens: Georgia University Press, 1992); Cristina L. Ruotolo, "James Weldon Johnson and the Autobiography of an Ex-Colored Musician," *American Literature* 72.2 (June 2000): 249–74; and Martin Japtok, "Between 'Race' as Construct and 'Race' as Essence: *The Autobiography of an Ex-Colored Man*," *Southern Literary Journal* 28.2 (1996): 32–47.

5. Johnson, *Autobiography of an Ex-Colored Man*, 3–4, 12–13.

6. Ibid., 46–48, 83–86.

7. Ibid., 46–47.

8. Ibid., 46.

9. Ibid., 66.

10. Paul Gilroy, *The Black Atlantic: Modernity and Double Consciousness* (London: Verso, 1993), 101.

11. Johnson, *Autobiography of an Ex-Colored Man*, 50–51.

12. Ibid., 56.

13. See Ruotolo and Japtok for further discussion of the narrator's motives.

14. Johnson, *Autobiography of an Ex-Colored Man*, 67. Ruotolo and Japtok both suggest that this philosophy is discredited by the millionaire's social and racial distance from African American life, by his advice to the narrator to renounce racial solidarity and the American South in favor of a self-seeking career in Europe, and by his ultimate suicide born out of disillusionment and ennui. Certainly, the spiritual and cultural purgatory to which the narrator is ultimately condemned is in part a result of his following the millionaire's advice to drop the pursuit of racial solidarity. But it must be noted that the millionaire never counsels the narrator to renounce black music or to pass as white. Indeed, he encourages the narrator to write "Negro themes" and even offers to sponsor him. His advice is against pursuing a career as a "Negro composer" in America, particularly in the American South. It is based in a realistic understanding of the prejudices and resistance the narrator will encounter there, an understanding that subsequent events at least partially vindicate. Thus, although the millionaire places self-preservation before racial solidarity, he urges the renunciation of neither Negro music nor Negro identity and is remarkably perceptive in his grasp of both American race relations (rigid, hierarchical) and cross-cultural relationships (fluid, radically egalitarian). Even while at his most race conscious, the narrator enjoys "a familiar and warm relationship" with the millionaire, whom he describes as "entirely free from prejudice" and "about all a man could wish to be" (56, 57, 67).

15. Johnson, *Autobiography of an Ex-Colored Man*, 90.

16. See Ruotolo, "James Weldon Johnson," 267–68.

17. Sheet music sales for "Under the Bamboo Tree" reached over 400,000 copies in the year after the song's publication in 1902. See Eugene Levy, "Ragtime

and Race Pride: The Career of James Weldon Johnson," *Journal of Popular Culture* 1 (1968): 357–70, and Levy, *James Weldon Johnson*, 75–98.

18. Johnson, *Along This Way*, 152–53.

19. Paul Oliver, "Selling That Stuff: Advertising Art and Early Blues 78s." Conference paper given at Criss Cross: Confluence and Influence in African American Music, Visual Art and Literature, University of Nottingham, June 18–20, 2004. A revised and expanded version of this paper appears in *The Hearing Eye: Jazz & Blues Influences in African American Visual Art*, ed. Graham Lock and David Murray (New York: Oxford University Press, 2009), 21–46.

20. In *Along This Way*, Johnson presents the decision to abandon his songwriting career as motivated by a temperamental inability to commit fully to the show business lifestyle. He trades its "feverish flutter" for the "stillness of the spirit" essential to the cultivation of his more serious literary sensibility (223).

21. Johnson, *Along This Way*, 335.

22. Johnson was himself a lawyer as well as a founding member, and from 1916 to 1930 secretary, of the civil rights organization the National Association for the Advancement of Colored People.

23. Strictly speaking, the narrator purports to avoid the issue of choice entirely, determining "neither [to] disclaim the black race nor claim the white race," but rather to "let the world take me for what it would" (90). Yet only paragraphs later he informs us that "I had made up my mind . . . I was not going to be a Negro" (91).

24. Johnson, *Autobiography of an Ex-Colored Man*, 41.

25. Langston Hughes, "The Negro Artist and the Racial Mountain" (1926), in *Portable Harlem Renaissance Reader*, ed. David Levering Lewis (New York: Penguin, 1995), 92, 94. See also Hughes's "When the Negro Was in Vogue" (1940) in the same volume, 77–80.

26. Sterling Brown, "Ma Rainey," in *The Collected Poems of Sterling A. Brown*, ed. Michael S. Harper (1980; reprint, Evanston, IL: TriQuarterly Books/ Northwestern University Press, 1996), 62.

27. Sterling Brown, "The Blues as Folk Poetry" (1930), in *The Jazz Cadence of American Culture*, ed. Robert G. O'Meally (New York: Columbia University Press, 1998), 540, 551; Brown, "Folk Literature" (1941), in *A Son's Return: Selected Essays of Sterling A. Brown*, ed. Mark A. Sanders (Boston: Northeastern University Press, 1996), 223; Brown, "Negro Folk Expression: Spirituals, Seculars, Ballads and Work Songs" (1953), in *A Son's Return*, 263; and Brown, "Stray Notes on Jazz" (1946), in *A Son's Return*, 267.

28. Richard Wright, *10 Million Black Voices* (New York: Arno Press, 1941), 130.

29. Ralph Ellison, "Richard Wright's Blues" (1946), in Ellison, *Shadow and Act* (London: Secker and Warburg, 1967), 94, 93, 78.

30. LeRoi Jones, *Blues People: Negro Music in White America* (New York: Morrow, 1963), 69, 94; Ellison, "Richard Wright's Blues," 89. Ellison famously took issue with Jones in a review of *Blues People*, chastising the younger writer for considering the blues "as politics" rather than "as art." See Ellison, "Blues People," in *Shadow and Act*, 257.

31. LeRoi Jones, *Black Music* (New York: Morrow, 1967), 183.

32. Calendar No. 567, 107th Congress, 2nd Session, S.RES 316. See the official Year of the Blues Web site at http://www.yearoftheblues.org/index.asp.

33. J. J. Phillips, *Mojo Hand: An Orphic Tale* (London: Serpent's Tail, 1987), 33, 105.

34. Houston A. Baker Jr., *Blues, Ideology, and Afro-American Literature: A Vernacular Theory* (Chicago: University of Chicago Press, 1984), 184.

35. Phillips, *Mojo Hand*, 73, 81–82.

36. Ibid., 46.

37. Ibid., 106.

38. Ibid., 107–8.

39. Ibid., 108.

40. Ibid., 109.

41. Baker, *Blues, Ideology, and Afro-American Literature*, 5.

42. Ellison, "Richard Wright's Blues," 78–79.

43. Jones, *Black Music*, 176.

44. Phillips, *Mojo Hand*, 136, 170.

45. Ellison, "Richard Wright's Blues," 93, 94, 90, and "Blues People," 255.

46. Jones, *Blues People*, 236.

47. Phillips, *Mojo Hand*, 85, 101.

48. Ibid., 49.

49. Ibid., 108.

50. Ibid., 29.

51. Ibid., 30 (emphasis in original).

52. Ibid., 66.

53. Ibid., 178.

54. Daphne Duval Harrison, *Black Pearls: Blues Queens of the 1920s* (New Brunswick, NJ: Rutgers University Press, 1988); Hazel Carby, "'It Jus Be's Dat Way Sometime': The Sexual Politics of Women's Blues," in *Unequal Sisters: A Multicultural Reader in U.S. Women's History*, ed. Ellen Carol DuBois and Vicki L. Ruiz (London: Routledge, 1990), 238–49; Angela Y. Davis, *Blues Legacies and Black Feminism* (New York: Vintage, 1999). The first song Eunice plays on Blacksnake's guitar is Blind Lemon Jefferson's epic of phallic sexual torment, "Black Snake Moan," which he recorded in 1926 (*Mojo Hand*, 26–27). *Mojo Hand*'s fascinating gender politics require much greater discussion than I can give them here. As the novel's subtitle indicates, it is a feminist re-telling of the Orpheus myth in which, on one level, the gender roles of Orpheus and Eurydice are reversed: in Phillips's version, it is the woman who follows her male object of desire into the underworld. On another level, though, the Greek myth's gender roles are adhered to but have their meaning subverted. The Orphic musician, Blacksnake, is duly dismembered by jealous and vengeful women, but their hostility is provoked not, as in the Greek myth, by his refusal to break a vow of fidelity to his dead wife but by his sexually exploitative mistreatment of women. Blacksnake's murder is a punishment killing for sexist attitudes and conduct. Moreover, instead of passing out of the world with him, as Orpheus's music does, Blacksnake's art is appropriated and transformed by those he

exploited. It is possible to read *Mojo Hand*'s complex interweaving of racial and sexual politics as an early instance of feminist critical engagement with the patriarchal bias and sexism of both the civil rights movement and the political and cultural wings of black nationalism. On these issues see Sara Evans, *Personal Politics: The Roots of Women's Liberation in the Civil Rights Movement and the New Left* (New York: Vintage, 1980), esp. chapter 4, "Black Power—Catalyst for Feminism."

55. Langston Hughes, "The Blues I'm Playing" (1934), in Lewis, *Portable Harlem Renaissance Reader*, 626 (ellipses in original).

WORKS CITED

Baker, Houston A., Jr. *Blues, Ideology, and Afro-American Literature: A Vernacular Theory.* Chicago: University of Chicago Press, 1984.

Brown, Sterling A. "The Blues as Folk Poetry." In *The Jazz Cadence of American Culture.* Ed. Robert G. O'Meally. New York: Columbia University Press, 1998. 540–51.

———. "Folk Literature." In Brown, *A Son's Return.* 207–31.

———. "Ma Rainey." In Sterling A. Brown, *The Collected Poems of Sterling A. Brown.* Ed. Michael S. Harper. 1980. Reprint, Evanston, IL: TriQuarterly Books/Northwestern University Press, 1996. 62–63.

———. "Negro Folk Expression: Spirituals, Seculars, Ballads and Work Songs." In Brown, *A Son's Return.* 243–64.

———. *A Son's Return: The Selected Essays of Sterling A. Brown.* Ed. Mark A. Sanders. Boston: Northeastern University Press, 1996.

———. "Stray Notes on Jazz." In Brown, *A Son's Return.* 265–74.

Carby, Hazel. "'It Jus Be's Dat Way Sometime': The Sexual Politics of Women's Blues." In *Unequal Sisters: A Multicultural Reader in U.S. Women's History.* Ed. Ellen Carol DuBois and Vicki L. Ruiz. London: Routledge, 1990. 238–49.

Davis, Angela. *Blues Legacies and Black Feminism.* New York: Vintage, 1999.

Ellison, Ralph. "Blues People." In Ellison, *Shadow and Act.* 247–58.

———. "Richard Wright's Blues." In Ellison, *Shadow and Act.* 77–94.

———. *Shadow and Act.* London: Secker and Warburg, 1967.

Evans, Sara. *Personal Politics: The Roots of Women's Liberation in the Civil Rights Movement and the New Left.* New York: Vintage, 1980.

Gilroy, Paul. *The Black Atlantic: Modernity and Double Consciousness.* London: Verso, 1993.

Harrison, Daphne Duval. *Black Pearls: Blues Queens of the 1920s.* New Brunswick, NJ: Rutgers University Press, 1990.

Hughes, Langston. "The Blues I'm Playing." In Lewis, *Portable Harlem Renaissance Reader.* 619–27.

———. "The Negro Artist and the Racial Mountain." In Lewis, *Portable Harlem Renaissance Reader.* 91–95.

———. "When the Negro Was in Vogue." In Lewis, *Portable Harlem Renaissance Reader.* 77–80.

Nick Heffernan

Japtok, Martin. "Between 'Race' as Construct and 'Race' as Essence: *The Autobiography of an Ex-Colored Man.*" *Southern Literary Journal* 28.2 (1996): 32–47.

Johnson, James Weldon. *Along This Way: The Autobiography of James Weldon Johnson.* 1933. Reprint, New York: Da Capo Press, 2000.

———. *The Autobiography of an Ex-Colored Man.* New York: Dover, 1995.

———. *God's Trombones: Seven Negro Sermons in Verse.* New York: Penguin, 1976.

Jones, LeRoi (Amiri Baraka). *Black Music.* New York: Morrow, 1967.

———. *Blues People: Negro Music in White America.* New York: Morrow, 1963.

Levy, Eugene. *James Weldon Johnson: Black Leader, Black Voice.* Chicago: University of Chicago Press, 1973.

———. "Ragtime and Race Pride: The Career of James Weldon Johnson." *Journal of Popular Culture* 1 (1968): 357–70.

Lewis, David Levering, ed. *The Portable Harlem Renaissance Reader.* New York: Penguin, 1995.

Oliver, Paul. "Selling That Stuff: Advertising Art and Early Blues 78s." In *The Hearing Eye: Jazz & Blues Influences in African American Visual Art.* Ed. Graham Lock and David Murray. New York: Oxford University Press, 2009. 21–46.

Phillips, J. J. *Mojo Hand: An Orphic Tale.* London: Serpent's Tail, 1987.

Ruotolo, Christina L. "James Weldon Johnson and the Autobiography of an Ex-Colored Musician." *American Literature* 72.2 (June 2000): 249–74.

Sundquist, Eric. *The Hammers of Creation: Folk Culture in African American Fiction.* Athens: Georgia University Press, 1992.

Wright, Richard. *10 Million Black Voices.* New York: Arno Press, 1941.

T W O   Blackface Minstrelsy and Jazz Signification
in Hollywood's Early Sound Era

Corin Willis

There is general agreement among cultural historians that whereas much of the power of jazz and blues still came across on radio and recordings,[1] the expressivity of African American music was closed down and contained in Holly-wood film. As Ann Douglas has noted, "Seeing was one thing, hearing another. Black musical performers had their biggest opportunities in the pure sound media."[2]

I want to examine this process of containment through a consideration of co-presence. Co-presence, a phenomenon that has attracted remarkably little critical attention, is the term I use to describe the widespread practice in early sound film of juxtaposing African American actors and performers with whites in blackface. A particular historical tension occurred when the African Americans involved in these co-present scenes happened to be jazz artists, since jazz had been central to the process whereby African American popular cultural performance had managed to break free from the minstrel trope at the turn of the twentieth century. I want to begin by looking at two film scenes from the early sound era as a way of establishing the parameters of what this chapter will have to say about jazz and black music in film. These scenes are the blackface "voodoo" dance in *The King of Jazz* (1930) and the feature debut of the African American dance act the Nicholas brothers in the minstrel show number in *Kid Millions* (1934).

The lack of an African American presence in *The King of Jazz* has been well recorded. Krin Gabbard notes, "A more elaborate, more thorough denial of the African American role in jazz is difficult to imagine."[3] Underlining the film's "sin of erasing black people from jazz"[4] is the lack of any black presence in its final number, "The Melting Pot of Music," which an announcer introduces thus: "the melodies of all nations are fused into one great new rhythm, JAZZ." There is, however, one extended moment of "black" presence in the film during the rendition of Gershwin's "Rhapsody in Blue." Paul Whiteman ends his spoken introduction to the number with the statement "jazz was born in the African jungle to the beating of the voodoo drums." Then, as the rhythmic opening drum sequence of "Rhapsody in Blue" begins, there is a cut to a low-angle shot of an almost naked man, his entire body covered in black oily makeup, dancing on a drum. Aided by his improbably large headdress, the man's "wild" dancing casts a huge shadow onto the blue setting behind.[5] The dance increases in its frenzy until the drums and the voodoo man suddenly stop. There is a cut to some showgirls and a white man, who begins to play the soothing clarinet section of the number.

Although Gabbard is extremely attentive to the invisible influence of minstrelsy elsewhere in the film, he does not mention the use of blackface in this scene but instead refers to the "black man's movements."[6] This ambiguity (the implication is that the man under the makeup is African American) is understandable because the film itself seems to have deliberately tried to conceal the actual ethnic identity of the man. The use of such unrealistically oily and dark blackface appears to suggest the dancer is white, yet there is no other self-reflexive pointer to a white performer, such as the exaggerated mouth or wig of minstrelsy.

This concealment of the dancer's ethnicity contributes to the concerted attempt to conjure up a black presence at this moment in the film. That this presence, so conspicuous by its absence in the rest of the film, is called up at this point is instructive because it occurs at the very moment that Whiteman (for white men in general) stakes his claim to the authorship of jazz, to the title "King of Jazz." In his spoken introduction, Whiteman has noted how the number was written for his celebrated 1924 concert at the Aeolian Hall. Now the clarinetist dances away from the camera toward a gigantic grand piano at the rear of the set. Its lid opens to reveal inside, suspended high above the floor, Whiteman and his orchestra. This is followed by a shot of Gershwin himself seated at a different piano, and this image, through a superimposition effect, floats through the air toward the Whiteman orchestra.

In itself this sequence of imagery is a consummate exposition of the contemporaneous understanding of jazz as the white "lifting" (the white men in the sky) of primitive black rhythm (the voodoo dancer enslaved to the drum) into musical form. What I want to highlight here, however, is the way in which blackface functions at this key ideological pressure point in the film to conjure up a sense of an actual African American presence. The most striking aspect of the voodoo dancer, a prophetic image for subsequent patterns of racial representation in 1930s film, is that (however hybrid and ambiguous in its form) it is the archaic blackface signifier that is called up to contain this "African American" presence and the potential of black musical expressivity in the film.

The King of Jazz was released in 1930, the year that Hollywood confirmed itself as the new home of minstrel-derived blackface.[7] Although the minstrel show had died out around the turn of the century and sound film itself had enacted the death throes of vaudeville, it became clear in the first years of the sound era that blackface would retain a prominent and visible place in American popular culture through its presence in Hollywood film. As David Butler has noted, the sheer scale of African American involvement in the evolution of jazz through the 1930s meant that Hollywood could not cling to a Whitemanesque policy of omission: "This total erasure of the vital black presence in jazz became less permissible during the Swing era."[8] So, in addition to being used to conjure up a sense of African American presence, blackface was frequently deployed alongside African American performers, as illustrated in *Kid Millions* in the second of our introductory scenes.

Harold and Fayard Nicholas followed in the footsteps of Duke Ellington and Cab Calloway in leaving a Cotton Club residency to make their first Hollywood feature film.[9] As was the normal practice in 1930s Hollywood, their appearance is restricted to a particular number in the film, in this case a minstrel show performance on a ship. Harold Nicholas begins the number by singing the opening section of the song, "I Want to Be a Minstrel Man," alongside a cohort of Goldwyn showgirls. Then both brothers join a blackfaced Eddie Cantor for an extended dance interlude during his performance of "Mandy."[10] The centerpoint of their screen appearance here is a display of their exuberant dancing skills. Yet, in this context, their role is to take on and project the physicality and bodily excess of the minstrel show "for real," as the Goldwyn girl minstrel troupe maintain their refined showgirl poise.

There is an extraordinary tension in this number, which debuts a new African American act alongside an established blackface act. On the one hand there is the sense of boundaries being broken when an African American male (albeit the child figure of Harold Nicholas) interacts with the white showgirls at the start of the number, and when both brothers share the stage and perform with the star of the film. And yet at the same time these "breakthroughs" are recuperated by the fact that Cantor is showcasing his famous blackface brand in this scene. Indeed, such was the perceived recuperation that this and other co-present numbers involving African Americans together with white film stars were an exception to the rule of the segregated number.[11] It is hard to imagine that cinemas in the South would have cut out a central scene by a leading star in their desire to avoid screening African American performance. There is also tension woven into the actual dancing of the Nicholas brothers, in the way that Cantor, eyes rolling, stands in between them and tries to take his turn, only for them to each take turns in holding him still as the other continues the call-and-response structure of their act.

The feature film debut of the Nicholas brothers in a minstrel show number raises complexities that will take the rest of this chapter to unravel. What I would like to highlight at this point is how clearly the intended function of co-presence is marked out in the extraordinary finale of the number and how the film attempts to resolve the tensions raised in the scene in favor of the racial containment of African American musical expression.

Having completed their dance routine, the Nicholas brothers exit from the side of the frame and seemingly from the film. Their departure acts as the cue for the chorus finale of "Mandy." The penultimate shot of the number begins as a long shot of the Goldwyn chorus girls holding tambourines over their faces. The shot is then transformed into a mid shot of Cantor as his minstrel mask appears from behind the tambourines in the foreground (Figure 2.1). Cantor begins the final refrain of the song: "Mandy—," then turns around for Harold Nicholas, who in some way has been affixed to Cantor's back, to close the number and complete the line, "—and me" (Figure 2.2). A final cut to an extreme long shot of the minstrel troupe, with Harold Nicholas suspended in the middle of it, concludes the scene. With this playful swivel, minstrel man Cantor seems to reveal so much about the conditions of co-presence in early sound film, where archaic minstrel-derived blackface forms clash against a youthful African American vernacular.

Blackface in 1930s Hollywood had largely lost its ability to stand in for an African American presence in the way that minstrelsy in the nineteenth century (at first with white but later also African American participation) had acted as the only "black" presence in American popular culture. At the same time, as I noted above, Hollywood's increasing utilization of black-inspired popular music meant that the total omission of black presence was untenable. *Kid Millions* demonstrates the way in which the floating presence of the blackface signifier in 1930s film attempts to make up for the loss of some of its racial currency by seeking to reattach itself to its African American referent in order to enact

a new cycle of minstrelization, if not by replacement, then through co-presence with African Americans. I should emphasize that I am not suggesting that the co-presence of blackface and African American vernacular forms was a universal practice in early sound film. At the same time, its occurrence does seem significant enough to justify further investigation.

Just a few weeks after the release of *King of Jazz*, Duke Ellington and his band began the process of making African American music visible in Hollywood when they appeared in *Check and Double Check* (1930), starring blackface act Amos 'n' Andy, and in doing so became the first African American jazz band to be credited in an otherwise white film.[12] Thereafter the list of African American artists to appear in co-present scenes in either a debut or early feature film appearance includes many of the best-known African American musicians and dancers of the era: Ivie Anderson (*A Day at the Races*, 1936), the Mills Brothers (*Operator 13*, 1934), the Hall Johnson Choir (*Dimples*, 1934), Bill Robinson (*In Old Kentucky*, 1934), Cab Calloway (*The Singing Kid*, 1936), and Louis Armstrong (*Artists and Models*, 1937). Other film sequences, in similar fashion to *King of Jazz*, used blackface to conjure up African American vernacular artists who were not actually present, such as Fred Astaire's blackfaced homage to Bill Robinson in *Swing Time* (1936) or the blackfaced mimicry of Cab Calloway in *Wonderbar* (1934). Still more films, such as Laurel and Hardy's *Pardon Us* (1931) and Cantor's *Ali Baba Goes to Town* (1937), involved uncredited African American jazz and blues artists in co-present scenes.

It is particularly striking that all the instances of co-presence with African American vernacular acts that I have been able to identify involve artists making either their first or a very early feature film appearance, almost as if blackface functioned as a racial marker early in the screen careers of those artists who gained Hollywood visibility. It is this sense of blackface working as a racial marker in co-present scenes that I want to explore further; that is, the way that blackface in early sound film functioned not to smother over and replace an African American presence in popular culture, as it had in the minstrel show and on the vaudeville stage, but instead to act as the most visible signifier of a wider mode of film perception and portrayal, which, to all intents and purposes, continued to minstrelize the actual African American presence that had now asserted itself in film. It is important first, however, to consider why co-presence, the defining feature of the racially charged persistence of blackface in sound film, has been so neglected in the debates on blackface and in film history generally.

Figure 2.1 (top)
Eddie Cantor. *Kid Millions,* 1934.

Figure 2.2 (bottom)
Harold Nicholas. *Kid Millions,* 1934.

Co-presence has been overlooked, I think, largely because of the shift away from the consideration of blackface minstrelsy as a practice of racial denigration to the exploration of its role in the construction of whiteness. The most influential work in this shift, which "rephrases the issues" in the study of blackface,[13] is Eric Lott's *Love and Theft: Blackface Minstrelsy and the American Working Class*, which argues against the "reigning view of minstrelsy as racial domination."[14] Lott delves underneath the racial markings of minstrelsy to find "cross racial desire" in the practice and redefines it as a "visible sign of cultural interaction."[15]

Brenda Dixon Gottschild has made a telling intervention into Lott's rephrasing of blackface minstrelsy that paves the way for a better understanding of the historical significance of the co-present nature of blackface in film. She argues that Lott's "musings privilege the psyche of the white male subject over and above the soma—the actual, mortal body—of the black male object. They separate white motives from black outcomes."[16] For her, the central component of minstrelsy is "the function and the effect of the minstrel mask on the black object (with function, here implying action)."[17] Gottschild's attitude to blackface minstrelsy is that the historical consequences of the medium on African Americans outweigh any other meaning to be found in the practice. She uses the phrase "minstrel trope" to indicate how minstrelsy continued to have a profound effect on African Americans,[18] even after it disappeared as a visible presence in American popular culture.

Herein lies the full significance of co-presence in early sound film. It acts as a unique visual record of the historical consequences of blackface minstrelsy on African Americans, with the minstrelization of their image occurring as a visible textual process. While each earlier phase of blackface (white minstrel shows, African American minstrelsy, and vaudeville) had operated along segregated lines, its final visibility in early sound film juxtaposed racial signifier with its referent so that "the function and effect of the minstrel mask" on African Americans is displayed. The persistence of blackface in sound film, seen as "minstrelsy's somewhat baffling afterlife" by Lott,[19] takes on a much clearer historical racial logic when its co-present nature is recognized.

Indeed, co-presence, the holding together of an African American presence with the constructed blackface signifier, resonates with many well-known critiques of the cultural representation of African Americans, from W. E. B. Du Bois's notion of "two-ness" to Ralph Ellison's *Invisible Man*. In recognizing the co-present nature of blackface in early sound film, we not only open up the significance that it has in the history of Hollywood's stereotyping of African

Americans; more specifically, we also uncover how blackface in early sound film acts as the most visible sign that the presentation of African American music in Hollywood was caught up in much broader historical cycles than might at first seem apparent.

In using this sense of a racially charged co-presence to ask why jazz did not cross unproblematically into the Hollywood film, we first need to address the definition of jazz. Krin Gabbard has noted how the "contemporary fashion" of 1990s jazz definition is one that "centers canonical geniuses."[20] African American artists dominate this modern jazz canon and yet, as Michael Rogin points out, "The 'jazz' of the Jazz Age, to be sure, was not the music of Jelly Roll Morton, King Oliver, Louis Armstrong and Fletcher Henderson."[21] As both Gabbard and Rogin make clear, the label "jazz" was almost exclusively applied in the 1920s and early 1930s to white performers such as Paul Whiteman. Moreover, this label was often attached to music that would not be recognized today as jazz.

Clearly, assigning authorship to jazz was a racially driven process, as Rogin states: "Almost without exception, popular-culture writing in the 1920s treated Negro primitivism as the raw material out of which whites fashioned jazz. Savage, not polyphonic, rhythm was heard in black music."[22] We can see this denial of black authorship in jazz in the writing of Gilbert Seldes. In relation to the "Negro" contribution to jazz, he wrote in 1924 that "the Negro is more intense than we are, [though] we surpass him when we combine a varied and more intelligent life with his instinctive qualities."[23] In creating his own racially exclusive jazz canon, Seldes wrote, "the greatest art is likely to be that in which an uncorrupted sensibility is *worked* by a creative intelligence."[24] We have already seen how *The King of Jazz* visualizes these sentiments. The intense and instinctive dancing of the blackfaced figure and the savage rhythm of the voodoo drum is lifted, via the sweeping movements of the white clarinetist, up to the heavens where Gershwin and Whiteman *work* it into jazz. It is also the belief in "natural black rhythm" that governed the way in which the Nicholas brothers were cast as the exuberant dance interlude to Irving Berlin's minstrel score in *Kid Millions*.[25]

Our two earlier moments from *The King of Jazz* and *Kid Millions* illustrate the two main themes that I draw from co-presence through the rest of this chapter. First, through the pulsating black figure on the drum and through the Nicholas brothers' gymnastic display of "natural" rhythm, co-presence demonstrates how there was an obsessive emphasis on the notion of an essentialized instinctive and rhythmic black body in Hollywood representations of African

American music and dance. Second, via the ambiguity of the blackfaced dancer (both a "real" and false presence at the same time) and by that closing exchange of minstrel mask for African American performer in *Kid Millions,* co-presence illustrates a music-film relationship whereby the fear of unknowable and hidden expressivity in black music and dance motivated the visual containment of African Americans through a particular form of representation, a process that we might call the minstrelization of the African American image.

I want for a moment to explore in more detail the way in which this key moment in *Kid Millions* negotiates the medium of minstrelsy, because it reveals how there is a deeper historical process of racial containment at work. Why is African American vernacular the subject of blackface racial play in this and other early sound films? What is the film attempting to restore in this moment of exchange between the archaic blackface signifier and youthful jazz expressivity? To address these questions, it is necessary to delve into the origins of minstrelsy itself.

Since Robert Toll's seminal 1974 study, *Blacking Up: The Minstrel Show in Nineteenth Century America*, it has generally been accepted that, regardless of its racist intent and form, the medium arose from extensive and serious white observation of African American cultural practice. One of the more fascinating aspects to emerge from this recognition of the ethnographic basis of minstrelsy, where a "dizzying series of inversions works through the simplest minstrel representation,"[26] is the fact that much of the cultural practice copied by white minstrels was already a resistant commentary *on* whites that had been structured by the conditions of slavery. According to Lisa Anderson, "What the white 'observers' of black culture were actually watching was often black people or performers 'signifyin'' on whites."[27] To understand the racial logic of minstrelsy and its particular means of containing African American vernacular, it is vital to recognize that it was gesture and performance, the African American body itself, that became the principal means of Signifyin(g) meaning that could not be spoken under the watchful eyes of whites.[28]

In his analysis of the "repertoires of black popular culture" that were possible for blacks under the restrictive conditions of white supremacy, Stuart Hall writes, "think of how these [black] cultures have used the body—as if it was, and it often was, the only cultural capital we had. We have worked on ourselves as the canvases of representation."[29] Hall's discussion of black popular culture illustrates how Signifyin(g) involved blacks developing strategies of "over-determination," where they used "heightened expressions, hairstyles, ways of walking, standing, and talking" as a means of "occupying an alien social space."[30] Overdetermined physical gestures, what Hall calls the "rhetorical stylization of the body," were necessary because, "excluded from the cultural mainstream, [they] were often the only performative spaces we had left."[31]

In addition to the use of the body, blacks also communicated Signified meaning in the face of white surveillance through overdetermined practices of looking, nods, winks, and knowing glances from the sides of their eyes. Gottschild cites an incident in Fanny Kemble's diary of slavery on a Georgia plantation in 1838–39 as a representative historical white encounter with the body and facial language of African American Signifyin(g). In the original text, Kemble describes how she visits the Infirmary, where the slaves put on their own mock ball to precede the white ball that will follow that evening (a scenario very similar to the cakewalk, which involved slaves parodying white dance): "It is impossible for words to describe the things these people did with their bodies, and, above all, with their faces, the whites of their eyes, and the whites of their teeth, and certain outlines which . . . they bring into prominent and most ludicrous display."[32]

Perhaps the most striking aspect of minstrelsy is that the very sources of Signified meaning in original African American cultural practice, expressive use of the body and overdetermined looks, were turned into the key racial signs of the minstrel copy. This is made clear in another primary source quoted by Gottschild, an anonymous description of Frank Pelham, member of the first minstrel troupe, the Virginia Minstrels, who exhibited "looks and movements comic beyond conception. He seemed animated by a savage energy. . . . His white eyes rolled in a curious frenzy."[33]

Much has been made of white "misrecognition" in minstrelsy. This position would seem to be in danger of underestimating the process of racial containment at work in the medium. The fact that the afterlife of the white minstrel show materialized as a direct racial containment of African American expression at key junctures for a century or more suggests that minstrelsy recognized and intercepted the Signified meaning of African American gestures all too clearly. If there is "genius" in the "fundamentally black" concept and practice of Signifyin(g),[34] then there was a certain horrifying brilliance in the containment of African American Signification that was at work within the contours of the minstrel mask. In short, minstrelsy denied the hidden meaning of Signifyin(g) and dragged its overdetermined and duplicitous gestures of body and face into the literal world of white racial signification, into the overdetermined racial features of the minstrel mask. We begin to see more clearly the nature of the racial work involved in any juxtaposition of blackface and African American performers in early sound film. But we still have a full turn of the "blackface lore cycle" to consider.[35]

A significant part of the tension in minstrelsy is that the power of black vernacular was being invoked by the practice of mimicry. Berndt Ostendorf makes this point in a wonderfully illustrative account of the historical process whereby jazz can be seen to have "passed through" minstrelsy. He describes how "jazz dance and tap dance clearly are a non Western presentation of the human body which was salvaged in minstrelsy and professionalised in jazz."[36] The crucial historical intervention that allowed the reflowering of African American Signifyin(g) in jazz was African American minstrelsy. Blacks largely took over the format in the later decades of the nineteenth century and used it to develop the key musical forms that emerged in the early twentieth century, notably ragtime and early jazz. As Lisa Anderson notes:

> The black minstrel show has come to be regarded as a "reclaiming" of slave dance and performance. It differs from white minstrelsy in that it gave theatrical form to "signifyin'" on white minstrelsy in the manner in which slaves practiced "signifyin'" on whites in real life.[37]

Ostendorf explains how African American minstrelsy especially, but also white minstrelsy, acted as the conduit that ultimately allowed African American Signifyin(g) expressivity to be reborn in jazz:

> minstrelsy got its start as the imitation of a dance step: Jim Crow. This dance involved the entire body. . . . Early jazz, as Handy and others have noted, struck listeners so forcibly because it called for the entire body. Many converts to jazz tell us that the initial effect of jazz was total. For many it was not just a music, it was a new body feeling and a new world view.[38]

Jazz positively reinscribed meaning into expressive black bodies that had been racialized by white minstrelsy. Ostendorf highlights "that one of the most important single heritages of minstrelsy is the versatility in the presentation of face, voice, and body on stage in music and dance."[39] He argues that the key component of jazz expressivity was the fusion between body and music,

Corin Willis

"the handling of the entire body as instrument and the handling of instruments as extensions of voice and body,"[40] and that this fusion reaffirmed a long-standing tradition in black culture (a point exemplified by Fanny Kemble's account of the music at that African American ball, in which she notes "the feats of a certain enthusiastic banjo player, who seemed to me to thump his instrument with every part of his body at once").[41]

If, as Stuart Hall has asserted, black people have historically "found the deep form, the deep structure of their cultural life in music,"[42] then it would seem that the technological innovation of adding sound to film, occurring as it did in the Jazz Age, was a moment of high promise for African American jazz expression. But as we return to that scene in *Kid Millions*, that playful exchange of minstrel man for African American performer, I hope that I have demonstrated how this juxtaposition works to restage the racial containment of African American vernacular that was embedded in the very origins and formal shape of the minstrel mask itself. Eric Lott has noted how "insistently blackface performance concerned itself with matters of the body,"[43] and it seems clear that one of the key racial functions of the revitalized blackface signifier in early sound film was the disruption of that fusion between body, instrument, and voice that had been restored in jazz. Blackface functioned once again in sound film to inscribe race into black bodies, which were objectified in the model of minstrelsy.

In assessing how jazz fared in 1920s–30s film, David Butler writes: "Fundamental to an understanding of the way that jazz has been used and represented in film is the dualism of mind and body."[44] This Eurocentric dualism marked jazz as inextricably bound up in an instinctive black body and explains why white jazz artists such as Whiteman and Gershwin had to be seen to "lift" the music through interpretation and mental activity. The presence of a racially charged blackface signifier in early sound film is a privileged textual site through which we can see how this mind/body dualism in the representation of "black" music was directly passed on from the minstrel show.

Numerous films in the early sound era repeated the use of blackface to mark out the racial difference of the unthinking and instinctive black body. Al Jolson's second film, *The Singing Fool*, depicts a vaudeville stage show in which white showgirls move from a ballerina routine to a raucous dance as blackfaced minstrel men. As classical music gives way to a more uptempo beat, the earlier ballerina poise of the showgirls is lost in blackface as they strike up a "spontaneous" dance with arms and legs flaying in awkward style. A similar scene occurs in the Bing Crosby film *Too Much Harmony* (1933), with showgirls interchanging between whiteface and blackface, with the latter motivating spontaneous and uncontrolled body movement. Fred Astaire's apparent homage to Bill Robinson in the "Bojangles" number of *Swing Time* begins with a surrealistic scene in which the blackfaced Astaire's feet are ballooned up to giant size. Here, as with the huge shadows cast by the voodoo dancer in *King of Jazz*, Hollywood's obsession with a literal overdetermined racial signification of the black body attempts to mask the art of expressive black vernacular.

All of the above scenes exemplify Gottschild's assertion that "the seat of difference is strongly centered in minstrel body language,"[45] only now in a new context that has direct consequences for African American vernacular expression in Hollywood film. This is demonstrated in the scenes of co-presence involving the onscreen juxtaposition of blackface with African American performers. In *Roman Scandals* (1933), Eddie Cantor uses his minstrel mask to pass as an "Ethiopian witch doctor" and becomes involved in a dance with "jazzy black maids,"[46] who dance with "hot verve and swing"[47] and whose body posture is markedly different from the white women they serve. In *Ali Baba Goes to Town*, Cantor adopts blackface and shouts "Hi de ho" in order to break down the language barrier with an "African" jazz band. The song he sings with them, "Swing Is Here to Sway," succeeds in forcing the surrounding white crowd to spontaneously break out into a jazz dance. In *Artists and Models* (1937), Louis Armstrong stands proud and erect in fusion with his trumpet as a blackfaced Martha Raye leads a crowd of African Americans, who literally crouch as they walk in "black" style to the beat of his music. Momentarily, Armstrong seems to soar above them as one of the closing shots shows him playing on a rooftop above the street before he is drawn into a minstrelizing "eyes to the side" pose, which is quickly caught by what I would term a racial cut—that is, an edit specifically timed to frame and freeze the character in a stereotypical "racial" pose or gesture (Figure 2.3).

The co-present scenes above capture as a visual process the way in which the "mortal body" of minstrelsy visited its racial consequences on African American vernacular long after the death of the minstrel show itself. In co-present scenes such as these, white stars like Cantor, Raye, and Astaire can be seen to interpret the blackness of the black music and dance forms so central to American popular culture, while leaving African Americans themselves grounded in the racial signification of the instinctive and rhythmic black body.

If co-presence is useful in demonstrating the separation of the expressive jazz body from jazz music, and that body's reduction to a racial sign of

difference, then it also helps to illuminate how there were formal features to this minstrelization of African Americans in film. Gottschild writes: "However, what has proven to be the most insidious level of minstrelization, from the Africanist perspective, is the way in which that influence has persisted in non-minstrel cultural forms."[48] The moment to which I have repeatedly made reference, that crucial swivel which exchanges minstrel mask for African American performer in *Kid Millions*, might easily be described as a minstrelization shot. The exchange confirms that the entire purpose of the shot is to implant the racial features of the minstrel mask into the viewer's perception of Harold Nicholas, and the timing of a racial cut to catch him in a wide-eyed pose only serves to confirm the effect. The use of similar shots of African Americans without the reminder of blackface in frame (such as the "eyes to the side" pose of Louis Armstrong noted above), or even more significantly in films without blackface, is a striking illustration of the minstrelization of the African American image in the "nonminstrel cultural form" of film. Minstrelization shots repeated the original racial work of the minstrel mask in the context of narrative film by transforming the overdetermination of Signified African American looks into overdetermined racial signs.

I will close my discussion of co-presence in the early sound era by examining a sequence in *A Day at the Races* that encapsulates my overall argument. Robert Crease has identified *A Day at the Races* as one of the first Hollywood feature films to employ the African American vernacular jazz dance form the Lindy Hop.[49] The Lindy appears in a scene, also involving the Hollywood feature debut of singer Ivie Anderson, toward the end of the film, when the Marx Brothers hide out in the African American living quarters of a race course while on the run from the police. It is a co-present scene because it ends with the Marx Brothers smearing oil on their faces to "look black" in an attempt to evade capture.

The build-up to the appearance of the Lindy is most notable for the repeated use of minstrelization shots to show the reaction of African Americans to the antics of Harpo Marx. Harpo walks around the living quarters playing a high-pitched pipe, which prompts a startled response from several African Americans, who cry, "Who dat man?" As with the minstrelization shot of Harold Nicholas in *Kid Millions*, the duration of the shots used to catch these reactions is timed specifically to capture a performed racial gesture, and the racial cuts used to end the shots are timed to trap the African Americans into a wide-eyed minstrel-like pose.

Corin Willis

At the very moment that the Lindy is introduced, the film signals its intention to racially mark and contain the expressivity of the dance with another minstrelization shot. The penultimate action before the entrance of the Lindy is a comical dance between Ivie Anderson and a fat African American man. The man completes his dance by spinning to a halt. There is a match-on action edit to a big close-up minstrelization shot that catches his performed (racial) gesture as he opens his mouth wide and pushes his eyes to the side to look at something offscreen (Figure 2.4). As with the earlier minstrelization shots I noted above, this one, too, enacts a particularly strong containment of an African American screen presence. Under normal circumstances, the cut to close-up in order to privilege a character's look is an empowering moment in film. Here, however, the audience's attention is primarily directed to the peculiarity of the man's racial expression, and his act of looking becomes part of his stereotypical containment in the film.

Within itself, this minstrelization shot works as a strong act of racial containment of the African American vernacular. The way in which the man's expression is overlaid onto the upstanding trumpet in the background works to dissipate the energy and virility of that most potent symbol in the African American jazz band and also to separate out and defuse the contribution of the body, physical and facial gesture, to jazz expressivity.

A brief shot now shows the background jazz band with their instruments jutting upward before there is a cut to a ground-level long shot and the Lindy dancers sweep into view, forcing Harpo offscreen. The Lindy Hoppers' ejection of Harpo seems to reassert the jazz vernacular that he has earlier stopped and controlled with his pipe. It seems to offer the hope, as did the Nicholas brothers' action of stopping Eddie Cantor from dancing in *Kid Millions*, that the infusion of a brand-new African American jazz act onto the Hollywood screen had the power to wrestle back some degree of autonomy for black performers.

As in *Kid Millions*, however, minstrelization shots are used to contain the expressivity of African American jazz performance. The first four shots of the dance stay in a long-shot setup, and this stylistic choice, together with the full-length shots of the dancers taken from ground level, help, as Robert Crease notes, to translate some of the key features of the Lindy to the screen.[50] Of the sixteen shots used to film the Lindy, only two break and disrupt this pattern of filming the dance in long shot. Shot five is a mid shot of a woman shaking her head from side to side, and shot six is a mid close-up of a man grinning and rolling his eyes. Both these shots are classic minstrelization shots (i.e., mid/

close-up framing, frontality, shot duration geared entirely around a performed racial gesture, and a cut timed to catch this gesture). The minstrelization shot of the female dancer, in particular, like the earlier shot of the fat man against the jazz trumpet, serves to disrupt the fusion of body performance with jazz instruments and music. It occurs as she performs an important move in the Lindy dance; she is "shown shaking her head and wagging her finger, doing the 'truckin',' a popular step that year."[51] The visual motif of the minstrelization shot, signaled prominently earlier in the sequence in the reactions of the African Americans to Harpo Marx, has grown in its insistence through the number until it acts as the point of rupture that breaks up and contains a historically significant infusion of black jazz vernacular onto the Hollywood screen.

The formal and conceptual manipulation of the blackness of African Americans in these minstrelization shots is emblematic of much wider formal practices of racial marking at work on African Americans in this and other early sound films. The effect here is such that the scene almost of itself seems to render the structuring influence of the minstrel trope as a visible presence. Indeed, when the blackface does eventually emerge, it appears to mark the thorough racial containment of the Lindy dancers, Ivie Anderson, and the other African American jazz performers in the scene. The police arrive and the Marx Brothers quickly smear oil over their faces in a rather unsuccessful attempt to disguise themselves. Here the "enfeebled" state of the blackface, its floating, almost ethereal presence, adds to, rather than detracts from, its racial significance in the scene. The racial power of minstrel forms had always resided not so much in terms of their mimesis or realism, but rather in terms of how they functioned historically in relation to African Americans and in their consequences and effect on them. If the Marx Brothers' "failed" minstrelsy seems to indicate that, nine years into sound film, the currency of blackface was breaking down, it nonetheless signifies and highlights a much more insidious process at work in the era of co-presence, where the original racial work of the minstrel mask was restaged within the contours of the African American screen image.

The co-present scenes in *Kid Millions* and *A Day at the Races*, along with similar scenes in many other films, make clear why, to use Richard Merelman's phrase, the "black cultural projection" of jazz did not cross onto the Hollywood screen,[52] as African American vernacular forms and artists were brought back under the glare of the very white minstrel gaze from which historically they had just emerged. This cinematic juxtaposition of black and blackface perfor-

56   Corin Willis

mance reactivated the racial function that had been embedded in the minstrel mask since its origins; that is, the racial containment of Signifyin(g) African American vernacular expression. In a process that Linda Mizejewski refers to as the "circular logic of blackface,"[53] Hollywood defused and denied African American jazz Signification through a practice of corporeal containment and visual minstrelization that mirrored the minstrel show's original racial containment of African American Signifyin(g).

NOTES

1. See, for example, Michelle Hilmes, *Radio Voices: American Broadcasting, 1922–1952* (Minneapolis: University of Wisconsin Press, 1997).

2. Ann Douglas, *Terrible Honesty: Mongrel Manhattan in the 1920s* (New York: Farrar, Straus and Giroux, 1995), 420.

3. Krin Gabbard, *Jammin' at the Margins: Jazz and the American Cinema* (Chicago: University of Chicago Press, 1996), 10.

4. Ibid., 14.

5. *The King of Jazz* was an early Technicolor film.

6. Gabbard, *Jammin' at the Margins*, 13.

7. Among other releases of 1930 in which blackface characters either pretend to be, or are perceived to be, "actually black" were those by the blackface comic acts Amos 'n' Andy (*Check and Double Check*) and Moran and Mack (*Anybody's War*), Eddie Cantor's film debut *Whoopee!*, and Al Jolson's *Big Boy*.

8. David Butler, *Jazz Noir: Listening to Music from "Phantom Lady" to "The Last Seduction"* (Westport, CT: Praeger, 2002), 44.

9. Herbert Goldman, *Banjo Eyes: Eddie Cantor and the Birth of Modern Stardom* (New York: Oxford University Press, 1997), 165.

10. The minstrel song "Mandy" was originally scored for Ziegfeld's 1919 "minstrel" Follies by Irving Berlin (Goldman, *Banjo Eyes*, 72). One hidden motivation for the co-presence in this scene in *Kid Millions* may be that this original Ziegfeld minstrel show involved Cantor playing end man opposite a blackfaced Bert Williams.

11. Thomas Cripps has highlighted the normal racial logic involved in the segregated number: "Black entertainers usually appeared in film segments without whites so they could be cut when the film was shown in the South." Thomas Cripps, *Slow Fade to Black: The Negro in American Film, 1900–1942* (1977; reprint, Oxford: Oxford University Press, 1993), 357.

12. Gabbard, *Jammin' at the Margins*, 167.

13. John Blair, "The Cultural Complexity of Blackface Minstrelsy," *American Quarterly* 47.3 (1995): 538.

14. Eric Lott, *Love and Theft: Blackface Minstrelsy and the American Working Class* (New York: Oxford University Press, 1995), 7.

15. Ibid., 6. Another example of the shift toward questions of "whiteness" is Michael Rogin's analysis of blackface in terms of its function as a medium of identity transfer, whereby immigrants were transformed into white Americans. See Michael Rogin, *Blackface White Noise: Jewish Immigrants and the Hollywood Melting Pot* (Berkeley: University of California Press, 1996).

16. Brenda Dixon Gottschild, *Digging the Africanist Presence in American Performance: Dance and Other Contexts* (Westport, CT: Praeger, 1996), 90.

17. Ibid., 89.

18. Ibid., 90.

19. Lott, *Love and Theft*, 240.

20. Gabbard, *Jammin' at the Margins*, 8.

21. Rogin, *Blackface White Noise*, 112.

22. Ibid., 113. The widespread perception that black rhythm was the "raw material" of jazz may also have been a reason why white jazz did not cross successfully onto the Hollywood screen. See Berendt Ostendorf, "Minstrelsy and Early Jazz," *Massachusetts Review* 12 (Autumn, 1979): 596; and Butler, *Jazz Noir*, 43.

23. Gilbert Seldes, *The Seven Lively Arts* (1924; reprint, New York: Sagamore Press, 1957), 96.

24. Ibid., 99 (emphasis in original).

25. I hope this makes clear why I think a variety tap dance act should figure in an account of the way in which jazz was contained in Hollywood's early sound era. In the 1920s and '30s, jazz was seen as part of a long-standing African American expressive tradition—that included blues, spirituals, ragtime, and dance—rather than as a separate and distinct form, and it was this expressive tradition that was the target of Hollywood's racial containment.

26. W. T. Lhamon Jr., *Raising Cain: Blackface Performance from Jim Crow to Hip Hop* (Cambridge, MA: Harvard University Press, 1998), 140.

27. Lisa Anderson, "From Blackface to 'Genuine Negroes': Nineteenth-Century Minstrelsy and the Icon of the Negro," *Theatre Research International* 21.1 (1996): 22.

28. Henry Louis Gates adopted the formulation "Signifyin(g)," which I retain throughout the chapter, to designate a process he has shown was central to the African American culture that preceded minstrel mimicry. Explaining how Signifyin(g) arose from the African tradition of the "double voiced," Gates writes: "Free of the white person's gaze, black people created their own unique vernacular structures and relished in the double play that these forms bore to white forms." Gates uses the capital "S" to differentiate the word's meaning from the normal white use of the term and brackets the "g" to indicate that this letter is not usually sounded when the word is spoken by African Americans. Henry Louis Gates Jr., *The Signifying Monkey: A Theory*

of African-American Literary Criticism (New York: Oxford University Press, 1988), xxiv–xxv, 46.

29. Stuart Hall, "What Is This 'Black' in Black Popular Culture?" In *Representing Blackness: Issues in Film and Video*, ed. Val Smith (New Brunswick, NJ: Rutgers University Press, 1997), 128–29.

30. Ibid., 129.

31. Ibid.

32. Frances A. Kemble and Frances A. Butler Leigh, *Principles and Privilege: Two Women's Lives on a Georgia Plantation* (1863; reprint, Ann Arbor: University of Michigan Press, 1995), 96.

33. Gottschild, *Digging the Africanist Presence*, 105.

34. Gates, *Signifying Monkey*, 46, 64.

35. Lhamon, *Raising Cain*, 225.

36. Ostendorf, "Minstrelsy and Early Jazz," 595.

37. Anderson, "From Blackface to 'Genuine Negroes,'" 17.

38. Ostendorf, "Minstrelsy and Early Jazz," 595.

39. Ibid., 594.

40. Ibid.

41. Kemble, *Principles and Privilege*, 97.

42. Hall, "What Is This 'Black,'" 128.

43. Lott, *Love and Theft*, 86.

44. Butler, *Jazz Noir*, 29.

45. Gottschild, *Digging the Africanist Presence*, 105.

46. Gerard Mast, *Can't Help Singing: The American Musical on Stage and Screen* (New York: Overlook, 1987), 119.

47. William Routt and Richard J. Thompson, "'Keep Young and Beautiful': Surplus and Subversion in *Roman Scandals*," *Journal of Film and Video* 42.1 (1990): 31.

48. Gottschild, *Digging the Africanist Presence*, 124.

49. Robert Crease, "Divine Frivolity: Hollywood Representations of the Lindy Hop, 1937–1942," in *Representing Jazz*, ed. Krin Gabbard (Durham, NC: Duke University Press, 1995), 213.

50. Ibid., 215.

51. Ibid.

52. Richard Merelman, *Representing Black Culture: Racial Conflict and Cultural Politics in the United States* (New York: Routledge, 1995), 2.

53. Linda Mizejewski, *Ziegfeld Girl: Image and Icon in Culture and Cinema* (Durham, NC: Duke University Press, 1999), 131.

WORKS CITED

Films

Artists and Models. Dir. Raoul Walsh. Paramount, 1937.

A Day at the Races. Dir. Sam Wood. MGM, 1937.

Kid Millions. Dir. Roy Del Ruth. MGM, 1934.

The King of Jazz. Dir. John Murray Anderson. Universal, 1930.

Texts

Anderson, Lisa. "From Blackface to 'Genuine Negroes': Nineteenth-Century Minstrelsy and the Icon of the Negro." *Theatre Research International* 21.1 (1996): 17–23.

Blair, John. "The Cultural Complexity of Blackface Minstrelsy." *American Quarterly* 47.3 (1995): 537–42.

Butler, David. *Jazz Noir: Listening to Music from "Phantom Lady" to "The Last Seduction."* Westport, CT: Praeger, 2002.

Crease, Robert. "Divine Frivolity: Hollywood Representations of the Lindy Hop, 1937–1942." In *Representing Jazz.* Ed. Krin Gabbard. Durham, NC: Duke University Press, 1995. 207–28.

Cripps, Thomas. *Slow Fade to Black: The Negro in American Film, 1900–1942.* 1977. Reprint, Oxford: Oxford University Press, 1993.

Douglas, Ann. *Terrible Honesty: Mongrel Manhattan in the 1920s.* New York: Farrar, Straus and Giroux, 1995.

Gabbard, Krin. *Jammin' at the Margins: Jazz and the American Cinema.* Chicago: University of Chicago Press, 1996.

Gates, Henry Louis, Jr. *The Signifying Monkey: A Theory of African-American Literary Criticism.* New York: Oxford University Press, 1988.

Goldman, Herbert G. *Banjo Eyes: Eddie Cantor and the Birth of Modern Stardom.* New York: Oxford University Press, 1997.

Gottschild, Brenda Dixon. *Digging the Africanist Presence in American Performance: Dance and Other Contexts.* Westport, CT: Praeger, 1996.

Hall, Stuart. "What Is This 'Black' in Black Popular Culture?" In *Representing Blackness: Issues in Film and Video.* Ed. Val Smith. New Brunswick, NJ: Rutgers University Press, 1997. 123–33.

Hilmes, Michelle. *Radio Voices: American Broadcasting, 1922–1952.* Minneapolis: University of Wisconsin Press, 1997.

Kemble, Frances A., and Frances A. Butler Leigh. *Principles and Privilege: Two Women's Lives on a Georgia Plantation.* 1863. Reprint, Ann Arbor: University of Michigan Press, 1995.

Lhamon, W. T., Jr. *Raising Cain: Blackface Performance from Jim Crow to Hip Hop.* Cambridge, MA: Harvard University Press, 1998.

Lott, Eric. *Love and Theft: Blackface Minstrelsy and the American Working Class.* New York: Oxford University Press, 1995.

Mast, Gerard. *Can't Help Singing: The American Musical on Stage and Screen.* New York: Overlook, 1987.

Merelman, Richard. *Representing Black Culture: Racial Conflict and Cultural Politics in the United States.* New York: Routledge, 1995.

Mizejewski, Linda. *Ziegfeld Girl: Image and Icon in Culture and Cinema.* Durham, NC: Duke University Press, 1999.

Ostendorf, Berndt. "Minstrelsy and Early Jazz." *Massachusetts Review* 12 (Autumn 1979): 574–602.

Rogin, Michael. *Blackface White Noise: Jewish Immigrants and the Hollywood Melting Pot.* Berkeley: University of California Press, 1996.

Routt, William, and Richard J. Thompson. "'Keep Young and Beautiful': Surplus and Subversion in *Roman Scandals.*" *Journal of Film and Video* 42.1 (1990): 31.

Seldes, Gilbert. *The Seven Lively Arts.* 1924. Reprint, New York: Sagamore Press, 1957.

Toll, Robert. *Blacking Up: The Minstrel Show in Nineteenth Century America.* New York: Oxford University Press, 1974.

Paging the Devil: Jazz and Blues Poetics

"Thanks, Jack, for That": The Strange Legacies of Sterling A. Brown

THREE

Steven C. Tracy

For poet Sterling Brown, mythic heroes represented a central concern for the African American artist, and the African American ballad and blues tradition was often the soul of his best work. He dealt with real-life heroes in "Remembering Nat Turner," "The Temple," and "Ma Rainey." He created his own ballad heroes in the "Slim Greer" poems, "Long Gone," "Johnny Thomas," and "He Was a Man" and described his reverence for little-known guitarist Big Boy Davis in "Odyssey of Big Boy." In poems like "Virginia Portrait" and "Coolwell Vignette," he dealt with the possibility that indeed common people could be heroic, and they represented for him, in his echoing of Carl Sandburg's line, the "Strong Men" whose connection to the group spirit and strength of the spirituals allowed them to "keep a-comin' on" and "git stronger." This preoccupation with heroes and the concern with their significance is expressed in microcosm—and nowhere better—in "Strange Legacies" (see pp. 75–76).[1] The poem demonstrates the relationship between myth-hero John Henry, real-life hero Jack Johnson, and the nameless poor couple so much a part of the heroic tradition despite their seeming distance from it. What makes the poem so remarkable is Brown's ability to mix the elements of the blues ballad and formal poetry into a slice of reality with the sweep of myth and history, and to establish how people need to challenge their perceptions of what heroes are in order to recognize the roots of the heroic in the common.

Brown's critics have recognized from the beginning down to the present day that folk material was of central importance to Brown's work. James Weldon Johnson, who in his own earlier work had despaired over the inadequacies of dialect poetry, praised Brown's folk poetry as making "beyond question, a distinctive contribution to American poetry."[2] Alain Locke, too, found that Brown was "able to compose with the freshness and naturalness of folk balladry,"[3] and not, as Jean Wagner points out, by simply copying formal elements:

> Sterling Brown's work takes issue with that of his predecessors in the sense that it represents a living rebuttal of the notion that a great gulf separates the outlook of the New Negro from the spirit exhibited in slave poetry. He is not satisfied . . . to borrow only the forms of his verse from the storehouses of folk poetry. He imbues himself with its spirit, its practical philosophy, its humor, and its speech.[4]

He did all of this, as Stephen Henderson points out, "without condescension, without sentimentality, and without fakery,"[5] and he did it with the intention to "extend rather than reflect meaning."[6] Echoing Whitman, Brown himself wrote that "the Negro poet must write so that whosoever touches his book touches a man,"[7] emphasizing the closeness of the literary aesthetic and production with communion with humanity. So his mining of the "accurate, imaginative transcripts of folk experience, with flashes of excellent poetry"[8] that he found in such folk material as the blues helped Brown to create what he called "living-people-lore."[9]

Such living-people-lore intends to capture what Joanne Gabbin terms Brown's "master theme," the existence, and necessity, of an "indomitable spirit" of "defiance and strength."[10] This spirit was not only a legacy of generations of African Americans who faced the nearly insurmountable odds of slavery, Reconstruction, and Jim Crow policies. It was also a social and economic necessity for the generation of African Americans for whom Brown was writing when the poem was published, in the year the Scottsboro Boys were convicted of rape in Alabama: 1931, after all, found Americans crippled by the Great Depression, African Americans doubly so. "Hard times don't worry me, I was broke when they first started out," Lonnie Johnson sang in 1937 on the recording "Hard Times Ain't Gone Nowhere."[11] This tune was coupled with another entitled "Something Fishy (Don't Lie to Me)," which, although not overtly political in its lyrics, might well express commentary on social and economic policies aimed at subordinating African Americans.

In "Strange Legacies," Brown mixes aspects of the oral and written traditions to help depict both the mythic and historical legacies that help empower the "common people" to recognize and employ their own heroism in circumstances that require heroes to perform amazing feats against incredible odds to survive. This is, in fact, to prevail in a hostile environment that plots their destruction

Steven C. Tracy

and is, conversely, destroyed when they are not eliminated or debased, but resolute. That resolution stems from the performance, style, content, and spirit of the folk tradition, which empowers a mythic hero who provides the "dramatic breakthroughs of the sacred (or the 'supernatural') into the World."[12] That, in turn, furnishes the opportunity for the historical figure to partake of that spirit and achieve a mythic status and, again, impart the heroic to the "ordinary"—to awaken average black people, including the speaker, to their own heroic nature. As Mark Sanders asserts, "These heroes do not occupy a fixed place in a static past but affect an ongoing present as the 'us' of the poem attempts to formulate the future."[13] Much like what scholars call a nodal ballad (in reference to "John Henry" and certain other ballads in the folk tradition), the poem we are presented with is not a continuous, chronological narrative, but rather presents a heartfelt and celebratory voice and space that creates, asserts, and affirms identity.

The mythic hero in the poem, of course, is John Henry. The earliest reference to John Henry occurs in E. C. Perrow's collection of songs gathered from east Tennessee mountain whites in 1905 and published in the *Journal of American Folklore*, though the earliest reference linking John Henry with the steam drill was collected in 1913 by Perrow from Kentucky mountain whites.[14] As Mac Edward Leach points out, the work songs, ballads, and legends that form the John Henry story complex are related to each other, though they sometimes differ widely in the presentation and content of material. The work songs have "no content pattern and only a general emotional core,"[15] though songs inspired by them, like Mississippi John Hurt's "Spike Driver Blues," do have more substantial content. In the ballads, Leach sees "a basic and unchanging core of narrative" that nonetheless shows "all sorts of variation in detail."[16] Finally, the legend has grown out of "an assortment of work songs, ballads, casual references, folk tales, and deliberate conscious invention" to transform John Henry from folk hero to popular hero.[17]

There is disagreement about whether John Henry, steel driver on the C&O or any American railroad, actually existed: Leach argues that there is "no sure evidence beyond the songs";[18] Richard Dorson asserts that "the evidence painstakingly gathered and skillfully evaluated by Chappell builds a powerful case for the historicity of John Henry at Big Bend"; and a recent book, *John Henry: The Untold Story of an American Legend* by Scott Reynolds Nelson, also makes a strong historical case for his existence.[19] In fact, the actual existence of one particular John Henry whose life inspired the story complex is of only peripheral importance. Brown's point in part is that the myth draws from reality, that "common folks" are the source of myths, creating and embodying them, though the embodiment is not always so obvious or identical. John Henry the figure is a paradigm, the "facts" of his life accepted for their spiritual accuracy and efficacy. The myths, then, connect to a significant communal past, a struggling present, and a projected future that assumes optimistically that the present can be survived as the past had been, honoring this space and time continuum by giving voice to the spirit and artistry of these various generations of survivors. Looking in detail at Brown's poem in relation to the folk tradition will allow us to better appreciate the depth and breadth of folklore and blues influence, and to see how texts of this nature might be more fully understood in such a context. What it will also reveal is Brown's special insider knowledge of the style and substance of African American folklore and his particular skills in establishing its legitimacy in belles lettres and in employing it for the aims of his work.[20]

Brown's description of the "John Henry" ballad (in his essay "Blues, Ballads, and Social Songs") combines the narrative outline with the spiritual essence of the ballad: John Henry is, in Brown's own words, "the steel driving hero of the Negro working class," who accepted "the challenge of the new-fangled steam drill" that threatened "his supremacy as a steel-drivin' man."[21] Though when a little baby John Henry foresaw and prophesied his own death, coming while he was at work with his hammer in his hand, he faced his destiny "like a natural man," occasionally faltering, laying down his hammer and crying in a number of variants collected by folklorists or recorded commercially, but never capitulating until his death. John Henry's ability to falter and cry, like other mythic heroes such as Gilgamesh and Christ, humanizes him, emphasizes his mortality and humanity even as he is about to commit the heroic act that will make him a hero. The commonness of his names, John and Henry, reemphasizes his generalized humanity. He is not an emperor, lord, or king, but he *is* John Henry as royally endowed as anyone who has walked the earth. He is truly of the people, by the people, and for the people.

Recognizing this unifying spirit in "John Henry," Sterling Brown uses elements of the blues ballad not only to unify his poem "Strange Legacies" but also to help unify his people's past, present, and future, their successes and failures, uncommon and common, as well as provide an aesthetic for the contemporary literary artist that is close to that of the masses of African Americans. (The accessibility of John Henry because of his humanity is a boon to Brown's poem.) This aim to unify is what also guides Brown's rare departures from the blues ballad in "Strange Legacies": one example is the speaker's direct address to John Henry using both his name and the pronoun "you," since John Henry is rarely, if ever, in the blues tradition addressed by the performer.[22] John Henry becomes, as do Jack Johnson and the nameless couple, a more immediate presence because of the speaker's direct address, and the speaker himself is elevated to the heroic status of seer and sayer even as he briefly chronicles the importance of the heroes. The various mythical and historical moments are compressed by the speaker into one aesthetic vision, so that the unity that the speaker emphasizes is both of space (geographically and on the page) and time. Brown begins the poem, after all, with "one thing" and ends with "one more try," and nine times throughout the poem draws speaker, subject, and audience all together through the use of the pronouns "us" and "we." The unity of effort, perseverance, and spirit is thus underscored by the closeness of the speaker with his subjects and audience.

The speaker's first address to John Henry comes in the form and language appropriate to the traditional "John Henry" blues ballad, indicating the speaker's familiarity with and respect for the folk tradition. Indeed, analysis of a typical performance of the ballad by a folk musician such as a harmonica player would yield even further valuable connections between Brown's poem and the tradition. One of the important things to emphasize about the performance of the blues ballad is this: that "John Henry" had widespread popularity—among both blacks and whites—and that it was a standard test piece, especially for slide guitarists and harmonica players alike. In both cases it is usually a solo piece. As a solo piece, it requires the performer to relay both the rhythms and melody of the piece, the chords and the lead lines, simultaneously, or at least skillfully enough to suggest simultaneity. Polyrhythms, of course, are a common feature of African American music, stemming most likely from the African roots side of the musical equation from which the blues emerged. It is possible to see this polyrhythmic element as a dynamic, galvanic community that recognizes its commonalities and diversities by unifying currents and counter-currents in a complex rhythmic performance, which—with its improvisations, whoops, and tempo changes—signals an African American cultural space that is broad and deep.[23] Similarly, the poem brings together three currents of a polyrhythmic community heroism: the mythic hero John Henry, the historical hero Jack Johnson, and the anonymous heroes, the old, nameless couple. They are united as social models through their courage and perseverance, but divergent in the ways they reflect the community.

The syncopation that is also involved in the performance of the "John Henry" ballad serves the purpose of calling attention to the spaces between the metronomic beats, which is always implied but frequently not stated.[24] These spaces embrace the possibilities beyond mundane and established regularity and can be seen as vernacular spaces, corresponding to the everyday language of the "common" people, who lie outside the mainstream, the "official" society, history, and culture of a country, whose historians and artists use a more "elevated" and "respectable" language to place themselves at a distance from the folk. The word "syncopation" stems etymologically from *syncope*, which refers to a skipped heartbeat, and thus sounds a kind of interruption to regularity and points to a stronger consciousness of what it means to live, deep down, physically and viscerally. These are the deep feelings that Brown tries to evoke in the polyrhythmic and syncopated elements that he hambones into his work.[25]

This connection to the rhythms, which helps identify the piece as African– and African American–derived, with churning chords as opposed to single notes, establishes a communal aesthetic and a group past in the performance of the song. But this type of rhythm might have been employed for a variety of songs—"Train Imitations," for example—so the frequently single-note melody line enters to establish the individual instance being presented, but always with its important relation to the group context musically. In fact, the use of a train-like churning rhythm for "John Henry" not only connects specifically to the story, but also evokes the symbol of the train so important in African American folklore. As a symbol of geographical mobility (especially important for the post-slavery ramblers who began to generate the blues), of spiritual transcendence, and of sexuality, among other things, the train serves as an important cultural symbol that creates a meaningful context for John Henry's story. It is significant that the polyrhythmic and syncopated elements of the performance, arising out of the interaction between multi-note chords and single-note melody line, provide a musical performance analogue of the relation of individual to community that Brown describes in his poem.

The five-line stanza marking the speaker's address to John Henry, beginning with line 11, takes the form of the often loose ten-bar musical stanza to which the ballad is sung:

> John Henry was a little teeny boy
> Settin' on his daddy's knee.
> He point his finger at a little piece of steel
> "Lawdy, that gon' be the death of me

Steven C. Tracy

Lawdy, that gon' be the death of me."
(Jimmie Owens, "John Henry")[26]

We see here the common folklore motif of the hero prophesying his own death, in this case a childhood prophecy, couched in the characteristic five-line stanza with the last two lines containing roughly the same words repeated for dramatic effect (in fact, some versions of this blues ballad repeat the line four times or more, or repeat the music for this line without singing, or feature some combination of the two). Art, in a very real sense here, becomes life—predicts it, sets out its trajectory and boundaries, and encompasses not only the life of John Henry, but the spirit that he passes along to the community too. Through the life of the ballad, the manner of communication and performance is passed along as well. Brown's poem, then, passes on a philosophy of living and a manner of communication that ultimately becomes a tribute both to John Henry and to those who follow in his tradition, speaker and audience included.

Brown also includes many of the essential elements of the ballad: John Henry's name is repeated for emphasis; his instrument, the hammer, is mentioned three times; his occupation, that of a steel driver, is referred to; and his pride (line 2 of Brown's stanza on Henry) is emphasized by its end rhyme with the defiance of death described in the last two lines of the stanza, which is itself celebrated through the repetition. David Evans has suggested that the blues ballad tends "to 'celebrate' events rather than relate them chronologically and objectively in the manner of other American folk ballads."[27] Brown's use of "John Henry" in "Strange Legacies" is clearly celebratory, fragmentary in the sense that it makes no attempt to relate the details of the complete story, but certainly whole in the broader spiritual sense that Brown seeks to emphasize. Brown's primary audience, after all, knows the story of John Henry in its general outline and specific variants but is listening now to another variant that drives to the core of the ballad even as it departs from it, or rather develops it to its contemporary usefulness.

The relation of events in "Strange Legacies" is also not chronological in the sense that John Henry's contest with the stream drill, if it actually took place, is generally dated in the 1870s. This was roughly sometime around the birth of Jack Johnson in 1878, who is addressed first in the poem, and perhaps forty years before Johnson defeated Jim Jeffries. The chronological time element is, then, fractured, and the poem is rearranged in a more delicate balance. This strategy is a combination of modernist techniques: sifting through the fragments of a contemporary existence that is informed by a meaningful past, we can sense a Picasso-esque cubist approach that is generated from an Einsteinian sense of the relativity of time and a Bergsonian sense of the way drama bends time to the consciousness of human beings. The lyric is used here as more of a fulcrum existing outside time, a soul center for the trinity of stanzas that find their unity in the spirit of John Henry and the style of "John Henry."

For if the speaker is the spiritual brother of John Henry—and he addresses him as such—the boxer who persevered against white American racism and defeated the white hope Jim Jeffries in 1910, keeping black hope alive, is a relative of John Henry as well: Jack, John's son. Johnson's given name at birth was, after all, John Arthur Johnson, connecting him even more closely to John Henry. Clearly the speaker of the poem feels a close kinship to the public figure, too, addressing him familiarly as "Jack," which itself has a kind of informal, vernacular ring by virtue of its function as a colloquial catch-all name used to refer to any other male who is being addressed by a speaker. One might say "Thanks, Jack" to any Tom, Dick, or Harry, but this common Jack, like John Henry, is a king. Like John Henry, he stands there "like a man," defying those who would say that he is not a man but an animal, and takes his "punishment . . . confident." Significantly, these two words, both dactyls, are rhymed in this stanza, emphasizing that confidence comes with the knowledge that one can take, even invite, punishment. The word "confident" gains from the dactylic shoving of the opening accented syllable, with its hard "c" initial consonant, in the face of the reader just as Johnson confronts Jeffries. But it also benefits from its status as one of only two one-word lines in the poem. The other, "Brother," addressed to John Henry, makes the point that the knowledge of brotherhood with John Henry, who proved that punishment could be confronted and overcome just in the act of confronting, inspires confidence in the individual and group. The difference between the two, that Jack Johnson prevails over Jim Jeffries and survives, while John Henry dies in his contest with the steam drill, sharpens the focus: it is the struggle and the spirit of the figures that binds them together, and the significance of the spirit, not the length of the life, that is important.

That Brown intends for us to compare the two figures is clear from his employment of seven-line stanzas with identical rhyme schemes (ABCBCDC) in his discussions of both figures. Johnson's grinning confidence contrasts with the heartsickness of John Henry, but finally their mettle is identical. Johnson is much more actively in control, as evidenced by Brown's use of the present

Steven C. Tracy

participles "taking" and "inviting," indicating Johnson's knowledge of the necessity to seize and welcome the punishment he is confident he can survive and overcome. The past-tense verbs of the corresponding stanza describing John Henry, lines 16–22, serve to make his experience more oppressive and his fate more circumscribed than Johnson's, but the help requested is requested in the present tense, for what is important about John Henry has survived. Johnson's loss of his title to another white hope, Jess Willard, in Cuba in 1915, receives no attention here because it is his ascent to the mountaintop, and the style with which he made the trip, taunting and challenging white authority, that made him the heir of John Henry. And it is what kept him alive in African American literary consciousness twenty years after Brown's poem, in places such as Ralph Ellison's *Invisible Man*.

That oppressiveness of John Henry's situation places him temperamentally closer to the "old nameless couple" than it does to Johnson. This is perhaps another reason why Brown placed his discussion of John Henry in the center of the poem's three sections, between the historically more documented figures. Certainly, since we have dealt with a couple of heroes who have provided legacies of strength and perseverance, we are now ready to confront the couple in Red River Bottom, who do not seem to possess the legendary status or physical stature of the other two figures. One thing they do possess is each other. They are the two who are one couple, who can put forth the kind of unified and collective effort for which Brown is calling in the poem. This couple is both literally and figuratively at the bottom, in the bottom lands and at the bottom of the socio-economic strata. They are also, it should be pointed out, at the bottom of the poem, since they do come last. But, as the periodic sentence Brown uses in this stanza emphasizes, sometimes that is where the reader finds the significant information. Perhaps more important, the reader anticipates finding revelation there. Like Langston Hughes, who deals with the bottom, the low-down, as the positive and valuable in his Simple stories, Brown sees the bottom not as the dregs, but the foundation, that genesis of existence crucial to meaningful survival.

At first it seems that the nameless couple are, in fact, rather passive. The present perfect verbs refer to activities completed in the past, but those "activities" seem to consist of watching helplessly while floods, boll weevils, droughts, cholera, and "the man" have preyed upon them. They "have seen" these things repeatedly, Brown repeating the words three times. He also repeats "out" thrice, continually chronicling their banishment from society and success. In fact, in contrast to Jack Johnson's "taking," "inviting," and "boring in" and John Henry's "sticking," the couple's only present participle is "muttering," hardly as active or resolute as those of Johnson and John Henry. Still, they seem to have grown heartsick like the John Henry of the blues ballad, and their final words, repeated in the manner of the final two lines of the poem's "John Henry" stanza, reflect their status as legendary heroes. They may be nameless, anonymous, considered by some to be insignificant, but Brown sees them as worthy of the status of heroes for always trying once more. Perhaps they are even greater heroes, more extraordinary, because they are "ordinary." They are, like their "porkers," stretched out, pulled by the tensions that threaten to assail to the snapping point poor black Americans in a hostile environment. And when, in fact, they repeat:

> "Guess we'll give it one mo' try.
> Guess we'll give it one mo' try."

they are saying that they'll give it one more try *twice*. In addition to the couple's speaking in the cadence, language, and form of art that is significant to them, that form, the blues ballad, with its repetition of the fourth line, carries the knowledge that their lives will be a repetition or series of "one more tries." Their incessant need to try is almost as formulaic in its reoccurrence as the repetition is formulaic in the "John Henry" blues ballad stanza.

Brown, then, has made folklore the repository of strength and wisdom of the past, present, and future, and he has done it in such a way as to seem not to be distorting the tradition, but revealing it as it is intuitively known by the "common people." Those common people have the ability to see it when it is embodied in the present and embody it themselves for the benefit of future generations. And Brown the artist has, in fact, defeated those who were claiming that African American folklore and dialect, and particularly the blues, were unworthy of serious consideration or unsuitable as a source for literary inspiration. This was especially important as the heyday of the Harlem Renaissance was fading and a focus on Leftist political dogma and naturalistic techniques was beginning to impact upon the use of folklore in African American literature. Brown's poems are his series of "one more tries." As in his great paean "Ma Rainey," where he brings together speaker, audience, and singer in one unified poem of community,[28] in "Strange Legacies" he unites his artistic aims with the aims of the nameless couple, to persevere, knowing of the conspiracy to defeat him.

Strange Legacies

One thing you left with us, Jack Johnson.
One thing before they got you.

You used to stand there like a man,
Taking punishment
With a golden, spacious grin;
Confident.
Inviting big Jim Jeffries, who was boring in:
"Heah ah is, big boy; yuh sees whah Ise at.
Come on in. . . ."

Thanks, Jack, for that.

John Henry, with your hammer;
John Henry, with your steel driver's pride,
You taught us that a man could go down like a man,
Sticking to your hammer till you died.
Sticking to your hammer till you died.

Brother,
When, beneath the burning sun
The sweat poured down and the breath came thick,
And the loaded hammer swung like a ton
And the heart grew sick;
You had what we need now, John Henry.
Help us get it.

So if we go down
Have to go down
We go like you, brother,
'Nachal' men. . . .

Old nameless couple in Red River Bottom,
Who have seen floods gutting out your best loam,
And the boll weevil chase you
Out of your hard-earned home,
Have seen the drought parch your green fields,

And the cholera stretch your porkers out dead;
Have seen year after year
The commissary always a little in the lead;

Even you said
That which we need
Now in our time of fear,—
Routed your own deep misery and dread,
Muttering, beneath an unfriendly sky,
"Guess we'll give it one mo' try.
Guess we'll give it one mo' try."

 To hear—and see—Steven Tracy play a solo harmonica/vocal version of "John Henry," please go to the *Thriving on a Riff* Web site at http://www.oup.com/us/thrivingonariff, where—courtesy of Document Records—you can also hear a solo harmonica version by DeFord Bailey and a guitar/vocal version by "Big Boy," who may be Big Boy Davis, the itinerant bluesman befriended by Sterling Brown and celebrated by him in the poems "Odyssey of Big Boy" and "When de Saints Go Ma'ching Home" (more details on the Web site).

NOTES

1. See Sterling A. Brown, "Strange Legacies," in *The Collected Poems of Sterling A. Brown*, ed. Michael S. Harper (New York: Harper and Row, 1980), 96–97. The other poems cited in this paragraph can also be found in this volume.
2. James Weldon Johnson, "Introduction to the First Edition of *Southern Road*," in *Collected Poems of Sterling A. Brown*, 17.
3. Alain Locke, "Sterling Brown: The New Negro Folk Poet," in *Voices from the Harlem Renaissance*, ed. Nathan Irvin Huggins (New York: Oxford University Press, 1976), 252.
4. Jean Wagner, *Black Poets of the United States* (Urbana: University of Illinois Press, 1973), 476–77.
5. Stephen Henderson, "A Strong Man Called Sterling Brown," *Black World* 19.11 (1970): 5.
6. Sterling Stuckey, Introduction, in *Collected Poems of Sterling A. Brown*, 9.
7. Sterling A. Brown, *Negro Poetry and Drama* (1937; reprint, New York: Atheneum, 1972), 80.
8. Sterling A. Brown, "The Blues as Folk Poetry," in *Folk-Say* 1, ed. Benjamin A. Botkin (Norman: University of Oklahoma Press, 1930), 339.

9. Sterling A. Brown, "The Approach of the Creative Artist: Remarks at a Conference on the Character and State of Studies in Folklore," *Journal of American Folklore* 59 (1946): 506.

10. Joanne V. Gabbin, *Sterling A. Brown: Building the New Black Aesthetic Tradition* (Westport, CT: Greenwood Press, 1985), 133.

11. Lonnie Johnson, "Hard Times Ain't Gone Nowhere," *Complete Recordings in Chronological Order (1937–1940)* (Document BDCD 6024, 1992).

12. Mircea Eliade, *A Mircea Eliade Reader*, ed. Wendell C. Beane and William G. Doty (New York: Harper and Row, 1975), 4.

13. Mark A. Sanders, *Afro-Modernist Aesthetics and the Poetry of Sterling A. Brown* (Athens: University of Georgia Press, 1999), 74.

14. Mac Edward Leach, "John Henry," in *Folklore and Society* (Hatboro, PA: Folklore Associates, 1966): 96–97.

15. Ibid., 93.

16. Ibid., 94.

17. Ibid.

18. Ibid., 95.

19. Richard Dorson, "The Career of John Henry," *Western Folklore* 24.3 (1965): 156; Scott Reynolds Nelson, *John Henry: The Untold Story of an American Legend* (New York: Oxford University Press, 2006).

20. Brown's insider knowledge of African American folklore is evident in many of his essays; see, for example, his "Negro Folk Expression: Spirituals. Seculars, Ballads, and Work Songs," *Phylon* 14 (1953): 45–61. Brown, of course, was not alone in either his interest in the John Henry legend or the employment of African American folklore in literature—precedents for the latter ranged from the dialect and rhythms of Paul Laurence Dunbar and James Weldon Johnson's mighty folk preachers to the spirituals, blues, ballads, jokes, and tales of Langston Hughes, Zora Neale Hurston, Jean Toomer, and Claude McKay—but critics from Johnson and Locke to Stuckey and Gabbin have recognized Brown's special relationship with the folk and folk materials. For another, more recent example of this recognition, see John S. Wright, "The New Negro Poet and the Nachal Man: Sterling Brown's Folk Odyssey," in *Black American Literature Forum* 23.1 (Spring 1989): 95–106. Other early interest in John Henry included scholarly studies by Guy B. Johnson, *John Henry: Tracking Down a Legend* (Chapel Hill: University of North Carolina Press, 1929) and Louis Chappell, *John Henry; A Folk-lore Study* (Frommannsche Verlag, W. Biedermann, 1933), and a novel (1931) and a musical play (1939, starring Paul Robeson), both called *John Henry*, both by Roark Bradford and both due to be republished by Oxford University Press in a single volume.

21. Sterling A. Brown, "Blues, Ballads and Social Songs," in *75 Years of Freedom* (Washington, DC: Library of Congress, 1943), 23.

22. However, in a version by Peg Leg Sam, the singer claims to have been a water boy who personally observed the events. Peg Leg Sam, "John Henry" (1972), on the LP *The Last Medicine Show* (Flyright 507/508, 1973).

23. Alan Lomax argues just such a point in his Cantometric studies, which, though somewhat controversial, seem solid on this point. See Alan Lomax, "Song Structure and Social Structure," *Ethnology* 1.4 (October 1962): 425–51.

24. Although I would be reluctant to say that polyrhythms produce syncopation, I would say that there are times when even the most highly developed technique of a harmonica soloist cannot manage all the notes of a polyrhythmic performance without some adjustment. This leaves the instrumentalist with little alternative but to anticipate or delay the beat in one of the rhythms in order to manage all of the rhythms that are being juggled. Of course, sometimes the rhythms are not being played at a particular point at all. A basic rhythm can be established by itself at the beginning of a performance that is frequently thereafter suggested only through emphasis in another rhythmic figure that is more involved or complicated. This is often the case with a metronome beat.

25. Brown certainly employs the syncopated rhythms of the "John Henry" ballad in his poem. To give just one example: the seven syllables of line 11 could be pronounced in a wooden manner that adheres to a metronomic beat, but the next line, which is nine syllables, requires a rushing of the pronunciation of "Henry," followed by three unaccented syllables that hurry us to the next accent on "steel." The following line, the longest of the three at twelve syllables, reproduces three unaccented syllables in a row on syllables three, four, and five, followed by two anapests, which makes it clip along after the opening iamb of the line. The fact that each poetic line would be performed in the folk tradition of the ballad in two bars of 4/4 demonstrates how the lines would be increasingly rushed to fit the musical time frame of performance. This would build momentum and crowd syllables into pre-beats and post-beats as well. This is not to say that other poems do not add extra syllables or vary accentual patterns in similar ways, but combined with the notion of the music as a "given" to the folk audience, it seems to be Brown's way of managing the rhythms and syncopation of performance.

26. Jimmie Owens, "John Henry" (1934), on the LP *Red River Runs* (Flyright-Matchbox 259, 1979).

27. David Evans, *Big Road Blues* (Berkeley: University of California Press, 1982), 44.

28. Sterling A. Brown, "Ma Rainey," in *Collected Poems of Sterling A. Brown*, 62–63.

WORKS CITED

Recordings

Johnson, Lonnie. "Hard Times Ain't Gone Nowhere." *Complete Recordings in Chronological Order (1937–1940)*. Document BDCD 6024, 1992.

Owens, Jimmie. "John Henry." 1934. *Red River Runs*. LP. Flyright-Matchbox 259, 1979.

Peg Leg Sam. "John Henry." 1972. *The Last Medicine Show*. LP. Flyright 507/508, 1973.

Texts

Bradford, Roark. *John Henry*. New York: Literary Guild, 1931.

———. *John Henry: A Play*. New York: Harper, 1939.

Steven C. Tracy

Brown, Sterling A. "The Approach of the Creative Artist: Remarks at a Conference on the Character and State of Studies in Folklore." *Journal of American Folklore* 59 (1946): 506–7.

———. "The Blues as Folk Poetry." In *Folk-Say* 1. Ed. Benjamin A. Botkin. Norman: University of Oklahoma Press, 1930. 324–39.

———. "Blues, Ballads and Social Songs." In *75 Years of Freedom*. Washington, DC: Library of Congress, 1943. 17–25.

———. *The Collected Poems of Sterling A. Brown*. Ed. Michael S. Harper. New York: Harper and Row, 1980.

———. "Ma Rainey." In *Collected Poems of Sterling A. Brown*, 62–63.

———. "Negro Folk Expression: Spirituals, Seculars, Ballads and Work Songs." *Phylon* 14 (1953): 45–61.

———. *Negro Poetry and Drama*. 1937. Reprint, New York: Atheneum, 1972.

———. "Strange Legacies." In *Collected Poems of Sterling A. Brown*, 96–97.

Chappell, Louis. *John Henry; A Folk-lore Study*. Frommannsche Verlag, W. Biedermann, 1933.

Dorson, Richard. "The Career of John Henry." *Western Folklore* 24.3 (1965): 155–63.

Eliade, Mircea. *A Mircea Eliade Reader*. Ed. Wendell C. Beane and William G. Doty. New York: Harper and Row, 1975.

Evans, David. *Big Road Blues*. Berkeley: University of California Press, 1982.

Gabbin, Joanne V. *Sterling A. Brown: Building the New Black Aesthetic Tradition*. Westport, CT: Greenwood Press, 1985.

Henderson, Stephen. "A Strong Man Called Sterling Brown." *Black World* 19.11 (1970): 5–12.

Johnson, Guy B. *John Henry: Tracking Down a Legend*. Chapel Hill: University of North Carolina Press, 1929.

Johnson, James Weldon. "Introduction to the First Edition of *Southern Road*." In *Collected Poems of Sterling A. Brown*, 16–17.

Leach, Mac Edward. "John Henry." In *Folklore and Society*. Hatboro, PA: Folklore Associates, 1966. 93–106.

Locke, Alain. "Sterling Brown: The New Negro Folk Poet." In *Voices from the Harlem Renaissance*. Ed. Nathan Irvin Huggins. New York: Oxford University Press, 1976. 251–57.

Lomax, Alan. "Song Structure and Social Structure." *Ethnology* 1.4 (October 1962): 425–51.

Nelson, Scott Reynolds. *John Henry: The Untold Story of an American Legend*. New York: Oxford University Press, 2006.

Sanders, Mark A. *Afro-Modernist Aesthetics and the Poetry of Sterling A. Brown*. Athens: University of Georgia Press, 1999.

Stuckey, Sterling. Introduction. In *Collected Poems of Sterling A. Brown*, 3–15.

Wagner, Jean. *Black Poets of the United States*. Urbana: University of Illinois Press, 1973.

Wright, John S. "The New Poet and the Nachal Man: Sterling A. Brown's Folk Odyssey." *Black American Literature Forum* 23.1 (Spring 1989): 95–105.

Phraseology: An Interview with Michael S. Harper

Graham Lock

Michael S. Harper was born in Brooklyn, New York, in 1938 and moved to Los Angeles at the age of thirteen. He attended graduate school in Iowa, then returned to California to teach before moving in 1970 to Brown University, where he is now University Professor and professor of English. His first book of poems, *Dear John, Dear Coltrane* (1970), was nominated for a National Book Award, and his many subsequent volumes have brought him numerous honors. Jazz has been a major presence in his poetry, both as theme and stylistic influence, and he has frequently returned to the music of John Coltrane, declaring (in 1990), "I guess Coltrane was my Orpheus."

Songlines in Michaeltree: New and Collected Poems appeared in 2000 and has been followed by four CD releases, including the self-produced three-disc *Selected Poems* (2004) and two collaborations with bass clarinetist Paul Austerlitz, *Double Take* and *Our Book on Trane: The Yaddo Sessions* (both 2004). He has co-edited three major literary collections: *Chant of Saints* (with Robert Stepto), *Every Shut Eye Ain't Asleep,* and *The Vintage Book of African American Poetry* (both with Anthony Walton). He has also edited *The Collected Poems of Sterling A. Brown* (1980), a book that proved very influential in reaffirming Brown's place in the first rank of American poets, and *I Do Believe in People: Remembrances of W. Warren Harper 1915–2004* (2005).

The interview took place in June 2003 in Saratoga Springs, where Michael Harper was in retreat at the Yaddo artist colony.

GL: I'd like to talk to you first about Sterling Brown. I know you edited his *Collected Poems.*

MSH: I also selected his poems for the National Poetry Series. He hadn't written any since the 1940s, but so many of his poems were so pioneering that he was an influence in many, many areas. I'm glad I did it and I'm glad I did the book, because the poems were brought back and made more available. There's a kind of reclamation that certain people just deserve.

It was a very important thing for Sterling's career, for his life, because you know he died in '89 and he was already retired when we made the decision to do the book. But I've never had a regret, not one. The poems stand up, after all these years. I had a little resistance from a couple of people; they said, well, the guy is old. I said, that's not the point. If we were talking about Keats . . . you know, Keats is not "old"; Milton . . . these people are not "old." They're classic.

GL: The aim of our book is to look at the influence of jazz and blues on other African American art forms, and vice versa, though our main emphasis is on the music's influence and our starting point is that it does have a special and central role in the culture. Would you agree with that?

MSH: Absolutely.

GL: And that there are certain historical reasons for this, to do with slavery and the fact that music was basically the only form of expression allowed?

MSH: Yes, all of that. And, of course, Sterling Brown did remarkable pioneering work, not only his essays, many of them on the blues, but *Southern Road*, *The Negro Caravan*, his work with the Gunnar Myrdal study, with the Federal Writers Project—all of that was extremely important.[1] And his collaborations with people like Ben Botkin, the whole slave narrative project, *Lay My Burden Down*—he was involved in that; he was involved in *Folk-Say*.

Sterling was going to do what he called *The New Negro Caravan* and he wanted he and I to be editors. He talked about this all through the '80s. He wanted to upgrade his notion of what the first *Caravan* had achieved. Of course, the impact of music was very important. I don't know what Sterling would have done, for example, with hip-hop; but it would certainly have been interesting, given some of his characterizations, given his famous prototype of the heroic figure who was semi-literate or illiterate, Big Boy Davis, the blues singer in "When de Saints Go Ma'ching Home," who was an actual man.[2] As Sterling used to say, "I learned the arts and sciences at Williams and Harvard; I learned the humanities at Lynchburg, Virginia." Which is to say that when he went to Lynchburg, Carter Woodson, who was one of his high school teachers, told him, you need to go and be immersed in your people. And Sterling had such extraordinary gifts as a scholar and a poet that even James Weldon Johnson said, in his introduction to *Southern Road*, that of all the poets, it was Sterling who best captured the genuine black folk idiom.

Sterling never characterized his efforts at folk speech in his poems as "dialect poetry." He would never call it that. He would say, "I am writing these poems in the folk idiom." The reason why Sterling said that is because he felt the values of black American speech . . . It was so penetrating, so laconic, and so resonant that to be in that speech community was to be given this information. What Sterling had was the ability to arrange it, because he studied—among other people—Shakespeare, Milton, Chaucer; he had what we call a classical education, Greek and Latin. So he could see the value of what his people had done; one could say a semi-literate or illiterate people, but you don't have to be literate to have a tradition. All of those great ballads that you know and grew up with, many of them anonymous, were crafted over generations by people who couldn't read and write. So it's not an anomaly for you to have a resonant past, which is captured by people who don't have a written tradition.

GL: Can I ask you about Sterling's poems? There are several that are either about, or influenced by, the blues and the spirituals, yet he doesn't seem to write very much about jazz. The only poem I know where jazz features is "Cabaret," and he portrays it in a negative light there.[3] But in his essays, he appears to like jazz as much as anything else.

MSH: Oh, Sterling had an incredible record collection. I'll tell you the story of "Cabaret" because it's very important. The reason why the poem is cast in the way it is, is because he was at a black and tan in Chicago in 1927, and Fletcher Henderson's was the band. And because of the impact of Tin Pan Alley on the blues, and music *period*, he decided he would have to, in legitimate fashion, critique the phoniness—this was during Prohibition. So remember it's Fletcher Henderson's band and he's talking about where these people, who are the entertainers, the dancers, really come from, right? Then, all of a sudden, the poem shifts into the levee, the 1927 Mississippi flood, and those black people chained to the levee. And, of course, Bessie Smith, "My heart cries out for muddy water."[4] Now Sterling didn't talk about it like this. He'd just read the poem. But it's a poem that has at least three levels to it. It's a very complicated poem, with various voicings. I think what he was after, certainly at the time, was an assault on Tin Pan Alley music as a substitute for the real blues, and the pressure that was put on theatrical people—what he'd call his people—to bastardize something that was really sacred to him.

If you look at the essays he did, you notice that he wrote a wonderful essay on Jelly Roll Morton, which was in *Black World*.[5] Sterling's favorite people were mostly piano players: he loved Willie "the Lion" Smith, he loved James P. Johnson, he loved the guy who played for the Mafia . . . Earl Hines. He knew all of that music. He had the record collection. He had the first blues ever recorded in the United States, 1920, "Crazy Blues" by Mamie Smith. He said he bought it when he was a student at Williams College, so he was a student of the blues way back. And so many of those poems are written with a blues consciousness to them. And, more than anything, when you look at his ballads . . .

> Look at old Scrappy puttin' on dog,
> Puttin' on dog, puttin' on dog,
> Look at old Scrappy puttin' on dog,
> Todle-oh-in' with his Jane.[6]

. . . the theme of people being pushed too far and the kind of style that couldn't be suppressed. The way in which his characters in the Slim Greer cycle were able to do impossible things: well, they were all based on people he knew. When he was tellin' those damn stories about the woman who . . . where Slim goes and plays the piano and all of a sudden he loses his sense of things and the cracker says to him, "No white man could play like that."[7] Sterling was just full of that kind of stuff. He loved to attack the conventions, the conventions of race. And, of course, the famous poem about all of the people laughing in the phone booth in Atlanta:

> Down in Atlanta,
> > De whitefolks got laws
> For to keep all de niggers
> > From laughin' outdoors.[8]

And they're all trying to get in the telephone booth to laugh! These kind of things. And the famous poem called "Slim in Hell," which was based on Orpheus and Eurydice: you know, Slim goes to Hell, which turns out to be Dixie. Sterling said to me one day, he said, every one of those places that

I mention in the poem, there was a race riot. Race riot in Waco, race riot in Rome, race riot in Vicksburg, every one of those place names. So Sterling had an extremely well-developed social conscience. And enormous courage.

GL: I was just puzzled that he had all these poems on blues and ballads and didn't write very much about jazz. Whereas Langston Hughes does include jazz and concentrates more on urban blues, while Sterling Brown seems to refer more to folk and rural blues.

MSH: Oh, I think that's true. Sterling was very much immersed in that. But he wrote those wonderful poems, you know, "They don't come by ones, they don't come by twos, but they come by tens."[9]

GL: Some critics have seen this aspect of his work as implicitly anti-modernist. The fact that he's looking at the rural rather than the urban, that he's into folk and blues—and using those forms—rather than commercial jazz. Do you think that's a fair comment?

MSH: Well, I think it's contrary to what I know about Sterling. I know he'd read "The Waste Land" in 1922. He was just out of Williams and into Harvard when he was reading *The Dial* and *The Double Dealer* and all of those damn poems. He knew Pound and he knew him early. But he would choose a Frost over an Eliot. It wasn't so much that he didn't appreciate what Eliot was doing, but he felt—I'm not sure Sterling ever said this, probably I intuited it—he didn't feel that Eliot had made the proper choice by becoming an Anglican and leaving the country. Here he was, born on the Mississippi River in St. Louis: why was it good enough for Twain but not good enough for him? Because Sterling was very much an Americanist. He believed in American literature. I mean, he was studying American literature when it was a new literature.

I think Sterling was so prescient on the arteries of blues and jazz and where they came from. He knew a tremendous amount about New Orleans; he knew a lot about Kansas City; and he learned this stuff early and he was writing about it early.[10]

GL: Can we talk about your own work? I'm particularly interested in your relationship with John Coltrane. I know you saw him play live . . .

MSH: Oh, many times.

GL: Did you know him to talk to?

MSH: Sure, sure. You gotta understand about Coltrane; Coltrane was not very talkative. He was very friendly but he was all business. I can remember . . . I first saw Coltrane play live in 1955, which was the year I graduated out of high school. I went to a school in Los Angeles called Dorsey High School, which had some famous people—Eric Dolphy went to the same school. Dolphy was older than me; he was not at school when I was there but people knew that Eric Dolphy had been to that school.

We had no black teachers at Dorsey when I was there, not one. Billy Higgins, who was a great drummer, went to Jefferson High School in Los Angeles, which had black teachers, so he was immersed in the musical tradition of his peers with a teacher who could mentor him. I went to a school which had been a predominantly white school in a border area. Los Angeles is a very segregated place and there was a dividing line, LaBrea Avenue; being on the other side of LaBrea Avenue put you in a different district. My father, who was working at the post office, bought a house in what had been an all-white neighborhood. We came out to L.A. in June and there were homes in our neighborhood that were bombed. I mean, it wasn't the South but homes in our geographic area were bombed. That's how much venom there was regarding the changeovers. This is 1951.

Robert Bone and a couple of other people who have written essays about this think that the thing that made me a poet was being cut loose from my native turf, Brooklyn, New York, at age thirteen, which I think is true. Everything I knew, including being born in the same house my mother was born in, all of that went and I had to start over again. I'd been to pretty good schools, too, but from the time I left Brooklyn until pretty much going into college, I went dead intellectually. I was like an automaton going to school. I was a fairly good student, but I wasn't challenged and I think I was in an emotional depression of sorts.

I had already known a great deal about music when I was in New York because my parents were big band people. They had a record collection; they went out. They heard Basie; they heard Jimmie Lunceford; they went to dances. I had listened to records of Bessie Smith and Billie Holiday; and I already knew about Parker, the bebop people, even when I was a kid. That was avant-garde music and that was what I was interested in.

Okay, Los Angeles had a music tradition also and they had a lot of guys who didn't travel. Dexter Gordon was from Los Angeles; Mingus was born in Arizona but he grew up in Los Angeles—I knew his older sister because she and I worked in the post office together. One of my teachers at undergraduate school was Christopher Isherwood, who encouraged me to write plays; I was writing one-act plays. I was talking in exotic speech, like a hipster. I was talking like Lester Young. And I was writing one-act plays. I don't think Isherwood was really interested in that, but he liked my spunk. I was an independent kid in that I wasn't a joiner and I didn't like gang fighting. I had been recruited to be a gang fighter in Brooklyn by the Nits and the Jellystompers—these were two very prominent gangs. The thing I didn't like about gang fighting was fighting strangers, people you didn't know. That struck me as being nuts, crazy, because I had a lot of people I did know who I didn't like. [*Laughs.*] I couldn't figure out why I was fighting people I didn't know and didn't have any grievance.

Years later, when Gwendolyn Brooks and I did a reading together at Brooklyn College, there was a question and answer period afterward and a guy raises his hand and he says, who was trying to recruit you when you were twelve or thirteen? I say, the Nits and the Jellystompers. He says, well, I'm a retired lieutenant from the Jellystompers. [*Laughs.*] This guy as old as me, sitting there in the audience. Gwendolyn Brooks was hysterical. She said to me, Michael, I didn't know you had such dark roots. [*Laughs.*]

She was, you know, Miss Chicago! Gwendolyn Brooks gave me my career. She took my book, *Dear John, Dear Coltrane*[11] . . . I had submitted it for a contest, the University of Pittsburgh Press. I didn't win—the judges were Robert Penn Warren, Denise Levertov, and Gwendolyn Brooks, and the woman who won was named Shirley Kaufman. Gwendolyn raised so much hell that they published my book too. She wrote me a letter—I didn't know her then—the first line "YOU WERE MY CLEAR WINNER" in capital letters. Then she sent me a telegram: they wanted to publish my book! So there was a contradiction: I didn't win the contest—why did they want to publish my book? What's going on? Well, what Gwendolyn had done was raise so much hell they published my book. Then the book was nominated for the National Book Award and I was in *Time* magazine and *that* gave prominence to my book.

As I think about it now, I first submitted my book to Wesleyan University Press and the word came back, we already have our black book: they'd already signed on *Swallow the Lake* by Clarence Major, so they had their black poet.

Then here I come with Gwendolyn selecting my book, and next thing you know I had a certain kind of prominence. I had to take advantage of it because I knew this would not come again. In America, you can be famous for fifteen minutes but then they're going to forget. That's why I decided to go to Brown University. I was living in San Francisco, and I was quite content to stay there, but I knew I had to go because the chance would not come again. Ronald Reagan was already governor. I thought what happened to California was gonna happen to the country and it sure as hell did. I said to myself—at the time I had two kids; now I have three—I gotta start thinking about family. So I moved.

But I was always both an outsider by choice, not a joiner, and an innovator in that jazz music was always at the heart of everything I did. At the same time, at graduate school in Iowa, I had studied with people who did nothing but write in rhyme and meter and they were all white teachers. But I was interested in the culture and phrasing of these great musicians, and when you look at a Michael Harper poem and you think to yourself, damn, he went to Iowa—why does he sound so different to everybody else? Well, it's phrasing; it's not the subject matter itself. I was interested in innovation. I'd read William Carlos Williams; I'd read all the people who were my contemporaries; I read all their dissertations, their poetry theses. But I was interested in putting into the language, and into the literature, those particular people who were most prominent to me: the jazz musicians. Their sonics, their phrasing.

GL: When you say you were influenced by the musicians' phrasing, are you talking in general terms or are there particular musicians you have in mind?[12]

MSH: By the time I was living in California, I already knew Parker. Parker died the year I was a senior in high school and I'd listened to a lot of his music. I was a classmate of Don Cherry; I knew who Ornette Coleman was, Billy Higgins—these were my contemporaries. And I listened to a lot of rhythm and blues—the Clovers, the Flamingos, all of them. But I never considered that serious music. Serious music was jazz music; and not big band jazz groups either, small groups, groups like Miles Davis, the MJQ, the Jazz Messengers, Horace Silver, Clifford Brown and Max Roach. I grew up on these people. I built up a record collection and heard a lot of live music. When Coltrane came to San Francisco, when I was teaching there in 1964, I heard every single session he played for those two weeks; matinees, whatever, I was totally absorbed.

GL: This wasn't the first time you'd seen him live, though?

MS: No, no, I'd heard Coltrane earlier. In fact, I didn't really like Coltrane playing with Miles Davis live. I felt he was being curtailed. Miles was very sparse and Coltrane was very large . . . open. And had a lot to say. I liked him in different contexts than the Miles Davis context. I loved it when he played in his own bands and when he finally broke away from Miles: he'd been with Miles twice and in between he'd been with Monk.

We were kind of watching him because there was no one . . . other than Sonny Rollins, and Rollins was his own category, even though Sonny was born in 1930. Sonny Rollins was a virtuoso musician, but there was something about Coltrane's *sound* that was like nothing else. And we knew that sound had been hard earned. We also worried because Elvin Jones was just unreal as a drummer. But that group was fantastic, and we also knew it wasn't gonna last long.

GL: How did you know that?

MSH: We had a sense of this, a sense that so much of the intensity of the times, of the apocalyptic . . . it was like a kind of projection. Coltrane was so powerful and so sweet. I mean, we knew his temperament. He wasn't any revolutionary except on the horn; he was very easygoing, very nice. He wasn't vitriolic like Miles. Coltrane was none of that. What is important about the music is that, no holds barred, they went anywhere they wanted to go. And they literally carried the country for five years. There was nothing like it. And if you ever heard them live, you never got over it.

There were other great musicians who were playing, Art Blakey; night after night, week after week; music was live and awake. Live music was important. We did not live on records. We bought the records but we understood that the records were supportive of the live world. We saw a lot of concerts; we saw the behavior of the musicians, their grace under fire. But musicians were always in the avant-garde; they were always pioneers, always ahead: in their style, in the way in which they looked at the world, in their willingness to break convention, in their absolute oblivion to restraint. They were cosmopolitan in the best sense. All you had to do was look at them. And we wanted to be like them. At the same time I'm going to school. I'm studying Milton. I'm an English major but my heart is not really in it. Except that I knew there was something about me wanting to make poems and write. It wasn't until I came back from Iowa—I was only there for a year, then I had to get a job—that I realized how hard I had to work to do this without compensation. Because there wasn't any money to be made, so you had to do it because you loved it. And I wasn't sure: I didn't really understand until I was in my mid-thirties that I was going to write poetry the rest of my life. Then I found out a very important thing: poetry chooses you, you don't choose it.

I'm kind of an anomalous figure. By the time I ended up being a person publishing books, I was also teaching the first black literature classes and the first black history classes in the institutions where I taught. So much of the need for those things came out of the community; it came out of the students. Without the black students raising hell in the 1960s, there would have been no revolution on the campuses, that's for sure. Brown University went from having a class of, let's say, two or four black graduates in '66, '67 to having 500 black students in '69, '70. That's an incredible revolution. That's just part of it, one little narrow part of the story.

What was catapulting us was the black revolutionary music. That was forcing us to teach courses we didn't have the expertise to teach but we felt needed to be taught. And so you filled the gap, whatever it was. I started in community colleges where the students had no tradition of books, but they were in school. Many of these people went to school part-time and worked part-time. All of my students were workers and there wasn't nothin' bourgeois 'bout none of 'em. They were all working-class kids and that was the wonder of it. I was trying to teach them how to read and write and I wouldn't let them fail. I would not allow them to fail. I knew that just because they were not well educated or well prepared, that had nothing to do with their ability. I knew they could do it, so I willed it. I was putting in some hard hours, but I was young. I had plenty of zoom.

GL: When you started writing poetry, were these the people you were writing for? Did you have a clear idea of who your audience was?

MSH: If you look at some of my early poems, I realized that when I was writing those poems I was in a dilemma about audience. The people I went to school with, they were really corny to me. They had no subject matter. And I had some style because I had those musicians as backup. I was not judgmental; I was searching. The neighborhood I'd lost could not be found.

GL: Your peers at school didn't share that musical culture?

MSH: First of all, they were white. The majority of them were white. This is in Los Angeles. And most of them were lame . . . meaning, for example, a person says, let's have a party. The black kids all understood that party meant dance; the white kids never meant that. They meant talk, they meant drink, maybe, but they didn't mean dance. So you got a lexicon problem.

Now, behind all of this was desegregation. The Kennedy years, when Kennedy became president, the atmosphere of the country changed: there was promise and hope and all of that. That was why I went to Iowa. I was in these workshops, in these seminars. I was studying the history of the English language, but I tried to translate that into the styles I loved, the music I loved, the life I loved. So I was reading all around and I was young; young enough not to understand that you weren't supposed to win. That is to say, the logical consequence of going to graduate school was to get a job. Well, where was that job going to be? It ain't gonna be Ohio State or Michigan State unless you're gonna get out and start publishing; and publishing meant in good magazines and that meant reading magazines, going to the library. This was very individual kind of stuff. When you're running around mostly with black men, many of them athletes, some with no ambition other than to get a job.

Part of it is about will, because there's nothing harder than trying to make a poem when nobody wants you to. You don't even know why you're doing this. It's not because W. H. Auden is writing, 'cause he ain't my hero, you know? Even though I had read Auden, he wasn't *my* hero. And I had no Langston Hughes in front of me, not at that time, though I knew who he was. I had Isherwood . . . but I had nothing but white teachers and most of my classmates were white, and I knew I wasn't! In America, *race* is always a component. Whether it's talked about or not. And in my case it wasn't, not at all.

I took seminars on Eugene O'Neill 'cause I was writing plays, but O'Neill's subject matter wasn't my subject matter. There were no August Wilsons then. Even the black playwrights were doing other things—not to mention production costs. If you were not connected with a Howard University or some other black university, how were you gonna get produced? Community theater? In Los Angeles you had the illusion that integration was the norm; but that was not the norm. You were going to class with white people, but you weren't socializing with them; you weren't partying with them. We had a segregated prom. We had two proms, a white prom and a black prom. The black prom started after the white prom was over, and the white prom was over at ten o'clock. See, we never desegregated in this country. I don't know where people get the idea we desegregated: we never desegregated.

The black community's just devastated now. The middle class has moved on. That presumes that you got some education, some skill, you stayed in school. But if you're poor, if you work in a factory and the factory goes elsewhere, what can you do? It used to be you could always get a job: at the post office, the city, something. It's not easy anymore; the economy's changed. In my generation, I've seen a lot of the ambition's gone. I think that in America, in my lifetime, I've seen everything come down to jobs.

I've worked in the same job since 1970 and I insisted on tenure. For some reason, I knew if I was gonna survive in the Ivy League, I had to have tenure. The strategies that we used, what has been called civil rights, were appropriated by everybody else and we were excluded again. Like, you're always competing with the same people.

The same is true in art. I'm sixty-five years old and the stuff that I'm doing I would have done whether people had paid me or not. What little reputation I have—I mean, I've published a few books—I don't think that this is an enormous achievement, really. But I've had freedom of choice to do what I wanted to do and I've done it. I've tried to articulate what I thought were the best attitudinal choices to take in the world, and I've tried to update my view of things, given what my allegiances are, what my loyalties are—and the erosion of those things, because we're all mortal, we only live for a little while.

I really love being an individual. I don't carry my race on my shoulder: it's too heavy a burden and it's hard enough to be honest in the world, no matter who you are. I think that James Baldwin said this best: "I want to be an honest man and a good writer." Well, that's a full-time job right there! [*Laughs.*]

The Coltranes of the world . . . now he was willing to give everything. But one of the reasons why Coltrane was unique was because of his strong religious views; he came out of a religious family. If you ask why Coltrane never went back to High Point, where he grew up, the answer was segregation. He hated it and took a stance against it, would not come back to his hometown because of the way he was treated as a child. He didn't feel it was right. Now the high moral tone of Coltrane's playing is, in part, his uniqueness. Because when you hear Coltrane, he sounds like nobody else.

GL: Why do you call it a moral tone?

MSH: Because I think it's religious. I think Coltrane's playing is . . . there's a spiritual element to it, which I think is religious. I don't mean it's not rigorous; I don't mean it's not demanding. But there is a religiosity to him.

GL: Do you think that quality was there from the start or did it come in at a particular time?

MSH: I think it's always been there, but he had to develop the techniques to actually express what he heard. What I love about Coltrane is that he never blasphemed or tried to tear down his teachers, the people that came before him. So that the Lester Youngs, the Coleman Hawkinses, he always played their tunes, their expression, with reverence. He honored them, which is not necessarily the norm in a very competitive world, where people are trying to get theirs.

When I think about black composers, the great ones, who have spent their lives . . . Benny Golson, for example, the guy who wrote "I Remember Clifford," or Ellington, who spent his whole lifetime writing tunes, I think about the respect that those musicians had playing together. I mean, what can we call that? That was a kind of fraternal order of excellence that is the epitome of style. And they did that in the teeth of segregation, being out there. We used to have a joke about Coltrane. Coltrane would play so intensely and his music would be so demanding that all of a sudden he'd just knock the doors down, you know, and people would always say, man, we didn't hear you knockin'. If you'd just have knocked, we'd have opened the door. But the point is, it took that kind of intensity.

Coltrane's certainly intense and some people, when they'd hear him, they'd think it was noise. It was not noise, it was conviction. Now, of course, that which sustains you . . . If you're gonna live in the world, you gotta figure out how to do it. I would say, discipline. There's got to be a bit of luck too, 'cause there are gonna be some ups and downs. The musicians' world is just tenacious and it's all dictated by the marketplace. If you don't have your own standards, so that you can live in hard times, you're not going to make it. Because the industry eats you alive. You gotta perform all the time. You gotta stay up all the time.

One of the reasons I don't enjoy readings so much anymore is because there's not enough time to compose. I'm here at Yaddo now having days where I can just sit down and reflect on what I want to do; but I can see the ruthlessness, driven by the marketplace, and what this does.

None of my art comes out of the academy. That doesn't mean I don't enjoy teaching, but the motivation to make the art is not about the academy. I don't know what it is about; maybe it's about the world, but it certainly isn't about the university. It's really important that people understand there's an accident, there's a tinkering quality with just playing with certain things, which ends up happening, and part of that is about phrasing. I happen to say things in a way other people don't. It's not that I'm trying to be unique, it's just the way I do it. I have a sense inside that this is not as good as I can make it. Sometimes I abandon it; I just give up, move on to other things.

For example, when I want to write a poem, let's say it's about Dexter Gordon—what I remember most about him is his sound. And his stance, you know, his uniqueness, comes across. Dexter Gordon was just unreal. He wasn't the innovator that Coltrane was or Parker was but there's nothing that says it's a bad thing to be a journeyman. Because he was one hell of a journeyman; and he carried a whole generation. We are looking for genius as the norm here, man—there ain't been no Coltrane since he died. We have gone since 1967 without having anybody like him, and we might not get him again. Now, are there other people out there? Yeah! A Wayne Shorter is wonderful but a Wayne Shorter ain't Coltrane and didn't fill his shoes. Nobody did. Nobody filled Parker's shoes.

When we talk about innovation, and we're talking by analogy . . . when I was introduced at a reading as a Keatsian poet, I was very pleased because John Keats is a hero of mine. I don't know where it comes from; I just appreciate . . . I learned what I could from him: he was a mentor to me in that he was a model. But he was long dead by the time I got to him. That's the hard part, to make art out of the living: it's easy to talk about Shakespeare and Milton; it's not easy to deal with the contemporary. I run into people all the time who want to talk to me as though I'm writing a concerto or a tango; I'm just writing a poem and if you want to put it in a category, you can. If it's a ballad . . . I haven't many ballads but I wrote a ballad for Bessie Smith.[13] I wasn't interested in doing that again. I was interested in doing that one time and then moving on to something else. I wasn't interested in replicating.

GL: You talk about dealing with the contemporary but most of your poems about Coltrane, for example, were written after he died. Do you still consider that as being contemporary?

MSH: Well, I want to say that the "Dear John, Dear Coltrane" poem,[14] I wrote that before he died. But what is it that Yeats said? Yeats said, "Memories are old identities"; who you were is who you are. That's what I'm saying. Until there comes to be another Coltrane, I'm content with who he was. Of course, it's about change; at the same time, it's about continuity. Therefore I'm never finished with Coltrane. I just wrote a poem about him two or three days ago.[15]

GL: I wanted to ask you . . . for example, in the Coltrane poems in *Chant of Saints*, when you're writing in his voice, as it were, do you research that or do you allow yourself poetic license?[16]

MSH: [*Laughs.*] I like the question. I'm gonna answer it in two ways, all right? You notice that there's a section in this book [*points to* Songlines in Michaeltree] called "My Book on Trane."[17] This is Tyner talking; well, Tyner is my take on this. And you'll notice that the poems in *Chant of Saints*, the three poems you mentioned, they're not organized the same way in *Songlines*. Part of that has to do with the editing; part of it has to do with the publisher. I don't like this arrangement [*points to* Songlines]; I had it imposed on me.[18]

Now those three poems I wrote because I had a poetic model, and the first poetic model I had was Frederick Douglass, the *Narrative of the Life*. I had that in mind because I had been thinking about Douglass, about his pioneering spirit, and I saw Coltrane as being that. I knew a great deal about his reasons for why he arranged his itinerary in the way he did, why he didn't fill up all the gaps, why they didn't rehearse, and why he was able to keep his freshness. Because there were certain things he didn't do. He was so gifted and understanding of what that particular group needed to make that music that he wasn't willing to compromise. And I love the stance that he took, that he wasn't willing to compromise. And, of course, what is the example? The example is the music; that there was a method to that. The music has its own uniqueness; it stands as itself; and when you compare it with the music played by others, there's nothing like it.

A lot of people think that some part of Coltrane's evolution is chaotic; that is to say, they don't understand it. None of the musicians I know who love Coltrane talk about him in terms of being chaotic. What I think they hear and see is the uncompromising stand that he takes on things. And that's the wonderful part of it. But Coltrane was a unique person. He was not articulate in the glib sense. He didn't do a lot of talking. I know because I was around him a lot.

Michael S. Harper *Interview*

He was not whimsical; he was joyous and friendly and available but he didn't have a lot to say. None of those people did when they played during that period: Elvin and Jimmy Garrison and McCoy, they didn't talk a lot. Their action was action. They played and they played wonderfully. And they enjoyed each other's company. It played out after a while. McCoy Tyner was devastated by this because he did not want to leave; he was forced out. Alice Coltrane forced him out because she wanted to play with Coltrane herself. That ruined the dynamics for me, because Alice Coltrane is not the kind of player that McCoy was. But nothing is here for all time.

This Tyner section, "My Book on Trane," is rather complicated because it talks about a period, the 1960s, and the pressures on those people, having to make sense of a society in enormous change when all they were were musicians; they were not philosophers. They were just, as best they could, trying to reflect what it is that they did best. Of course, there's a lot of excess to this because you're trying to live in tumultuous times and everybody wants to make this coherent. That is to say, subject to a plan, as though they know the results. Well, as Ralph Ellison said, life is to be lived.

GL: This may be a very mundane sort of query but, for example, I didn't know who you were talking about in "My Book on Trane" when you refer to the guy who lost a leg.

MSH: That's Julius Hemphill.

GL: But that didn't happen in the 1960s; he came later.

MSH: Sure he was later, but that's not the point.

GL: Well, you just said it was about the 1960s.

MSH: It is about the 1960s, but it's not literally about the 1960s. See, Hemphill losing his leg, the actual losing of the leg, or what drove me to talk about it was then, when I wrote it, but he was emblematic of people who had taken the same risks beforehand and had no name. They were just casualties. They were in the tradition, you know, but they're not necessarily people who had names. Hemphill . . . I know that was Hemphill I was talking about. I know it came later. We're not talking about it being frozen; we're talking about the kind of archetypes that are put in place, which are fluid in a sense because there's a certain amount of replication.

GL: Okay, but in what sense, then, is this seen through the eyes of McCoy Tyner?

MSH: It's not only him; it's not exclusively him.

GL: But didn't you say the whole sequence was supposed to be as seen through his consciousness?

MSH: It is, but it's not only his. Another way of putting it is that there are things that we have not talked about. I don't think we have to. I saw him play recently and we had a nice conversation; I saw him at Iridium last New Year's with Michael Brecker, and he was wonderful! He had a piece he played called "Traveling" and it reminded me a great deal of Hemphill. Hemphill was a great innovator but he was a man who at the compositional level was way ahead of his time.[19] And was therefore emblematic of a certain series of people who played with Coltrane at the time when Coltrane was at his zenith—I'm thinking about the Albert Aylers of the world. Some of these people are not named but they're meant to make up a kind of composite, and the composite is attitudinal. For those particular places where there's not an even gloss, that's maybe my own intuition failing. I'm not saying I'm perfect. There's a lot of Monk in that sequence too. And also . . . Miles always wanted to hire Tyner; Tyner would never play for him because of the way Miles had treated Coltrane. Even after Coltrane was dead, Tyner didn't want anything to do with Miles. This is instinct, I guess; Miles was not an easy person to play for.

GL: You said you were going to answer the question in two ways. Have you done that?

MSH: [*Laughs.*] I don't know.

GL: [*Laughs.*] Okay. I'm curious . . . you're still writing about musicians, but apart from one or two pieces—I know "Audio" is dedicated to Julius Hemphill—they're all musicians from the '60s or earlier. I'm wondering why you haven't written about later musicians.

Michael S. Harper *Interview*

MSH: I have. I have written about other people; I haven't felt the need to publish it. For example, I'm doing something now on Wayne Shorter. I've been thinking about him for a while.

GL: Oh yes, there's a poem about him in *Songlines*.

MSH: There are other things I've done on him that I haven't published. They're mostly about the impact of him and Milton Nascimento, the things that he did with the discovery of Brazilian music and what the Brazilian music means. I sit on stuff a long time. Just because I don't publish it doesn't mean I'm not thinking about it. Hemphill happened to be somebody that I did concerts with and I knew him really well at a certain period of his life.

I'm doing some more contemporary things now with a guy on bass clarinet, Paul Austerlitz. I'm beginning to sound things because I feel there's a need . . . I call it duets or duos, and the poem is my part, but the person I'm collaborating with is writing his own music. Therefore he's not playing backup for me but he's using my poems to generate a music that he will write for himself. He's a colleague of mine at Brown. I like his playing and I like his sound: he plays a lot of music from Latin America, the Caribbean.[20]

I decided it might be nice to go into the studio and find whether we have some rapport. I want to do some of this stuff live but I don't want it to be just live; I want us to be informed about what we're trying to do.[21] I haven't thought about this really, in a serious way, since about 1970, when I did a series of recordings with a cello player called Ron DeVaughan.[22] The point is that I have a sense of wanting to bring alive not only the phrasing but the orchestration of some of the poems and see whether I can find somebody who can respond equally on his own terms. I'm also thinking about this for voice, trying to find somebody to sing. I don't know what'll happen but I'm becoming more and more venturesome.

I wrote this poem for Dexter Gordon, for his eightieth birthday, which just took place, and it's about his Denmark experience, when he was in Copenhagen. I've brought it along so I'm going to read it to you. It's called "Tattoo" and it's written in couplets. [*Reads*]:

Tattoo

Though a simple rose under your skin
I look up the bugle ritual of recall

for sailors to regroup   soldiers at parade rest
and your sister who could not read as a child

needing you for sustenance   now you want it removed
Copenhagen (for me) is Tivoli played by Dexter Gordon

his love for that city   broad and low in balladry
for making the sound of recall a lullaby

with his name on it   he would love to see your tattoo
his magic at composition a call to Basie/Ellington

Hamp and two full days of practice at seventeen
with the makers of bebop   just off the train from LA

the son of a doctor whose doctoring gave such a smile
in the lower registers he was Mr. "Blue Note" (tenor)

he would venture his signature on conventions ROSE
and turn courtly in the madrigal   play you a hymn

and take you to his church (which was always the road)
so you know why you came from the north   a town

just out of sight from Copenhagen   and in this poem
provided your sister that special speech of signals

so the faerytale of being pricked into song
just under the skin was the song of a tent show

the tattooist fully sober and without shaky hands
and just beneath the surface of your blood

Cezanne's Polynesian sorcerer   so genial in profile
that eating your salad is a school of painting

primal in the garden of the artist's magic circle
where every gesture is the canon of tattoo

I don't know where this came from. I was listening to his music; I was with some woman who began to tell me a story. She happened to be from Denmark, not from Copenhagen. The next thing you know I'd written the poem.

GL: Do you usually write quickly?

MSH: Sometimes I do; sometimes I'll start a poem and I'll just stop somewhere because I don't know where it should go. Generally speaking, when I'm really called to something, it comes very fast.

GL: Do you rework a lot?

MSH: It depends. So much of it has to do with the sound. And when I say phrasing, I don't mean only the arrangement of the words; I mean the periodic sentence. Where I want the details.

GL: The cadences?

MSH: It's not only cadences; it's also delay. When I say periodic sentence, I mean a sentence that waits until the end to give you the predicate and the subject. It's like a solo that gives you a certain kind of suspense but is also building toward something. And what the building is, is the theme, the thematic of it. Sometimes it has to be discovered. It's not only something that you start out with as an idea and just bring it to completion; it's more than an idea. In fact, it's the performance of it.

When I first started writing this poem, I didn't know what the relationship was between Gordon, who had just asserted himself in the poem, and the story that the young woman was telling me, which was more about her than her sister, who I'd never met: she's just a convention. But the tattoo was a rose tattoo and the rose is a convention in courtly love. And so much of what I was saying about Dexter Gordon's playing has to do with his respect for the ballad and the stories that are told in the ballad. The poem just took over. Now "tattoo" means emblem, but it's also a superimposition of a reality. A kind of . . . [*sighs*] emblem's all right, a metaphor, you know?

I sent it as a gift to Dexter Gordon's widow and she responded and liked it. They had this eightieth birthday ceremony and Bob O'Meally read my poem. They invited me to come but I had something else on. Of course, in an ideal world I would have liked to do this reading with Paul Austerlitz. He's never seen the poem but I'd have given it to him and said, why don't you write music for it? I might still give it to him because I'm really interested in the music that's suggested by my poem, which is outside of it and which can be responded to equally by a person who has the same kind of conviction in his own art. It's not about my poem alone. I like his attitude because he wants to meet me where the art is.

NB. A few months later, Michael Harper sent me two further poems about Dexter Gordon, which he had just written. These are reprinted below, with his permission.

Digesting Dexter Gordon @ 80

Effortless vibrato in all registers
lovely speaking voice   on ballads   unassailable

[When I was green at 21 he waltzed into Sunset
Blvd Renaissance matinee   blowing glorious]

Marshall Royal had him audition for the road
left school in LA for Fort Worth   Texas

could translate everyone   'statesman of reed'
we christened him   regular   in ensemble settings

a little behind the beat   ready to take charge   now
(loved Mr. Pork Pie Hat   even when not with Basie)

why he loved Maxine?   consult the ledger
management akin to godliness   even when over the edge

Repeat Button

I usually don't indulge   Dexter Gordon
now past his 80th year   "Don't Explain"

over and over Maxine sent me this double cd
and after "Tattoo" seized me last summer

I revisit heartwork   once heartache
as a righteous sideman   on the road

when he got out of Chino   Renaissance
Club matinee on Sunset Blvd   cheering

his brim was up   still knockkneed
a grin   sweeping in from the Pacific

like the pro he was a little early
the beat as steady as his heartbeat

which had straddled generations of song
(the microsurgery of such support   at odd

hours   in the postal airmail section
where an old Mingus sat   taking names

the Watts local about to go out of service
'our people' never becoming "your people"

his attitude)   at Tivoli   maestro of Blue Note
with his brief commentary   a mastery

of our one idiom   no one could steal
"I been down so long that down don't worry me"

ever
never

—All three poems © Michael S. Harper, 2003

To hear Michael S. Harper read a selection of his poems on different musicians,
including John Coltrane, Dexter Gordon, Julius Hemphill, and Bessie Smith,

with music by Paul Austerlitz on bass clarinet, please go to the *Thriving on a Riff* Web site at http://www.oup.com/us/thrivingonariff. Courtesy of Michael S. Harper and Paul Austerlitz.

NOTES

1. Several of Brown's essays on the blues are reprinted in Sterling A. Brown, *A Son's Return: Selected Essays of Sterling A. Brown*, ed. Mark A. Sanders (Boston: Northeastern University Press, 1996). *Southern Road*, Brown's first book of poems, was originally published in 1932; it is reprinted in Sterling A. Brown, *The Collected Poems of Sterling A. Brown*, ed. Michael S. Harper (1980; reprint, Evanston, IL: TriQuarterly Books/Northwestern University Press, 1996). *The Negro Caravan*, a landmark collection of material on African American culture and life, was co-edited by Brown, Arthur P. Davis, and Ulysses Lee (1941; reprint, New York: Arno Press, 1969).

2. Brown, "When de Saints Go Ma'ching Home," in *Collected Poems of Sterling A. Brown*, 26–30.

3. Brown, "Cabaret," in *Collected Poems of Sterling A. Brown*, 111–13.

4. "Muddy Water," recorded by Bessie Smith in 1927, is a sentimental Tin Pan Alley song, the lyrics of which Brown threads through "Cabaret" in telling counterpoint to his descriptions of the appalling conditions African Americans were forced to endure in the wake of the 1927 Mississippi flood. For a detailed account of the poem's complexities and different levels, see Mark A. Sanders, *Afro-Modernist Aesthetics and the Poetry of Sterling A. Brown* (Athens: University of Georgia Press, 1999), 77–81.

5. Sterling A. Brown, "Portrait of a Jazz Giant: 'Jelly Roll' Morton," *Black World* (February 1974): 28–48.

6. Brown, "Puttin' on Dog," in *Collected Poems of Sterling A. Brown*, 239. He also reads this poem on Sterling A. Brown, *The Poetry of Sterling A. Brown* (Smithsonian Folkways SF47002, 1995).

7. Brown, "Slim Greer," in *Collected Poems of Sterling A. Brown*, 78.

8. Brown, "Slim in Atlanta," in *Collected Poems of Sterling A. Brown*, 81.

9. Brown, "Old Lem," in *Collected Poems of Sterling A. Brown*, 180. Also on Brown, *The Poetry of Sterling A. Brown* CD.

10. For a more extensive discussion by Michael S. Harper of the life and work of Sterling Brown, see Graham Lock, "Br'er Sterling & the Blues: An Interview with Michael S. Harper," in *After Winter: Selected Writings on the Art and Life of Sterling A. Brown*, ed. John Edgar Tidwell and Steven C. Tracy (New York: Oxford University Press, forthcoming).

11. Michael S. Harper, *Dear John, Dear Coltrane* (1970; reprint, Urbana: University of Illinois Press, 1985).

12. Harper also discusses the influence of jazz on his poetic phrasing in Michael S. Harper and Aldon Lynn Nielsen, "Conversation," in *The Furious Flowering of African American Poetry*, ed. Joanne V. Gabbin (Charlottesville: University Press of Virginia, 1999), 77–85.

13. Michael S. Harper, "Last Affair: Bessie's Blues Song," in *Songlines in Michaeltree: New and Collected Poems* (Urbana: University of Illinois Press, 2000), 63–64. (Michael Harper reads this poem on the *Hearing Eye* Web site.)

14. Michael S. Harper, "Dear John, Dear Coltrane," in both Harper, *Dear John*, 74–75, and *Songlines*, 25–26.

15. For detailed discussions of Harper's poetry in relation to both Coltrane's music and the genre of the "Coltrane poem," see Kimberly W. Benston, "Renovating Blackness: Remembrance and Revolution in the Coltrane Poem," in *Performing Blackness: Enactments of African American Modernism* (London: Routledge, 2000), 145–86; Michael Borshuk, "'Here Where Coltrane Is': Jazz, Cultural Memory, and Political Aesthetics in the Poetry of Michael S. Harper," in *Swinging the Vernacular: Jazz and African American Modernist Literature* (New York: Routledge, 2006), 121–58; Sascha Feinstein, "The John Coltrane Poem" in *Jazz Poetry: From the 1920s to the Present* (Westport, CT: Praeger, 1997), 115–42; and Günter H. Lenz's article, "Black Music and Black Poetry; History and Tradition: Michael Harper and John Coltrane," in *History and Tradition in Afro-American Culture*, ed. Günter H. Lenz (Frankfurt: Campus Verlag, 1984), 277–326.

16. Michael S. Harper, "Three Poems," in *Chant of Saints: A Gathering of Afro-American Literature, Art, and Scholarship*, ed. Michael S. Harper and Robert B. Stepto (Urbana: University of Illinois Press, 1979), 408–12.

17. Harper, *Songlines*, 167–81.

18. In *Chant of Saints* the order of the poems is: "Peace on Earth," "A Narrative of the Life and Times of John Coltrane: Played by Himself," and "Driving the Big Chrysler across the Country of My Birth"; in *Songlines* the order is "Narrative," "Driving," "Peace."

19. For an idea of the scope of Julius Hemphill's compositional activities, see, for example, *Roi Boyé and the Gotham Minstrels* (1977; reissue, Sackville SK2CD 3014/5, 2001); *Flat Out Jump Suite* (1980; reissue, Black Saint 120040-2, 2003); and *One Atmosphere* (Tzadik TZ 7090, 2003). He also made numerous other recordings, including several with the World Saxophone Quartet, of which he was a founding member.

20. Paul Austerlitz is also the author of *Jazz Consciousness: Music, Race, and Humanity* (Middletown, CT: Wesleyan University Press, 2005).

21. The resulting CD features two different live versions of the same set of poems. Paul Austerlitz and Michael S. Harper, *Double Take: Jazz Poetry Conversations* (Innova 604, 2004).

22. Ron DeVaughan is probably better known to jazz aficionados under his later Islamic name of Abdul Wadud: he has recorded with numerous players, including Arthur Blythe, Anthony Davis, Julius Hemphill, and James Newton.

SELECTED WORKS

Recordings

Austerlitz, Paul, and Michael S. Harper. *Double Take: Jazz Poetry Conversations.* Innova 604, 2004.

———. *Our Book on Trane: The Yaddo Sessions.* YADDO 1, 2004.

Brown, Sterling A. *The Poetry of Sterling A. Brown.* Smithsonian Folkways SF47002, 1995.

Harper, Michael S. *Selected Poems.* Self-published three-CD set, 2004.

———. *Use Trouble.* Modo, 2003.

Hemphill, Julius. *Flat Out Jump Suite.* 1980. Reissue, Black Saint 120040-2, 2003.

———. *One Atmosphere.* Tzadik TZ 7090, 2003.

———. *Roi Boyé and the Gotham Minstrels.* 1977. Reissue, Sackville SK2CD 3014/15, 2001.

Texts

Austerlitz, Paul. *Jazz Consciousness: Music, Race, and Humanity.* Middletown, CT: Wesleyan University Press, 2005.

Benston, Kimberly W. *Performing Blackness: Enactments of African-American Modernism.* London: Routledge, 2000.

Borshuk, Michael. *Swinging the Vernacular: Jazz and African American Modernist Literature.* New York, Routledge, 2006.

Brown, Joseph A. "Their Long Scars Touch Ours: A Reflection on the Poetry of Michael Harper." *Callaloo* 26 (Winter 1986): 209–20.

Brown, Sterling A. *The Collected Poems of Sterling A. Brown.* Ed. Michael S. Harper. 1980. Reprint, Evanston, IL: TriQuarterly Books/Northwestern University Press, 1996.

———. "Portrait of a Jazz Giant: 'Jelly Roll' Morton." *Black World* (February 1974): 28–48.

———. *A Son's Return: Selected Essays of Sterling A. Brown.* Ed. Mark A. Sanders. Boston: Northeastern University Press, 1996.

Brown, Sterling A., Arthur P. Davis, and Ulysses Lee, eds. *The Negro Caravan.* 1941. Reprint, New York: Arno Press, 1969.

Chapman, Abraham. "An Interview with Michael S. Harper." *Arts in Society* 11 (1975): 462–71.

Feinstein, Sascha. *Jazz Poetry from the 1920s to the Present.* Westport, CT: Praeger, 1997.

———. "John Coltrane and Jazz Poetics: An Interview with Michael S. Harper." *Indiana Review* 12 (1989): 1–12.

Harper, Michael S. *Dear John, Dear Coltrane.* 1970. Reprint, Urbana: University of Illinois Press, 1985.

———. *The Fret Cycle.* N.p.: Effendi Press, 2005.

———, ed. *I Do Believe in People: Remembrances of W. Warren Harper 1915–2004.* Providence, RI: Effendi Press, 2005.

———. Liner notes. *John Coltrane.* LP. Prestige 24003, 1972.

———. *Songlines in Michaeltree: New and Collected Poems*. Urbana: University of Illinois Press, 2000.

Harper, Michael S., and Aldon Lynn Nielsen. "Conversation." In *The Furious Flowering of African American Poetry*. Ed. Joanne V. Gabbin. Charlottesville: University Press of Virginia, 1999. 77–85.

Harper, Michael S., and Robert B. Stepto. *Chant of Saints: A Gathering of Afro-American Literature, Art, and Scholarship*. Urbana: University of Illinois Press, 1979.

Lenz, Günter H. "Black Poetry and Black Music; History and Tradition: Michael Harper and John Coltrane." In *History and Tradition in African American Culture*. Ed. Günter H. Lenz. Frankfurt: Campus Verlag, 1984. 277–326.

Lock, Graham. "Br'er Sterling & the Blues: An Interview with Michael S. Harper." In *After Winter: Selected Writings on the Art and Life of Sterling A. Brown*. Ed. John Edgar Tidwell and Steven C. Tracy. New York: Oxford University Press, forthcoming.

O'Brien, John. "Michael Harper." In *Interviews with Black Writers*. Ed. John O'Brien. New York: Liveright, 1973. 94–107.

Rowell, Charles H. "'Down Don't Worry Me': An Interview with Michael S. Harper." *Callaloo* 13.4 (Autumn 1990): 780–800.

Sanders, Mark A. *Afro-Modernist Aesthetics and the Poetry of Sterling A. Brown*. Athens: University of Georgia Press, 1999.

Stepto, Robert B. "Michael Harper's Extended Tree: John Coltrane and Sterling Brown." *The Hollins Critic* 30.3 (June 1976): 1–16.

Young, Al, Larry Kart, and Michael S. Harper. "Jazz and Letters: A Colloquy." *Triquarterly* 68 (Winter 1987): 118–58.

FIVE

Paul Beatty's *White Boy Shuffle* Blues: Jazz Poetry, John Coltrane, and the Post-Soul Aesthetic

Bertram D. Ashe

My plan is to listen to everything recorded before 1975 in alphabetical order," says Nick Scoby to Gunnar Kaufman, narrator and protagonist of Paul Beatty's first novel. "No white band leaders, sidemen cool. No faux African back-to-the-bush bullshit recorded post-1965. Though I'm going to make an exception for Anita O'Day," he adds, "she could pipe."[1] So begins the pointed jazz commentary in *The White Boy Shuffle*.[2] From Cannonball Adderley in the fourth chapter to Sarah Vaughan in the twelfth and final chapter, Gunnar's best friend Scoby intently listens to jazz under headphones. Along the way, this jazz-from-A-to-, well, -V exploration provides a template for Beatty's larger views on jazz and its cultural connection to the written word. All of Beatty's books—two each of fiction and poetry—explore both the compatibility and the tension between jazz and poetry.

That compatibility—and that tension—emerges from Beatty's use of the African American vernacular tradition. Ralph Ellison once famously wrote, "Without the presence of Negro American style our jokes, our tall tales, even our sports would be lacking in the sudden turns, the shocks, the swift changes of pace (all jazz shaped) that serve to remind us that the world is ever unexplored, and that while a complete mastery of life is mere illusion, the real secret of the game is to make life swing."[3] Beatty's novels and poetry include many such vernacular gestures. The books explore numerous facets of African American expressive culture, including basketball, hair, and dance, as well as "Negro American style" in everyday life: conversation, storytelling, and joke telling on stoops of urban brownstones, children playing the dozens on schoolyard playgrounds, even the oral nature of the black classroom. When Gunnar Kaufman's mother moves her family from Santa Monica to "the 'hood,'"[4] Beatty spoofs the intensity of Gunnar's immersion into an oral, black world, where traffic signals "blinked a furious 'Hurry the fuck up!'" and phone operators answered requests for information "with a throaty 'Who dis?'"[5] The black vernacular tradition not only permeates Gunnar's everyday world, but also serves as a cultural base for each of Beatty's books. Besides *The White Boy Shuffle,* perhaps Beatty's best-known work, he has published two well-regarded volumes of poetry, *Big Bank Take Little Bank* (1991), and *Joker, Joker, Deuce* (1994). His second novel, *Tuff,* arrived in the year 2000. So Beatty is living two literary lives, one as a poet, one as a novelist. Instead of allowing that separation to implicitly speak for itself, however, Beatty made the protagonist of his first novel a poet—as is the protagonist's father in his second novel. Beatty, as a result, has placed himself in the intriguing position of having extant collections of poetry and novels that compellingly critique that phenomenon *The White Boy Shuffle* refers to as "the American poet."[6]

But the four books have more in common than poetry—jazz figures in each book too. Curiously, Beatty employs a jazz aesthetic in his poetry and fiction, while his novels also crisply interrogate poets who romanticize jazz musicians—in this case, John Coltrane—for poetic ends.[7] Along the way, Beatty inadvertently demonstrates his place in the post-soul aesthetic. I use the word *inadvertently* because Beatty has said he feels absolutely no allegiance to the post-soul—even though his work places him solidly within that aesthetic.[8]

Post-soul is a term popularized by cultural critics Nelson George and Mark Anthony Neal that describes a post–civil rights school of African American artists and writers.[9] Trey Ellis, in his post-soul manifesto, "The New Black Aesthetic," makes several observations about post-soul artists and writers, including the notions that these artists are trans-cultural, that they have "changed, crossed, and flouted existing genres according to their own eclectic inspirations"; that a "telltale sign" of the work of the post-soul is their "parodying of the black nationalist movement"; and that these artists often represent in their work that which they often are themselves: "cultural mulattoes," blacks who were either born or came of age in the post–civil rights movement era and were "educated by a multi-racial mix of cultures."[10] These artists, argues Ellis, "no longer need to deny or suppress any part of [their] complicated and sometimes contradictory cultural baggage."[11]

Beatty demonstrates this cross-cultural stance in each of his books. In *The White Boy Shuffle,* as alluded to above, Gunnar Kaufman moves, early in the novel, from integrated Santa Monica to all-black Hillside. Gunnar's experiences include traversing and immersing himself in the worlds of an urban, black vernacular-drenched junior high, a barely integrated suburban Los Angeles high school, the angry, Rodney King–verdict-riot-fueled streets of the same city, as well as a bizarre, single-day-in-the-classroom stint at Boston University. While the novel centers on black characters, it also includes major Latino and Asian characters and, all told, credibly explores the multi-cultural, post–civil rights American cultural landscape. Similarly, in *Tuff*, there are a variety of characters of differing races, socio-economic levels, and political perspectives, including Inez, a politically active Asian American female character who is loosely based on Yuri Kochiyama, a 1960s associate of Malcolm X, and Spencer Throckmorton, a politically conservative black rabbi. Beatty is, indeed, interested in the post–civil rights movement "cultural mulatto." But he also employs, in each novel and collection of poetry, the African American vernacular tradition. Beatty's use of the black vernacular undergirds his implicit argument for an expansive sense of blackness, as he pokes holes in the ideology of those who would reduce essential blackness to such signifiers as revolutionary poetry, John Coltrane, and the jazz aesthetic.

While it is true that Beatty's work—both poetry and fiction—is grounded in the black tradition and maintains a formal relationship with jazz, he also interrogates the way in which black cultural commentators have long compared black literature unfavorably to black music. Amiri Baraka, writing as LeRoi Jones, argued that "it is impossible to mention the achievements of the Negro in any area of artistic endeavor with as much significance as in spirituals, blues and jazz. There has never," he contended, "been an equivalent to Duke Ellington or Louis Armstrong in Negro writing, and even the best of contemporary literature written by Negroes cannot yet be compared to the fantastic beauty of the music of Charlie Parker."[12] Baraka's argument was not exactly a novel pronouncement even in 1962—Richard Wright suggested something similar in his "Blueprint for Negro Writing" twenty-five years earlier, and it was not even new then: James Weldon Johnson made much the same point in his preface to *The Book of American Negro Poetry* as early as 1921.

So when Gunnar Kaufman and Nick Scoby argue, late in *The White Boy Shuffle*, over "the finiteness of music,"[13] the words sound more than a little familiar. Responding to Gunnar's suggestion that music inherently has only so many songs that it is possible to play, Scoby counters by saying that time makes music "infinite":

See, if Charlie Parker had played Dixie, it would be like colorizing *Birth of a Nation*. It'd be a different tune but the same tune. You dig? You'd be hearing it differently and its meaning would change. Because a musician has they own sense of time and experience of time. For Parker, time was a bitch. He wouldn't play Dixie as no happy-go-lucky darky anthem. He'd play it as a "I'm mad and I *know* them cotton-picking niggers was mad," piss-on-their-graves dirge.[14]

Then Scoby explicitly compares the act of playing music with the act of writing poetry: "The page is finite. Once you put the words down on paper, you've fossilized your thought. Bugs in amber, nigger."[15]

What is surprising is that Beatty's poetry—and his fiction—critiques Scoby's idea that words on paper equate "fossilized . . . thought." Formally, Beatty's poetry ranges from long, sweeping poems to short, four-line pieces. Occasionally, italicized lines slash through his poems, either as song lyrics or as snatches of familiar commercials ("*how many licks does it take to lick a tootsie roll lollipop/a one/ a twoooo/a thrrrrreeeee*").[16] He writes about hip-hop and black cultural figures, but his poems also regularly include lyrics from or references to "soft rock" singers such as Barry Manilow and James Taylor. Sometimes the italicized lines are simply recognizable quotations. Whatever the source—television game shows or *The Jetsons* or skateboard culture lingo ("*oh wow radical/im stoked*")[17]—the tension between the free-floating stanzas and the cross-cutting italicized phrases creates a fluid, jazz-like poetry that *swings*, by which I mean (to paraphrase Albert Murray's description of swing) it becomes percussive "incantation," calling up rhythmic responses in the listener/reader.[18]

Many of Beatty's poems also rhyme, although not in the traditional rhyming couplets form. Instead, the poems consist of short phrases that seem to drift almost randomly about the page, appearing anywhere from the far-left margin to the far-right. Perhaps most important, the poems have little to no punctuation—no capital letters, no commas, no periods, no apostrophes. This is perhaps the most crucial consideration, given Lynne Truss's description of the importance of punctuation in *Eats, Shoots and Leaves: The Zero Tolerance Approach to Punctuation*: "The earliest known punctuation," she relates in a chapter on commas, was a "system of dramatic notation . . . advising actors when to breathe. . . . For a millennium and a half, punctuation's purpose was to guide actors, chanters and readers-aloud through stretches of manuscript, indicating the pauses, [and] accentuating matters of sense and sound."[19] Punctuation today has a similar goal. "On the page," contends Truss, "punctuation performs its grammatical function, but in the mind of the reader it does more than that. It tells the reader how to hum the tune."[20]

Beatty's poetic origins are in spoken word. He became involved with the Nuyorican Poets Café at the beginning of the poetry slam movement, winning the 1990 New York Poetry Slam. Not surprisingly, then, Beatty's poems are decidedly oral—it is somewhat difficult, because of the lack of punctuation, to tell exactly when the end of a line occurs, but when reading them aloud some of the breaks seem to signal themselves naturally. This clever black vernacular gesture almost ensures that the poems will be read aloud at some point; indeed, they seem to beg to be read that way. When that happens, though, when his poems are read aloud and interpreted—performed—they seem to exist in the moment, precisely the way Scoby insists music does and poetry cannot. In part, it is because the phrases must swing themselves loosely into a constantly shifting "place," given the fact that no punctuation exists to tell the reader exactly "how to hum the tune." Consider this excerpt from Beatty's poem "Sitting on Other People's Cars," from 1994's *Joker, Joker, Deuce*:

> this mingus CD
> reminds you of me
>
> our friendship workshop
> where nat hentoffian gizzard driven
> record jacket criticism rhythms
> trickled from the starsky n hutch spinout swirl
>
>   in the crown of yo head
>   ran down
>   your back
>   with the bumpidy syncopation
>
>   of a bestfriends knuckle
> rubbin up and down your spine
>
> till some drummers high hat tapped
> the side of your neck
> did you get the chills
>   yeah kinda[21]

Beatty's poetry is, indeed, "musical." It is as if he is consciously attempting to blur that sense of the finite, of that paper-margin boundary that, Scoby argues, marks the superiority of jazz over poetry. Beatty certainly refers to a jazz master in his poem, Charles Mingus. But beyond that reference, the question becomes how, and to what extent, does Beatty infuse a jazz sensibility into his poetry? To what extent does he counter Scoby's contention that poetry can (un)profitably be compared to "bugs in amber"?

The answer is in the punctuation, or lack thereof. Truss states that one "distinct function" that grew out of the "mixed origins of modern punctuation" is "[t]o point up—rather in the manner of musical notation—such literary qualities as rhythm, direction, pitch, tone and flow."[22] In the case of "Sitting on Other People's Cars," there is, as with all of Beatty's poetry, nary a comma, period, or exclamation point to be found. If Truss's analogy with musical notation is valid, Beatty's refusal to punctuate his poem leaves a great deal of the work of interpretation to the reader. As a result, the interpretation of the poem varies, perhaps moreso than for poems that do not participate in a jazz aesthetic. Phrases like "in the crown of yo head" are completely free to be interpreted as the end of the previous line, as in "trickled from the starsky n hutch spinout swirl/in the crown of yo head." But that same line could also be read as beginning the next stanza: "in the crown of yo head/ran down/your back/with the bumpidy syncopation."

There are other ways the poem nods its head to jazz. Literally at the moment that Beatty is making overt reference to jazz-like syncopation—complete with the "tapp[ing]" of a "drummers high hat," he's also using a call-and-response moment to heighten the touch: "did you get the chills/yeah kinda." Indeed, with the draining of punctuation from the poem, Beatty suggests an even stronger sense of vernacular call-and-response: the poem's indeterminate "call" demands the reader's interpretive "response" in a way that ultimately suggests a participation in the jazz aesthetic.

Beatty also uses the jazz aesthetic in poems that are not jazz-oriented (though many of his poems do have jazz references). I could exhaust even the most enthusiastic reader with examples of his swinging poetic voice, but a representative moment that occurs in "Twix. Caramel, Not Peanut Butter," from *Big Bank*, will suffice. Beatty's poignant poem about a young woman attempting to navigate the sometimes treacherous terrain of African American fraternities and sororities contains this segment:

> she too wuz once a fine fine
> scholar ath-uh-lete
> out of tupelo, mississippi

till she pulled ligaments
in her sanity
when she discovered the vanity of bein AKA

aint deep enough
to keep niggahs from dissin you

good evening big sister
be missin you

til death rips me apart
from a black tie red cummerbund jesus
who lights farts in the dark

singin   *ballpark franks they plump when you cook 'em*[23]

This excerpt demonstrates the variety and volume of with-and-against, competing-yet-complementary voices that Beatty melds into a poem—something like the different musicians of a jazz quintet taking turns soloing onstage. The first soloist is the voice resembling a white southern head football coach, drawling "fine fine/scholar ath-uh-lete/out of tupelo, mississippi." The "leader," the narrator, resumes control momentarily, and then an Alpha Kappa Alpha pledge, a little sister, contributes "good evening big sister/be missin you/til death rips me apart," until the jingle singer from the Ballpark Franks commercial briefly takes his place in front of the mike. Certainly, the sense of a collaborative wholeness that emerges from the use of these rotating voices nods to a poetic jazz sensibility, but the excerpt also swings, as does virtually every Beatty poem, with its own sense of rhythmic attitude.

Further, and perhaps most important, that sense of line-break indeterminacy that I refer to above in "Sitting on Other People's Cars" is also present here. The lack of clarifying punctuation not only allows the poem to swing, but it also obscures exactly when the line or thought should be completed. At first read, it appears that an oral rendering of the poem would signal a period at the end of "mississippi." But the "till" that begins the next line suggests that perhaps there is a ghost comma after "mississippi" rather than a period. And there appears to be another implied comma after "sanity," as well, and maybe an open dash after "dissin you" and a close dash after "missin you" that maintains a certain coherence until "til death rips me apart" and the close of the lyric from the commercial jingle. But that's just what *I* hear; that's my interpretation, my sense of how "Twix" should be read—my own listening *response*, if you will, to Beatty's poetic *call*. The poem will inevitably change slightly, perhaps significantly, depending on the reader-cum-listener's relationship to the black vernacular tradition and/or the poem itself.

While Beatty moved away from publishing poetry after *Joker, Joker, Deuce*,[24] he did not move away from jazz. He employed the same jazz aesthetic in *The White Boy Shuffle* as he did in his poetry. Beatty's novel is, indeed, "jazz shaped," as Ellison wrote, complete with "sudden turns," "shocks," and "swift changes of pace"[25] in its narrative structure, voice, and plot. The book-wide prologue/chapters/epilogue construct, for instance, instantly recalls the head/solos/head musical structure of straight-ahead jazz. But between the prologue and epilogue the novel's twelve chapters are sliced into five sections, each titled with a popular saying from the black community. Within the chapters are occasionally sub-titled sections that appear seemingly at random, in much the same way italicized lines seem to emerge from out of nowhere in Beatty's poetry. In chapter 2 there are explanations for the meaning of the colors "Blue" and "Psychedelic" ("When you're young, psychedelic is a primary color," Gunnar explains) and "White" and "Black."[26] Chapter 2 also includes good-bye letters to the classmates and friends he will miss. In chapter 4 Scoby indoctrinates Gunnar into black street culture by having him acquire "new sneakers, new basketball, and new haircut."[27] But each acquisition is described as a specific cultural moment, with its own titled section: "The Shoes";[28] "The Haircut";[29] and "The Ball."[30] Then there are poems, drawings, e-mail from Nike Camp in chapter 7, a worldwide satellite broadcast in chapter 11—each of these divergent, disruptive voices and placements emerges like the abrupt and surprising flights of a jazz soloist from within the context of the supporting groove, lending an improvisational sensibility to the narrative at large. The result is something like John Szwed's description of the multi-voiced group of musicians Miles Davis assembled to play on *Kind of Blue*: "John Coltrane's astringency on tenor is counterpoised to Cannonball Adderley's soulful alto, with Davis moderating between them as Bill Evans conjures up the still lake of sound on which they walk. Meanwhile, the rhythm team of Paul Chambers and Jimmy Cobb seem prepared to keep time until eternity."[31]

But while the structure of the novel eagerly makes room for continuity as well as sudden shifts and turns, the voice Beatty employs swings throughout, imparting a strong sense of plot-level improvisation. Below, Gunnar Kaufman recalls Ralph Ellison's speechmaking protagonist from *Invisible Man* as he takes the stage at a Boston University political rally. Having just seen a plaque that displays Martin Luther King Jr.'s words, "If a man hasn't discovered something he will die for, he isn't fit to live," Gunnar tells the crowd:

> So I asked myself, what am I willing to die for? The day when white people treat me with respect and see my life as equally valuable to theirs? No, I ain't willing to die for that, because if they don't know that by now, then they ain't never going to know it. Matter of fact, I ain't ready to die for anything, so I guess I'm just not fit to live. In other words, I'm just ready to die. I'm just ready to die.[32]

Beatty displays, here, both vernacular repetition and a sense of improvisation. The "willing to die" and "ready to die" phrases commingle with the "if they don't know . . . they ain't never going to know" phrases, building upon each other until the end of the riff. This is a rhythmic passage, and it swings. And yet, the sense of fluid improvisation, the sense of not knowing quite what one is saying as one says it—let alone what one might say next—is evident in the contrasting response his comments get from his pregnant wife and his best friend: Scoby is nodding in agreement, while Yoshiko gestures toward her distended belly and yells, "What the fuck are you talking about?"[33] The plot-oriented improvisational nature of the novel becomes clear as the rest of the narrative subsequently focuses on the complexities of "freedom through suicide";[34] before too long, death poems float to Gunnar from black folk all over the nation. The above passage, then, is not only an improvisational, call-and-response example of *White Boy Shuffle*'s swinging jazz voice, but the novel's "Emancipation Disintegration"[35] conclusion is also effectively launched by Gunnar's improvisational speech.

So Nick Scoby's contention that poetry is necessarily fixed like "bugs in amber" is opposed not just by Beatty's poems; it is also opposed by the "jazz shaped" structure, voice, and plot of *The White Boy Shuffle* itself. In a sense, Beatty's manipulation of punctuation, his swinging, rhythmic riffs and his scattered, non-specific line breaks in his poetry, as well as his combination of swinging novelistic voice and offbeat narrative surprises in his fiction, "colorize" his writing in exactly the way Scoby suggests can only happen in music. To paraphrase Scoby, then, the use of a jazz aesthetic makes a poem "a different

[poem] but the same [poem]." Depending on when and where the listener/reader hears Beatty's breaks, "You'd be hearing it differently and its meaning would change," because Beatty's poetry has its "own sense of time and experience of time."[36]

It might seem odd—it is odd—that an author's extant poetry would oppose such a decisive argument made about poetry in his novel, but such is the poetic and fictional world of Paul Beatty. What is odder still, however, is that while Beatty, like other poets, utilizes a jazz aesthetic in his poetry, unlike some other poets—black poets in particular—he refuses to romanticize the relationship between poetry and jazz. Beatty's portrayal of the poet in his novels critiques that very idea. Recall that Trey Ellis argued above that "a telltale sign" of the post-soul aesthetic is the "parodying of the black nationalist movement."[37] In his discussion of black poets and their allegiance to John Coltrane, Beatty deftly executes what I refer to as an allusion-disruption strategy. Lisa Jones, in her post-soul handbook *Bulletproof Diva*, suggests more than once that, in this post–civil rights era, one can "both endorse and poke fun at . . . [black] nationalism."[38] The difference here is that Beatty stops far short of "endors[ing]" black nationalism.

There is, after all, an explicit link between black nationalism and the Black Arts Movement. Larry Neal calls the Black Arts Movement "the aesthetic and spiritual sister of the Black Power concept" and insists that "both relate broadly to the Afro-American's desire for self-determination and nationhood. Both concepts are nationalistic."[39] Black Arts poets often looked to jazz musicians for inspiration. Kimberly Benston includes several such poets in his discussion of "the myriad poems directly inspired by Coltrane. The 'Coltrane poem,'" continues Bentson, "has, in fact, become an unmistakable genre of black poetry and it is in such works—by Ebon, [Haki] Madhubuti, Sonia Sanchez, Carolyn Rodgers, A. B. Spellman, and [Michael] Harper, to list but a few—that the notion of music as the quintessential idiom, and of the word as its prelude and annunciator, is carried to an apex of technical and philosophic implication."[40]

It is not surprising, then, that Beatty offers his critique of this deep, emotional connection to the notion of "music as the quintessential idiom" by focusing on the case of John Coltrane. Indeed, when I first read that Nick Scoby, in *The White Boy Shuffle*, would "listen to everything recorded before 1975 in alphabetical order,"[41] the absence of any mention of John Coltrane startled me somewhat. Recall that when Scoby makes his initial pronouncement in the middle of the fourth chapter, he is listening to Cannonball Adderley; twenty pages later in that same chapter, we discover he's listening to Toshiko Akiyoshi. The next time any mention is made of Scoby's alphabetical romp through jazz, Gunnar reports, "He's listening to Miles Davis and refuses to come outside."[42]

Back in 1996, when *The White Boy Shuffle* was first published, the lack of a specific moment when Nick Scoby listened to John Coltrane seemed like either an oversight or simply the author's preference. Anyway, I reasoned, while there are regular mentions of Scoby's progress, there is no exhaustive list of who he did and did not listen to. It is entirely possible, I thought then, that in the fictional world of the novel Scoby did listen to John Coltrane; he just did it offstage, while our narrative attention was forced elsewhere. It was only after *Tuff* was published four years later that I became convinced that Beatty had intentionally, specifically not mentioned Coltrane in his first novel.

Tuff is set in the year 2000, and about halfway through the novel the protagonist, a young man named Winston "Tuffy" Foshay, has a telling encounter with his father, Clifford, a black nationalist poet who appears to be still living in the 1960s. This is where Beatty's chief post-soul allusion-disruption gesture takes place. In this particular scene, Winston has had a disagreement with his father, and he therefore insists that his father and his friends leave his house. "Now bounce!" says Tuffy, "Before you motherfuckers start talking about John Coltrane." "No need to bring Coltrane into this," replies one of Clifford's friends. As the scene plays out, the reason for the absence of Coltrane in *The White Boy Shuffle* becomes clear. When his father and his friends prepare to leave, Tuffy begins "beat[ing] a rhythm on the tabletop, mocking their poetry as they skulked down the hallway":

> *Coltrane be superbad.*
> *Coltrane be black love.*
> *Coltrane be a love supreme. A love supreme.*
> *Coltrane be a burrito supreme. A burrito supreme.*

"You call that poetry?" asks Tuffy. "I admit," he continues, "when y'all used to bogart my tape deck, I liked that nigger's music. That fucking horn would calm you down like a back rub. But after listening to you clowns write about his shit, I can't stand his music. Whenever I hear one of his tunes I think about your bullshit poetry. Y'all must be killing the nigger's record sales."[43]

Bertram D. Ashe

Tuffy has a point—if not about Trane's record sales, then certainly about the abundance of, and virtual religious fervor inherent in, the "Coltrane poem." Indeed, the poetic jab that Tuffy takes at his father and his father's Black Arts friends recalls Michael S. Harper's well-known poem "Dear John, Dear Coltrane" and its famous "*a love supreme, a love supreme*" refrain,[44] as well as, of course, the chant John Coltrane's quartet made on the original recording. Then Beatty links it to, of all things, the Burrito Supreme, a popular entrée at fast-food restaurant Taco Bell.

Clearly, Beatty is offering a strident critique of what he seems to see as empty hagiography and his position conforms to his dismissal of poets he refers to as "bullshit Purveyors of Truth."[45] Another allusion-disruption scene occurs in *The White Boy Shuffle* when Beatty seems to signify on the famous "we want 'poems that kill'" line from Baraka's 1969 poem "Black Art."[46] In reaction to the Rodney King verdict that acquitted the Los Angeles Police Department officers who were captured on videotape beating King, Gunnar Kaufman feels, "A rage that couldn't be dealt with in a poem."[47] Moments later he writes, "The American poet was a tattletale, a whiner, at best an instigator. . . . The day of the L.A. riots I learned that it meant nothing to be a poet."[48] In a sense, then, Beatty's critique of Tuffy's father's black nationalist obsession with John Coltrane folds easily into a distrust of the revolutionary work of the "American poet."

Beatty provides an exclamation point on his critique of the Black Arts Movement version of this American poet in a chapter from *Tuff* titled "The Reading":

> After invoking the requisite Yoruba spirits, Clifford was finally ready to read. There was a cannonade of shotgun fire, and Winston turned to leave. There was no purpose in his staying; he knew the program by heart. Poems about Clifford's expatriation to Cuba: repetitive paeans layered with images of mangos, rusty automobiles, sugarcane, and raven-haired beauties who like to fuck until the roosters crow. To break the revolutionary reveille there would be some poems about basketball, drums, and of course John Coltrane.[49]

Poets such as Clifford Foshay, or, perhaps, Amiri Baraka, for that matter, make careers of searching for or expressing a black nationalist "Answer," as Beatty puts it, to black problems. But Beatty has no investment in that search. "Everybody wants this big meta-Answer," he said in an interview. "There are questions and answers in [my work], but they're not these big . . . there's no panacea. No panacea. And I know people don't like that shit, but that's how I see it."[50] As such, his work suggests that he finds the Black Arts Movement's elevation of John Coltrane one more false note, if you will, coming from poetic "bullshit Purveyors of Truth." "Part of the real reason why I started writing, at some level, wasn't to find answers, it was just to explore," explains Beatty. "For me, the place where I'm most comfortable is on the threshold. Am I hot or cold? What's this perfect temperature, is it 72? 73? You know what I mean? That's the stuff I find fun. The stuff where you're in this space and both things are happening at the same time."[51]

Beatty's perspective on black art—as well as his demonstrated poetic and novelistic stances—places his work squarely in the post-soul aesthetic, even though Beatty, like many artists whose work links them with the post-soul school, would prefer not to be confined to a particular identifiable aesthetic. It is not difficult to see why an artist would resist being placed in any ideological box. But the issue is complicated for black artists. Studio Museum in Harlem curator Thelma Golden, in her introduction to the Freestyle exhibition's catalog, writes, "For me, to approach a conversation about 'black art,' ultimately meant embracing and rejecting the notion of such a thing at the very same time."[52] Similarly, when asked by London's *The Independent* whether he was a black writer, Beatty answered, "Well, I'm black and I'm a writer, so, yes, I am a black writer. But I also have big feet and wear glasses. Why should I be expected to be The Real Thing? Who has decided that I should be the spokesman for the whole black experience?"[53] From Golden's perspective, the post-soul (although she prefers the term *post-black*) is "characterized by artists who [are] adamant about not being labeled as 'black' artists, even though their work [is] steeped, in fact, deeply interested in, redefining complex notions of blackness."[54] Even if she had used Beatty's name in that sentence, she could not have described his perspective and work more closely.

Some readers do not appreciate that perspective. Ishmael Reed complains, in a *Village Voice* review of *Tuff*, that Beatty "needs a vision."[55] Likewise, Hal Hinson, in *Salon*, feels the novel lacks "any sort of moral or philosophical center."[56] And Ken Foster, of the *New York Times*, writes, "For all Beatty's powerful observations, it's hard to see a clear lesson or message beneath his work. From *Tuff* one gets the sense that nothing matters to Beatty more than anything else, that there is nothing worthy of emotional investment or political belief."[57] Beatty agrees, to an extent, with all three: "I don't have an articulated vision. I'll

Bertram D. Ashe

never have that. There's obviously things I believe in, and give a fuck about, but it's not a prophetizing vision." Beatty's work is "basically talking about the contradictions within saying you have a vision,"[58] and he opposes the idea of serving up the "Answer" that some readers, reviewers, and critics seem to want from him. "I'm interested in contradictions," he continues in *The Independent*, "but that doesn't mean that I have any responsibility to come up with any resolutions. I've had reviewers being angry with me for failing to solve the entire race issue single-handedly."[59] He will not. He cannot. But what he can and does do, as he puts it, is "explore." And, ultimately, Paul Beatty's complex, four-book exploration—of poets, of jazz and poetry, of jazz poetry, and his ultimate denigration of the valorization of jazz and poetry—conspires to embed him in the post-soul, a "post-liberated" aesthetic,[60] to use Greg Tate's term, that peers deeply into blackness, in all its complicated variety.

Beatty's line-by-line work, then, his formal poetic output on the page does, indeed, validate the idea of a jazz poetry. As Charles O. Hartman suggests in his book *Jazz Text*, "contemporary American poetry is vitally interested—as many poets are personally interested—in two of the central principles of the jazz art: improvisation . . . and 'voice.'" These two principles, among others, point "toward yearnings in poetry—often yearnings away from the printed page—that make jazz the land of heart's desire."[61] Beatty just might agree with Hartman—about poetic form, anyway. But he would likely oppose the idea of viewing jazz musicians (John Coltrane being the most obvious example) as musical "Purveyors of Truth" to be emulated by poetic "Purveyors of Truth." After all, Nick Scoby never made it to Z in his jazz-listening odyssey. He was listening to Sarah Vaughan on the day he took his own life. Perhaps Scoby's incomplete quest is one last way for Beatty to argue that using jazz as a poetic vehicle might work wonders, but one should stop short of elevating mere players of music, however great, into jazz gods.

NOTES

The author would like to thank Crystal Anderson, Daphne Brooks, Diana Cruz, and O'Donavan Johnson for their valuable contribution to the writing of this essay.

1. Paul Beatty, *The White Boy Shuffle* [subsequently referenced as *WBS*] (Boston: Houghton Mifflin, 1996), 67.

2. While the brief conversations about jazz between Gunnar and Scoby sprinkled throughout *The White Boy Shuffle* are not significant to the plot, jazz is, I argue below, of great formal significance to the novel.

3. Ralph Ellison, "What America Would Be Like without Blacks," *The Collected Essays of Ralph Ellison* (New York: Modern Library, 1995), 582.

4. Beatty, *WBS*, 41.

5. Ibid., 49.

6. Ibid., 131.

7. Although he does not use the term *jazz aesthetic*, Charles S. Johnson explains the idea: "Jazz is not so much music as method. The poetry which goes by the name is a venture in the new, bold rhythms characteristic of the music. And, although it has come, curiously, to express the fierce tempo of our contemporary life, it is also its vent. For jazz, more than being rhythm, is an atmosphere." See Charles S. Johnson, "Jazz Poetry and Blues," *Carolina Magazine* (May 1928): 16.

8. As he revealed during the author's interview with Beatty, 16 August 2001.

9. See Nelson George, *Buppies, B-Boys, Baps, and Bohos: Notes on Post-Soul Black Culture* (New York: HarperPerennial, 1994) and *Post-Soul Nation* (New York: Viking, 2004); see also Mark Anthony Neal, *Soul Babies: Black Popular Culture and the Post-Soul Aesthetic* (New York: Routledge, 2002).

10. Trey Ellis, "The New Black Aesthetic," *Callaloo* 12.1 (Winter 1989): 234, 236, 235.

11. Ibid., 235.

12. LeRoi Jones, *Home: Social Essays* (New York: William Morrow, 1966), 106–7.

13. Beatty, *WBS*, 204.

14. Ibid., 204–5. Scoby's specific use of Charlie "Bird" Parker's saxophone playing as an expression of anger on the part of African Americans recalls Baraka's similar suggestion in his 1964 play *Dutchman*: "Charlie Parker? Charlie Parker. All the hip white boys scream for Bird. And Bird saying, 'Up your ass, feeble-minded ofay! Up your ass!' And they sit there talking about the tortured genius of Charlie Parker. Bird would've played not a note of music if he just walked up to East Sixty-seventh Street and killed the first ten white people he saw. Not a note!" In *The Norton Anthology of African American Literature*, 2nd ed., ed. Henry Louis Gates Jr. and Nellie Y. McKay (New York: W. W. Norton, 2004), 1958.

15. Beatty, *WBS*, 205.

16. Beatty, *Big Bank Take Little Bank* (New York: Nuyorican Poets Café, 1991), 31.

17. Ibid., 22. Beatty's "cultural mulatto" post-soul tendencies are very much on display in such mixes of references.

18. Defining swing is, of course, a notoriously difficult task. For Murray, music swings "so long as it has the idiomatic rhythmic emphasis that generates the dance-step response. In other words, the incantation must be so percussion oriented that it disposes the listeners to bump and bounce, to slow-drag and steady shuffle, to grind, hop, jump, kick, rock, roll, shout, stomp, and otherwise swing the blues away." Murray's description of swing rightly recalls black vernacular call-and-response: he sees it in relational terms, moving between

musician and listener. Beatty's poetry swings, then, in that it provides a similarly percussive "incantation" between poet and reader/listener. See Albert Murray, *Stomping the Blues* (New York: McGraw-Hill, 1976), 144.

19. Lynne Truss, *Eats, Shoots and Leaves: The Zero Tolerance Approach to Punctuation* (New York: Gotham Books, 2004), 72.

20. Ibid., 71.

21. Paul Beatty, *Joker, Joker, Deuce* (New York: Penguin, 1994), 34.

22. Truss, *Eats, Shoots and Leaves*, 70.

23. Beatty, *Big Bank*, 46–47.

24. Beatty expresses his feelings about poetry and fiction this way: "You know, everyone when I read expects some show, some shit that I've never, ever, ever done. And it's all kind of based on something, I don't fucking know what. Mostly based on what they expect [from], you know, 'black poets,' whatever that means to them. . . . And I got very uncomfortable with it, but [while]I was uncomfortable, it wasn't like I got this conscious decision to stop [writing poetry]. What I really started to do was write *White Boy Shuffle*, and so then I didn't have any time to write any poetry, and then writing fiction was just far more interesting. So it kind of all worked together in a good way, and I could say the same shit [in *White Boy Shuffle*] and make fun of poetry—which is always fun to do." Author's interview with Beatty, 16 August 2001.

25. Ellison, "What America Would Be Like," 582.

26. Beatty, *WBS*, 34–35.

27. Ibid., 92.

28. Ibid., 88–90.

29. Ibid., 90–91.

30. Ibid., 92.

31. John Szwed, *So What: The Life of Miles Davis* (New York: Simon & Schuster, 2002), 174–75.

32. Beatty, *WBS*, 199–200.

33. Ibid.

34. Ibid., 201.

35. Ibid., 2.

36. Ibid., 205.

37. Ellis, "New Black Aesthetic," 236.

38. Lisa Jones, *Bulletproof Diva: Tales of Race, Sex, and Hair* (New York: Anchor Books, 1994), 24.

39. Larry Neal, *Visions of a Liberated Future: Black Arts Movement Writing* (New York: Thunder's Mouth Press, 1989), 62.

40. Kimberly W. Benston, "Late Coltrane: A Re-Membering of Orpheus," in *Chant of Saints: A Gathering of Afro-American Literature, Art, and Scholarship*, ed. Michael S. Harper and Robert B. Stepto (Urbana: University of Illinois Press, 1979), 416. Sascha Feinstein also includes an entire chapter, "The John Coltrane Poem," in his *Jazz Poetry: From the 1920s to the Present* (Westport, CT: Greenwood Press, 1997), 115–42.

41. Beatty, *WBS*, 67.

42. Ibid., 99.

43. Paul Beatty, *Tuff* (New York: Alfred A. Knopf, 2000), 111. Notice the similarity between this novelistic description of a sensual and emotional reaction to jazz—"That fucking horn would calm you down like a back rub"—and the poetic description from "Sitting on Other People's Cars," where the "rhythms" from Charles Mingus's music "ran down/your back/with the bumpidy syncopation/of a bestfriends knuckle/rubbin up and down your spine" (34). In tandem, these references suggest, particularly when the "bestfriend" gets "the chills" later in the poem, that Beatty feels jazz allows a listener to "chill," so to speak, while also simultaneously producing "chills"; the music is, he suggests, both spine-soothing and spine-tingling at the very same time.

44. It is worth mentioning that Michael Harper, his Coltrane poetry notwithstanding, is not generally considered a Blacks Arts Movement poet.

45. Author's interview with Beatty, 16 August 2001.

46. See Amiri Baraka, "Black Art," reprinted in Gates and McKay, *Norton Anthology of African American Literature*, 1943.

47. Beatty, *WBS*, 131.

48. Ibid., 131–32.

49. Beatty, *Tuff*, 129.

50. Author's interview with Beatty, 16 August 2001.

51. Ibid.

52. Thelma Golden, Introduction, *Freestyle* (New York: Studio Museum in Harlem, 2001), 14.

53. Graham Caveney, "Sweet Talk and Fighting Words," *Independent*, 22 July 2000, 9.

54. Golden, Introduction, 14.

55. Ishmael Reed, "Hoodwinked: Paul Beatty's Urban Nihilists," *Voice Literary Supplement*, 11 April 2000, 135.

56. http://dir.salon.com/books/review/2000/05/15/beatty/index.html.

57. Ken Foster, "Boy in the 'Hood," *New York Times*, 7 May 2000, 7, 25.

58. Author's interview with Beatty, 16 August 2001.

59. Caveney, "Sweet Talk and Fighting Words," 9.

60. Greg Tate, *Flyboy in the Buttermilk: Essays on Contemporary America* (New York: Simon & Schuster, 1992), 200.

61. Charles O. Hartman, *Jazz Text: Voice and Improvisation in Poetry, Jazz, and Song* (Princeton, NJ: Princeton University Press, 1991), 4.

WORKS CITED

Baraka, Amiri. "Black Art." In Gates and McKay, *Norton Anthology*, 1943–44.

———. *Dutchman*. In Gates and McKay, *Norton Anthology*, 1946–60.

Beatty, Paul. *Big Bank Take Little Bank*. New York: Nuyorican Poets Café, 1991.

———. *Joker, Joker, Deuce*. New York: Penguin, 1994.

———. *Tuff*. New York: Alfred A. Knopf, 2000.

———. *The White Boy Shuffle*. Boston: Houghton Mifflin, 1996.

Benston, Kimberly W. "Late Coltrane: A Re-Membering of Orpheus." In *Chant of Saints: A Gathering of Afro-American Literature, Art, and Scholarship*.

Bertram D. Ashe

Ed. Michael S. Harper and Robert B. Stepto. Urbana: University of Illinois Press, 1979. 413–24.

Caveney, Graham. "Sweet Talk and Fighting Words." *Independent*, 22 July 2000, 9.

Ellis, Trey. "The New Black Aesthetic." *Callaloo* 12.1 (Winter 1989): 233–51.

Ellison, Ralph. "What America Would Be Like without Blacks." In *The Collected Essays of Ralph Ellison.* New York: Modern Library, 1995. 577–84.

Feinstein, Sascha. *Jazz Poetry: From the 1920s to the Present.* Westport, CT: Greenwood Press, 1997.

Foster, Ken. "Boy in the 'Hood." *New York Times*, 7 May 2000, 7, 25.

Gates, Henry Louis Jr., and Nellie Y. McKay, eds. *The Norton Anthology of African American Literature,* 2nd ed. New York: W. W. Norton, 2004.

George, Nelson. *Buppies, B-Boys, Baps, and Bohos: Notes on Post-Soul Black Culture.* New York: HarperPerennial, 1994.

———. *Post-Soul Nation.* New York: Viking, 2004.

Golden, Thelma. Introduction. *Freestyle.* New York: Studio Museum in Harlem, 2001. 14–15.

Hartman, Charles O. *Jazz Text: Voice and Improvisation in Poetry, Jazz, and Song.* Princeton, NJ: Princeton University Press, 1991.

Johnson, Charles S. "Jazz Poetry and Blues." *Carolina Magazine* (May 1928): 16–20.

Jones, LeRoi. *Home: Social Essays.* New York: William Morrow, 1966.

Jones, Lisa. *Bulletproof Diva: Tales of Race, Sex, and Hair.* New York: Anchor Books, 1994.

Murray, Albert. *Stomping the Blues.* New York: McGraw-Hill, 1976.

Neal, Larry. *Visions of a Liberated Future: Black Arts Movement Writing.* New York: Thunder's Mouth Press, 1989.

Neal, Mark Anthony. *Soul Babies: Black Popular Culture and the Post-Soul Aesthetic.* New York: Routledge, 2002.

Reed, Ishmael. "Hoodwinked: Paul Beatty's Urban Nihilists." *Voice Literary Supplement*, 11 April 2000, 135.

Szwed, John. *So What: The Life of Miles Davis.* New York: Simon & Schuster, 2002.

Tate, Greg. *Flyboy in the Buttermilk: Essays on Contemporary America.* New York: Simon & Schuster, 1992.

Truss, Lynne. *Eats, Shoots and Leaves: The Zero Tolerance Approach to Punctuation.* New York: Gotham Books, 2004.

Giving Voice: An Interview with Jayne Cortez

Graham Lock

Jayne Cortez was born in Arizona in 1936 and grew up in Los Angeles. She played bass, cello, and piano in high school, then tried her hand at painting and drama before settling on poetry as her chosen means of expression. Don Cherry lived in the same L.A. neighborhood and would call around to hear her collection of hot new bebop 78s. In 1954 she introduced him to Ornette Coleman, to whom she was later briefly married. (Their son Denardo, now a renowned drummer, performs and records with each of his parents.)

Cortez moved to New York in 1967 and her first books—*Pissstained Stairs and the Monkey Man's Wares* (1969), *Festivals and Funerals* (1971), and *Scarifications* (1973)—helped to establish her as a major voice among Black Arts poets. In 1974 she made her first recording (with bassist Richard Davis) and in 1980 formed her own band, the Firespitters, with whom she has now recorded some half dozen titles, the most recent of which are *Taking the Blues Back Home* (1996), *Borders of Disorderly Time* (2003), and the compilation *Find Your Own Voice* (2006). She has continued to publish books of poems too, focusing on both musical and political subjects (she is a committed political organizer); *Jazz Fan Looks Back* (2002) collects together many of her music-related pieces.

We met in the Harmolodic Studios in East Harlem, New York City, in April 2004.

GL: You were a big bebop fan as a teenager?

JC: Yes, I first heard Charlie Parker and other musicians playing bebop on the radio in Los Angeles in the late '40s and I bought those recordings on 78s. The music was different from the recordings of my parents. Their collection was mainly big bands, like Duke Ellington and Count Basie, and some blues recordings. I played those 78s over and over and my parents would say, "Can you please turn that down?" [*Laughs.*]

I was very attracted to the music of Charlie Parker, Thelonious Monk, Fats Navarro, Bud Powell, Lester Young, and others. As a young girl, I used to go to jam sessions in our community. We had young musicians who played in garages or in the park on Sunday afternoons. I guess I got a lot of ear training.

GL: Were you also going to dances, listening to different kinds of musics?

JC: Yeah, not just bebop but blues, rhythm and blues . . . In the '50s in Los Angeles, there was a lot of rhythm and blues, and people like T-Bone Walker, Roy Milton, Big Jay McNeilly. I used to hear Johnny Otis and his group, with Big Mama Thornton and Little Esther Phillips; they would play at teenage dances. Later, in the late '50s and early '60s, I heard a lot of country blues—Howlin' Wolf, John Lee Hooker, Lightnin' Hopkins—at the Troubador Club and at the Ash Grove in Los Angeles.

GL: Can I ask about your political background too? You made a trip to the South in 1963 that proved very influential?

JC: I went to Greenwood, Mississippi, to work with the Student Non Violent Co-ordinating Committee in a voter registration project. I think participating in the civil rights movement made me more aware of black history, black resistance, and the struggle for black freedom. I learned much more about politics, domination, and the world. It was during this time that I started mixing politics and art.

GL: When did you begin to read with musicians?

JC: That was also in 1963. I would read my work alone and with music.

GL: What kind of musicians? Jazz musicians?

JC: In Los Angeles I performed with Horace Tapscott and his group, and with saxophone players like Curtis Amy, Teddy Edwards, and Arthur Blythe. In 1967, when I arrived in New York City, I read with trumpeter Clifford Thornton and his group. In the 1970s and '80s, I also worked in other venues on the East Coast: for example, I performed in several concert series organized by Bill Cole at Dartmouth College. Those events included players such as Julius Hemphill, Abraham Adzinyah, Jerry Gonzales, Sam Rivers, Joe Daley, Warren Smith, Vishnu Woods . . .

GL: I'm intrigued because you seem to have worked with both bebop musicians and free jazz musicians, yet the jazz journalism from the '60s and '70s suggests there was a big split between them.

JC: Maybe generational splits and splits based on new technology. Musicians are always experimenting; some in free time, others in standard time and in no time. Louis Armstrong's music was called early jazz, but Louis Armstrong was playing Louis Armstrong. I mean, there are all these tags and limitations. Musicians cross many lines and spaces; they have their own approaches, their own concepts.

I wanted to collaborate with different musicians; I also wanted my poetry to be the focus, the center post. I'm interested in the possibilities and in the intensification of those possibilities. My hope is to eliminate certain musical references and fixtures, so I like collaborating with musicians in an improvisational call-and-response way.

GL: You knew some avant-garde people very early: Ornette, Don Cherry . . .

JC: Don and I grew up in the same neighborhood in south Los Angeles. I was definitely attracted to music that was taking the next step. But I didn't have anything against people who wanted to stay on the same step, because they were also friends. I introduced Don to Ornette. At that time Don was still playing with his high school friends and was not in the avant-garde realm. He learned a great deal from Ornette.

GL: Did knowing all these musicians change your idea of the music you wanted with your poetry?

JC: Not really. That idea was based not on what kind of music I wanted, but on who did I want to work with? That was the interest. I never thought about what kind of music, because whatever it was, it was going to be based on my poetry. I've worked with kora players, djembe players, saxophonists, guitar players, et cetera, and I've worked with musicians from different parts of Africa, Latin America, and the USA. I like collaborating with various musicians.

GL: You made your first recording in 1974.[1] Why did you choose to bring out a record?

JC: Well, I had the books and I had already been reading my work with music, so I wanted to make a recording. I thought about Richard Davis—he's a great bass player; I thought it would be interesting to see what would happen between the two of us. I had never performed with Richard and at the recording session he did not want to rehearse, so we just did it! Which is the same way I worked with the great bassist Ron Carter on *Borders of Disorderly Time*: we never did rehearse.[2] We just came to the studio, listened, responded, and recorded.

GL: How have you chosen the different instrumentations you've used since that first record?

JC: What happened is, I started working with Denardo. He was playing drums with me; and he said, let's get a band. [*Laughs.*] I wanted a guitar player on that second recording, *Unsubmissive Blues*; Bern Nix was available, and I had worked with Bill Cole and Joe Daley so we went to a studio and recorded.[3] That was around 1980. Then, as I started to get more performances, I was able to hire a bass player as well as Bern and Denardo, so we started to increase. The next recording, in 1982, I used the musicians who had been working with me.

You could say that Denardo and I started the band in 1980 and instead of just playing a concert and whatever happens happens, now we have an actual band that can respond to my work. It's not that I don't want to work with other groups; I do sometimes, but it's an advantage when you have a group of people who know that the center is going to be your poetry; that they have to take whatever it is from there and run with it, make a U turn and bring in fresh ideas.

GL: Has working with a band changed the way you work?

JC: I don't know if it's changed. Maybe there are two or three pieces that developed out of rehearsal, so in that sense my work can change. For the most part, I sit in my room and write. Sometimes in rehearsal something will happen spontaneously and I'll say, that's good, I can use what happened there. But that's rare.

GL: Has working with a band affected the way you perform? Made it more musical, say?

JC: One of the problems for me is that when I'm working in concert, all of those instruments are so powerful and I have just this voice. This is a speaking voice, it's not a singing voice—a singing voice can get right up there with the instruments; in a speaking voice, you really can't do that. It's always been a challenge to me: how to project, how to bring my voice up, with all of this music behind me.[4]

I feel like in some situations I can't go low, I can't vary my tone, because of having to stay at a high pitch just to be heard. You can do it in rehearsal but when you get to the concert and you have to use somebody else's microphone, somebody else's equipment, some other engineer, it's another story.

GL: Have you ever been tempted to sing? Because you don't just speak, you kind of go with the music.

JC: Sometimes I go with the rhythm . . . I guess it's a speak-chant type thing. [*Laughs.*] But no, I don't think about singing. The other thing is that the way I write is not within the song form. There are many more words, many more images. You just can't sing that. Or maybe you can, but I've never tried.

GL: When you began to work with musicians, did that change how you thought about a poem? I mean, as something to be performed, say, rather than as something on the page?

JC: No. I have many pieces that will never be performed with music. They just wouldn't fit within that pattern of what I'm trying to do. But they're right there on the page and they're right there in my voice, because I can read them by myself to audiences. I do a lot of readings without music.

GL: The poems basically have to work on the page?

JC: Right. They usually work on the page. And if they work with music, then fine; if not, I leave them on the page.

GL: How does the recording process work for you? You've said you rehearse but you've also written in your liner notes that some tunes are collectively improvised.

JC: It's mostly collectively improvised. Except for the last recording, *Borders of Disorderly Time*: Denardo wrote a lot of the tunes and I decided to see how that would work. I found that interesting too, because we were having to deal with the tune as well. I want to be able to do it every which way.

GL: When you collectively improvise a tune, how does that work? Do you begin by reading the poem?

JC: When we rehearse, I just read the piece, then we talk about it and everybody finds their line; they focus and build. That's kind of how it works. We all have to listen very intensely and act on what we hear.

GL: Before you rehearse, do you already have an idea . . . not of a tune but of a mood, perhaps, that you'd like the music to express?

JC: Usually I'll have . . . like, this is definitely not a carnival piece! [*Laughs.*] Or this is more a blues, you know. Mainly whatever the piece is about, that sets the mood. For "Bumblebee," the piece where I'm talking about Big Mama Thornton, I was using the word "Bumblebee" because she used it on her recording about Bumblebee, so the musicians felt like they would be bumblebees . . . [*hums*] . . . like that. [*Laughs.*] That image came up and it worked. We buzzed all over the place.[5]

Sometimes there are surprises. I can be working on something and it's not seeming to work, then Denardo or the bass player will say, well, let's try it another way, and that does the trick.

GL: Do *you* improvise?

JC: I alter things in performance. Like I said, I have to stay at one pitch level in order to get over the instruments—I'm not like a vocalist who's singing with the horns—but there's quite a lot of improvising that goes on. I never approach a piece in the same way twice; however it sounds today, it'll sound different tomorrow. What's down on paper is the guideline and we just take off from that.

GL: You mentioned earlier that you had worked with Julius Hemphill. Can you say a little more about that?

JC: I met Julius and his family back in 1970, 1972. We performed together in Chicago, then when he came to New York, we performed with Bill Cole in New York and at Dartmouth College. We worked together every year for at least seven years.

Julius composed some beautiful music and organized the World Saxophone Quartet. It's really a drag that Ken Burns, who did the TV series on jazz, stopped in 1960, because I think the '60s, '70s, '80s, and '90s are all so important to the story of jazz. When they stopped there, they did not include the work of Julius Hemphill, David Murray, et cetera, which was just incorrect. And they left out the whole loft scene, which was full of independent directions. I keep thinking, if I ever get a lot of money [*laughs*], I'm going to make a film on jazz the way I see it, and Julius would be a big part of that.

GL: Why do you think people have so many problems with free jazz and what happened after 1960? It seems as if they simply don't know how to deal with it.

JC: I think it's just that they can't be free. Maybe they feel safe with something that's more familiar to them. They're stuck in a conservative way of thinking and they can't move on.

GL: Does race play a part in this? I'm thinking of Marion Brown's comment that white people have a real problem accepting that black people can do abstract art of any kind,[6] which might explain the press hostility to free jazz and the fact that so many black abstract painters are still being overlooked.

JC: Definitely. Well, they're being overlooked because white people own the so-called art market and if they want you in, you're in; and if they don't, you're out. Usually you're out. Which is okay with me because I don't think you should stop what you're doing based on that fact: and it is a fact in the United States and in Europe too. But that's not why we are creating. Once you become aware of who you are and what you want to do, there are many more places to go to play and many more opportunities to read and collaborate with other artists in Africa and the rest of the third world. You can't stop working on abstract work or avant-garde work or any kind of work because so-and-so doesn't like it or because someone feels threatened because you are black and your work is strong.

GL: Is this why you've published your own books and CDs?

JC: It's why I started Bola Press. I don't have to worry about censorship. I don't have to worry about those restrictions or about being published or recorded. And when I do publish my work in other publications or record with other companies, it's because they want my work as it is. I just move ahead. I find that having my own company and handling a lot of my own work has given me unlimited freedom.

GL: Are there not financial constraints?

JC: There are, yes. I'm sure that when I did the recording with Verve, they had more money to spend on distribution, and distribution is available to them because of who they are. There's the difference—but not in terms of the quality of the work, because that's in my hands.

GL: You said before that you don't use song form; you don't seem to use blues form either, even when you're doing a blues.

JC: No, I'm using the blues before the blues was twelve bars. [*Laughs.*] But you can tell it's a blues by the music and by the feeling; and even the music is going over bounds, back to what it was before we bottled it in twelve bars or forward into what it is in that moment.

GL: How about other poets working with musicians, have they been an influence on you? Like Langston Hughes with Mingus?[7]

JC: I heard Langston's work with Mingus but I think our approaches to music and poetry are different. He uses music as a background for his work. Most of the music on the recording with Mingus was written, not improvised. And our poetic views are different, though he is one of my favorite poets. Our approach to the blues is also different; he uses a blues form for his blues. But I really did like his work with Mingus; I liked the fact that they did something together.

GL: Talking about your approach to the blues, can you say a little more about that? For instance, in your "Statement" in the notes to the *Taking the Blues Back Home* CD,[8] you say the disc is "focused on the basic progressive aspects of the blues in the deepest sense." Is it possible to explain that phrase in more detail?

JC: Usually, when you hear the blues, you're not hearing the political part of it; you're hearing a musician saying, "I'm lovesick" or "I'm travelin', honey." I wanted to take on the things that are not said in those relationships, and to talk about the things that the blues are a part of; talk about race, talk about wars, talk about the environment. I think there are only a few blues singers who talk about war. But maybe war is underneath the blues—because the blues is so coded; you have to know the combination to find it. I wanted my take on various experiences and conditions and solutions to be an out-front kind of blues.

GL: Was "Taking the Blues Back Home" itself a response to a specific event? [*See pp. 134–36.*]

JC: Not an event: I wanted to take up that issue. Okay, you're going to ask why! [*Laughs.*] Because the blues stealers are stealing, you know, and they're making a mess of things. I mean, we're not talking about the same blues here. I'm talking about slavery, the transatlantic slave trade, about slave dungeons, and 400 years of consequences. I'm talking about struggle and resistance and the bitterness inside of me. I'm not talking about how the slaveholder has the blues, I'm not talking about entertainment; I'm talking about black freedom and how to make a better world.

GL: Do you think jazz has been stolen too? Are there jazz stealers around?

JC: I don't know . . . how can I say this? Like, you see people who are singing the blues—they're taking what's already been done and putting it out there as if it was their own; they're making thousands and thousands of dollars off it, while the people who created it have nothing. I don't think this is happening as much in jazz. But there are people improvising off of jazz licks and saying that they're doing something different, so they don't have to acknowledge that the source is the black experience in jazz. In terms of the blues, you just have to say, listen, you can't take somebody's voice, you're actually taking the way they talk and pretending like it's yours! It's a minstrel show. That's why I wrote "Taking the Blues Back Home." I believe you have to find your own voice and use it.

GL: You've talked before of the blues as "instinct and relief," that it's about "being real and surreal." Can you explain that a little?

JC: Instinct, intuition, it all plays a part in the writing. The work is emotional, intellectual—everything is there. It's natural, supernatural, surreal, in dreams. It's associations, juxtapositions of images and words, based on a real situation, on inventions. I put it all together. That's the way I think.

GL: When you write about real people, like the musicians you've known, is there ever a tension between the surreal and fantasy elements in your writing and a need for historical accuracy, historical truth?

JC: I don't think so. I think it's all about imagination, invention, and transformation. I think the combination is the truth.

GL: When you write about musicians, have there been instances when you've adapted your style to try to reflect their music?

JC: I guess it won't happen, even if you try, because your thoughts and feelings are going to be so different from what was happening at the time of the music. It's all a point of departure.

Okay, I wrote a poem about Miles Davis, "A Miles Davis Trumpet," because I was invited to read at a memorial for Miles Davis at St. John the Divine.[9] [*See pp. 136–39.*] I don't think the piece actually captures his music, but it captures my feelings about his music, about him, and about the time he lived in.

GL: You've never tried to "capture the music"?

JC: Oh, that's impossible! Everything I'm doing is based on words. You have two different things going on: the music is one thing and the verbal is another.[10] And I'm not writing words *to* the music, like Eddie Jefferson; I don't write like that.

GL: I meant to ask you earlier . . . You said you're not a singer, but did jazz singers and blues singers not influence you at all?

JC: No, though I like a lot of those people: Billie Holiday, Ella Fitzgerald, Betty Carter. But no, because I can't do what they do; I'm not trying to sing.

GL: I was thinking perhaps more in terms of attitude.

JC: No, my attitude is pretty much mine. [*Laughs.*] My work has always had attitude.

Taking the Blues Back Home

I'm taking the blues back home
I'm taking the blues back to where
the blues stealers won't go

I'm taking the blues back home
because the blues stealers like to steal
when they think they have nothing of their own
I'm taking the blues back home
I'm taking the blues back to the fire of the spirits
I'm taking the blues back to the
damp undergrowth
I'm taking the blues back to where
the blues stealers won't go
I'm taking the blues back home

I'm taking the blues out of the mouths of the stealers
I'm taking the blues out of the western stream

I'm taking the blues back before somebody sings
"Ain't nobody's business if I steal your blues"
I'm taking the blues back home
I'm taking the blues back home
before Robert Johnson comes from
the graveyard to say
"The blues has been crapped on"
I'm taking the blues back to the crossroads
I'm taking the blues back to the bush
I'm taking the blues back to the place
where the blues stealers won't go
I'm taking the blues back home before
Langston Hughes returns to say
"They've taken my blues again and gone"
I'm taking the blues back home
I'm the owner of the blues
& I'm taking the blues back home

The blues that came to me from the slave dungeons
the blues that came to me from the death trails
the blues that came to me from my ancestors
the blues that came to me in a spell that tells me
through birth that I'm the owner of the blues
from a long time ago
I'm the owner of the blues from a long
long long long time ago
I'm the owner of the blues
& even if somebody says
they have a right to sing the blues
I'm still the owner of the secrets in the blues
from a long time ago
I'm the owner of the blues
& even if somebody pays to play & use the blues
I'm still the owner of the blues
from a long time ago
I'm the owner of the blues
& I'm taking the blues back home

I'm taking the blues back to where
the blues stealers won't go
I'm taking the blues back home
I'm taking the blues back home

A Miles Davis Trumpet

There are the ivory trumpets from Africa
the silver trumpets found in drawings
on walls of Egyptian tombs
telescoping trumpets from China
trumpets that live in Tibet
Spanish-speaking trumpets of Spain
& then
there is
that trumpet
with solitary feeling of sound
splashing through rough woodshed of Charlie Parker
splashing the sound of distance
                in trumpet
                against orchestra
trumpet circling within box
                of a box
           of controlled settings
      trumpet
patinaed with layers of rust & spit
grooving inside the groove surface
trumpet
with bell of funk fired up
in middle extremities
between bass & treble
thunder & whistle
Unmuzzled cheeks of brass
inflated storm of mutes

elastic electric Elegba
that trumpet

There are the oceanic shell trumpets
buzzing Southern Indian trumpets
natural Arabian trumpets
fast-talking Cuban trumpets
European-inspired valve trumpets
trumpets with great ears
& husky tones & avant-garde ways
trumpets   fanfaring   dirging   parading
& giving military salutes

There are
side-blown trumpets
side-winder trumpets
straight trumpets
sweet trumpets
Satchmo trumpets
Oliver trumpets
Bolden trumpets
Little Jazz trumpets
Red trumpets
Rex trumpets
Dorham trumpets
curved trumpets
Dizzy trumpets
Clark trumpets
Hot Lips trumpets
Fats trumpets
pocket trumpets
Cootie trumpets
Farmer trumpets
Brownie trumpets
Cherry trumpets
& then there is
that short dark popping trumpet

covered in a mask of
New York hipness & fame
that trumpet
with another hairdo
another change of aspirations
another half-nelson in
a constellation of dust
another motif in
      terrycloth turban
another hoarse voice of
Orin to ti Orunwa
that trumpet

That trumpet
with the sound of chance
the sound of prediction
the sound of invention
the sound of migration & madness
& fluidity of solitude
& mathematical flurries
& blasted bridges
& dynamism within
collectivity of the hunt
that trumpet
with jom
with spirit
with secret sound systems hidden
behind sunglass fetishes
that trumpet
has a throat
which sits outside
of its body
sits on top of the wind
on top of the band
with explosive pucks
mystical rain spittle
aboriginal tongue toot toots

that trumpet

that trumpet is

the militant   mellow   melodic   magical

miraculous   minimalist   Miles Davis trumpet

that trumpet

To hear Jayne Cortez read her poem "A Miles Davis Trumpet," with music by Ron Carter on bass, please go to the *Thriving on a Riff* Web site at http://www .oup.com/us/thrivingonariff. Courtesy of Jayne Cortez and Bola Press.

NOTES

1. Jayne Cortez, *Celebrations and Solitudes* LP (Strata East SES 7421, 1974).

2. Jayne Cortez and the Firespitters, *Borders of Disorderly Time* (Bola Press BLP, 2003).

3. Jayne Cortez, *Unsubmissive Blues* LP (Bola Press BP 8001, 1980).

4. Cortez was indeed already talking about this problem in the early 1980s. See D. H. Melhem, *Heroism in the New Black Poetry: Introductions and Interviews* (Lexington: University Press of Kentucky, 1990), 204.

5. On Jayne Cortez and the Firespitters, *Taking the Blues Back Home* (Harmolodic/Verve 531 918-2, 1996).

6. Quoted in A. B. Spellman, "Not Just Whistling Dixie," in *Black Fire: An Anthology of Afro-American Writing*, ed. LeRoi Jones and Larry Neal (New York: William Morrow, 1968), 159.

7. Langston Hughes, with Charles Mingus and Leonard Feather, *Weary Blues* (1958; reissue, Verve 841 660-2, 1990).

8. Jayne Cortez, "Statement," in liner notes to Cortez and the Firespitters, *Taking the Blues Back Home*, n.p.

9. On Cortez and the Firespitters, *Borders of Disorderly Time*.

10. For a persuasive counter-argument (at least in reference to a written poem), see T. J. Anderson III's discussion of Cortez's use of bebop phrasing and rhythm in "Why Not" (an homage to vocalist Babs Gonzalez), which Anderson cites as "a good example of how Cortez can adapt language to a particular musical style." T. J. Anderson III, *Notes to Make the Sound Come Right: Four Innovators of Jazz Poetry* (Fayetteville: University of Arkansas Press, 2004), 141–44; Jayne Cortez, "Why Not," *Jazz Fan Looks Back* (Brooklyn, NY: Hanging Loose Press, 2002), 83–84.

SELECTED WORKS

Recordings

Cortez, Jayne. *Celebrations and Solitudes*. LP. Strata East SES 7421, 1975.

———. *Everywhere Drums*. Bola Press BP 9001, 1990.

———. *Unsubmissive Blues*. LP. Bola Press BP 8001, 1980.

Cortez, Jayne, and the Firespitters. *Borders of Disorderly Time*. Bola Press BLP 2003, 2003.

———. *Cheerful & Optimistic*. Bola Press BLP 9401, 1994.

———. *Maintain Control*. Cassette. Bola Press BP 8601, 1986.

———. *Taking the Blues Back Home*. Harmolodic/Verve 531 918-2, 1996.

———. *There It Is*. Cassette. Bola Press, BP 8201, 1982.

Cortez, Jayne, and the Firespitters with Special Guests. *Find Your Own Voice: Poetry and Music 1982–2003*. Bola Press BP20-04, 2006.

Hughes, Langston, with Charles Mingus and Leonard Feather. *Weary Blues*. 1958. Reissue, Verve 841 660-2, 1990.

Texts

Anderson, T. J., III. *Notes to Make the Sound Come Right: Four Innovators of Jazz Poetry*. Fayetteville: University of Arkansas Press, 2004.

Bolden, Tony. *Afro-Blue: Improvisations in African American Poetry and Culture*. Urbana: University of Illinois Press, 2004.

———. "All the Birds Sing Bass: The Revolutionary Blues of Jayne Cortez." *African American Review* 35.1 (2001): 61–71.

Christian, Barbara T. "There It Is: The Poetry of Jayne Cortez." *Callaloo* 26 (Winter 1986): 235–39.

Cortez, Jayne. *Coagulations: New and Selected Poems*. London: Pluto Press, 1984.

———. *Jazz Fan Looks Back*. Brooklyn, NY: Hanging Loose Press, 2002.

———. *Somewhere in Advance of Nowhere*. New York: Serpent's Tail, 1996.

———. "Statement." In liner notes to Jayne Cortez and the Firespitters, *Taking the Blues Back Home*. N.p.

Feinstein, Sascha. "Returning to Go Someplace Else: An Interview with Jayne Cortez." *Brilliant Corners* 3.1 (Winter 1998): 52–71.

Melhem, D. H. *Heroism in the New Black Poetry: Introductions and Interviews*. Lexington: University Press of Kentucky, 1990.

Neilsen, Aldon Lynn. *Black Chant: Languages of African-American Postmodernism*. Cambridge, UK: Cambridge University Press, 1997.

Spellman, A. B. "Not Just Whistling Dixie." In *Black Fire: An Anthology of Afro-American Writing*. Ed. LeRoi Jones and Larry Neal. New York: William Morrow, 1968. 159–68.

Wilmer, Val. "Jayne Cortez and the Unsubmissive Blues." *The Wire* (August 1985): 18–21.

———. "Jayne Cortez: The Unsubmissive Blues." *Coda* (February/March 1990): 16–19.

"Out of This World": Music and Spirit in the Writings of Nathaniel Mackey and Amiri Baraka

David Murray

In a short piece called "Body and Soul," Al Young describes first hearing Coleman Hawkins's classic version of that song. Young sets the piece and his hearing of it in 1939, in the context of World War II and the New York World's Fair, but he then talks about his sense of the music itself as going beyond these points of time and material circumstances. "I knew what a body was, but what was a soul? Was it like a breeze?" Finally he has an image of it as an essence. "Essence in this instance is private song, is you hearing your secret sorrow and joy blown back through Coleman Hawkins, invisibly connected to you and played back through countless bodies, each one an embodiment of the same soul force."[1] We could see this as a sort of Neoplatonic view of music. As the soul transcends the body, so music expresses an ideal or transcendent form through physical sound. Such abstract talk of the material and spiritual may seem rather far from jazz, but attention to these ideas is justified, I think, because the standard hierarchy that ranks the ideal or spiritual as higher than the material, or the earthly, the earthy, has often been seen to be challenged or overturned in African and African American tradition and expression, and music has been seen as a key site for this challenge. In this case, Al Young's vision of the music being played back through countless bodies is important, because it invokes a community and continuity that physically persists. This potential solidarity of many thousands gone, the idea of the material bodies in which black cultural non-material resources have been carried and handed down, suggests something that is both material and non-material, a "changing same" to take LeRoi Jones's term, to be discussed later. It is the relation between the material and the spiritual or ideal with which I am particularly concerned in exploring the way two writers, LeRoi Jones/Amiri Baraka and Nathaniel Mackey have explored African American music as a cultural resource and spiritual touchstone.

The investment in African American music as an expression of spiritual interiority and authenticity not found so readily in literature or art can be observed both in the early white fascination with spirituals and other folk expressions, and most notably developed by Du Bois.[2] The attitude toward blues and jazz, as they developed, was more ambivalent, as can be seen in the writers of the Harlem Renaissance, as well as Du Bois. Associated with the modernity, migration, and commercialization that some saw as diluting the core of African American culture as it had developed in the South, these forms may have been viewed suspiciously, but music as a whole was still seen as more fundamentally related to the continuities and spiritual values of black life by many writers and painters. Houston Baker has described the effort in the period to "capture the sound of a racial soul and convert it into an expressive product equivalent in beauty and force to Afro-American folk songs or ecstatic religious performance."[3]

When the painter Aaron Douglas, for instance, was encouraged by Winold Reiss to think about primitive or atavistic connections, stimulated by the masks and fetishes used by the European modernists, he found himself resorting to sound, when trying to "objectify with paint and brush what I thought to be the visual emanations or expressions that came into view with the sounds produced by the old black song makers of the antebellum days, when they first began to put together snatches and bits from Protestant hymns, along with half remembered tribal chants, lullabies and work songs."[4] This idea of African American music acting as a spiritual link across generations has a strong political and cultural resonance but it has also been criticized for the risk it runs in essentializing and idealizing music and its role. Ronald Radano, for instance, has argued that for the Black Aesthetic critics music was made to act as the signifier of what he calls "a primordial African-based culture." In fact, he says, they were more interested in literature, with the result that music really functioned in their writings and speeches as "a supplement, an exoticized Other that enhanced the sense of mystery and spirit informing the stable grounds of the text." While he accepts that later critics have made this more complex, he is still uneasy with Gates's and Baker's tendency to what he calls "an ahistorical devotion to a 'vernacular' grounding that is reformulated in the postmodern lexicon of elusiveness: signifyin(g), the blues matrix, etc."[5] Whether this is entirely fair to what Baraka or Larry Neal were doing or not, it does open up some of the issues that I want to explore in Mackey and Baraka, namely, what it means to talk of spirit or source and how music is used in this discussion.

David Murray

Both Nathaniel Mackey and LeRoi Jones/Amiri Baraka began as poets with a deep engagement and involvement with the more innovative and experimental aspects of American poetry. Mackey has written on Robert Duncan and Charles Olson as well as on Caribbean and African American poets, and LeRoi Jones, as he then was, as editor of *Yugen*, published many beat and experimental writers. Baraka later rejected many of these concerns, in line with his changing allegiances to black nationalist and Marxist politics, but what both writers continue to share is a concern with poetic innovation and African American music. For Baraka, this has involved him in claims for the immediate social relevance of music, often linked to a political platform, as well as various performances with musicians.[6] Mackey has taken a more detached and cerebral approach, though he, too, has performed his work with jazz musicans,[7] but I want to argue that his use of jazz is perhaps ultimately more probing than Baraka's and offers us a way of looking at some of the most common uses and invocations of music in African American writing. Though their common concern is the idea of a spiritual power that has its roots in African American traditions, Mackey's ideas go beyond Baraka's in significant ways.

Baraka's commitment to African American music, evidenced not only in the path-breaking *Blues People* of 1963 and the later collections, *Black Music* of 1967 and *The Music* of 1987, but also in numerous poems and essays, is clear, and what runs through it is an investment in aspects of African American music as the site of an original and continuing cultural essence or resource—what he has called in an important essay "The Changing Same." Here he reflects a wider investment in orality and aurality, rather than literacy, as a privileged area of African American cultural heritage and continuity. For him it is natural that a people coming from a mainly oral culture, and deprived for years of literacy as a means to join an American mainstream, would see music and oral expression as an important cultural resource, and one that was sustainable right in the heart of white culture, even while it was being overheard and appropriated by whites.

> There was always a border beyond which the Negro could not go, whether musically or socially. . . . [A]t some point, always, he could not participate in the dominant tenor of the white man's culture. It was at this juncture that he had to make use of other resources, whether African, subcultural or hermetic. And it was this boundary, this no man's land, that provided the logic and beauty of his music.[8]

Furthermore, whereas the acquisition of literacy can be seen as a potentially alienating as well as an empowering process, in that its processes of individuation may cause separation from the communal and traditional culture, music has been seen as a dynamic and communally rooted process, and its main elements of performance and improvisation have been seen as crucial to its survival and strength. So, like many other writers, Baraka privileges black music as occupying the heart of black culture in ways that literature has not.

One of Baraka's arguments for putting more trust in music as cultural resource, though, has to do with class as well as race. Literacy could be seen as more the province of the black middle classes than black music, with its associations with urban working class and rural folk (and Baraka tends to be dismissive of the more trained early musicians or those playing music popular with whites, like ragtime). As a result, literature and the visual arts, which were often the province of the bourgeoisie, were more likely to be dislocated from the deeper cultural and spiritual currents of African American life. In his quest to connect up with his community Baraka therefore refers back to music, rather than the legacy of individual writers, who have often not represented what he needs—in fact he is largely dismissive about his literary precursors. While the early *Blues People* provides a large historical narrative, Baraka's changing political views have meant that he has wanted to champion particular musical forms and styles as more expressive of what he sees as the quintessential qualities of African American culture. This has meant a suspicion of many popular and commercial forms, which seemed to espouse forms of extreme individualism. "New Black Music is this: Find the self, then kill it."[9]

One of Baraka's key formulations stresses the idea of process and movement as opposed to fixity. He uses the term *swing* to make his point, seeing the systematization and deadening effect of the big bands as exemplifying the movement from swing as a verb, an activity, to swing as a noun, a thing, or commodity. (This clearly relates to the important role of improvisation, rather than working from a pre-composed score, but this quality is also relevant to the historical process by which black people survived expropriation and domination. For Baraka, what survived was the process, not the object.) Though much of the material culture and social structure of the slaves disappeared in the Middle Passage, what was the realm of the intangible survived. "Music, dance, religion, do not have *artifacts* as their end products, so they were saved."[10] At a more general level this is also the argument that African Americans were led to invest even more in the idea of immaterial power, and in fact the area of the immaterial, the spiritual, as the area of power.

On the one hand, then, there is the idea of music as an expression of its cultural context, something that reflects and expresses the specificity of place and time, of roots and routes. In this way it creates solidarity and tells the tales of the tribe. But on the other hand, it also contains the possibility of going beyond this people and this time. Baraka sees in the New Black Music, and in Albert Ayler and Coltrane in particular, something else, related to the surviving religious traditions, and he calls these musicians "God-seekers." Though this music may have begun by defining itself in social comment, "Once free, it is spiritual. But it is soulful before, after, any time, anyway."[11]

In this way the music is transcendent of the conditions of its production and contains an aspiration toward something more. (This could present a problem for the later Marxist and materialist Baraka, though it could presumably be seen as a form of utopian thinking, which at least keeps in the culture an idea of something beyond what exists.) In a fairly recent recording with Hugh Ragin and David Murray, Baraka recites a poem, "Message from Sun Ra," in which the message is "The world is in transition, your world and your condition."[12] In keeping with Sun Ra's claims, it is supposedly in "Jupiter-language," and I would suggest that this sort of use of Sun Ra demonstrates Baraka's refusal to give up on the idea of an alternative spirit world—and perhaps also on a sense of humor.

These two aspects of music, the rooting in experience and the capacity to aspire to something else, have been identified by Craig Werner in two strands of music, so that "clarifying realities" are represented by the blues and "envisioning possibilities" are represented by gospel.[13] Clearly it is reductive to make such categorical distinctions, the point often being the inextricability of the two aspects, as Graham Lock brings out so clearly in his study *Blutopia*, but the formulation does point to the two functions whereby music operates in relation to the physical world of history and to the spiritual or beyond.[14]

It is important to stress that for Baraka the capacity of art, whether music or writing, to perform this second role is related to its formal capacities and not just its content. As Mackey's sympathetic essay on him brings out very well, Baraka's own work has "an obliquity or angularity"[15] that allows for a complexity, and an oscillation between the certainties of a materialist interpretation of the world and a sense of a penumbra of other possibilities. This is not just a resort on Mackey's part to a New Critical or liberal idea that art should be complex and therefore above and beyond politics, or an implicit justification of his own apparently less politically engaged position, but an awareness that even in his most politically engaged poems, such as "Black Dada Nihilismus," Baraka sees and uses the disruptive power of what does not seem to fit or make sense. Earlier Baraka had suggested, "Perhaps one way Negroes could force institutionalized dishonesty to crumble, and its apologizers to break and run, would be to turn crazy, to bring out a little American Dada, Ornette Coleman style."[16] Mackey picks up a phrase from Baraka's description of a John Tchicai solo ("It slides away from the proposed") and uses it to describe one of the strengths of some of Baraka's writing. "The obliquity, the sliding away from the proposed we find in many of Baraka's poems" (and which Mackey also finds in Monk, Dolphy, and others) reflects a sense of the constraints and determinations of the world but also "a vigilant sense of any reign or regime of truth as susceptible to qualification."[17]

Baraka's Marxism does not entail an absolute determinism, and there is a clear awareness of the ways in which cultural expression and, in particular, African American music is more than its determinants. Mackey quotes with approval some lines from Baraka:

> What is encumbered sings to
> change its meaty box. The dirt
> is full of music.[18]

that reflect Mackey's own concern with the relation of "Body and Soul" and its expression in music and provide a bridge into his work.

Mackey's ongoing series of novels, with the collective title *From a Broken Bottle Traces of Perfume Still Emanate*, has a narrator who plays in jazz ensembles variously known as the Mystic Horn Society, the Deconstructive Woodwind Chorus, the Crossroads Choir, and the Boneyard Brass Octet, and much of the writing is directly about their performances. Mackey's major poetic work, spread across a number of volumes, "The Song of the Andoumboulou," actually refers to an African myth about singers, but the poems draw on a much larger range of music. (He has also written about flamenco and other world musics.)

His novels are made up entirely of letters from the protagonist, who signs himself N., to someone known only as "Angel of Dust" (and in the name we

David Murray

see the typical conjunction in Mackey of spiritual and material, heavenly and earthly).[19] In one letter we get his response to an argument that Angel of Dust has apparently made about the need for a clear belief in an original source (like a religious faith in God or a culturally centered belief like Afrocentrism). Angel of Dust has asked N. to distinguish between what comes from a source and what is about a source—between "'what speaks of speaking of something, and what (more valuably) speaks *from* something, ie where the source is available, becomes a re-source rather than something evasive, elusive, sought after.'" N. responds with a defense of his focus on loss and absence rather than the assertion of presence. "We not only can but should speak of 'loss' or . . . speak of *absence* as unavoidably an inherence in the texture of things." His "pre-occupation with origins and ends is exactly that: a pre- (equally post-, I suppose) occupation." He distinguishes between the supposed solidity of Angel's world and "the world my 'myriad words' uncoil." His world is not "insubstantial, unreal or whatever else. Only an other (possibly Other) sort of solidarity." It is "an unlikely Other whose inconceivable occupancy glimpses of ocean beg access to" and he ends the letter by insisting, "Not 'resource' so much for me as re:Source."[20]

The distinction here is an important if apparently abstruse one. If we assume that there is a point of origin and absolute presence that precedes and transcends the day-to-day world of our material senses—a God—then artists and others may be able to access that spirit or power, and speak, or be spoken through, from the source. On the other hand, if we take a post-structuralist view that questions such claims for presence, then all we can ever do is write *about* it, and in doing so bring into being or sustain a flickering sort of presence created through the processes of difference and deferral inherent in representation itself.[21] What is crucial is that to insist on absence is not to reject all dealings with the idea of presence, as a resource, but to see the two terms in a dynamic relation, with the idea of source and spirit being questioned and historicized rather than taken for granted. Mackey is aware of the importance of being able to claim and connect with a historical and geographical origin in Africa but he approaches with caution the merging or eliding of this with the idea of a cultural and hence a spiritual wholeness. Instead he explores the lack of wholeness. He wants to foreground those black linguistic and musical practices that emphasize process and invention rather than a return to a supposed fixed identity or essence, and he wants "a countertradition of marronage, divergence, flight, fugitive tilt." In his essay "Other: From Noun to Verb" he takes up

Baraka's remarks about swing as noun and verb, referred to earlier, but argues that the "non-recognition of black artistic othering" has been due to the fact that African Americans are treated as a fixed quantity (a noun) defined by race. "Artistic othering has to do with innovation, invention, and change. . . . Social othering has to do with power, exclusion, and privilege, the centralizing of a norm against which otherness is measured, meted out, marginalized. My focus is the practice of the former by people subjected to the latter."[22]

In other words, he wants attention to the formal processes by which black artists have dismantled the limiting labels of identity (and he quotes approvingly Jones's dictum "Find the self, then kill it"), and for him this means focusing on lack rather than a presumed spiritual plenitude.[23] In his second letter to Angel of Dust, N. introduces the idea of a physical lack: "However much I may in the end/beginning turn out to have been courting a 'lack' I intend to keep that tail-biting lizard in mind. Aren't we all, however absurdly, amputees?"[24]

Mackey's poem "Grisgris Dancer" is based on an Afro-Caribbean figure, whose use of what were called fetishes, gris-gris, or charms has been melodramatically and negatively presented as a form of malign superstition by white observers. The practices of the "backwardswalking / twoheaded / woman," do not offer any simple solace or remedy for

>   All the gathered
>   ache of our
>
>   severed selves,
>   all the
>   windowless light.[25]

and the idea of severance here relates to an important idea in Mackey. From the Caribbean writer Wilson Harris he takes the idea of music operating like a "phantom limb" for peoples of the African diaspora. Harris saw music as a rich cultural resource because it was a powerful and resonant reminder of what had been lost in the destruction of cultures and people in slavery and its aftermath, and he described this in figures of loss, amputation, and absence—an idea taken up by later writers. Saidiya Hartman sees the recognition of loss as

> a crucial element in redressing the breach introduced by slavery. This recognition entails a remembering of the pained body, not by way of a simulated

David Murray

wholeness but precisely through the recognition of the amputated body in its amputatedness, in the insistent recognition of the violated body as human flesh, in the cognition of its needs and in the anticipation of liberty. In other words, it is the ravished body that holds out the possibility of restitution, not the invocation of an illusory wholeness or the desired return to an originary plenitude.[26]

For Harris, music is a reminder of what had once been there. It is a reminder of absence that is a feeling of presence—as if the leg is still there. We could say it is an absence felt as a presence, or a feeling of presence that points toward an absence. "The phantom limb reveals the illusory rule of the world it haunts."[27] In other words, the awareness of absence, expressed as a false presence, can be a sort of resource in itself. "The phantom limb is a felt recovery, a felt advance beyond severance and limitation that contends with and questions conventional reality." It is "a feeling for what is not there that reaches beyond as it calls into question what is. . . . The phantom limb haunts or critiques a condition in which feeling, consciousness itself, would seem to have been cut off."[28] This means that music can function to reveal a spiritual dimension that is experienced as something physical, but that points to more than itself. "The world, music reminds us, inhabits while extending beyond what meets the eye, resides in but rises above what is apprehensible to the senses."[29] This is not the same, though, as saying that when we listen to music we enter a separate spiritual realm, or experience a spiritual presence, because what interests Mackey is the way in which its effects are associated with absence and loss.[30] We are all orphans but "in back of 'orphan' one hears echoes of 'orphic,' a music that turns on abandonment, absence, loss. . . . Think of the black spiritual 'Motherless Child.' Music is wounded kinship's last resort."[31] Music, then, can be a phantom reminder of what is not here, but is playing a positive role, in keeping alive in the mind a utopian possibility, and of course black music has also pointed beyond the present and actual in more direct historical ways as a response to slavery and oppression, so this reaching or pointing beyond has both a social and a metaphysical dimension.[32]

It is typical of Mackey to refuse to separate out the social and the theoretical. The musical phenomenon of call-and-response, for instance, is usually seen as an expression of a social relation as well as a musical form, but Mackey has another take on this. As well as the communal context, and the relation between individual and group in communal assent, he wants to look at the ways in which "*assent* can be heard to carry undertones or echoes of *ascent* (*accents* of ascent),"[33] and he also refers to this in an account of a performance in *Bedouin Hornbook* (the first volume of *From a Broken Bottle . . .*), when he describes the flute player fulfilling for a moment the dreams of the oppressed. "An almost clandestine appeal, its claim was that were there no call the response would invent one."[34] This could be taken at the social level, suggesting that revolution comes from below, that the people create and call into being their leader, but it also connects up with the idea of what is seen as the secondary or belated state of mundane life bringing into being what is supposed to precede it, namely what is supposed to have been there from the beginning, the primary or originary. But we may only experience this as phantom, ghost, rather than as pure or unmediated soul or spirit, since the sublime can only be seen as an aesthetic phenomenon, the creation of an effect, rather than the evocation of a spiritual presence.

In his fiction Mackey literalizes these ideas, often to comic effect. He refers to a tenor player whose solo has a "'phantom' reach" and then typically brings this down to earth with humor by suggesting that he perhaps achieved this through smoking a joint soaked in embalming fluid.[35] Equally he plays with the idea of music as transcending itself, when one of the band, Penguin, seems to create a balloon from his horn, which floats above the band. The balloon contains a message, like those in comic strips, and it is borne aloft by circular breathing. It creates a sensation, with audiences not sure what they have actually seen, and the band not sure what is happening, either, but the narrator typically improvises on it, and on the idea of a balloon, in a way that is both highly intellectual and abstract and at the same time led by sound—something that we could trace back to one of his poetic influences, Robert Duncan and his tone leading and punning. In the book Mackey has already performed a set of improvisations and variations on the name of a member of the band, Penguin—a flightless bird, whose wings are just stubs, or nubs—just quills and feathers—that are related to pens and writing. And this is itself related to a recurrent dream of a figure of a woman drummer called Penny.

He then performs a similar flight of improvisation on the word *balloon*, which he sees as B'Loon (as in B'Fox or Brer Fox, as well as the African form of many names) and he relates this to the waterbird, the loon, which is associated with Native American Earthdiver myths, in which the loon dives deep to be able to bring up some mud, which grows to become our world. So we have a conjunction of aerial flight, with its associations of transcendence, with the lowest and most earthly. "Are the balloons mud we resurface with, mud we situate ourselves upon, heuristic precipitate, axiomatic muck, unprepossessing mire?"[36]

David Murray

Mackey's concern, then, is with music's power to link the material and the spiritual, by pointing toward something not physical, transcendent. In some ways this may seem a conventional enough claim for music as transcendent, but Mackey has an important twist in formal terms here. For him the reaching beyond does not happen by abstraction, by achieving a Platonic or pure form that is greater than the actual sound, in other words through transcending the material, the sound, and achieving a purity that is independent of the sounds heard, but by stressing and stretching the sounds themselves. In other words, when you stress the materiality of the sound so that you go to the edge of its signifying system (if, when speaking you exaggerate the sounds of the words, the sibilants for instance), you draw attention to the material sounds, not to the semiotic system, the language by which you are being understood. Similarly, to stretch at the very edge of an instrument's or voice's range, or beyond, is to risk losing meaning (interfering with the semiotic system of music) but also, paradoxically, sometimes to create the sense of pointing toward something else outside or beyond it. It is this that can give the sense of yearning, or aspiring—in other words, the effect of the sublime. For instance, when a voice or an instrument soars and strains, we become aware of the physical medium but we are also directed beyond it. Mackey's narrator talks, for instance, about the role of the falsetto and puns on the idea of the "strangulated tenor." Talking about Al Green, he says, "I've long marveled at how all his going on about love succeeds in alchemizing a legacy of lynchings—as though singing were a rope he comes eternally close to being strangled by." He describes this as a "metavoice," bearing the weight of "a gnostic transformative desire to be done with the world." The "false" voice "creatively hallucinates a 'new world.'" "What is it in the falsetto," he asks, "that thins and threatens to abolish the voice but the wear of so much reaching for heaven?" Not just the falsetto, but the moan and the shout can explore "a redemptive unworded world."[37]

It is the breaking and stretching, what he calls the rasp and creak of sound and forms under pressure, that interests him and he mentions, for instance, Rahsaan Roland Kirk's many voicings and breathings over the flute he is playing. He also develops the idea, related to the idea of the phantom, of a language, or a sound being corrupted, or invaded from outside. In Coltrane he finds sometimes an "unruly agonistic sound in which it seems that the two articulations are wrestling with one another, that they are somehow one another's contagion or contamination."[38] This is not dialogical, or call-and-response in any communal sense, but something that threatens, or promises to pollute or transform the intended sound. He links this elsewhere to possession as this is found in voo-doo, where one is said to be "ridden" by a spirit, or loa, like a horse. In his poem "Ohnedaruth's Day Begun" he describes such a possession of a jazz musician:

> We play "Out of
> This World" instead, the riff hits
> me like rain and like a leak in my
> throat it won't quit. No reins whoa
> this ghost I'm ridden by[39]

In talking about the poem, he says it was written for John Coltrane ("Out of This World" is a number that Coltrane recorded,[40] and of course is a very appropriate title for this theme), and he refers to "a surge, a runaway dilation, a quantum rush you often hear in Trane's music, the sense that he's driven, possessed—*ridden*—as it's put here."[41] The idea of being transported, in all its senses, is taken up and developed in Mackey's poetry. In "Song of the Andoum-boulou" he uses the idea of a train journey to express, traditionally enough, the idea of a movement or quest for something perhaps unattainable. The train is variously located in Spain, then in Brazil, but is often more abstract.

> It was a train we were on,
>   peripatetic tavern we
> were in, mind unremittingly
>   elsewhere, words meaning
>   more
>   than the world they
> pointed at,   asymptotic
>   tangent,   Ahtt it
> was called . . .[42]

The vehicle is less important than its ability to go beyond the limits of earth.

> was a boat we were on, bus we were
> on, sat on a train orbiting abject
>   Earth . . .

As well as suggesting Sun Ra's use of images of space travel, including orbiting monorails and satellites, this also invokes the African American use in sermons

of the gospel train, and the underground railroad referred to obliquely in spirituals:

> Would-be train we'd
>   heard about in sermons, songs,   to ride
>   was to bid exile goodbye. Ride meant to
>   be done with waiting

and he folds this into more jazz-based references:

> Gnostic sleeper stowed
>   away on
>   the boat we rode, runaway sunship, Trane's
>   namesake music's runaway ghost . . .[43]

Mackey, then, is fascinated by the impurities, by the edges of the medium,
where it gets invaded by something else, and where we feel the rasp and creak,
the physical characteristics of the medium itself. This connects up with what
Olly Wilson has identified as the "heterogeneous sound ideal" of African American music. According to Wilson, whereas Western music has aimed increasingly for a blending of sounds, African and African American music has sought
a wide range of contrasting timbres, even within a single line, to create a different
texture, and this can involve the full continuum of vocal sounds ranging from
speech to song.[44] Mackey puts this in a more formal and theoretical context, in
arguing that it is on the edges, where it is most stretched and threatened, that we
are aware of both the absolute materiality of the sound and its capacity to point
toward something more. Mackey refers several times to the striking description
by the Dogon people of the sound made by the shuttle and block in the process
of weaving, as the "creaking of the Word." This is because for them the creation
of cloth and the creation of language are intimately related. Thus the web of
language is not just a figure of speech, or even a metaphor for speech, but an
assertion of the unity of the material and the immaterial, cloth and word, textile
and text.[45]

What attracts Mackey here is not just the idea of the inextricability of material and spiritual but the idea of friction, of strain or incompleteness in this
fusion. "It is the noise upon which the word is based, the discrepant foundation

of all coherence and articulation, of the purchase upon the world fabrication affords. Discrepant engagement, rather than suppressing or seeking to silence that noise, acknowledges it." This "antifoundational acknowledgement of founding noise"[46] is, I think, fundamental to his scrupulously post-structuralist stance, so that Michael Harper's description (in a brief introductory statement to Mackey's *Eroding Witness*) of Mackey making and restoring disparate connections and working toward "the reconstruction of a spiritual wholeness despite the fragmentation of the body" may be going further than Mackey himself would, in its suggestion of a unity to be returned to. Mackey's own poetry employs a number of techniques that decenter a self or single point of control and allow for "the cultivation of another voice, a voice that is other than that proposed by one's intentions, tangential to one's intentions, angular, oblique . . . That sliding away wants out."[47]

The idea of voice is crucial here, in its implication—its invocation—of presence, and he is interested in the ways in which that voice can be influenced and informed by more than the conscious self. Like a number of American poets, he refers to Lorca's use of the *duende*, which he describes as "a kind of gremlin, a gremlinlike, troubling spirit," which can inhabit or haunt the artist.[48] It is heard or overheard in the deepest and most disturbing parts of the work, is beyond mere technique, and is the expression of spirit.[49] But Mackey stresses two aspects, which others often do not. One is the idea of dissonance, what he describes as "trouble in the voice. . . . It has to do with trouble, deep trouble," ultimately unredeemable loss and death.[50] The other important aspect is its racial dimension. Mackey refers to Lorca working with "the black aesthetic of Spain," in an essay in which Mackey invokes the possible Egyptian origins of gypsies. He recalls the advice given to Lorca by a gypsy singer, "What you must search for and find is the black torso of the Pharoah" and "All that has dark sounds has *duende*" (or black sounds, depending on the translation, as Mackey points out).[51]

Mackey's work is a deliberate and often witty challenge to the idea of spirit or source as something outside and separate from the material, to be achieved through leaving or transcending the physical. In other words, he insists on body *and* soul rather than body *or* soul: in doing so, he draws on and contributes to the rich expressions of this in African American music, and he uses post-structuralist approaches to avoid the essentialism and exceptionalism that haunt so many claims for the music.

I have concentrated in this chapter on the distinctive relation between the realms of the material and spiritual in African American music, and used Mackey's provocative deconstructive approach in his poetry and prose to help me. If this has meant sometimes using Baraka as something of a foil to Mackey, this is not to deny the depth of his long-standing engagement with music and its social significance. Indeed, I would argue that the obliquity and "sliding away" that Mackey points to in Baraka's poetry are crucial elements, too often obscured by attention to his more direct and programmatic assertions.

Both writers find in African American music a stance that roots us in the material world, even as it refuses to accept that this world is all there is. While Baraka emphasizes this as a social as well as a spiritual resource, an approach taken up by Houston Baker, among others, Mackey is more concerned to explore the formal implications, but also to show how taking this seriously means collapsing the binaries of material and spiritual—an approach that means questioning the uncritical privileging of spirituality, wherever it is found. He demonstrates how African Americans have created a powerful aesthetic, which combines spiritual power with concrete realities, which finds spirit at the edges of the ordinary and at the heart of the earthly, in the mud of the earth-diving loon and in addressing angels of dust.

To hear Nathaniel Mackey read his poem "Song of the Andoumboulou: 20," with music by Royal Hartigan on reeds and Hafez Modirzadeh on percussion, please go to the *Thriving on a Riff* Web site at http://www.oup.com/us/thriving onariff. Courtesy of Nathaniel Mackey and Spoken Engine Co.

NOTES

1. Al Young, "Body and Soul," in *Moment's Notice: Jazz in Poetry and Prose*, ed. Art Lange and Nathaniel Mackey (Minneapolis: Coffee House Press, 1993), 250–51. See also the use made of Hawkins's recording in Jayne Cortez's poem, "No Simple Explanations," which is dedicated to Larry Neal, in *Jazz Fan Looks Back* (Brooklyn, NY: Hanging Loose Press, 2002), 42.

2. See Jon Cruz, *Culture on the Margins: The Black Spiritual and the Rise of American Cultural Interpretation* (Princeton, NJ: Princeton University Press, 1999); and Ronald Radano, "Denoting Difference: The Writing of the Slave Spirituals," *Critical Inquiry* (Spring 1996): 506–44.

3. Houston A. Baker, *Afro-American Poetics: Revisions of Harlem and the Black Aesthetic* (Madison: University of Wisconsin Press, 1988), 101.

4. Quoted in Richard J. Powell, *The Blues Aesthetic: Black Culture and Modernism* (Washington, DC: Washington Project for the Arts, 1989), 35. In Douglass's original unpublished manuscript, titled "The Harlem Renaissance," he has added and then crossed out, "These later became early outlines of our spirituals, sorrow songs and blues." Unpublished MS, 18 March 1923, Special Collections, Fisk University Library, Nashville, Tennessee.

5. Ronald Radano, "Soul Text and the Blackness of Folk," *Modernism/modernity* 2.1 (1995): 72, 73.

6. For a brief survey of some recent recordings that feature Baraka, see Aldon Nielson, "Real Song," *Shuffle Boil* 2 (Summer 2002): 25–26.

7. See Nathaniel Mackey, *Strick: Song of the Andoumboulou 16–25* (Spoken Engine Co. [no catalog number], 1995), on which Mackey is accompanied by multi-instrumentalists Royal Hartigan and Hafez Modirzadeh.

8. LeRoi Jones, *Blues People* (New York: William Morrow, 1963), 80.

9. Amiri Baraka, *Black Music* (New York: Apollo, 1968), 176. Exactly which music should be espoused in accordance with particular political views was a complicated issue. Did Motown or avant-garde jazz really represent the people and their best interests? For an account, see Brian Ward, *Just My Soul Responding: Rhythm and Blues, Black Consciousness and Race Relations* (Berkeley: University of California Press, 1998).

10. Jones, *Blues People*, 16.

11. Baraka, *Black Music*, 193.

12. Included as a part of Hugh Ragin's "When Sun Ra Gets Blue," on *An Afternoon in Harlem* (Justin Time JUST 127-2, 1999).

13. Craig Hansen Werner, *Playing the Changes: From Afro-Modernism to the Jazz Impulse* (Urbana: University of Illinois Press, 1994), 269.

14. Graham Lock, *Blutopia: Visions of the Future and Revisions of the Past in the Work of Sun Ra, Duke Ellington, and Anthony Braxton* (Durham, NC: Duke University Press, 1999).

15. Nathaniel Mackey, "The Changing Same: Black Music in the Poetry of Amiri Baraka," in *Discrepant Engagement: Dissonance, Cross-Culturality, and Experimental Writing* (Cambridge: Cambridge University Press, 1993), 43.

16. Quoted in ibid., 41.

17. Ibid., 43.

18. Ibid., 46.

19. We also see Mackey's typical practice of threading references to black music throughout his text, either explicitly or as playful allusion. Here "Angel of Dust" calls to mind the Penguins' doo-wop classic "Earth Angel," a response apparently confirmed when we learn that one of N's fellow band members is named Penguin.

20. Nathaniel Mackey, *Eroding Witness* (Urbana: University of Illinois Press, 1985), 50. The first letters actually appeared in his collection of poetry, before the novels themselves developed.

David Murray

21. Mackey does not refer to Derrida, but his work probably offers the most sustained parallel critique to Mackey's.

22. Mackey, *Discrepant Engagement,* 285, 265.

23. Ibid., 275.

24. Mackey, *Eroding Witness,* 54.

25. Ibid, 17.

26. Saidiya Hartman, *Scenes of Subjection: Terror, Slavery and Self-Making in Nineteenth-Century America* (New York: Oxford University Press, 1997), 74. See also Adam Gussow, *Seems Like Murder Here: Southern Violence and the Blues Tradition* (Chicago: University of Chicago Press, 2002).

27. Mackey, *Discrepant Engagement,* 236.

28. Ibid., 235.

29. Ibid., 232.

30. As Devin Johnston puts it: "These figures of ghostliness and absence and incompletion are meant to suggest a spiritual supplement to the world that both invests it with a certain urgency and divests it of any ultimacy." In "Nathaniel Mackey and Lost Time: 'The Phantom Light of All Our Day,'" *Callaloo* 32.2 (2000): 5.

31. Mackey, *Discrepant Engagement,* 232.

32. Lawrence W. Levine, *Black Culture and Black Consciousness: Afro-American Folk Thought from Slavery to Freedom* (New York: Oxford University Press, 1977), 19–55.

33. Nathaniel Mackey, *Bedouin Hornbook* (Los Angeles: Sun and Moon Press, 1997), 25.

34. Ibid., 115–16.

35. Ibid., 118.

36. Nathaniel Mackey, *Atet A.D.* (San Francisco: City Lights, 2001), 121.

37. Mackey, *Bedouin Hornbook,* 62, 63.

38. Nathaniel Mackey, "Cante Moro," in *Sound States: Innovative Poetics and Acoustical Technologies,* ed. Adelaide Morris (Chapel Hill: University of North Carolina Press, 1997), 205.

39. Mackey, *Eroding Witness,* 73.

40. In 1962 on *Coltrane* (Impulse! 12152, 1997) and in 1965 on *Live in Seattle* (Impulse! GRP 21462, 1994).

41. Mackey, "Cante Moro," 203. The reference to a leaking of sound here might recall the hostile criticism of Coltrane, in which one critic, Ira Gitler, said that "his horn actually sounds as if it is in need of repair." Quoted in C. O. Simpkins, *Coltrane: A Biography* (Perth Amboy, NJ: Herndon House, 1975), 157.

42. Nathaniel Mackey, *Whatsaid Serif* (San Francisco: City Lights, 1998), 22–23. Ellipses in original. This poem is also included on Mackey's CD *Strick*.

43. Mackey, *Whatsaid Serif,* 100. Ellipses in original.

44. Olly Wilson, "The Heterogeneous Sound Ideal in African-American Music," in *Signifyin(g), Sanctifyin', and Slam Dunking: A Reader in African American Expressive Culture,* ed. Gena Dagel Caponi (Amherst: University of Massachusetts Press, 1999), 157–71.

45. Marcel Griaule, *Conversations with Ogotemmeli: An Introduction to Dogon Religious Studies* (London: Oxford University Press, 1965), 28, 29, 73.

46. Mackey, *Discrepant Engagement*, 19.

47. Mackey, "Cante Moro," 201.

48. Ibid., 195.

49. It is interesting to note that in one of the most imaginative and articulate of jazz autobiographies, Sidney Bechet describes a similarly unsettling compulsion. "So many of [the musicianers] had something inside them and it wouldn't let them rest. It was like there was something in that song deeper than a man could bear, something he could hear calling from the bottom of his dreams. . . . It was that stirring, all that night sound there was at the bottom of the song all that long way back making itself heard." Sidney Bechet, *Treat It Gentle: An Autobiography* (1960; reprint, New York: Da Capo Press, 1978), 204.

50. Mackey "Cante Moro," 196.

51. Ibid., 195.

WORKS CITED

Recordings

Coltrane, John. *Coltrane*. 1962. Impulse! 12152, 1997.

———. *Live in Seattle*. 1965. Impulse! GRP 21462, 1994.

Mackey, Nathaniel. *Strick: Song of the Andoumboulou 16–25*. Spoken Engine Co. [no catalog number], 1995.

Ragin, Hugh. *An Afternoon in Harlem*. Justin Time JUST 127-2, 1999.

Texts

Baker, Houston. *Afro-American Poetics: Revisions of Harlem and the Black Aesthetic*. Madison: University of Wisconsin Press, 1988.

Bechet, Sidney. *Treat It Gentle: An Autobiography*. 1960. Reprint, New York: Da Capo Press, 1978.

Cortez, Jayne. *Jazz Fan Looks Back*. Brooklyn, NY: Hanging Loose Press, 2002.

Cruz, Jon. *Culture on the Margins: The Black Spiritual and the Rise of American Cultural Interpretation*. Princeton, NJ: Princeton University Press, 1999.

Griaule, Marcel. *Conversations with Ogotemmeli: An Introduction to Dogon Religious Studies*. London: Oxford University Press, 1965.

Gussow, Adam. *Seems Like Murder Here: Southern Violence and the Blues Tradition*. Chicago: University of Chicago Press, 2002.

Hartman, Saidiya. *Scenes of Subjection: Terror, Slavery and Self-Making in Nineteenth-Century America*. New York: Oxford University Press, 1997.

Johnston, Devin. "Nathaniel Mackey and Lost Time: 'The Phantom Light of All Our Day.'" *Callaloo* 32.2 (2000): 563–70.

Jones, LeRoi. *Black Music*. New York: Apollo, 1968.

———. *Blues People*. New York: William Morrow. 1963.

Lange, Art, and Nathaniel Mackey, eds. *Moment's Notice: Jazz in Poetry and Prose*. Minneapolis: Coffee House Press, 1993.

Levine, Lawrence W. *Black Culture and Black Consciousness: Afro-American Folk Thought from Slavery to Freedom*. New York: Oxford University Press, 1977.

Lock, Graham. *Blutopia: Visions of the Future and Revisions of the Past in the Work of Sun Ra, Duke Ellington, and Anthony Braxton*. Durham, NC: Duke University Press, 1999.

Mackey, Nathaniel. *Atet A.D.* San Francisco: City Lights, 2001.

———. *Bedouin Hornbook*. Los Angeles: Sun and Moon Press, 1997.

———. "Cante Moro." In *Sound States: Innovative Poetics and Acoustical Technologies*. Ed. Adalaide Morris. Chapel Hill: University of North Carolina Press, 1997. 194–212.

———. *Discrepant Engagement: Dissonance, Cross-Culturality, and Experimental Writing*. Cambridge: Cambridge University Press, 1993.

———. *Eroding Witness*. Urbana: University of Illinois Press, 1985.

———. *Whatsaid Serif*. San Francisco: City Lights, 1998.

Nielson, Aldon. "Real Song." *Shuffle Boil* 2 (Summer 2002): 25–26.

Powell, Richard J. *The Blues Aesthetic: Black Culture and Modernism*. Washington, DC: Washington Project for the Arts, 1989.

Radano, Ronald. "Denoting Difference: The Writing of the Slave Spirituals." *Critical Inquiry* (Spring 1996): 506–44.

———. "Soul Texts and the Blackness of Folk." *Modernism/modernity* 2.1 (1995): 71–95.

Simpkins, C. O. *Coltrane: A Biography*. Perth Amboy, NJ: Herndon House, 1975.

Ward, Brian. *Just My Soul Responding: Rhythm and Blues, Black Consciousness and Race Relations*. Berkeley: University of California Press, 1998.

Werner, Craig Hansen. *Playing the Changes: From Afro-Modernism to the Jazz Impulse*. Urbana: University of Illinois Press, 1994.

Wilson, Olly. "The Heterogeneous Sound Ideal in African-American Music." In *Signifyin(g), Sanctifyin', and Slam Dunking: A Reader in African American Expressive Culture*. Ed. Gena Dagel Caponi. Amherst: University of Massachusetts Press, 1999. 157–71.

iii

Until the Real Thing: Biography,
Autobiography, and Other Fictions

Blaxploitation Bird: Ross Russell's Pulp Addiction

John Gennari

> *What's hard is to circle about him and not lose your distance, like a good satellite, like a good critic.*
>
> —Julio Cortázar, "The Pursuer"

RECORDING BIRD, WRITING BIRD

In "The Pursuer," a short story by the Argentine writer Julio Cortázar, a Parisian jazz critic named Bruno obsesses over his relationship with the genius musician Johnny Carter, whose unparalleled musical exploits are matched by equally extraordinary acts of personal dissolution. Bruno, the narrator, considers himself Johnny's friend. He has written a well-received biography of Johnny, which has enhanced the saxophonist's reputation with the Parisian intelligentsia. He also has made a habit of intervening to save Johnny from bouts of highly erratic, irresponsible behavior. Forever protesting his own innocence and forbearance, Bruno seemingly earns his cultural capital by cleaning up the mess of Johnny's childish bohemian lifestyle. Yet, as literary critic Doris Sommer has brilliantly argued, the very language of "The Pursuer" reveals Bruno's uneasiness and paralyzing self-doubt. As a matter of established convention, Bruno the intellectual is expected to impose order and stable meaning on the discordant life and work of his artistic subject. But throughout the story Johnny's "disarming lucidity"—his superior intelligence and technical appreciation of his own work—continually stokes Bruno's anxiety about his purpose and identity as a critic.[1]

The details of the story plainly reveal Johnny as a literary stand-in for the legendary bebop alto saxophonist Charlie Parker, to whom Cortázar in fact dedicates the story *in memoriam*. Parker died in 1955 at the age of thirty-four.

He was canonized immediately by a legion of cult worshipers, including Greenwich Village hipsters who festooned New York subways and building walls with the graffiti tag, "Bird Lives!" Many likened Parker to the poet Dylan Thomas, who had died a year earlier under circumstances similarly hospitable to the romantic myth of the tragic artist. Cortázar encourages this affiliation by using as an epigram a line he attributes to Thomas, "Oh make me mask," and then by having Johnny mouth these words at his moment of death. Like Parker himself, whose death certificate fixed the age of his heroin- and alcohol-saturated corpse at fifty-three, Johnny is a man of many masks, a chameleon-like character who constantly eludes the pursuit of critics and coroners alike. The problem with his biography, Johnny tells Bruno, is that "what you forgot to put in is me."[2]

If Cortázar's Bruno is right to say that Johnny's (Bird's) true biography is in his records, then all the more reason to be fascinated by the story of the relationship between Charlie Parker himself and his first real-life biographer, Ross Russell (1909–2000). Driven by a feeling for Parker that he characterized as "an obsessive thing [that] was almost like a disease,"[3] Russell wrote first *The Sound* (1961), a novel whose protagonist is based on Parker, and *Bird Lives!* (1973), a full-length Parker biography. When Martin Williams, one of several confidants privy to the soul-searching that Parker had elicited from his biographer, congratulated Russell on the publication of *Bird Lives!*, he observed: "It's as though *The Sound* had to be got out of the way . . . for you to reach the inner layers of your own being and Parker's."[4]

Russell's literary and critical/historical representations of Charlie Parker bear the traces of a complicated personal relationship dating to the 1940s, when Russell owned Dial Records, one of the small independent labels that first recorded Parker playing with small groups in the new bebop style.[5] Russell, who launched the Dial record company in 1945 as an adjunct to his retail record store in Hollywood, was the producer of seven recording sessions with Parker in 1946 and 1947. Parker also recorded for Savoy Records from 1944 to 1948, and cut sides for Norman Granz's Clef, Mercury, and Verve labels from 1946 to 1954. But, as Edward Komara has suggested, because of their more limited distribution and high quality of technical craftsmanship, Parker's Dial sides—including versions of "Ornithology," "Yardbird Suite," "A Night in Tunisia," "Max Making Wax," "Dexterity," and "Drifting on a Reed"—held special interest for record collectors and musicians.[6]

The significance of Parker's Dial sessions was never, however, simply a matter of commodity exchange: several of them, by virtue of the extraordinary circumstances of their unfolding, immediately became part of Bird mythology, grist for the legend mill that shaped perceptions of Parker in both life and death. Parker's very first recording for Dial, "Moose the Mooche," cut in Los Angeles in March 1946, was a tribute to his local heroin connection, Emry "Moose the Mooche" Byrd, a Central Avenue paraplegic pusher who made his way around jazz clubs in a wheelchair. The Moose mooched the profits from this recording and several others from Parker's first Dial session: Parker, it seems, had signed over his rights to Byrd, an agreement Russell learned of in a letter postmarked from San Quentin Prison.[7]

At his second Dial recording session in July 1946, Parker, malnourished, pumped with alcohol and inferior-quality narcotics, and depressed over recent public attacks on his music, was in the throes of a mental breakdown. In a surreal episode that for Miles Davis and Howard McGhee constituted the very definition of exploitation, Russell insisted on continuing with the session in spite of Parker's obvious distress. The brother of Russell's business partner, a psychiatrist, supplied Parker with an emergency dose of phenobarbital. Russell literally propped Parker up to the recording mike, holding him in place from behind as Parker played. Later that night, Parker snapped: after twice appearing in his hotel lobby in just his socks and then setting fire to his room, Parker wrestled with blackjack-wielding policemen before being cuffed and muscled off to the psychopathic ward of the east L.A. county jail. When McGhee and Russell found him there ten days later, Parker was slated to go to a maximum security prison for the criminally insane. Russell's intercession helped move him instead to the Camarillo State Hospital, where he spent six months before being released into Russell's custody in January 1947.[8]

The wrenching, anguished version of "Lover Man" that came of the July 1946 Dial session has been called Parker's most poetic statement on record, while the tunes Parker recorded in a February 1947 Dial session after his Camarillo release—"Relaxin' at Camarillo," "Cheers," "Stupendous," and "Carvin' the Bird"—have struck many listeners as his most joyous and optimistic. Parker himself was incensed that Russell released "Lover Man," feeling that the record caught him playing beneath his abilities. He also accused Russell of committing him to Camarillo as leverage to force him to renew his breached contract. Russell has said very little about his decision to release "Lover Man." Writer Elliott Grennard witnessed the recording session and claimed that Russell decided to release the record after Grennard's short story, "Sparrow's Last Jump," inspired by the session, was published in *Harper's* in May 1947. In a New York nightclub in December 1954, in a last brush with Parker just months before the saxophonist's death, Russell was warned that Parker was carrying a gun and threatening to shoot him, and that it would be in everyone's best interest if he left the premises.[9]

While some musicians have claimed that Russell was a "money-grubbing record company executive intent on exploiting the musicians under his contract," the jazz historian Ted Gioia has argued that Russell's financial investment in bebop was a "godsend" to L.A. boppers like Teddy Edwards, Wardell Gray, and Dexter Gordon.[10] Gioia contends that it was the absence of Dial—Russell moved the company to New York in 1947 and dissolved it in 1954—or other independent companies recording and marketing the harder bop style which cleared the way for the cool sound more popular with white musicians and audiences to secure West Coast dominance by the mid-1950s. Whatever effect Russell's Dial recordings had in shaping the jazz marketplace, however, it was inevitable that Russell himself would loom as a symbol of the jazz establishment, the white-dominated class of club owners, record company executives, union officials, personnel managers, and booking agents. For black musicians in particular, Russell was easily targeted as The Man—a designation which subjected him to an uneasiness and vulnerability beyond that which Cortázar ascribes to his fictional critic-biographer Bruno. Miles Davis slandered Russell as "a jive motherfucker who I never did get along with because he was nothing but a leech, who didn't never do nothing but suck off Bird like he was a vampire."[11]

Russell's anxiety over this image was no less acute when he turned to the task of representing Parker in words rather than on wax. "Since you are a writer yourself, as well as a musician, and knew Bird," Russell wrote to the composer and performer David Amram in 1969, shortly after Amram had published a memoir and Russell was starting serious work on *Bird Lives!*, "you well appreciate the complexity of the job of trying to do an honest biography of Bird, especially for a person like myself who is white, middle class, and whose relations with Bird were colored by the inevitable entrepreneur-creative artist relationship."[12]

Parker was by all accounts a supremely difficult person—in Ralph Ellison's judgment, "one whose friends had no need for an enemy, and whose enemies had no difficulty in justifying their hate."[13] Davis, bitter over having been constantly harangued for drug fix money and made to watch Parker receive sexual favors, remembered Parker as "a great and genius musician . . . [but] also one of the slimiest and greediest motherfuckers who ever lived in this world."[14] When Russell lamented to Amram "the persistent image my memory holds of Bird as a willful psychopath,"[15] his concern was not the faithfulness of his memory, but whether his recollections would be perceived as tainted by the nature of his relationship with Parker. Russell hoped that by adopting the pose of the dispassionate critic and historian he would distance himself from the stereotype of the parasitic music industry operator and the ingratiating White Negro. Among cold war–era liberal jazz critics, in fact, Russell was known not as a hipster but as an important pioneer of a self-consciously elevated, analytical, and historical style of jazz writing. In 1948 and 1949, in the midst of the scorched-earth debates over bebop, Russell stepped back from the sectarian battle lines and wrote a series of acclaimed articles for *Record Changer* tracing connections between bebop and earlier jazz traditions, focusing particularly on the line of stylistic descent from Lester Young to Parker.[16] Russell's evolutionary framework strongly influenced those critics (Whitney Balliett, Nat Hentoff, Martin Williams, Dan Morgenstern) who later became the theorists and tribunes of a jazz "mainstream."

Between *The Sound* and *Bird Lives!* Russell published the highly regarded *Jazz Style in Kansas City and the Southwest* (1971), which subsequently has become a staple of jazz history courses.[17] Even in his fiction, Russell could show a fine, subtle touch in describing the nuances of jazz performance:

> Hassan's ride cymbal began to vibrate, pumping its shimmering sound across the bandstand. He was playing six notes to the bar, And-One-TWO, And-Three-FOUR, but the notes seemed to run together so that the big cymbal, with light splashing off its gentle coolie-hat curves, had a musical pulse of its own.[18]

The *New Yorker*'s Balliett embraced Russell as a model of the "coolheaded professional critic"; Hentoff and Williams, both of whom credited Russell with helping them overcome an initial distaste for bebop, solicited contributions from him for the *Jazz Review*; Williams urged Russell to join him in writing for the *Evergreen Review* because "they need someone besides me and the beatniks."[19] These ascendant critics (all born in the late 1920s) claimed Russell (born in 1909) as a father figure of the jazz critical fraternity. He was certainly a colorful figure for this role. In the late 1950s, while these thirty-something urbane men were making their way in the world of New York middlebrow cultural journalism, Russell, pushing sixty, embittered from his record company experience, was running a golf course outside of Worcester, Massachusetts, and dabbling in the Canadian stock market. Returning to California in the 1960s, Russell eked out a living writing publicity for a motor speedway, selling pictures and reviews to jazz magazines, and teaching jazz history in adult education programs. His unpublished fiction from the period includes soft-core pornography (one pulp story titled "The Girl Who Liked Muscles" details erotic goings-on between a call girl and a boxer), stories about dope smuggling, motorcycle racing, and dune buggy culture, and a book-length thriller featuring an assassination attempt on a character patterned after Herbert Marcuse.[20] Hearing that one of Russell's late 1960s adjunct teaching gigs was at the University of California at San Diego, Martin Williams wrote him, "Just wait until Ronald Reagan finds out about *you*!"[21]

Despite the esteem for his jazz criticism, in other words, Russell was no New Critical man of letters, and his eccentric interests defied the reigning image of the postwar jazz intellectual as aspiring sophisticate. Unbeknownst to the New York critics, in fact, Russell had cut his writing teeth covering sports for a California local newspaper and penning crime and sex thrillers for pulp magazines from 1936 to 1941. Russell spent years working on an unpublished biography of Raymond Chandler, convinced of his superior understanding of both the poetics of pulp and the Southern California of Chandler's imagination.[22] In the 1970s, discussing the crafting of his novel *The Sound* and his in-progress Parker biography with English professor-turned-popular culture critic Albert Goldman, Russell emphasized his enduring affinity with the *Black Mask* school of pulp writing, which he described as a graphic, visually oriented approach in which the writer's point of view is epitomized in the taut interplay of character, setting, and situation.[23] *The Sound*, originally titled *The Hipsters*, can be read as an updating of the overlapping hard-boiled and film noir genres, shifting focus from the Depression-era gangster and private dick to the late 1940s jazz milieu that Russell knew well. Nevertheless, Russell realized he courted serious controversy by engaging Charlie Parker as a vexing social subject rather than as a bloodless object of musical analysis—and one who fascinates but, in the manner of Cortázar's Johnny Carter, also makes claims on his interpreters.

Writing Charlie Parker into history has proved to be a difficult task. During his lifetime, Parker was given short shrift in the jazz press and either completely neglected or tortuously misrepresented in the mainstream media.[24] The black press was no better: the African American writer John A. Williams has noted that the severest criticism levied against Parker at the time he was committed to Camarillo came from "the pretentious Negro press of Los Angeles."[25] Few newspapers of any kind ran an obituary for Parker, and several that did failed to list his proper name, burying him as "Yardbird Parker." *Life* published a big story on bebop at the height of Parker's career but failed to mention him, concentrating instead on cabalistic subcultural emblems such as Dizzy Gillespie's secret handshake. In his one surviving television appearance, Parker, billed second to trumpeter Gillespie, stares down Earl Wilson, the ingratiating emcee who spouts platitudes about jazz's color- and creed-blindness before asking if the musicians have anything to say before they play. "They say that music speaks louder than words, so we'd rather voice our opinion that way," Parker says through gritted teeth. The fact that Gillespie garnered more mainstream recognition than Parker might suggest that Parker's marginality was more a function of his artistic persona than of his race. Black musicians like Gillespie skilled in the role of the comic entertainer better fit both the racial codes and the leisure desires that prevailed among most white and black Americans in the 1940s and 1950s. The drummer Art Blakey said that Parker held no special meaning for black people because "they never heard of him."[26] Blakey, who often lectured his audiences on jazz's orphan status in its own family, was exaggerating for effect. But it is surely significant that the group which gave Parker his strongest public embrace, the "beatniks," did so as a counter-cultural impulse of rebellion against the hypocrisies and banalities of American society. Ralph Ellison argued that these educated, white middle-class youth seized on Parker as a "thrice alienated" figure—as a black man, a drug addict, and an artist of the avant-garde—in fellowship with their own struggles for creativity and meaning in a culture of mass conformity plagued by the threat of nuclear annihilation.[27]

Ellison's observation that the dominant image of Charlie Parker was as a "white" hero underscores the racial crossover dynamics at work in most Bird mytho-biography. Nat Hentoff suggests in *Jazz Is* that "more than any critic or biographer, it would more likely be a novelist, a black novelist, who might eventually illuminate those parts of the cold inner darkness that finally took over all of Bird."[28] But when Hentoff endorsed the 1988 film *Bird* in a very friendly interview with director Clint Eastwood, he implicitly validated Eastwood's claim to an authenticity based on having grown up in Oakland, California, "around this kind of music" and hence knowing the "black experience . . . as well as any white person around."[29] The sternest critics of *Bird* were unimpressed with Eastwood's feel for black culture. Stanley Crouch panned the film as an exercise in "crude hipster mythology" that removed Parker from the "bittersweet intricacies of African American life." "[Eastwood's *Bird* is] just a colored man with a saxophone, a white girlfriend, and a drug problem," Crouch wrote. "When he dies you are almost relieved."[30]

Crouch's critique of Eastwood's film provides a brief glimpse into the racial politics shaping the memory of Charlie Parker in our own turn-of-the-millennium moment. But the battle over Parker's memory—the Bird legend, if you will—began just as soon as Parker died in 1955. In what follows—a close reading of Ross Russell's pulp novel *The Sound*, buttressed by an analysis of the novel's reception in both the U.S. jazz critic fraternity and in the U.S. mainstream press—I aim to stake out some of the crucial territory in that long battle.

PULP ADDICTION

The Sound, a largely forgotten and neglected jazz novel, was published by E.P. Dutton in 1961. It is not the cloth Dutton first edition, however, but the 1962 Macfadden paperback, with all of its pulp novel trimmings, that most effectively conveys the novel's bid for singular authenticity in the depiction of the jazz life. "Of the few novels that have seen the jazz world from the inside, *The Sound* is unique," screams the promotional pitch on the paperback's back cover. Promising such picaresque features of "the real jazz world" as "the tawdry grime of quick love in a nightclub dressing room" and "the grip, the choking stranglehold of heroin on a trumpeter who is a national hero," the novel leads the reader to expect a "convincing" and "honest" story that "pounds to an absorbing finish."[31]

Writers often distance themselves from the mercenary promotional rhetoric with which publishers adorn their work, but in the case of *The Sound* one is struck by a strong affinity between the tabloidal back cover and the contents of the novel itself. The novel is full of juicy narrative hooks; cheap thrills; countless incidents of "quick love" marked by varying degrees of tawdriness; luridly precise descriptions of narcotics trade and usage; terse and idiomatic popular culture details intensifying the novel's sense of contemporaneity; carefully etched cityscapes suggesting, in the manner of Dashiell Hammett, Raymond Chandler, and Edward Hopper, the inner emotional lives of their inhabitants.

Knowledgeable readers of *The Sound* immediately recognized it as a *roman à clef*, the trumpeter character Red Travers a stand-in for Charlie Parker. Travers is a musical genius of Mozartian heft, the "High Priest of the New Sounds,"[32] a heroic but tragic romantic artist who singlehandedly turns the jazz world on its head, simultaneously becoming increasingly consumed by his own excesses and ultimately destroying himself. To Bernie Rich, the white middle-class, master's-degree-holding pianist who serves as *The Sound*'s third-person narrator, Travers embodies the "Negro core of jazz,"[33] a holy grail of emotional, existential truth. Steeped in the ancient blues, but now a "heedless Pied Piper adrift in the carnival of postwar confusion,"[34] Travers played like "he had a grudge against the world."[35] Despite his misanthropy, however, he's an orgiastic cult hero to a national horde of hipsters, a man of Rabelaisian appetites, consuming food, drugs, and sex in epic, almost mythical proportions. Living only for these appetites and for his music, he is childish, rude, dishonest, and paranoid. He is "fiercely possessive" of his sexual partners, whom he mounts with "empowering virile odor and primitive genital force."[36] Flamboyantly generous one moment, sinister and violent the next, Travers compels from his tribal followers a mixture of hero worship, morbid fascination, and horror.

He's smart—devilishly so. In spontaneous protest of an Italian club owner's rapacity, he improvises a medley of Italian folk songs and opera arias, fracturing their familiar forms with hyper-fast bop tempi and chord progressions. But he's also out of control: he follows this brilliant satire by urinating in the club's telephone booth. His intelligence is that of the street-smart pimp: he has the wiles and cunning to survive the day, but has no vision of the future, much less an understanding of his artistic importance and potential place in history. He treats record sessions and club dates not as cultural work, but as sources of quick cash to feed his habit.

In private correspondence with Russell about *The Sound*, Martin Williams registered skepticism about the Red Travers character, which he simply assumed to be inspired by Russell's relationship with Charlie Parker. Williams had been introduced to bebop in Los Angeles during a World War II stint in the navy, and he was a frequent visitor to Russell's record store. The two men respected each other's critical intelligence, and Russell had solicited Williams's opinion about the novel. In a critique that Russell found penetrating, Williams wondered whether the novel's structuring as a melodrama had led Russell to render moralistic judgments about his character's basic humanity, and in so doing had made it impossible for the reader to grasp Travers's (Parker's) complexity and greatness. By employing the melodramatic form, Williams argued, Russell narrowed the terms by which the Travers/Parker character could be assessed: he could only be either a good man or a bad one. Counting himself lucky never to have met Parker, Williams hinted that Russell's vexed personal relationship with Bird had clouded his efforts. *The Sound* was too much like a detective story, Williams contended, "where the whole point is to find the guilty one and point the finger, and it is always somebody else. In life it is never really somebody else, but everybody."[37] Russell wrote back protesting his own innocence, and defending his choice of the melodramatic literary mode:

> In trying to cast the material of Bird's life and Bird's time, I was struck by its own melodramatic qualities. What else was his life, considered as a series of biographical events . . . than a melodrama? [How] else can you evaluate Lover Man, Camarillo State Hospital, pissing on the floor of a night club, disembarking from a stopped train in the middle of a desert to look for a doctor and a fix, drinking iodine, and winding up on a slab in a morgue?[38]

Albert Goldman was more sanguine about *The Sound*, calling it "a slightly disguised but essentially faithful portrait of . . . the greatest embodiment of the jazz life, Charlie Parker." Esteeming the novel as "a courageous piece of work," Goldman credited Russell with "a love for his subject . . . so great that he can admit all the evil, all the coarseness, all the egotistical violence of Parker and yet make us admire the extraordinary strength and truth of his genius."[39] Leonard Feather, well-known as an early critical supporter of bebop and as an intimate of Parker's, also recognized Bird in Red Travers, but his assessment of the character and of Russell's novel was just the opposite of Goldman's. Despite crediting Russell with having "been more a part of the [jazz] scene than any previous writer" and for a "very well-developed awareness of the struggle between art and business," Feather took umbrage at *The Sound*'s "dreadful cliches and stock characterizations," its "farrago of pseudo-philosophical reflections and wildly exaggerated hip talk," and the "tiresome inevitability of [its] link between jazz and narcotics." Feather's judgment was withering: "Charlie Parker," he wrote, "understood more about Ross Russell than Ross Russell understood about Parker."[40] Feather preferred to remember Bird "when he had the drugs under control and was able to lead the life of the square, driving to Coney Island for hot dogs and beer, charming my [British] father by assuming his best upper class accent and making eloquent small talk."[41]

As Feather notes, *The Sound* revels in the post-war vernacular of jazz musicians and their ardent followers. Russell's Menckenite interest in an authentic

John Gennari

American language directs his ear to the hip argots of sexual desire and racial negotiation. One of his male characters describes another's sexual ineptitude as putting him "on the Jersey side of the snatch play."[42] His ultra-hip white female protagonist declares herself "a queer for spades." She has big eyes for Red Travers even though he's "one stud that just can't tog up"[43]—that is, not a good dresser. A hipster lamenting an instance of southern bigotry says, "Like somebody got to straighten them peckerheads on the corn pone side of the black and white split."[44] The black drummer Hassan, who has hipped himself to "the Mohammedan thing," wearing soft leather slippers, learning a smattering of Arabic, and carrying around English translations of the Koran and Omar Khayyam's *The Rubaiyat* ("The craziest, dad. The original jive! Old Omar really laid down a righteous spiel!"),[45] discovers the advantages this mask holds for dealing with Jim Crow:

> Like, I'd walk up to some big fat-assed cracker policemans and fold my hands inside my sleeves and bow and ask him directions, like where the A-rab consulate was located . . . Yes, daddy, this rig makes it every time below the line.[46]

Leonard Feather's dismissal of *The Sound* singles out Hassan's voice as especially affected—"a heavily caricatured combination of Wingy Manone, Babs Gonzales, and the first edition of Cab Calloway's *Jive Dictionary*." In retrospect, Russell's rhetorical strategies are less interesting for the degree of their authenticity, their fidelity to a "real" jazz world and its argot, than they are as evidence of Russell's self-positioning as a figure of ethnographic and critical white intellectual authority. One cannot help but notice, on this count, the heterosexist and racial anxieties coursing through the novel, nor the way in which exoticized Others are brought on stage to allay these anxieties into some sort of narrative resolution. Raymond Chandler hyped *his* virility, for example, by describing an effeminate male character as speaking softly "in the manner of a sultan suggesting a silk noose for a harem lady whose tricks had gone stale."[47] Russell, for his part, makes the drug peddler of *The Sound* a homosexual with campy orientalist touches: named Fat Girl (and loosely modeled after the bebop trumpeter Fats Navarro), the character has "large, liquid eyes that swam under beautifully modeled lids and lashes," reminiscent of an "eastern idol."[48] When the oversexed black trumpeter invites the libidinally challenged white pianist to "go three in the feathers," the "chick" who is "hip to the play" is a Puerto Rican exotic dancer.

"I mean these Spic women really give you something in the feathers," Red says to Bernie.[49]

In a rhetorical maneuver elevating the tough-minded masculinity of the jazz critic/expert over the soft-boiled femininity of the jazz fan, Russell describes the hipster cabals in jazz clubs as sharing "the same figure-S postures, the same inscrutable faces, bright eyes, and soft-wristed feminine gestures."[50] Such gender coding of jazz authority may partially account for the overwhelmingly positive reception *The Sound* enjoyed among the leading white jazz critics, excepting Feather and Williams. Given late 1950s jazz critics' anxieties over their own intellectual legitimacy and their progressive liberal efforts to propagandize the middle-class "normality" of the jazz musician, these critics might have been expected to condemn the foregrounding of kinky sex and hard drugs in Russell's depiction of the jazz life. Significantly, however, with the exception of Feather's heated pan and Williams's exacting but friendly rebuke, the major jazz critics pronounced Russell's novel not just a success but something of a landmark statement. Nat Hentoff called *The Sound* "the first real jazz novel."[51] Ralph Gleason's review in the *San Francisco Chronicle* said that "Ross Russell has written one of the very few fictional treatments of the jazz world that has validity." In a review in the *Village Voice* that he admitted was hard to write because of his jealousy, Robert Reisner, a fellow Bird chronicler, declared *The Sound* "the finest novel ever written about jazz."[52]

Interestingly, the mainstream press, habitually denounced by the critics for pushing a jazz-junk-sex line, appeared in its reception of *The Sound* to have fully adopted the critics' jazz-as-good-works missionary posture. Deeming the book as "not for libraries," the *Library Journal* charged Russell with harming jazz and "abet[ting] the squares by perpetuating a stereotype of the musician as ignorant, amoral, and dope-destroyed."[53] A *Newsweek* review titled "Jazz and Junkies" absolved Russell on the junk theme ("Beethoven had his red wine and cirrhosis of the liver; the late jazz master Charlie Parker had his drugs") but lamented the "revolting cliches of hipster talk ('Like, solos from another planet, man! Dig!')."[54] Robert Reisner and several other jazz critics, including Dan Morgenstern and Whitney Balliett, defended Russell against these attacks.[55] Clearly, Russell had touched a nerve with the jazz critical fraternity. Reisner suggested a subtext:

No one could have written the book except Mr. Russell and perhaps a few other ofays who found themselves pioneering proselytizers of an unappreciated art created by embittered and exploited Negroes. Some of these white mid-dlemen in the [1940s] were talented men in certain other areas, but because they were so affected by what they heard, they pushed their own personali-ties into the background and touted jazz, carrying the monkey of inferiority on their back in the form of always knowing it was the Negro who created the music. It was . . . a psychic immolation on the cross of jazz.[56]

Reisner, who produced a series of Charlie Parker performances in 1953 and '54 at a downtown New York club called The Open Door, was the Village hipster of the jazz critical establishment, a man who liked to say that he based his life on the holy trinity of sex, jazz, and psychoanalysis.[57] Where Balliett wrote with cosmopolitan sophistication in the *New Yorker*, Hentoff and Williams sought *Partisan Review*–level credibility in the *Jazz Review*, and Morgenstern tried to elevate the discourse of the fan magazines *Down Beat* and *Metronome*, Reisner fit jazz into the alternative cultural format of the *Village Voice* and relished plac-ing freelance pieces in *Playboy* and the more specialized stroke books *Nugget* and *Cavalier*. He was convinced that "art is a form of sublimation and is cre-ated by neurotics and compulsion-ridden people, not by the happy, nine-to-five family man."[58] Reisner's purpose in putting together his 1962 collection of oral testimonies, *Bird: The Legend of Charlie Parker*, was to show Bird as the su-preme icon of hipsterism, an anarchic, amoral spirit, overcivilized to the point of decadence.

While other critics were not of the intellectual temperament to hang themselves in "psychic immolation" on the "cross of jazz," martyrs to the cause of guilt-ridden white privilege, what is notable in their response to *The Sound* is an avoidance of the book's full reckoning with racial politics, an avoidance so conspicuous as to invite speculation of subconscious anxieties. Feather and other critics may have disagreed over Russell's depiction of a Charlie Parker-like character, but they were united in assuming that their main responsibility in passing judgment on *The Sound* was to assess Russell's handling of *this* char-acter. But what is much more interesting about the book, and what the book's narrative strategy in fact highlights, is the drama of the pianist Bernie Rich's anguished struggle with his whiteness: his feelings of sexual and artistic inad-equacy, his castrating sense that for all of his assets—masters workshops with Schoenberg, compositional and arrangement skills that ensure steady employ-ment with a Kenton-like big band, a Greenwich Village apartment with a small Steinway grand and state-of-the-art hi-fi equipment—he nevertheless finds himself taking coital seconds on the shopworn blonde groupie with whom he has bonded in common worship of a black junkie. Son of a doctor, Bernie often finds Red's world "as remote from his own experience as the witch doctor's art lies from the practice of clinical medicine."[59] But when Bernie, chasing some of Red's magic, turns to heroin and needs Red's guidance on shooting up, he's struck by the thought, while watching Red neatly tap a vein, that this ghetto god would have made a good doctor. Whitney Balliett was being optimistic, if not obtuse, when he said that "Russell miraculously makes the white reader see himself with the black man's eyes."[60] For what *The Sound* actually does is make the white reader see himself through the eyes of a white man facing his own benighted vision of blackness.[61]

Bernie learns something about the new jazz: he overcomes some of his Brubeckish earnestness and becomes a solid "feed pianist," a good chord man clearing the runway under Red's virtuosic flights. But what he really learns is that jazz "was still the language of the Negro, the Negro's gift to culture." And it's his conceit—as it was of many white jazz critics—that "the Negro still didn't understand that he had made [this gift]."[62] Hung up on this aesthetic and intellectual asymmetry, Bernie defaults to a position of white safety and power. When he takes a pass on the *ménage à trois* proposed by Red, he backslides into squareness, but also, in the logic of the narrative, saves his life. At the end of the novel, in what Russell describes as a "show of Latin melodramatics," the dancer pulls "the old Spanish streetwalker's trick."[63] Feigning affection, she asks for a goodbye kiss—Red is headed to France, where an incurably Afrophiliac Parisian critic has arranged some concert dates. With catlike swiftness (if not a clear motive) she pulls a knife and slashes him from temple to chin. After Red chases her through the streets of Spanish Harlem, disarms her, and plunges the knife into her stomach, a cop shoots Red, and watches him die. In an epilogue saturated with knowing irony, Bernie is comfortably ensconced as the musical director of a Hollywood studio, laying tracks for a B-movie about an up-from-the-ghetto jazz musician. "Originally the kid had been colored," Russell writes, "but it hadn't taken them long to make him white."[64] It's a pulp fiction ending, but one with a twist. The cop, significantly, is a black man, one of the first on the Harlem force, hired with precisely this sort of incident in mind. Who, after all, could "raise the ugly cry of race prejudice," the narrator cynically suggests, in a case of one black killing another?[65]

And who's to blame, really, when a musician doesn't understand—as Travers in an earlier scene apparently doesn't, and as Russell badly needed to believe

Charlie Parker didn't—that when it comes to making music, "the cream of the thing isn't the cash in hand—it's the [royalty] revenue over the years . . ."?[66] It is difficult not to conclude that the subtext of Russell's novel is an implicit but unmistakable plea for absolution from the charge of racial exploitation in his own dealings with Parker. The political economy Russell sets up in *The Sound* accurately reflects the racial colonialism of the actual post-war jazz world: Red Travers and the other black musicians control the expression of the "Negro core of jazz" while performing on the bandstand, but every other aspect of the *sound*'s fate as creative property—its codification and commodification as notated and recorded *music*—is controlled by whites.

Despite his trenchant critique of Hollywood's deracination of black jazz, Russell is complacent about this racial division of labor in the jazz community itself; indeed, he naturalizes and romanticizes this division, suggesting that to have things otherwise would be to undermine the roles that blacks and whites have chosen for themselves. Hence, as a matter of principle, he has Red Travers eschewing the act of writing down his music. "If you got the music inside, why, you don't need no notes set down on papers, by somebody else, you got your own, and they're better," he says.[67] When Bernie "inadvertently" steals one of Red's unwritten compositions—inadvertent because it is only in hindsight that he realizes how thoroughly Red's musical ideas have colonized his mind—he voluntarily gives Red the composer's credit and suggests that the two form a writing partnership. "You have a fortune kicking around in your head but it isn't worth a dime until somebody helps you mine it," Bernie tells Red.[68] But when Red's erratic work habits undermine the partnership, Bernie concludes that it was futile to challenge the natural order of things. A paragon of white paternalism, Bernie is sure he knows what's best for his black friends: he's concerned about Red's well-being, but in the manner of one whose job it is to be concerned.

Bruno, the character in Julio Cortázar's story "The Pursuer," says that the truth about Charlie Parker is in his records. But even if that's so, we would still want to pursue the stories of the people who made those records. The story of Ross Russell—first as Parker's record producer, then as his mythologizer— is an especially important one, not least because of the far-ranging influence of the stories he told about Charlie Parker. Many of the same white jazz critics who embraced *The Sound* as a trenchantly illuminating portrait of the 1940s jazz world also esteemed Russell's Parker biography *Bird Lives!*

as an authoritative insider's account. It fell to black reviewers outside the jazz critical fraternity—notably Hollie West and Ishmael Reed—to call out some of the absurdities of Russell's portrayal of Parker as a proto-blaxploitation hero, a revision of the pulp hipster anti-hero of Parker's double in *The Sound*.[69]

Grappling with the mystery, complexity, and roiling messiness of Charlie Parker has been a preoccupation and signature gesture for two of this generation's most influential jazz critics—Stanley Crouch, who remains devotedly at work on the Parker biography he began to research in 1982; and Gary Giddins, who in 1987 published the book *Celebrating Bird: The Triumph of Charlie Parker* and directed a film documentary of the same name. Giddins aims to rescue Parker from Russell's pulp-blaxploitation sensationalism by figuring him as a kind of American artist-hero. "His life," Giddins writes, "is what his music overcame. And overcomes."[70] Just the right romantic note on which to canonize Bird as America's rebel outlaw-cum-artistic genius, ready-made for Ken Burns's Mount Rushmore, flying high above Ross Russell's obsessions and guilt.

NOTES

This chapter is an edited extract from John Gennari's book *Blowin' Hot and Cool: Jazz and Its Critics* (University of Chicago Press, 2006) and is reprinted by permission. © 2006 by the University of Chicago. All rights reserved. An early draft of this material was published in the magazine *Brilliant Corners* in 1997.

1. Julio Cortázar, "The Pursuer," in *Blow-Up and Other Stories*, trans. Paul Blackburn (New York: Pantheon, 1967), 182–247; Doris Sommer, "Grammar Trouble for Cortázar," in *Proceed with Caution, When Engaged with Minority Writing in the Americas* (Cambridge, MA: Harvard University Press, 1999), 211–33.
2. Cortázar, "Pursuer," 238.
3. Russell, quoted in a story by Robert Lawrence in the *San Diego Union* sometime after the 1973 publication of *Bird Lives!* The date and page number are obscured on the copy of the article I read in Box 5, Ross Russell Collection at the Harry Ransom Humanities Research Center, University of Texas at Austin. I wish to thank the Harry Ransom Center for the use of this collection, which is hereafter cited as RRC/HRHRC.
4. Martin Williams, letter to Ross Russell, 3 March 1973. Box 1B-35, RRC/HRHRC. Despite his admiration for Russell's grasp of Parker's character,

Williams, not uncharacteristically, also had a litany of complaints about Russell's "carelessness" in matters of discographical detail.

5. After serving in the merchant marine in World War II and a brief stint at Lockheed Aircraft, Russell opened a record store in Hollywood. Initially stocking the early jazz and swing music he had grown up on, Russell's Tempo Music Store was the West Coast analogue to Milt Gabler's Commodore shop in New York. Later diversifying beyond its traditionalist clientele, Tempo became the place where young musicians like Joe Albany, Dodo Marmarosa, Stan Getz, Zoot Sims, and Dean Benedetti came to listen to new bebop releases. In emulation of Gabler's Commodore label, Russell started Dial Records in 1945 as an adjunct to his retail operation. But as bebop became more popular and Russell began to squeeze marginally higher profits out of record production—Russell's financial returns, company records show, were never very substantial—the Dial label took precedence over the Tempo retail operation. Russell relocated Dial to New York in 1947, shifting its focus to contemporary classical music, before moderate sales and high stress led him to close down the label in 1954. Ross Russell, "Symposium Keynote Address," in *The Bebop Revolution in Words and Music*, ed. Dave Oliphant and Thomas Zigal (Austin: University of Texas Press, 1994), 19–20; Richard Lawn, "From Bird to Schoenberg," in *Perspectives on Music: Essays on the Collection at the Humanities Research Center*, ed. Dave Oliphant and Thomas Zigal (Austin: University of Texas Press, 1985), 137–47; Edward Komara, "The Dial Recordings of Charlie Parker," in *The Bebop Revolution*, 79–103.

6. Komara, "Dial Recordings," 80. Parker's Dial recordings have been collected on *Charlie Parker on Dial: The Complete Sessions* (Spotlite SPJ-CD4-101, 1993).

7. Ross Russell, *Bird Lives! The High Life and Hard Times of Charlie (Yardbird) Parker* (New York: Charterhouse, 1973), 214, 216.

8. For overall accounts of the "Lover Man" session and its aftermath, see Gary Giddins, *Celebrating Bird: The Triumph of Charlie Parker* (New York: Beech Tree, 1987), 94; Russell, *Bird Lives!*, 228–41; and Ted Gioia, *West Coast Jazz: Modern Jazz in California, 1945–1960* (New York: Oxford University Press, 1992), 24–27. Miles Davis's remarks are in Davis (with Quincy Troupe), *Miles: The Autobiography* (New York: Simon & Schuster, 1989), 93. Howard McGhee's account came in an interview with Scott DeVeaux: see DeVeaux, "Conversation with Howard McGhee: Jazz in the Forties," *Black Perspective in Music* 15.1 (Spring 1987): 75.

9. For assessments of "Lover Man," see Giddins, *Celebrating Bird*, 94; and Gioia, *West Coast Jazz*, 24. For Russell's account of the Camarillo affair, see his testimony in *Bird: The Legend of Charlie Parker*, ed. Robert Reisner (1962; reprint, New York: Da Capo, 1977), 200–201. Grennard's claim is made in Reisner, *Bird*, 98. Parker's nightclub threat is reported by Leonard Feather, "Book Shows Life and Hard Times of 'Yardbird' Parker," *Huntsville* (Ala.) *Times* [syndicated from *Los Angeles Times* news service], 11 March 1973, 28.

10. Gioia, *West Coast Jazz*, 22.

11. Davis, *Miles*, 89.

12. Ross Russell, letter to David Amram, 18 October 1969. Box 1, folder 10, RRC/HRHRC.

13. Ralph Ellison, "On Bird, Bird-Watching, and Jazz," in *Shadow and Act* (New York: Random House, 1964), 229.

14. Davis, *Miles*, 65.

15. Russell, letter to Amram.

16. Russell's essays were anthologized under the heading "Bebop" by editor Martin Williams in his *The Art of Jazz: Essays on the Nature and Development of Jazz* (New York: Oxford University Press, 1959).

17. Ross Russell, *Jazz Style in Kansas City and the Southwest* (Berkeley: University of California Press, 1971).

18. Ross Russell, *The Sound* (1961; reprint, New York: Macfadden Books, 1962), 34.

19. Whitney Balliett, "The Demon, the Tenderfoot, and the Monolith," *New Yorker*, 8 July 1961: 68; Martin Williams, letter to Ross Russell, 20 February 1961. Box 1B-35, RRC/HRHRC.

20. Box 9 ("unpublished fiction"), RRC/HRHRC.

21. Martin Williams, letter to Ross Russell, 12 January 1967. Box 1B-35, RRC/HRHRC.

22. Research notes and miscellany related to Raymond Chandler biography. Boxes 10, 11, and 12, RRC/HRHRC.

23. Ross Russell, letters to Albert Goldman, 22 January 1970 and 29 August 1977. Box 1A-8, RRC/HRHRC.

24. For discussion of Parker's treatment by the mainstream media see Giddins, *Celebrating Bird*, 9–20; and Jon Panish, *The Color of Jazz: Race and Representation in Postwar American Culture* (Jackson: University Press of Mississippi, 1997), 44–45.

25. John A. Williams, *Flashbacks: A Twenty-Year Diary of Article Writing* (Garden City, NY: Anchor Press/Doubleday, 1973), 228.

26. Ellison, "On Bird," 228. Ellison's essay was a review, originally published in *Saturday Review* in 1962, of the Robert Reisner-edited collection *Bird: The Legend of Charlie Parker*, in which the Art Blakey quote appeared.

27. Ellison, "On Bird," 228.

28. Nat Hentoff, *Jazz Is* (New York: Random House, 1976), 194.

29. Nat Hentoff, "Flight of Fancy," *American Film* (September 1988): 25–31.

30. Stanley Crouch, "Bird Land," *New Republic*, 27 February 1989, 25–31.

31. Russell, *Sound*.

32. Ibid., 22.

33. Ibid., 101.

34. Ibid., 55.

35. Ibid., 21.

36. Ibid., 30.

37. Martin Williams, letter to Ross Russell, 16 February 1961. Box 1B-35, RRC/HRHRC.

38. Ross Russell, letter to Martin Williams, 24 March 1961. Box 1B-35, RRC/HRHRC.

39. Albert Goldman, "The Art of the Bebopper," *New Leader*, 2 October 1961, 32.

40. Leonard Feather, "Book Review [The Sound]," *Down Beat*, 8 June 1961, 44.

41. Feather, "Book Shows Life and Hard Times of 'Yardbird' Parker," 28.

42. Russell, *Sound*, 77.

43. Ibid., 120.

44. Ibid., 79.

45. Ibid., 50.

46. Ibid., 49.

47. Philip Durham, "The 'Black Mask' School," in *Tough Guy Writers of the Thirties*, ed. David Madden (Carbondale: Southern Illinois University Press, 1968), 78.

48. Russell, *Sound*, 74.

49. Ibid., 128.

50. Ibid., 10–11.

51. Nat Hentoff, letter to Ross Russell, 19 February 1961. Box 1B-17, RRC/HRHRC.

52. Robert Reisner, "The Sound," *Village Voice*, 8 June 1961, 11.

53. Colin Clark, "The Sound," *Library Journal* (July 1961): 2494.

54. "Jazz and Junkies," [unsigned], *Newsweek*, 5 June 1961, 47.

55. Dan Morgenstern, "Books [The Sound]," *Metronome*, September 1961, 36–37; Balliett, "Demon, the Tenderfoot, and the Monolith," 68–69.

56. Reisner, "Sound," 11.

57. Reisner, *Bird*, 26; see also Gary Giddins, "The Death of a Hipster: Bob Reisner, 1921–74," *Village Voice*, 28 February 1974, 42–43, 47.

58. Reisner, *Bird*, 19.

59. Russell, *Sound*, 36.

60. Balliett, "Demon, the Tenderfoot, and the Monolith," 68.

61. Jon Panish, in an insightful reading of *The Sound*, suggests that "Russell's construction of African American experience in the novel is hollow and primitivistic because it refers not to anything specific to African Americans in American history—for example, racism or their musical tradition—but to the universal experience of the misunderstood and suffering artist and to the existing stereotypes about African American musicians." Panish, *Color of Jazz*, 63.

62. Russell, *Sound*, 101.

63. Ibid., 181–82.

64. Ibid., 186.

65. Ibid., 184.

66. Ibid., 126–27.

67. Ibid., 131.

68. Ibid., 126.

69. Hollie West, "The Bird: His Music and His Lifestyle," *Washington Post*, 1 April 1973, 1, 6; Ishmael Reed, "Bird Lives!" *New York Times Book Review*, 25 March 1973, 3–4. I examine Russell's *Bird Lives!* and the book's critical reception in "Race-ing the Bird: Ross Russell's Obsessive Pursuit of Charlie Parker," chapter 7 of my book *Blowin' Hot and Cool: Jazz and Its Critics* (Chicago: University of Chicago Press, 2006), 299–338.

70. Giddins, *Celebrating Bird*, 120.

WORKS CITED

The Ross Russell Collection at the Harry Ransom Humanities Research Center, University of Texas at Austin, is cited below as RRC/HRHRC.

Recordings

Parker, Charlie. *Charlie Parker on Dial: The Complete Sessions*. Spotlite SPJ-CD4–101. 1993.

Texts

Balliett, Whitney. "The Demon, the Tenderfoot, and the Monolith." *The New Yorker,* 8 July 1961, 68–69.

Clark, Colin. "The Sound." *Library Journal* (July 1961): 2494.

Cortázar, Julio. "The Pursuer." In *Blow-Up and Other Stories*. Trans. Paul Blackburn. New York: Pantheon, 1967. 182–247.

Crouch, Stanley. "Bird Land." *New Republic*, 27 February 1989, 25–31.

Davis, Miles [with Quincy Troupe]. *Miles: The Autobiography*. New York: Simon & Schuster, 1989.

DeVeaux, Scott. "Conversation with Howard McGhee: Jazz in the Forties." *Black Perspective in Music* 15.1 (Spring 1987): 64–78.

Durham, Philip. "The 'Black Mask' School." In *Tough Guy Writers of the Thirties*. Ed. David Madden. Carbondale: Southern Illinois University Press, 1968. 51–79.

Ellison, Ralph. "On Bird, Bird-Watching, and Jazz." In *Shadow and Act*. New York: Random House, 1964. 221–32.

Feather, Leonard. "Book Review [The Sound]." *Down Beat*, 8 June 1961, 44.

———. "Book Shows Life and Hard Times of 'Yardbird' Parker." *Huntsville* (Ala.) *Times* [syndicated from *Los Angeles Times* news service], 11 March 1973, 28.

Gennari, John. *Blowin' Hot and Cool: Jazz and Its Critics.* Chicago: University of Chicago Press, 2006.

Giddins, Gary. *Celebrating Bird: The Triumph of Charlie Parker*. New York: Beech Tree, 1987.

———. "The Death of a Hipster: Bob Reisner, 1921–74." *Village Voice,* 28 February 1974, 42–43, 47.

Gioia, Ted. *West Coast Jazz: Modern Jazz in California, 1945–1960*. New York: Oxford University Press, 1992.

Goldman, Albert. "The Art of the Bebopper." *New Leader*, 2 October 1961, 32.

Hentoff, Nat. "Flight of Fancy." *American Film*, September 1988, 25–31.

———. *Jazz Is*. New York: Random House, 1976.

———. Letter to Ross Russell, 19 February 1961 [Box 1B-17, RRC/HRHRC].

"Jazz and Junkies." [unsigned] *Newsweek*, 5 June 1961, 47.

Komara, Edward. "The Dial Recordings of Charlie Parker." In *The Bebop Revolution in Words and Music*. Ed. Dave Oliphant and Thomas Zigal. Austin: University of Texas Press, 1994. 79–103.

Lawn, Richard. "From Bird to Schoenberg." In *Perspectives on Music: Essays on the Collections at the Humanities Research Center*. Ed. Dave Oliphant and Thomas Zigal. Austin: University of Texas Press, 1985. 137–47.

Morgenstern, Dan. "Books [The Sound]." *Metronome*, September 1961, 36–37.

Panish, Jon. *The Color of Jazz: Race and Representation in Postwar American Culture.* Jackson: University Press of Mississippi, 1997.

Reed, Ishmael. "Bird Lives!" *New York Times Book Review*, 25 March 1973, 3–4.

Reisner, Robert. "The Sound." *Village Voice*, 8 June 1961, 11.

———, ed. *Bird: The Legend of Charlie Parker.* 1962. Reprint, New York: Da Capo, 1977.

Russell, Ross. "Bebop." In *The Art of Jazz: Essays on the Nature and Development of Jazz.* Ed. Martin Williams. New York: Oxford University Press, 1959. 187–214.

———. *Bird Lives! The High Life and Hard Times of Charlie (Yardbird) Parker.* New York: Charterhouse, 1973.

———. *Jazz Style in Kansas City and the Southwest.* Berkeley: University of California Press, 1971.

———. Letter to David Amram, 18 October 1969 [Box 1, folder 10, RRC/HRHRC].

———. Letter to Albert Goldman, 22 January 1970 [Box 1A-8, RRC/HRHRC].

———. Letter to Albert Goldman, 29 August 1977 [Box 1A-8, RRC/HRHRC].

———. Letter to Martin Williams, 24 March 1961 [Box 1B-35, RRC/HRHRC].

———. Research notes and miscellany related to Raymond Chandler biography, Boxes 10, 11, and 12, RRC/HRHRC.

———. *The Sound.* 1961. Reprint, New York: Macfadden, 1962.

———. "Symposium Keynote Address." In *The Bebop Revolution in Words and Music.* Ed. Dave Oliphant and Thomas Zigal. Austin: University of Texas Press, 1994. 19–20.

Sommer, Doris. "Grammar Trouble for Cortázar." In *Proceed with Caution, When Engaged with Minority Writing in the Americas.* Cambridge, MA: Harvard University Press, 1999. 211–33.

West, Hollie. "The Bird: His Music and His Lifestyle." *Washington Post*, 1 April 1973, 1, 6.

Williams, John A. *Flashbacks: A Twenty Year Diary of Article Writing.* Garden City, NY: Anchor Press/Doubleday, 1973.

Williams, Martin. Letter to Ross Russell, 16 February 1961 [Box 1B-35, RRC/HRHRC].

———. Letter to Ross Russell, 20 February 1961 [Box 1B-35, RRC/HRHRC].

———. Letter to Ross Russell, 12 January 1967 [Box 1B-35, RRC/HRHRC].

———. Letter to Ross Russell, 3 March 1973 [Box 1B-35, RRC/HRHRC].

NINE

How Many Miles? Alternate Takes on the Jazz Life

Krin Gabbard

It should come as no surprise that almost all jazz autobiographies are heavily edited, ghostwritten, or both. If nothing else, consider the enormous differences between the life experiences of jazz artists—especially African American jazz artists—and the lives of the whites and Europeans who established the genre of autobiography long before jazz artists arrived on the scene. Miles Davis's autobiography is not entirely typical of African American jazz self-narrative, if only because Davis and his co-author Quincy Troupe received a substantial advance from Simon & Schuster when they signed a contract for a book everyone suspected would become a best seller. With very few exceptions, other black jazz artists who have tried to tell their stories between the covers of a book have not been so richly rewarded. *Miles: The Autobiography* does resemble the others, however, in being radically rewritten at several stages as it moved from the subject's actual words to the published draft. In spite of these changes, a portrait of Miles Davis emerges that is fairly consistent from page to page. Even though Davis sought to separate himself from this portrait, it may actually have been the image he wished to project toward the end of his life.

Many jazz artists, of course, possess substantial verbal skills. The 1981 documentary film *Imagine the Sound* places several jazz musicians in front of the camera, including Archie Shepp, Paul Bley, and Bill Dixon. They are all remarkably articulate and quick witted. Eric Porter has exhaustively refuted the stereotype of the mumbling, inarticulate black jazz artist in *What Is This Thing Called Jazz?*, an intellectual history of jazz based entirely on utterances by the musicians themselves.[1] Think also of the witty, often learned lyrics that Jon Hendricks set to improvised jazz solos, many of them so convoluted as to seem beyond the reach of versification.

Among autobiographies by black jazz artists, *Boy Meets Horn* holds up as an immensely readable and entertaining work by cornetist and composer Rex

Stewart.[2] A mainstay of bands led by Fletcher Henderson and Duke Ellington during the first half of the twentieth century and the owner of an immediately recognizable style as a soloist, Stewart wrote regularly for jazz periodicals before publishing *Boy Meets Horn*. He surely did not hand his editors a manuscript in need of drastic rewriting.

Nevertheless, jazz scholars lack a larger study of the many instances of co-authorship involving important jazz autobiographies. We are fortunate to have some fascinating auto-narratives by jazz musicians, but we have no overarching account of the extent to which we are actually hearing the musicians' voices as well as why these voices are so elusive. Some claim that Billie Holiday never even read *Lady Sings the Blues*, the book that William Dufty cobbled together from a few conversations with the singer, her newspaper interviews, and his own fantasies.[3] Albert Murray has been candid about exhaustively researching the career of Count Basie before interviewing Basie for a few piquant comments and then sitting down to write *Good Morning Blues: The Autobiography of Count Basie*.[4] Similarly, novelist Don Asher was sufficiently intrigued by the music of Hampton Hawes to interview him extensively, listening carefully for the cadence of the pianist's speech. The result is *Raise Up Off Me*, a compelling, often startling account of Hawes's life as a jazz musician and heroin addict, told in the first person but basically written by Asher.[5]

Charles Mingus, by contrast, spent several years producing an autobiographical manuscript of almost 1,000 pages, at times calling it *Half Yaller Schitt-Colored Nigger*. Mingus hired and fired several editors who thought they could turn the pages into a publishable book, and the autobiography was rejected by several publishers before it was eventually published as *Beneath the Underdog* in 1971.[6] Mingus had the good fortune to encounter Nel King, a New York–based editor and screenwriter who had seen Mingus perform in clubs.[7] A great fan of his music, King convinced Mingus that she could prepare and then sell his book. She reduced the manuscript by more than half, contributing numerous descriptive passages to flesh out the narrative. Mingus's early drafts were mostly series of conversations, usually about sex. Although King pared down the book's focus on sexuality, a comparison of *Beneath the Underdog* to Mingus's typescript (now at the Library of Congress) reveals that Nel King actually expanded those sections of the book in which Mingus boasts about his career as a pimp. As David Yaffe has observed, King was not the only editor who decided that readers expect stories from red-light districts when they read about jazz artists. Mingus, by the way, distanced himself from the book, asserting that he only wrote it for the money and that he considered it deeply compromised.[8]

Writing in the afterword to the updated edition of *Straight Life*, Laurie LaPan Miller Pepper speaks of her initial delight at the stories she heard when she first met the alto saxophonist Art Pepper. As the two drew closer, eventually marrying in 1974, Laurie noticed that the stories took on new, often contradictory details as Pepper retold them. When she decided to write her husband's autobiography, she asked to hear his stories again and again, regularly stopping him for clarification and insisting that he avoid exaggeration and embellishment.[9] The result is a fascinating, often harrowing account of a self-destructive musical genius. As the book makes clear, however, Art Pepper himself had little of the self-discipline necessary for the actual writing of a book as heartfelt and as carefully constructed as *Straight Life*.

Sidney Bechet may have been a superb raconteur with the imagination of a great fabulist, but it is likely that others were responsible for some of the poetry and narrative flow that distinguishes his autobiography, *Treat It Gentle*.[10] Poet and essayist John Ciardi worked with Bechet in the early stages of the book and may even have been responsible for creating the story of Bechet's grandfather Omar that is the most memorable part of the book. Never mind that both of Bechet's grandfathers were Creoles and that, unlike the Omar of *Treat It Gentle*, neither was ever a slave. Nevertheless, Twayne, the press that had commissioned the book, shelved the project before Ciardi and Bechet had finished. When the distinguished English author Desmond Flower heard of an unpublished autobiography of Bechet, he contacted the musician and began the work of completing the book. There are a handful of tapes at the Hogan Archive in New Orleans that provide some information about the final stages of the collaboration between Bechet and Flower. Unfortunately, there is little else on which to base a compelling account of how the book was co-written. The crucial tape in the Hogan includes a conversation in which Flower is quizzing Bechet about what he had previously said, essentially editing his text. The tapes also suggest that Bechet had a habit of rambling and losing the thread of his story. Gabriel Solis, who has exhaustively investigated the writing of *Treat It Gentle*, has said that some of what Bechet spoke into the tape recorder had to be omitted, often because it was simply not true.[11] Although hardly a congenital liar, Bechet was willing to manufacture details if he thought it made a better story.[12] Solis believes that much of what is in the book is verbatim Bechet but that many passages were added to give continuity to the narrative. At different moments in the process,

Ciardi and Flower were probably responsible for phrasing the added material to make it read like Bechet's voice.[13]

As for the two giants of jazz who dominated twentieth-century American music, both Duke Ellington and Louis Armstrong had their own distinctive ways with words. We know that letters flowed profusely from the portable typewriter that was almost always with Louis Armstrong during his many years on the road. Only a small selection of these letters, some of them running to several pages and many addressed to people whom Armstrong only knew as correspondents, have been published.[14] By contrast, Armstrong's first autobiography, *Swing That Music* (1936), was extensively edited and rewritten. When Armstrong sat down to write his second autobiography, *Satchmo: My Life in New Orleans* (1954), he may have been gun-shy about telling all, recalling how his words had been taken away from him the last time. The result was a book that pleased his editors, who cleaned up his spelling and punctuation but made few substantive changes.[15] William Kenney, however, has argued that Armstrong found subtle ways of expressing himself in spite of the pressure he felt to make his prose more acceptable to mainstream (i.e., white) readers. For example, in *Satchmo* he speaks adoringly of Bix Beiderbecke, even calling him godlike. At one point we read: "Whenever we saw him our faces shone with joy and happiness, but long periods would pass when we did not see him at all."[16] Kenney suggests that Armstrong—who may have regarded Beiderbecke and the members of his cult with something less than reverence—managed to construct an account that did not rouse his editors to take up the red pencil at the same time that it contained a telling trace of ambiguity.[17] If left to his own devices, Armstrong was clearly capable of writing his own story with wit and clarity. This was definitely the case when he produced a long, handwritten document in a hospital bed the year before he died.[18] But if Kenney is right, anyone who delves into *Swing That Music* and *Satchmo: My Life in New Orleans* must read between and around the lines to know what the author intended to say.

The creation of Duke Ellington's autobiography is a different story altogether. Constantly on the road and constantly composing music, Ellington had little time to read, let alone to write. His debonair stage persona and his *faux* English accent were part of a carefully constructed facade. In fact, Ellington suffered from stage fright and tended to repeat a handful of formulaic phrases from the stage. When forced to improvise his announcements, he was capable of calling the Swedish singer Alice Babs "the essence of [pause] musical [long pause] epitome," being sure to use the French pronunciation of "essence." And as James Lincoln Collier has ruefully observed, a casual reading of the lyrics that Ellington wrote for his songs and sacred concerts suggest that he did not have a natural gift as a lyricist.[19] To further complicate matters, Ellington continually postponed the actual writing of his book even after he had set aside time to conduct interviews with his friend and palace guardsman, Stanley Dance. After a concert or a tour, the two would sit down to talk, but Ellington would turn away, silently watching old movies on television.[20]

Dance went about collecting statements that Duke made on and off the record, with and without requests for specific information, much of it scrawled on napkins and the backs of envelopes. Dance then stitched it all together to produce *Music Is My Mistress* in 1973, a year before Ellington's death. The book is full of glowing praise for almost everyone that Duke ever met, inspiring critics to sniff out a bit of damning amid the occasional faint praise as well as the few significant omissions. Ellington was clearly unwilling to open up his private life to Dance, omitting all mention of his encounters with gangsters, racists, and the many unscrupulous figures who exploited him over the years.

Ellington always wore a mask in public, setting it aside only for a handful of intimates. He may have learned his lesson early when, in an unguarded moment in 1935, he attacked Gershwin's *Porgy and Bess* because it failed to capture the real spirit of its black characters. A reporter for the periodical *New Theatre* was present, and Ellington's criticisms created a minor scandal when they subsequently appeared in print.[21] For the rest of his life, Ellington strove to speak only with humor and urbanity in public and conscientiously avoided candor. Duke's solution to living in white America has not appealed to all black jazz artists, but Ellington's practice is a revealing one. His reluctance to disclose his inner self in his autobiography may have stemmed from an African American man's reluctance to relive the humiliations and dangers he faced throughout his career. We should not be surprised that Ellington relied so heavily on Stanley Dance and that so many other jazz artists either worked closely with co-writers or saw their writings reworked by editors.

Having read the critical literature on African American autobiography, I find it unusual if not surprising that Ellington was reluctant to publish his story. In a tradition that begins with the slave narrative, black authors have sought to alert the world to their sufferings and to reclaim the personhood that had been denied them. Hampton Hawes and a handful of other black jazz artists can be understood as part of this tradition, but many more—and Armstrong

Krin Gabbard

is the foremost example—tended to put a happy face on their encounters and soft pedal the dark side of their experiences as African Americans. Holiday and Ellington were mostly uninterested in publicizing their lives, but when the time came, they seized the occasion to document their status as celebrities and to settle a few scores. And they were happy to cash the checks.

Like Ellington, Miles Davis was persuaded to write an autobiography by the offer of a large cash advance. And he, too, left out a great deal when he spoke with his co-author. Davis and Quincy Troupe first worked together when Troupe was assigned by *Spin* magazine to interview Davis in 1985. Apparently Davis was pleased with his first interactions with Troupe, who was then a published poet and critic. In 1991 Troupe became a professor of literature at the University of California at San Diego. After he was appointed poet laureate of the state of California in 2002, a background check revealed that he had claimed to hold a degree from Grambling College when in fact he had never graduated. Troupe subsequently resigned as poet laureate after holding the position for less than five months. He also gave up his chair at UCSD.[22]

When Simon & Schuster approached Davis's agent with a contract for an autobiography, Davis chose Troupe as his collaborator. The men spoke for many hours, engaging in disjointed, almost stream-of-consciousness conversations. Neither man seemed intent on constructing a chronological narrative. Troupe then marked up the transcripts of the interviews before drafting a manuscript that was then heavily edited by an editor or editors at Simon & Schuster. The precise number of editors who worked on the book is in dispute. Jack Chambers, one of Davis's first biographers, says that Troupe told him that "a whole committee" of editors worked on the book after he turned it over to the publishers.[23] But John Szwed, the author of a more recent biography of Davis, has said only one editor was empowered to alter Troupe's text.[24] The transcripts of Troupe's interviews with Davis, often heavily marked with Troupe's changes, constitute a large stack of papers at the Schomburg branch of the New York Public Library in Harlem.

Troupe had to edit his own questions out of the transcript and then rephrase Davis's statements so that they read like what Troupe believed to be the authorial voice of Miles Davis. On some level, he got it right. Many critics who reviewed the published text actually remarked upon how much the book sounded like Miles.

For example, when Davis recalls hearing Billy Eckstine's band in St. Louis in the early 1940s, Troupe added some colorful descriptions to a rather simple account of Sarah Vaughan's voice, and he changed other passages to give Davis's language more of a vernacular feel, such as inserting "and she was a motherfucker too" in Davis's characterization of Vaughan. Troupe may have been trying to make Davis sound more like an urban black man speaking casually, even in passages where the transcripts show Davis speaking with perfect standard American grammar. In one instance, Troupe initially changed Davis's entirely grammatical phrase "she used to sing" to "she be singing," which was then changed again, either by Troupe or the editor(s), to "she'd be singing" in the final, published version. Davis no longer sounds illiterate, but he does sound more vernacular.

In another passage, Davis speculates about how his voice arrived at that whispery, raspy sound it acquired in the 1950s. In his actual statements in the transcript, he appears uncertain, but he does seem willing to allow that, like Louis Armstrong and Dizzy Gillespie, he might have acquired such a voice simply by playing the trumpet for much of his life. He firmly denies that his voice changed when he could not resist yelling at Morris Levy, who ran the New York club Birdland after his brother Irving Levy had been knifed outside the club. (The tabloids were fond of calling the incident a "bebop murder.") Many journalists have dutifully reported the story that Davis ruined his voice by speaking truth to Levy's power. It is a useful story, even if Davis seems determined to debunk it. Troupe or the editors do not completely ignore what Davis said, but in the published book the story has been rewritten to portray him as acting against his better judgment and raising his voice to a hustler from the music business.

These transcripts suggest an entirely different set of problems than those that were raised in the first years after the book appeared. In the first reviews, critics were ambivalent about Davis's extreme honesty. They tended to admire him for telling the truth, but many had troubles with his unpleasant characterizations of Charlie Parker and John Coltrane, as well as himself. Before many actually read *Miles: The Autobiography*, they surely knew the sensational story about Davis sitting in a cab with Parker, who told him to turn his head away while he simultaneously ate fried chicken and was fellated by a young woman. Many will also recall hearing about Davis asserting that an unwashed, drug-addicted John Coltrane picked his nose on the bandstand and ate the contents. And most disturbingly, it was widely known that Davis bragged about his

Krin Gabbard

treatment of women in the presence of two policemen who showed up at his apartment while his wife, Cicely Tyson, hid downstairs after she had called the police to report that Davis was beating her.

The reception history of *Miles: The Autobiography* took a new turn when Stanley Crouch published a review in *The New Republic* in 1990, alleging that whole passages were taken directly from *Milestones*, Jack Chambers's biography of Miles Davis.[25] Crouch juxtaposed several passages from both books, leaving no doubt that there were major similarities between the two. In a new edition of his *Milestones*, published in 1998, Jack Chambers was kind to Troupe, suggesting that Davis was reading the first edition of Chambers's book at the same time that he was giving his interviews to Troupe.[26] Regardless, it is clear that Troupe needed some help in finishing his book after Davis became ill and would not sit for further interviews. Joanne Nerlino, the young art dealer who traveled with Davis during the last years of his life, told me that Davis tired of answering Troupe's questions after several sessions.[27]

A great deal of material in *Miles: The Autobiography* is not in the transcripts. It is entirely possible that there were conversations between Troupe and Davis that are not in the transcripts, but I am fairly certain that Troupe—or the editors at Simon & Schuster—added a great deal of material based on what was already in print about Davis. There was no other way they could produce so complete an account of his life. The transcripts, for example, contain nothing like the many passages in *Miles: The Autobiography* such as this: "After I did the Birdland gig, I think I recorded with Lee Konitz, as a sideman, for Prestige. Max Roach was on that date and George Russell and some other guys I have forgotten."[28] The phrases "I think" and "I have forgotten" are very common throughout the book. To me it suggests that someone has filled in personnel on their own in order to flesh out the history. But Davis is made not to sound like a jazz geek who can rattle off the complete personnel at every recording session. Nevertheless, the constant citations of personnel throughout *Miles: The Autobiography* ultimately served an important purpose for Miles Davis.

I t may be too much to ask for the real Miles Davis, whoever that might be. But I think we can ask, who is the Miles Davis of *Miles: The Autobiography*? Permit me a detour before I address this question.

In the 1940 MGM musical *Strike Up the Band*, Mickey Rooney and Judy Garland have, as is often the case, "put on their own show," forming a dance band with their high school friends. When they perform for Paul Whiteman and the members of his band, Jimmy (the hero played by Mickey Rooney) takes an extended drum solo. Whiteman is sufficiently impressed to invite him backstage. Behaving in a supremely avuncular fashion, Whiteman tells Jimmy that a former member of his own orchestra is forming a band and that he needs a drummer. He tells Jimmy that the job is his if he can start immediately. Overjoyed, Jimmy accepts the job and runs home to tell his mother.

Jimmy's saintly mother, however, urges him not to take the job, explaining that he has no business walking out on the members of his own band, who still need him for an imminent, all-important contest. Back with Whiteman, Jimmy explains why he cannot take the job while Whiteman listens in his dressing gown. (The matter of the dressing gown shall remain unexplored, at least for now.) Whiteman is satisfied with Jimmy's explanation and seems on the verge of sending him back home. But instead he sits down and delivers a remarkable speech to Jimmy. By today's standard, the speech represents a primitive attempt to theorize about the appeal of jazz. It can also be heard as standard Hollywood procedure, giving audiences a reason to like the music they already like.

Having told Jimmy about the star status of bandleaders like himself, Fred Waring, Kay Kyser, and Glenn Miller, he then points out how these men bear great responsibilities along with their fame:

> Rhythm can either excite the worst in us or bring out the best. Take that little fellow out on the street, Jimmy. Teach him to blow a horn and he'll never blow a safe. You know, rhythm is really a wonderful thing. Sometimes I think rhythm almost runs the world. In a little baby, the first thing that starts is his rhythm. His little heart starts beating. And every different city has a different kind of rhythm. And in your own car, if the engine's missing and jerking, or you feel the bump of a flat tire, it's the rhythm that tells you something's wrong. And if you call a doctor, the first thing he does is check your rhythm. He feels your pulse to find if your rhythm is solid and your beat's strong. So, Jimmy, when we get to the last eight bars of the big tune, the old ticker kinda slows down. No matter what's wrong with us, the last thing to stop is our rhythm.

Jimmy stares at Whiteman in awe, and the scene ends. He then goes on to win the contest and the affections of his girlfriend, played by Judy Garland.

Whiteman was fifty when *Strike Up the Band* was shot in 1940. He made a few recordings in the 1940s but spent most of the decade as music director for ABC radio. During the early years of television, he hosted *Paul Whiteman's*

TV Teen Club, in which he spoke to young performers much in the style he established with Mickey Rooney in *Strike Up the Band*. The television show ran from 1949 until 1954, introducing the world to Bobby Rydell, a regular who achieved some fame in the next few years, as well as to Dick Clark, who read the program's Tootsie Roll commercials. Whiteman retired in the 1950s and passed away in 1967. At the height of his career in the 1920s, when he was called, without irony, the King of Jazz, Whiteman employed some of the best white jazz artists. He was even an influence on some great black artists. Fletcher Henderson says that he listened to Whiteman's records before he left Georgia for New York in 1922.[29] Henderson is, of course, the best candidate for the title Inventor of Big Band Jazz as We Know It. Duke Ellington said that when he arrived in New York, all he wanted to do was lead a band that sounded like Henderson's. Paul Whiteman deserves at least a small share of the credit for Henderson's achievements.

But in 1940, when Whiteman appeared in *Strike Up the Band*, his glory days were over. As those scenes suggest, he was happy to present himself as an *éminence grise* providing employment and fatherly advice to a promising young musician. In the film, he is not at all the boastful, hard-partying, often cynical businessman who emerges in statements by many of the musicians who worked for him. Instead he speaks in aphorisms built on strained metaphors.

Whiteman was relatively young when he wrote his autobiography, called simply *Jazz*, in 1926. Miles Davis, by contrast, was over sixty when he began working on his autobiography. But like Whiteman, Davis's star was fading when he agreed to play a role in the film *Dingo*, directed by Rolf de Heer.

Dingo, released one year after Davis's death in 1991, has a bit in common with *Strike Up the Band*. The film begins in Australia when a young man marvels at the performance of Billy Cross (the Miles Davis character) after his airplane makes an emergency landing in the outback. To the delight of the young protagonist, the band gives a free concert to the locals on the landing strip near the plane. As he gets back on the plane, Miles's character tells the young boy to come see him whenever he's in Paris. Our Australian hero grows up to be a trumpeter as well as a hunter of dingoes, those predatory desert dogs we all know from Meryl Streep's performance in *A Cry in the Dark*, not to mention Julia Louis-Dreyfus's imitation of Streep on a famous episode of *Seinfeld*. When John, the Australian protagonist played by Colin Friels, thinks he is ready, he packs up his horn and heads to Paris.

When the Australian trumpeter first encounters Billy Cross in Paris, the older musician does not greet him in a conventional manner. Instead, he immediately delivers an aphorism that the Australian must decipher: "You know that old expression, 'The grass is greener on the other side?' It's true. You look down, you see grass and dirt. You look straight ahead, you see green grass. Think about it." Billy Cross then invites his guest into his music studio, clearly taking him under his wing but without the usual verbal cues. Although Cross has retired from playing the trumpet, John eventually manages to coax him into performing in a Paris jazz club. At least according to the film, the young Australian acquits himself well. Later that night, as they walk through the streets of Paris (vaguely recalling Jeanne Moreau's night walk in the 1957 film *Lift to the Scaffold,* with its memorable music by Davis), Cross warns his acolyte about the dangers of the jazz life. But he also announces that he and his band will record one of John's tunes. According to Cross, they will call it "Dogs of the Desert." Like Whiteman, Davis agreed to play a role that is a radically cleaned-up version of himself. In their respective films, Whiteman and Davis take an active interest in helping young musicians. And both deliver scripted speeches full of fatherly advice, tired metaphors, and conventional truisms.

I would argue that *Miles: The Autobiography* is part of the same process of self-rehabilitation that Davis undertook with *Dingo*. Davis was always intimately involved in the creation and maintenance of a public image, more so than the vast majority of jazz artists. This included his conspicuous consumption of expensive sports cars and stylish clothing as much as his erratic behavior. In 1964, for example, Davis famously spent a mere five minutes with a reporter for *Time* magazine before showing him to the door. That interview was supposed to put Davis on the cover of *Time* magazine—Thelonious Monk ended up on the cover instead.[30] Twenty-five years later, Davis's willingness to submit to several days of filming and taking orders from a relatively inexperienced movie director for a film as inauspicious as *Dingo* was an equally dramatic act of self-definition. Much the same can be said of the hours when he agreed to speak with Quincy Troupe, even if he may have grown tired of the process at some point.

The black feminist writer Pearl Cleage spoke for many when she publicly wondered how she could have fallen in love with the music of someone who was capable of abusing Cicely Tyson and virtually every other woman he claimed to have loved.[31] *Miles: The Autobiography* presents a problem that has little to do with Quincy Troupe's mediations of what Davis actually told him. How do you reconcile the violent, confrontational bully with the genius who created so many moments of extraordinary musical beauty? You probably cannot, although Robin Kelley can be convincing when he invokes the pimp aesthetic to explain Davis.

> Listening for the pimp in Miles ought to make us aware of the pleasures of cool as well as the dark side of romance. We get nostalgic for the old romantic Miles, for that feeling of being in love, but who understands this better than the mack, that despicable character we find so compelling and attractive?[32]

Others have tried to explain Davis's dark side in terms of his many years of drug abuse. Before he developed a drug habit, the young Miles Davis was, in the words of Stephanie Stein Crease, "a pussycat."[33] Nevertheless, John Szwed has been criticized—very unfairly, I think—for writing a biography of Davis in which he refuses to offer a single unifying account of Davis's character. The closest he comes is in quoting passages such as one by trumpeter Art Farmer, who was himself profoundly influenced by Davis. According to Farmer, "Miles plays the way he'd like to be."[34] In *Miles: The Autobiography*, however, Davis emerges as someone who, deep down inside, really is the way he plays. Someone who might even be capable of gently mentoring a young acolyte as in *Dingo*. In spite of his nasty public image, the autobiography suggests that, down deep, the real Miles is as tender as his most romantic solos. For example, near the middle of the book, Davis talks about the time he came to blows with Max Roach, who had accused Davis of having sex with his wife, Abbey Lincoln.

> I tried to explain to Max that all I had ever done to Abbey Lincoln was give her a haircut. Someone had told Max that I had "trimmed" Abbey—and he thought that meant that I had fucked her. When he started to scream at me and choke me, I just hit him with an uppercut and knocked him down. Dropped him right there. He was screaming, and I had tried to leave once or twice but he wouldn't let me. . . .
>
> Man, that was some real sad shit to be up in. That wasn't the real Max Roach screaming in that club at me, just like it wasn't the real Miles Davis who had been a junkie all them years. Drugs was talking for Max and so when I hit him like I did, I didn't feel like I was hitting the real Max that I knew. But that shit hurt me real bad, real bad, and I went home and cried like a baby in Frances's [Davis's second wife] arms that night, all night.[35]

Those who know his life story might assume that the real Miles—the inner Miles—is the egotistical monster who abused women. The account of his confrontation with Max Roach is one of several sections in the autobiography that seeks to reverse that perception, suggesting that the tender trumpet solos and not the notorious behavior off the bandstand represent the inner Miles.

It is this lifelong effort to construct a public image that makes *Miles: The Autobiography*, not to mention all biographies of Davis, so unsatisfying. Like many African Americans who have sought to tell their own stories, Davis—and to a larger extent Quincy Troupe—has attempted to create a coherent life narrative in spite of the oppressive uncertainty and danger of life in white America. But because he came from an affluent family and was able to use his musical talent to great advantage, Davis was able to try on many identities.

In the autobiography, compiled at the end of his life, Davis was busy justifying himself and villainizing his antagonists. But all the old Miles Davises make this work difficult if not impossible. And of course, the book itself is generically and even ontologically unstable.

For me, an intriguing aspect of this book is its close attention to the discographical details of Davis's career. Very few of the people who played with Davis, even for brief periods, are left out of the narrative. Troupe or someone at Simon & Schuster probably did this on their own, but it is also possible that Davis had his own reasons for insisting that all the names of the musicians he hired be included. At some stage in the process, he may have instructed Troupe to look up all those discographical details and add them to the narrative. Someone else probably added all those passages with "I think" and "I forget" that make Davis seem cool and insouciant but also respectful of his sidepeople.

To complicate matters even more, when the autobiography was published, Davis insisted that he did not actually talk that way. And as we know, he had a legitimate point. Davis even complained about the photograph on the back cover, insisting that he was smiling too broadly. He actually told a few interviewers that he never even read the galley proofs of the book.

On the one hand, because of the orality—real and constructed—of *Miles: The Autobiography*, it has much in common with African American literary traditions. On the other hand, the book is too ploddingly thorough to have the kind of focus and piquancy we find in the best jazz autobiographies, such as those of Charles Mingus, Sidney Bechet, and even Louis Armstrong. It would be hard to imagine the Mingus of *Beneath the Underdog* pausing to carefully list the personnel in each of his bands as does the narrator of *Miles: The Autobiography*.

Among the many Miles Davises that have been promoted, marketed, distributed, and analyzed, one objected strongly to the photograph of "a white bitch" on the cover of his 1957 LP, *Miles Ahead*. In his biography of Davis, John Szwed traces the history of this record, on which Davis played with a large orchestra arranged and conducted by Gil Evans. The LP was first released with the photograph of a white female model in a sailboat on its cover. After Davis protested, Columbia Records re-released the LP with a photograph of Davis playing his trumpet. The same music was in circulation with two different covers. Then, at about the same time that Davis was being interviewed by Troupe for the autobiography, the music was issued on CD "electronically rechanneled for stereo." Because mono recordings had been reworked in fake stereo, many considered this version inferior to what was on the original LP issue. In addition, brief, orchestrated passages that linked the individual cuts on the LP and helped make the original so distinctive were eliminated. After numerous complaints from listeners, the album was released again on CD using original takes, but some of the tracks were still in fake stereo. In addition, some of the linking passages were remixed, and an entirely new passage was added to connect selections that were previously separated because they were on different sides of the LP. In 1997, *Miles Ahead* was reissued again, this time in an elegantly packaged box that collected all of Davis's recordings with Gil Evans. The box included newly discovered true stereo versions of the old mono takes and the restoration of the original interludes.[36] In addition, the photograph of the white woman on the sailboat, long a fetishized object for collectors pursuing every shard of Davis's recordings, was included in the box set.

So what is the true version of *Miles Ahead*? We would not be asking this question if Davis were a minor talent who never worked with a genius like Gil Evans. There would have been no pressure for repeated issues of what is basically the same music. And we would not be asking, what is the true story of Miles Davis? were he not a brilliant and highly mercurial performer who labored hard not to be pigeonholed. Like any one of the *Miles Ahead* discs, *Miles: The Autobiography* is only one rendering of the artist's story. And like the Paul Whiteman of *Strike Up the Band*, as well as the Miles Davis of *Dingo*, the Miles Davis of *Miles: The Autobiography* wants to be remembered as a sensitive, philosophically inclined elder statesman, who nurtured a long list of younger artists, their names carefully inscribed in his own version of his life story. Even if Davis never bothered to construct any of these lists in his many hours of speaking with Quincy Troupe, those lists are entirely consistent with the aging, reflective Miles Davis who agreed to appear as an idealized version of himself in *Dingo*.

NOTES

1. Eric Porter, *What Is This Thing Called Jazz? African American Musicians as Artists, Critics, and Activists* (Berkeley: University of California Press, 2002).
2. Rex Stewart, *Boy Meets Horn*, ed. Claire P. Gordon (Ann Arbor: University of Michigan Press, 1991).
3. Farah Jasmine Griffin, *If You Can't Be Free, Be a Mystery: In Search of Billie Holiday* (New York: Free Press, 2001), 23; Billie Holiday with William T. Dufty, *Lady Sings the Blues* (Garden City, NY: Doubleday, 1956).
4. Albert Murray, *Good Morning Blues: The Autobiography of Count Basie* (New York: Random House, 1985).
5. Hampton Hawes and Don Asher, *Raise Up Off Me* (New York: Coward, McCann, and Geoghegan, 1974).
6. Charles Mingus, *Beneath the Underdog* (New York: Knopf, 1971).
7. Gene Santoro, *Myself When I Am Real: The Life and Music of Charles Mingus* (New York: Oxford University Press, 2000), 183.
8. David Yaffe, *Fascinating Rhythm: Reading Jazz in American Writing* (Princeton, NJ: Princeton University Press, 2006), 164.
9. Art Pepper, and Laurie Pepper, *Straight Life: The Story of Art Pepper*, updated ed. (New York: Da Capo, 1994), 478.
10. Sidney Bechet, *Treat It Gentle* (1960; reprint, New York: Da Capo, 1978).
11. Gabriel Solis, conversation with the author, 27 September 2004.
12. John Chilton, *Sidney Bechet: The Wizard of Jazz* (New York: Oxford University Press, 1987), 292.
13. Solis, conversation with the author, 27 September 2004.
14. In Thomas Brothers, ed., *Louis Armstrong, In His Own Words: Selected Writings* (New York: Oxford University Press, 2001). Brothers has carefully preserved Armstrong's orthographical eccentricities.
15. Dan Morgenstern, conversation with the author, 1 October 2004.
16. Louis Armstrong, *Satchmo: My Life in New Orleans* (New York: Prentice-Hall, 1954), 209.
17. William Howland Kenney, "Negotiating the Color Line: Louis Armstrong's Autobiographies," in *Jazz in Mind: Essays on the History and Meanings of Jazz*, ed. Reginald T. Buckner and Steven Weiland (Detroit: Wayne State University Press, 1991), 51.
18. This document is included in Brothers's anthology.
19. James Lincoln Collier, *Duke Ellington* (New York: Oxford University Press, 1987), 295.

Krin Gabbard

20. Mercer Ellington, with Stanley Dance, *Duke Ellington in Person: An Intimate Memoir* (Boston: Houghton Mifflin, 1978), 172.

21. See Mark Tucker, ed., *The Duke Ellington Reader* (New York: Oxford University Press, 1993), 114–17.

22. "UCSD's Quincy Troupe Resigns," *San Diego Union-Tribune*, 3 December 2002. Available at http://www.signonsandiego.com/news/metro/20021203-1116-troupe.html.

23. Jack Chambers, *Milestones: The Music and Times of Miles Davis* (New York: Da Capo, 1998), xxiii.

24. John Szwed, conversation with the author, 3 June 2004.

25. Stanley Crouch, "Play the Right Thing," *New Republic*, 12 February 1990, 30–37.

26. Chambers, *Milestones*, xxvi.

27. Joanne Nerlino, conversation with the author, 28 May 2001.

28. Miles Davis with Quincy Troupe, *Miles: The Autobiography* (New York: Simon & Schuster, 1989), 147.

29. Walter C. Allen, *Hendersonia: The Music of Fletcher Henderson and His Musicians*, Jazz Monographs 4 (Highland Park, IL: Walter C. Allen, 1973), 4.

30. Quincy Troupe, *Miles and Me* (Berkeley: University of California Press, 2000), 25.

31. Pearl Cleage, "Mad at Miles," *Deals with the Devil and Other Reasons to Riot* (New York: Ballantine, 1993), 39.

32. Robin D. G. Kelley, "Miles Davis: A Jazz Genius in the Guise of a Hustler," *New York Times*, 13 May 2001, Arts and Leisure: 7.

33. Stephanie Stein Crease, conversation with the author, 15 August 2002.

34. John F. Szwed, *So What: The Life of Miles Davis* (New York: Simon & Schuster, 2002), 403.

35. Davis, *Miles*, 254.

36. Szwed, *So What*, 144.

WORKS CITED

Films

Dingo. Dir. Rolf de Heer. GeVest Australia Productions, 1991.

Imagine the Sound. Dir. Ron Mann. Ontari Productions, 1981.

Strike Up the Band. Dir. Busby Berkeley. MGM, 1940.

Texts

Allen, Walter C. *Hendersonia: The Music of Fletcher Henderson and His Musicians*. Jazz Monographs 4. Highland Park, IL: Walter C. Allen, 1973.

Armstrong, Louis. *Satchmo: My Life in New Orleans*. New York: Prentice-Hall, 1954.

———. *Swing That Music*. 1936. Reprint, New York: Da Capo, 1993.

Bechet, Sidney. *Treat It Gentle*. 1960. Reprint, New York: Da Capo, 1978.

Brothers, Thomas, ed. *Louis Armstrong, In His Own Words: Selected Writings*. New York: Oxford University Press, 2001.

Chambers, Jack. *Milestones: The Music and Times of Miles Davis*. New York: Da Capo, 1998.

Chilton, John. *Sidney Bechet: The Wizard of Jazz*. New York: Oxford University Press, 1987.

Cleage, Pearl. "Mad at Miles." In *Deals with the Devil and Other Reasons to Riot*. New York: Ballantine, 1993. 36–43.

Collier, James Lincoln. *Duke Ellington*. New York: Oxford University Press, 1987.

Crouch, Stanley. "Play the Right Thing." *New Republic*, 12 February 1990, 30–37.

Davis, Miles, with Quincy Troupe. *Miles: The Autobiography*. New York: Simon & Schuster, 1989.

Ellington, Duke. *Music Is My Mistress*. Garden City, NY: Doubleday, 1973.

Ellington, Mercer, with Stanley Dance. *Duke Ellington in Person: An Intimate Memoir*. Boston: Houghton Mifflin, 1978.

Griffin, Farah Jasmine. *If You Can't Be Free, Be a Mystery: In Search of Billie Holiday*. New York: Free Press, 2001.

Hawes, Hampton, and Don Asher. *Raise Up Off Me*. New York: Coward, McCann and Geoghegan, 1974.

Holiday, Billie, with William T. Dufty. *Lady Sings the Blues*. Garden City, NY: Doubleday, 1956.

Kelley, Robin D. G. "Miles Davis: A Jazz Genius in the Guise of a Hustler." *New York Times*, 13 May 2001, Arts and Leisure: 1, 7.

Kenney, William Howland. "Negotiating the Color Line: Louis Armstrong's Autobiographies." In *Jazz in Mind: Essays on the History and Meanings of Jazz*. Ed. Reginald T. Buckner and Steven Weiland. Detroit: Wayne State University Press, 1991. 38–59.

Mingus, Charles. *Beneath the Underdog*. New York: Knopf, 1971.

Murray, Albert. *Good Morning Blues: The Autobiography of Count Basie*. New York: Random House, 1985.

Pepper, Art, and Laurie Pepper. *Straight Life: The Story of Art Pepper*. Updated ed. New York: Da Capo, 1994.

Porter, Eric. *What Is This Thing Called Jazz? African American Musicians as Artists, Critics, and Activists*. Berkeley: University of California Press, 2002.

Santoro, Gene. *Myself When I Am Real: The Life and Music of Charles Mingus*. New York: Oxford University Press, 2000.

Stewart, Rex. *Boy Meets Horn*. Ed. Claire P. Gordon. Ann Arbor: University of Michigan Press, 1991.

Szwed, John. *So What: The Life of Miles Davis*. New York: Simon & Schuster, 2002.

Troupe, Quincy. *Miles and Me*. Berkeley: University of California Press, 2000.

Tucker, Mark, ed. *The Duke Ellington Reader*. New York: Oxford University Press, 1993.

"UCSD's Quincy Troupe Resigns." *San Diego Union-Tribune*. 3 December 2002. Available at http://www.signonsandiego.com/news/metro/20021203-1116-troupe.html.

Yaffe, David. *Fascinating Rhythm: Reading Jazz in American Writing*. Princeton, NJ: Princeton University Press, 2006.

Krin Gabbard

iv

Second Balcony Jump: Unsettling the Score

"A Rebus of Democratic Slants and Angles":
To Have and Have Not, Racial Representation, and Musical Performance in a Democracy at War

Ian Brookes

And there's the picture—it's almost certain to offend me in some kind of way. If there're Negro actors in it the roles they play will be offensive; and if it's a play with no part at all for Negroes, if you get to thinking about it, you resent the fact of seeing the kind of life shown you'll never be able to live.

—Chester Himes, *If He Hollers Let Him Go* (1945)

To Have and Have Not was released in late 1944, the penultimate year of the war. It was produced by Warner Brothers, directed by Howard Hawks, and starred Humphrey Bogart and Lauren Bacall. Seen today, the film may be presented as part of an art-house auteur retrospective of Hawks where directorial concerns are pre-eminent; or in star terms as a Bogart vehicle; or by genre as romantic thriller or tangential film noir. If seen on television or obtained from a video store, it would probably be classified as "classic" Hollywood and packaged with studio-era nostalgia. Its listing descriptions invariably emphasize the on-screen "chemistry" between Bogart and Bacall, usually with reference to their off-screen romance during the making of the film. Clearly, the ways in which we view the film now are different from how it was seen on first release and so, too, are its meanings. One largely overlooked aspect of the film, I suggest, is its significance in the cultural politics of racial representation during wartime, particularly in the context of what was being widely billed as "a democracy at war." And although the film's music has attracted little interest—except about whether Bacall's singing was dubbed by Andy Williams[1]—the musical sequences play a key narrative role in wartime racial discourse. In this chapter, I consider the ways in which the film works as a narrative refraction of the racial politics of wartime democracy and, to this end, I highlight the musical sequences and their relation to the narrative themes of conversion and resistance.

Wartime audiences experienced the film in wartime circumstances, and three reception factors can be usefully taken into account. First, with wartime attendance at American cinemas running at approximately ninety million per week, a substantial percentage of the population was seeing on a regular basis a considerable number of wartime releases. Second, the film was shown as part of what was then called the "staple program," which typically included—in addition to an A picture like this one—a low-budget B feature, together with a combination of newsreels, documentaries, and shorts. Much of this material comprised public information and propaganda produced under the auspices of government departments, notably the Office of War Information (OWI) and the War Department. There were also many war charity appeals and both A and B films often ended with the "minuteman" logo and the exhortation to buy war bonds on sale at the theater. Cinema-going acquired new meaning as the locus of wartime community. As Thomas Doherty has pointed out, "theaters were natural places to disseminate information, sell war bonds, hold rallies, solicit money for charities, and collect scarce goods for the war effort." Front-of-house displays often featured the juxtaposition of film publicity with anti-Axis propaganda. The same cinemas provided emergency accommodation for servicemen in transit. Music played a social role with "community sings" of hymns and patriotic songs and, especially after Pearl Harbor, theater programs universally included "The Star-Spangled Banner." Moreover, the cinema virtually doubled as a national church when, on momentous occasions such as D-day, "managers-turned-deacons led audiences-turned-congregations in recitations of the Twenty-third Psalm or the Lord's Prayer."[2] Third, cinemas, like the armed forces, were racially segregated. Theaters were either divided into racially segregated blocks or separated as "race houses" for black cinemagoers.[3]

Although wartime cinema has often been seen as escapist entertainment, audiences could hardly escape from the ubiquitous presence of the war. When those audiences saw *To Have and Have Not*, it was in the filmic context of a program combining both official and entertainment productions, both being underwritten by wartime concerns. Narrative meaning, then, was generated not only by the film per se but also by its relation to the program's other narratives, and by the social context in which they were viewed. Here, as Thomas Schatz has suggested, "virtually all of Hollywood's major genres were affected by the war and might in some way be included under the general rubric of 'war film.'"[4] In other words, the inscription of wartime factors can be found throughout the body of wartime films, irrespective of their traditional generic classification. Thus, film narrative, as cultural text, and filmgoing, as social practice, were both *of* the war. Films were viewed ineluctably through the prism of wartime experience in the context of "a democracy at war."

Although "democracy" was being signaled as the unifying national ideology of wartime, there was a stark dichotomy between the realities of African American experience of military service and America's imputed democratic credentials. While the armed services were subject to the "custom and habit" policy of rigid segregation, there remained an absurd disparity between the official wartime discourse of "a democracy at war" and the atrocious realities of segregation and exclusion, which obtained throughout the military in much the same way as they did everywhere else. Even blood plasma was segregated.[5] As the war got under way, African American groups began to challenge the military's discriminatory practices and, by extension, those in society at large. The Pittsburgh *Courier*—the largest circulation black newspaper—inaugurated the Double V campaign, pressing simultaneously for victory over fascism abroad and racism at home. These factors triggered intense concern with the issue of screen representations of black Americans. In 1942 the OWI published guidelines for the industry in the "Government Information Manual for the Motion Picture Industry." "Show democracy at work," the manual exhorted, "in the community, the factory, the army." To this end, the manual also called for representations of racial diversity, although within limits. "Show colored soldiers in crowd scenes; occasionally colored officers," it advised.[6] As wartime became a crucible of disaffection about military racism, the penultimate year of the war would see a diverse range of filmic representations of African Americans that were iconoclastic in their challenge to the racial status quo.

The narrative iconography of wartime, especially the version produced by Hollywood, saw vast disparity between the theory and practice of democracy. Screen representations of blacks had been dominated hitherto by familiar stereotypes, predominantly as domestics or entertainers. More often than not they were excluded from the screen altogether and remained, to borrow Ralph Ellison's defining racial metaphor, invisible. Widespread condemnation of traditional screen stereotypes appeared in various African American publications. A major academic study of race relations and the mass media identified several of the characteristics habitually associated with the archetypal black servant and entertainer. These included "ignorance, superstition, fear, servility, laziness, clumsiness, petty thievery, untruthfulness, credulity, immorality or irresponsibility."[7]

Screen representations of black musical performance became a particular concern. It had become standard industry practice for self-contained musical performances by black artists to be interpolated in narratives as sequences that could readily be cut prior to exhibition in southern states. Alternatively, there were "segregated" musicals, such as *Stormy Weather* (1943) and *Cabin in the Sky* (1943), in which all-black musical performances could be generically consigned to racial ghettos. Elsewhere, representations of racial integration were systematically opposed. In *Stage Door Canteen* (1943), for example, depictions of black and white dancers sharing the same dance floor were deleted in advance of southern distribution.[8] Otherwise, southern boards vigilantly applied their own excisions to any films in which black representations strayed too far from their view of acceptable stereotypes, especially if there was any suggestion of inter-racial fraternization. Scenes depicting racial integration were permissible only within prescribed limits, and, as Doherty has succinctly noted, there were three such permissible areas: "presocial" (children), "antisocial" (convicts), and "offshore" (foreign locales).[9] Black groups challenged such practices. *The Crisis*, for example, a magazine of the National Association for the Advancement of Colored People (NAACP), campaigned for film producers to "include Negroes naturally and easily in a script in parts which are not stereotyped."[10]

An important generic form for depictions of racial integration was the combat film. Here, wartime democracy was represented through what Jeanine Basinger has called "the concept of the unified group," mobilized by wartime necessity "to bring our melting pot tradition together to function as a true democracy."[11] The democratically constituted platoon, given as a microcosm of American society, became a staple element in such films, where the platoon's strength and integrity derived from its multi-ethnic, multi-racial diversity. The platoon often featured one lone African American serviceman, such as Kenneth Spencer in *Bataan* (1943), Rex Ingram in *Sahara* (1943), and Ben Carter in *Crash Dive* (1943), each "democratically" integrated within a unit to which in reality he could not conceivably belong. And of course, as the place-name titles indicate, these far-flung locations in the Far East, North Africa, and the remote reaches of the Atlantic were all safely distanced from American soil.

So, too, was the Martinique setting for *To Have and Have Not*. The film was a reworking of another foreign-locale narrative, *Casablanca* (1942). Both films

Ian Brookes

featured Humphrey Bogart as a tough, cynically detached American expatriate, a resolutely *un*partisan outsider, apparently motivated by self-interest and willfully uninvolved in wartime conflict. "I stick my neck out for nobody," says Rick in *Casablanca*, and when Harry Morgan is questioned about his "sympathies" in occupied Martinique, he replies, "minding my own business." In both films, each situated in Vichy-controlled territories, he will eventually join the cause of the Free French in support of a Resistance leader.

In both films, we can see in the Bogart figure instances of what Dana Polan has called the "conversion narrative."[12] The occurrence of this conversion principle was so common in wartime films that it virtually constituted a generic category of its own. Here, the recalcitrant individual cannot or will not participate in the collective war effort and remains disengaged from any purposeful wartime role. The conversion narrative oversaw a transformation in attitude, leading ultimately to a willing acceptance of a citizen role in accordance with national war aims.[13]

Bogart's casting in this conversion context would become a significant narrative force in *To Have and Have Not*. *Casablanca*'s Rick was a pivotal role in the reconfiguration of Bogart's star persona, a shift away from the gangster roles with which he had been associated in the late 1930s, such as *Dead End* (1937), *Angels with Dirty Faces* (1938), *The Roaring Twenties* (1939), and *High Sierra* (1941). The early 1940s saw the development of an increasingly complex and ambivalent Bogart persona through roles such as private eye Sam Spade in *The Maltese Falcon* (1941). Following *Casablanca*, Bogart appeared in a series of other war films, usually involving combat, such as *Across the Pacific* (1942), *Sahara* (1943), and *Passage to Marseilles* (1944). Before *To Have and Have Not*, he appeared in *Report from the Front* (1944), a short made for the OWI with scenes of his recent foreign tour entertaining the troops. These roles worked cumulatively to produce for Bogart a credible serviceman persona. His Harry Morgan carried traces of his combat-film persona, which served to authenticate the characterization. Even his scarred lip, which had lent a note of realism to his earlier tough-guy roles, here connoted a former combatant. Bogart's Morgan is characterized with soldierly professionalism. Not only can he handle a boat and a gun with practiced skill, but he also performs a surgical operation in makeshift conditions resembling a field hospital, clearly demonstrating that he has treated similar combat casualties in the past.

As the Bogart persona was being transfigured into *Casablanca*'s romantic loner, the role also saw him associated with a black character, the singer-pianist

Sam (Dooley Wilson). Sam's characterization has been disparaged for conforming to traditional stereotypes: "little more than an updated combination of faithful servant and entertainer," complained one film historian.[14] But it is clear that the relationship between the two men signals a desegregated integrity that transcends reductive stereotyping formulas. Certainly, no one is closer to Rick than Sam and, for the period, such a relationship was an audacious rebuttal of traditional black stereotypes. Although the narrative has an ideological investment in Rick's conversion, it is not necessarily one that accorded with the kind of message to be found in the official productions overseen by the OWI and the War Department. Indeed, the film was officially distrusted because its message was seen as insufficiently clear: "OWI reviewers . . . disliked what they interpreted as Bogart's cynicism. They wanted him to announce his conversion to the Allied cause with a ringing peroration for democracy."[15] Nevertheless, the relationship between Rick and Sam is indicative of another aspect of "democracy," and the bond between them bespeaks a connection between black and white that was then remarkably untypical. Sam's role is integrated within the narrative as altogether beyond that of any stereotypical servant or entertainer.[16] He personalizes the circumstances of Rick's conversion, especially through the film's famous signature tune, "As Time Goes By." The changing meanings of the song, reprised throughout the narrative, provide a musical refraction of Rick's emotional life from a sympathetic perspective: as the soundtrack to his romantic idyll with Ilsa (Ingrid Bergman) in pre-war Paris and, ultimately, as the theme for their reconciliation and his conversion.[17]

Bogart's Rick in *Casablanca* can be seen as a precursor to his Harry in *To Have and Have Not*. Here, too, the Bogart persona was being configured through a role predicated on concerns with wartime democracy and the narrative principle of conversion. We first see Harry at work, as the skipper of a fishing boat hired by Johnson (Walter Sande). Johnson, a vacationing businessman who cuts a ludicrous figure in his safari suit and pith helmet, is situated in the narrative as a "slacker," a representative figure of the unacceptable face of wartime Americanism. Harry, in contrast, is the consummate professional, an experienced and skillful seaman. Although he appears as the archetypal Bogartian loner, Harry is characterized in these early scenes with a deeply rooted sense of social commitment and an unwavering sense of social responsibility to those around him. He is steadfastly loyal to his crew and resolutely defends them against Johnson's tirades. He retains the "rummy" Eddy (Walter Brennan),

Ian Brookes

mindful that he was "a good man once," and looks after him with affection. We can see in Harry a kind of unofficial platoon leader with both professional and personal loyalty to those in his "unit."

Harry is central to the narrative imperative of conversion, but not in the sense that he must learn obedience to the call of duty. Rather, it is for him a question of choice arising from personal conviction. When he ultimately decides to join the Resistance cause, Frenchy (Marcel Dalio) asks him why. "Well, I don't know," answers Harry. "Maybe because I like you and maybe because I don't like them." This is no doctrinal answer. As Robin Wood has suggested, the film "embodies one of the most basic anti-fascist statements the cinema has given us." The power of its anti-fascist sentiment derives from within Harry himself, not from any ideologically determined stance he is supposed to adopt. Harry's involvement is existential and, as Wood suggests, instinctual. "The distinction *To Have and Have Not* insists on is that between the application of calculated, official force imposed from above, and the spontaneous expression of the individual's sense of moral outrage."[18]

As in *Casablanca*, musical ambience plays a crucial role in the expression of the film's anti-fascist concerns, especially through what we might call the narrative's racial *mise en scène*. The first musical sequence contributes to the narrative in several ways. Amid the bustle of the bar-room, Bogart's Morgan is sitting alone at a table. The camera slowly zooms in as he lights a cigarette with Cricket (Hoagy Carmichael) at the piano vamping an introduction to "Am I Blue?" As the song gets under way, Johnson makes a clumsy pass at Slim (Lauren Bacall), who pushes him away. She gets up and walks over to the band to escape Johnson's unwanted attentions, drawn toward the more sympathetic space occupied by the musicians. Standing by Cricket's piano as he sings the song, she begins humming along with the tune until he invites her to "take over" and she joins him in an impromptu duet. Their performance of the song ends with the enthusiastic approval of both the audience and the band. The song works as a kind of knowing commentary on both Slim and Harry, each having suffered an unhappy love affair. The grimacing Cricket mocks the melancholy sentiment of the song, aware that the eye contact between Harry and Slim presages their romance. The song also provides the means for Slim to prove herself eligible for membership in the characteristically Hawksian world of masculine professionalism and camaraderie.[19] Her low vocal register, which surprises and delights Cricket, initiates her as "one of the boys" and, hence, a "soldier" in the anti-fascist cause.[20]

The sequence establishes the narrative's central location as a crowded, racially integrated space in which a considerable number of black patrons—many, significantly, in uniform—constitute a remarkable presence.[21] There is no precise demarcation between audience and musicians, many of whom are also black, with an informal group loosely clustered around the piano. The performance resembles a jam session getting under way as Cricket begins picking out the tune as others casually join in, like the drummer nonchalantly putting down his newspaper before taking up his brushes. It is spontaneous, improvisational: it seems that anyone could join in as Slim does. The scene occurs between two others in which the as-yet unconverted Bogart uncompromisingly rejects all entreaties to help the Resistance cause. "I can't afford to get mixed up in your local politics," he tells Frenchy. At the same time, there is an implication that the clientele at large are already opposed to the Vichy administration, that the space of the hotel is itself the site of collective resistance to the power of the fascist regime imposed upon it. Here, the visual planes established by the camera effectively democratize the action. Both Harry and Slim are socially embedded in the "local politics" of the multi-racial musicalized space, inextricably positioned in a field of view within that space. And it is here, through the narrative themes of conversion and resistance, that we can see a challenge to segregation and the racial status quo of wartime in the making.[22]

Following the "Am I Blue?" sequence, the action shifts away from the barroom as the camera follows Slim and Harry up the stairway. At the same time, the band begins another tune. With no prearranged schedule, a voice is heard calling for "Star Dust"—a jokey reminder of Carmichael's well-known composition—but the band spontaneously launches into an instrumental version of "Limehouse Blues." The guitar-centered arrangement with its propulsive rhythm is unmistakably reminiscent of the pre-war recording by Django Reinhardt and the Quintette du Hot Club de France. The song works on several signifying levels. It provides a note of realism in that Martiniquans would credibly play music redolent of pre-war France. It suggestively evokes Nazi-occupied France via Vichy-controlled Martinique. And it invokes the spirit of Reinhardt himself, who was by then internationally renowned as the first, if not the only, outstanding European jazz musician.

Reinhardt's reputation in America had been growing since before the war when a number of prominent black musicians, including Benny Carter and Coleman Hawkins, played with him in Paris, and later he become popular with GIs in France. Wartime France witnessed phenomenal enthusiasm for

Ian Brookes

jazz, particularly swing.[23] Swing, as the only available form of American culture in France, became a symbolic force of resistance to the Occupation for the French, who "subtly expressed their hostility toward the Nazis in this fad for American music."[24] The Djangoesque rendition of "Limehouse Blues" also implies an affinity between the gypsy Reinhardt and the black musicians playing it here: jazz-playing gypsies, like blacks, were doubly damned by Nazi ideology, both musically and racially. The tune also demonstrates how "background" music does not quite remain in the background: even when the focus of narrative interest, Harry and Slim, moves away, the sound of the music—and all it signifies—permeates the hotel building.

The film's racial *mise en scène* was noted with approval in the African American press. "Is Hollywood Yielding?" asked Jackie Lopez in the *Chicago Defender* in an article as much a news item as it was a review:

> The stiff lipped complaining we've been tossing Hollywood way may have some bearing on the fact that the movie town is viewing the race with new eyes. Every now and then we get the delightful little shock of seeing our own portrayed as interesting human beings, rather than as the lowest of the low. . . . Did you see all those beautiful black faces drifting in and out of the cafe in which most of the story takes place? Did you see them drinking at the bar, sitting at the tables, shifting in and out among the whites, talking, laughing, dancing—like anyone else? The story takes place in Martinique, true. But as I remember, Hollywood has, in the past, stuck to her white-man-super tales even if the story had only one white man in it. If he drank at a bar and there were no other white men to drink with him, he drank alone. I believe, anyway, that this honest to goodness reality made "To Have and Have Not" that much finer a picture.

"Hollywood has potentialities," she concluded, "it's about time they start showing."[25]

For Lopez, the significance of the film has nothing to do with any individual in it (as, say, in the combat film), but rather with the naturalized representation of what she calls "the race" and "our own." For her, the film's impact—its "delightful little shock"—derives from the dynamics of racial integration, what she describes as the "drifting in and out of" and "shifting in and out among" prominent throughout the film. What she finds remarkable is the ordinariness of this interaction. As her terms suggest, she is describing here a kind of interweaving that constitutes the film's racial fabric, a fabric resistant to the kind of cuts otherwise exercised as a matter of routine. She is also claiming, of course, that the *Defender*'s campaign challenging Hollywood's racial stereotyping was having some effect.

Other reviewers noted the film's racial *mise en scène* and its democratic ramifications. "The 'hepness' of this film is all over it," noted John McManus in *New York PM*. "It is like a rebus of democratic slants and angles. If you look for them, they're in every scene. . . . 'To Have and Have Not,'" he said, "has a healthy, democratic flesh tone, and it is not only skin deep."[26] Like Lopez in the *Defender*, McManus saw "democracy" in the narrative underwritten by "skin tone." But he is also alluding to something else here, as indicated by his recurrent use of *hep*, a voguish term in jazz vernacular. Jazz, as swing historians have pointed out, was mobilized in the cause of wartime Americanism.[27] Its improvisational creativity and democratic co-operation—indeed, its very African American credentials—were enlisted in the national war effort, where jazz, especially swing, served as the antithesis of fascism, Axis martial culture, and Nazi racial ideology. "Of all the arts," said Sterling A. Brown in 1945, "jazz music is probably the most democratic." What Brown meant by *democratic* was not only a band's demonstrable multi-racial composition (he cites the model of Benny Goodman's late 1930s quartet with Teddy Wilson and Lionel Hampton), but also the freedom of expression inherent in collective improvisation, specifically the jam session. "The mixed band," says Brown, "meets up with difficulties, especially in the South" (not unlike its Hollywood counterpart). "But completely democratic are the jam sessions," he suggests, "where Negro and white musicians meet as equals to improvise collectively."[28]

The production working practices on *To Have and Have Not* can also be seen as analogous to jazz improvisation.[29] Hawks, an inveterate on-set improviser, oversaw an exceptional degree of collaboration with the cast in the development of the script. Peter Wollen has described the director's characteristic *modus operandi* when Hawks "would slow down the whole production while everybody stood around, encouraging his collaborators to throw out ideas until he got a scene exactly the way he wanted it. He rarely stuck strictly to his script while shooting, always looking for ways of introducing a new element into familiar material."[30] Similarly, Lauren Bacall recounted in her autobiography how she and others involved in a particular scene began each morning on the set with Hawks when they "would sit in a circle in canvas chairs . . . and read the scene" together. Like the collaborative improvisation of a jam session, the original script would be collectively developed with the incorporation of new

Ian Brookes

dialogue suggested by the actors. "After we'd gone over the words several times and changed whatever Bogie or Howard thought should be changed, Howard would ask an electrician for a work light . . . and we'd go through the scene on the set to see how it felt. Only after all that had been worked out did he call [cinematographer] Sid Hickox and talk about camera set-ups."[31] The extent to which this on-set working process reshaped the production is evident in the numerous changes to the original screenplay.[32] The resultant script, with its typically repetitive dialogue, can be seen in itself as a series of musical refrains. As John Fawell has pointed out, "Hawks loved to repeat his lines, to use them over and over again, to play with them, work variations off them and to develop them according to the development of his characters."[33]

Central to the narrative's musicality is the figure of Carmichael's Cricket. Carmichael was widely known as the composer of "Star Dust" and other standards, but his role as Cricket cannot be seen simply as a casting strategy designed to exploit the celebrity of the singer-songwriter through a role in which he would play "himself" (even though Carmichael's own self-deprecating accounts of his screen roles would contribute toward that impression).[34] Although he recounted that he "ended up by writing all the background music for the picture," his musical contribution cannot be relegated to the background, nor can his Cricket role be seen as marginal.[35] According to jazz scholar Krin Gabbard, Carmichael "usually played a kind of asexual trickster figure who commented on the action from the outside."[36] While it is true that Cricket is in some ways an outsider, he is by no means an extraneous figure or a disinterested commentator. His role is indispensable to the narrative's concerns with racially integrated musical performance as a force against fascism. If his performative mask equips him with a certain insouciance and inscrutability, there is no doubt about where his loyalties lie. Cricket's resistance to the fascist occupation is disguised through the easygoing manner of his trickstering persona. Unlike Harry, Cricket would be incapable of armed resistance and could not conceivably become a soldier in the Resistance cause. His opposition to fascism's racial ideology is expressed musically, enacted nightly through his involvement with the racially mixed band and played out through jazz, a musical form denounced and proscribed throughout the Third Reich.

The casting of Carmichael may appear to contradict my argument that the film represents a certain advancement in screen representations of African Americans, and it may seem retrogressive that the Cricket role should be played by a white rather than a black actor-musician, especially after the precedent established by Dooley Wilson's Sam in *Casablanca*. Carmichael, in this context, could be seen to have usurped a role that was "obviously" a black one.[37] Nevertheless, the Carmichael persona, through Cricket, is characterized *sui generis* as a racially "hybridized" figure, situated in a racially indeterminate or intermediate space, and working as a kind of bridge between black and white social and cultural categories. It is through Cricket that the narrative naturalizes the inter-racial grouping of the band and, by extension, the inter-racial society we see as an active presence in the hotel.

Cricket appears rooted in what seems to be his natural environment, permanently seated at his piano in the hotel bar-room, where he is almost always surrounded by the black musicians in the band. It is from here that he contributes an ironic musical commentary on the unfolding events. When, for example, Johnson is inadvertently shot dead in the bar, Cricket provides a wryly appropriate accompaniment to his unmourned demise, a mockingly lugubrious rendition of Gustave Lange's melodramatic perennial, "The Flower Song." ("Cut it out, Cricket," says Harry, while obviously appreciating the musical joke.) In "Hong Kong Blues," Cricket is explicitly identified with the plight of a black musician as he narrates "the story of a very unfortunate colored man who got [a]rrested down in old Hong Kong," an opium-addicted piano player marooned abroad, yearning to return home "to the land of the free" but, like Cricket in Martinique, forever exiled.[38]

In the finale, Cricket reprises the song he has been working on earlier, "How Little We Know." Cricket's playing segues into a swelling orchestral arrangement, the romantic theme for Harry and Slim, signifying by conventional means their romantic future. But the song also serves as the theme for their departure, with Eddy, to Devil's Island and the perilous mission they have undertaken to rescue the Resistance leader Pierre Villemars. The final sequence begins when Cricket strikes up an impromptu upbeat chorus of "How Little We Know," its syncopated rhythm providing a jaunty accompaniment for the trio's exit. Slim sashays out with a slinky-hipped motion while a smiling Harry takes her arm and, with Eddy's jerky alcoholic walk, all draw their walking tempo from the rhythm of the band. As they stride out purposefully onto the street, the outcome of their mission remains uncertain. Nevertheless, their uptempo departure represents an affirmatively defiant march against a fascist enemy abroad and, by narrative implication, its "fascist" counterpart at home.

Ian Brookes

NOTES

1. Williams did record Bacall's songs for use on the soundtrack, but Hawks thought that "she sounded better" than he did. "It was all her singing," Hawks claimed. Quoted in Joseph McBride, *Hawks on Hawks* (Berkeley: University of California Press, 1982), 130. See also Todd McCarthy, *Howard Hawks: The Grey Fox of Hollywood* (New York: Grove Press, 2000), 377.

2. Thomas Doherty, *Projections of War: Hollywood, American Culture, and World War II* (New York: Columbia University Press, 1993), 82, 84.

3. On segregated black cinemas, see Douglas Gomery, *Shared Pleasures: A History of Movie Presentation in the United States* (London: BFI, 1992), 155–70.

4. Thomas Schatz, *Boom and Bust: American Cinema in the 1940s* (Berkeley: University of California Press, 1999), 222.

5. See Jack D. Foner, *Blacks and the Military in American History: A New Perspective* (New York: Praeger, 1974), 140.

6. Cited in Clayton R. Koppes and Gregory D. Black, *Hollywood Goes to War: How Politics, Profits, and Propaganda Shaped World War II Movies* (New York: Free Press, 1987), 67; Richard R. Lingeman, *Don't You Know There's a War On? The American Home Front, 1941–1945* (New York: G. P. Putnam's Sons, 1970), 184.

7. The study catalogued the "principal stereotypes of the Negro in the American mind." L. D. Reddick, "Educational Programs for the Improvement of Race Relations: Motion Pictures, Radio, the Press, and Libraries," *Journal of Negro Education* 13.3 (Summer 1944): 369.

8. Doherty, *Projections of War*, 221–22.

9. Ibid., 210.

10. The editorial cited *Going My Way* (1944) as an exemplary demonstration of such inclusion. "Score for the Movies," *The Crisis* 51.10 (October 1944): 312.

11. Jeanine Basinger, *The World War II Combat Film: Anatomy of a Genre* (New York: Columbia University Press, 1986), 36–37.

12. Dana Polan, *Power and Paranoia: History, Narrative, and the American Cinema, 1940–1950* (New York: Columbia University Press, 1986), 75–76.

13. Studio advertising linked both films to a discourse of wartime citizenship: "TO HAVE AND HAVE NOT (which takes up entertainment-wise where 'Casablanca' left off!) serves thunderous notice that *'combining good picture-making with good citizenship'* is a *permanent* Warner policy." [Advertisement] "*To Have and Have Not*: Pressbook," Warner Brothers, 1944, unpaginated.

14. Donald Bogle, *Toms, Coons, Mulattoes, Mammies, and Bucks: An Interpretive History of Blacks in American Films*, rev. ed. (New York: Frederick Ungar, 1989), 140.

15. Clayton R. Koppes and Gregory D. Black, "Blacks, Loyalty, and Motion-Picture Propaganda in World War II," *Journal of American History* 73.2 (September 1986): 400.

16. "It is clear," argues Thomas Cripps, "that [Sam] is to be taken for an equal." He "is in on everything." Rick's café, after all, is a joint venture in which Sam retains a financial interest; he also remains privy to the lovers' affair and, intimately, "shares their pain." Thomas Cripps, *Slow Fade to Black: The Negro in American Film, 1900–1942* (1977; reprint, New York: Oxford University Press, 1993), 370–73.

17. The music in *Casablanca* has two narrative functions. When a group of German soldiers starts singing "Die Wacht am Rhein," French loyalists retaliate with an impassioned chorus of "La Marseillaise," drowning out the Germans in a symbolic victory for the Free French. The national anthem is mobilized as an official expression of nationalist sentiment. "As Time Goes By," in contrast, plays privately rather than publicly, indexed emotionally to the narrative trajectory of Rick's conversion.

18. Robin Wood, *Howard Hawks*, rev. ed. (London: BFI, 1981), 26, 30. For Wood's astute reading of the film, see 25–32. Hawks himself affected a lack of interest in the political dimensions of *To Have and Have Not*. See Peter Bogdanovich, "Howard Hawks: The Rules of the Game," in *Who the Devil Made It: Conversations with Legendary Film Directors* (New York: Ballantine, 1998), 332.

19. See, for instance, the quasi-military masculine enclave in Hawks's "proto-combat" film, *Only Angels Have Wings* (1939).

20. Bacall underwent voice training at Hawks's insistence to acquire the requisite low register for the role. See Lauren Bacall, *Lauren Bacall: By Myself* (London: Jonathan Cape, 1979), 85–86.

21. There is a questionable narrative logic about the presence of so many uniformed black servicemen in territory under Vichy administration. Hawks appears indifferent to representation of realistic detail here: clearly, he is more concerned with the visual impact of these racially integrated scenes and their naturalized depiction of black service personnel. It is worth noting that in 1943, the year preceding the release of the film, Martinique changed its allegiance to support the Free French and the Allied cause. So although the narrative present is set early during the Vichy administration ("in the summer of 1940, shortly after the fall of France"), the film was produced *after* it was replaced by the Free French. By 1944, then, the sight of uniformed black servicemen at large was suggestive of an Allied military presence on the island and an intimation of incipient victory.

22. In one of the few locations away from the hotel, the injured Resistance fighter Beauclerc (Paul Marion) is given refuge by a black family living on the outskirts of town, and it is within the space of this black community that Harry is first drawn into the Resistance cause.

23. See, for example, Charles Delaunay, *Django Reinhardt*, trans. Michael James (1961; reprint, New York: Da Capo, 1982), 101, 122–25.

24. Gilbert S. McKean, "The Fabulous Gypsy," *Esquire* (June 1947), reprinted in Ralph J. Gleason, ed., *Jam Session: An Anthology of Jazz* (New York: G. P. Putnam's Sons, 1958), 143.

25. Jackie Lopez, "Is Hollywood Yielding?" *Chicago Defender*, 24 March 1945, 20.

Ian Brookes

26. John T. McManus, "Vichy, Bogart, and a Dame," *New York PM*, 12 October 1944, reprinted in *Motion Picture Critics' Reviews* 1.23 (16 October 1944): 214.

27. See Lewis A. Erenberg, *Swingin' the Dream: Big Band Jazz and the Rebirth of American Culture* (Chicago: University of Chicago Press, 1998), 181–210; David W. Stowe, *Swing Changes: Big Band Jazz in New Deal America* (Cambridge, MA: Harvard University Press, 1994), 141–79.

28. Sterling A. Brown, "Spirituals, Blues, and Jazz," *Tricolor* (1945), reprinted in Gleason, *Jam Session*, 26. The jazz short *Jammin' the Blues*, released on the same staple program as *To Have and Have Not*, was an early attempt to represent the "democratic" jam session within a documentary format. But although producer Norman Grantz resisted Warner Brothers' pressure to replace Barney Kessel, the group's only white musician, the guitarist was placed in shadow and his hands darkened with berry juice to safeguard the film's sales in the South. Yet *Jammin' the Blues* did initiate a transformation in the aesthetics of racial representation by producing a different *look* for jazz that was self-consciously artistic. Drawing on the black-and-white, low-key lighting of film noir expressionism and jazz's emergent "cool" aesthetic (associated with the film's tenor saxophonist, Lester Young), the film presented the group as serious musicians, described in the voice-over commentary as "great artists." This was a radical departure from conventional jazz iconography, which had typically depicted musicians as zany vaudevillian clowns or as uniformed members of the sleek, corporate formality of big band swing. See Charles Emge, "On the Beat in Hollywood," *Down Beat*, 1 December 1944, 6, and Larry Hollis and Eddie Ferguson, "Barney Kessel," *Cadence* (August 1987): 12–13. My thanks to Victor Schonfeld for supplying me with a copy of the Kessel interview. For further discussion of the film, see Arthur Knight, "*Jammin' the Blues*, or the Sight of Jazz, 1944," in *Representing Jazz*, ed. Krin Gabbard (Durham, NC: Duke University Press, 1995), 11–53.

29. The cultural status of jazz provided a narrative subject for Hawks's *A Song Is Born* (1948), a "jazz" remake of his *Ball of Fire* (1941). A group of cloistered professors is working on an encyclopedic history of music, which they regard as belonging exclusively to the past. Their work is repeatedly disrupted by various exponents of modern music, namely, jazz, including two black window cleaners ("Buck and Bubbles"), who introduce the bemused academics to boogie-woogie; the nightclub singer Honey (Virginia Mayo); and various real-life jazz musicians, both black and white, whom Professor Frisbee (Danny Kaye) encounters on a tentative foray into the jazz world. The narrative satirizes the scholars' unworldliness and draws on long-standing debates about the cultural status of jazz, specifically through the question of its academic recognition. Jazz also works here to subvert traditional social values. The academy, a refuge from post-war social realities, is irrevocably disturbed by Honey, the sexually alluring *femme fatale* who brings into this (all-white) sanctuary not only the music itself but also many of the characteristics often imputed to a jazz *demi-monde*: licentiousness, vice, criminality, and, not least, racial desegregation. In this Hawksian narrative, jam-session jazz becomes a radical force with the power to challenge the status quo of the *ancien régime*,

not only musically, but socially, sexually, and racially as well. Nevertheless, studio hostility to depictions of racially integrated bands had continued after the war. Hawks recounted how, during the making of *A Song Is Born*, the studio, RKO, told him, "Look, now, don't get the Negroes and the white musicians too close together." Hawks characteristically claimed that he refused to comply with any such studio diktat: certainly, the film's jam-session sequences—featuring Louis Armstrong, Benny Goodman, Tommy Dorsey, Lionel Hampton, and others—demonstrate once again Hawks's narrative realization of a racially integrated *mise en scène*. See McBride, *Hawks on Hawks*, 87.

30. Peter Wollen, Introduction, in *Howard Hawks: American Artist*, ed. Jim Hillier and Peter Wollen (London: BFI, 1996), 3.

31. Bacall, *Lauren Bacall*, 96.

32. For an account of these changes, it is instructive to compare the original screenplay with the filmed version. See Bruce F. Kawin, "Notes to the Screenplay," in Kawin, *To Have and Have Not* (Madison: University of Wisconsin Press, 1980), 185–223.

33. John Fawell, "The Musicality of the Filmscript," *Literature Film Quarterly* 17.1 (January 1989): 45.

34. Carmichael recounted in his autobiography how he became typecast in the role. "I was mentioned for every picture in which a world-weary character in bad repair sat around and sang or leaned over a piano." Hoagy Carmichael with Stephen Longstreet, *Sometimes I Wonder. The Stardust Road & Sometimes I Wonder: The Autobiographies of Hoagy Carmichael* (1965; reprint, New York: Da Capo, 1999), 268–69.

35. Ibid., 268.

36. Krin Gabbard, *Jammin' at the Margins: Jazz and the American Cinema* (Chicago: University of Chicago Press, 1996), 260.

37. On Carmichael as a racist construct, see Roger Hewitt, "Black Through White: Hoagy Carmichael and the Cultural Reproduction of Racism," *Popular Music* 3 (1983): 33–50.

38. For a discussion of Carmichael's idiosyncratic song, see Richard M. Sudhalter, *Stardust Memory: The Life and Music of Hoagy Carmichael* (New York: Oxford University Press, 2002), 199–202.

WORKS CITED

Films

Casablanca. Dir. Howard Hawks. Warner Brothers, 1942.
A Song Is Born. Dir. Howard Hawks. RKO, 1947.
To Have and Have Not. Dir. Howard Hawks. Warner Brothers, 1944.

Texts

Bacall, Lauren. *Lauren Bacall: By Myself*. London: Jonathan Cape, 1979.
Basinger, Jeanine. *The World War II Combat Film: Anatomy of a Genre*. New York: Columbia University Press, 1986.

Bogdanovich, Peter. "Howard Hawks: The Rules of the Game." In *Who the Devil Made It: Conversations with Legendary Film Directors*. New York: Ballantine, 1998. 256–378.

Bogle, Donald. *Toms, Coons, Mulattoes, Mammies, and Bucks: An Interpretive History of Blacks in American Films*. Rev. ed. New York: Frederick Ungar, 1989.

Brown, Sterling A. "Spirituals, Blues, and Jazz." *Tricolor*, 1945. Reprinted in Gleason, *Jam Session*. 17–26.

Carmichael, Hoagy, with Stephen Longstreet. *Sometimes I Wonder. The Stardust Road & Sometimes I Wonder: The Autobiographies of Hoagy Carmichael*. 1965. Reprint, New York: Da Capo, 1999. 157–313.

Cripps, Thomas. *Slow Fade to Black: The Negro in American Film, 1900–1942*. 1977. Reprint, New York: Oxford University Press, 1993.

Delaunay, Charles. *Django Reinhardt*. 1961. Trans. Michael James. Reprint, New York: Da Capo, 1982.

Doherty, Thomas. *Projections of War: Hollywood, American Culture, and World War II*. New York: Columbia University Press, 1993.

Emge, Charles. "On the Beat in Hollywood." *Down Beat*, 1 December 1944, 6.

Erenberg, Lewis A. *Swingin' the Dream: Big Band Jazz and the Rebirth of American Culture*. Chicago: University of Chicago Press, 1998.

Fawell, John. "The Musicality of the Filmscript." *Literature Film Quarterly* 17.1 (January 1989): 44–49.

Foner, Jack D. *Blacks and the Military in American History: A New Perspective*. New York: Praeger, 1974.

Gabbard, Krin. *Jammin' at the Margins: Jazz and the American Cinema*. Chicago: University of Chicago Press, 1996.

Gleason, Ralph J., ed. *Jam Session: An Anthology of Jazz*. New York: G. P. Putnam's Sons, 1958.

Gomery, Douglas. *Shared Pleasures: A History of Movie Presentation in the United States*. London: BFI, 1992.

Hewitt, Roger. "Black Through White: Hoagy Carmichael and the Cultural Reproduction of Racism." *Popular Music* 3 (1983): 33–50.

Hillier, Jim, and Peter Wollen, eds. *Howard Hawks: American Artist*. London: BFI, 1996.

Hollis, Larry, and Eddie Ferguson. "Barney Kessel." *Cadence* (August 1987): 5–18, 30.

Kawin, Bruce F., ed. *To Have and Have Not*. Madison: University of Wisconsin Press, 1980.

Knight, Arthur. "*Jammin' the Blues*, or the Sight of Jazz, 1944." In *Representing Jazz*. Ed. Krin Gabbard. Durham, NC: Duke University Press, 1995. 11–53.

Koppes, Clayton R., and Gregory D. Black. "Blacks, Loyalty, and Motion-Picture Propaganda in World War II." *Journal of American History* 73.2 (September 1986): 383–406.

———. *Hollywood Goes to War: How Politics, Profits, and Propaganda Shaped World War II Movies*. New York: Free Press, 1987.

Lingeman, Richard R. *Don't You Know There's a War On? The American Home Front, 1941–1945*. New York: G. P. Putnam's Sons, 1970.

Lopez, Jackie. "Is Hollywood Yielding? Writer Sees Improvement in Type of Parts Given Negroes." *Chicago Defender*, 24 March 1945, 20.

McBride, Joseph. *Hawks on Hawks*. Berkeley: University of California Press, 1982.

McCarthy, Todd. *Howard Hawks: The Grey Fox of Hollywood*. New York: Grove Press, 2000.

McKean, Gilbert S. "The Fabulous Gypsy." *Esquire*, June 1947. Reprinted in Gleason, *Jam Session*. 36–47.

McManus, John T. "Vichy, Bogart, and a Dame." *New York PM*, 12 October 1944. Reprinted in *Motion Picture Critics' Reviews* 1.23 (16 October 1944): 214.

Polan, Dana. *Power and Paranoia: History, Narrative, and the American Cinema, 1940–1950*. New York: Columbia University Press, 1986.

Reddick, L. D. "Educational Programs for the Improvement of Race Relations: Motion Pictures, Radio, the Press, and Libraries." *Journal of Negro Education* 13.3 (Summer 1944): 367–89.

Schatz, Thomas. *Boom and Bust: American Cinema in the 1940s*. Berkeley: University of California Press, 1999.

"Score for the Movies." *The Crisis* 51.10 (October 1944): 312.

Stowe, David W. *Swing Changes: Big Band Jazz in New Deal America*. Cambridge, MA: Harvard University Press, 1994.

Sudhalter, Richard M. *Stardust Memory: The Life and Music of Hoagy Carmichael*. New York: Oxford University Press, 2002.

"*To Have and Have Not:* Pressbook." Warner Brothers, 1944.

Wood, Robin. *Howard Hawks*. Rev. ed. London: BFI, 1981.

Ian Brookes

"No Brotherly Love": Hollywood Jazz, Racial Prejudice, and John Lewis's Score for *Odds Against Tomorrow*

David Butler

African American involvement in Hollywood's "golden age" of the 1930s, '40s, and '50s tends to be discussed in terms of either its absence or its misrepresentation, particularly through the narrow range of stereotypes analyzed in depth by Donald Bogle.[1] I want to focus here on a film that offers a genuine example of cultural "criss-cross." Released in 1959, *Odds Against Tomorrow* features a remarkable score by John Lewis (of the Modern Jazz Quartet) as well as a starring role for Harry Belafonte, whose company, HarBel Productions, produced the film.

Lewis's score is all the more remarkable when seen in the context of the scoring opportunities that were available to African American, and specifically jazz, musicians at the time. Although the 1950s brought a greater use of jazz elements in Hollywood film music, it was still white musicians (particularly those clustered around the California-based Stan Kenton Orchestra, such as Shorty Rogers, Shelly Manne, and Pete Rugolo) who were given the majority of these new opportunities. Even then, the way that jazz was employed by Hollywood was often related to a narrow range of narrative functions and situations. I will discuss briefly the music used in *Sweet Smell of Success* (1957), which had a limited input from Chico Hamilton, before I consider Lewis's excellent score for the late noir *Odds Against Tomorrow*. These two musicians, together with Duke Ellington, who worked on *Anatomy of a Murder* (1959), were among the first black composers to be entrusted with the scoring duties on a major American film, although in Hamilton's case that trust was almost immediately withdrawn again.

First, it is necessary to place these films in the overall context of jazz's relationship with Hollywood. The presentation and use of jazz in mainstream Hollywood films has long been riddled with inaccuracies, myths, and omissions, often shaped by racism and a Eurocentric perspective.[2] This misrepresentation became a constant source of frustration for those in the jazz community;

in 1953, for example, the leading jazz journal *Down Beat* ran an article with the headline "Little of Jazz Interest in 25 Years of Sound Films," while in 1980 the veteran broadcaster Willis Conover complained that jazz musicians appeared in Hollywood productions as either entertainers or "dangerous drug-users or other kinds of criminals."[3] Jazz became a convenient musical signifier of immorality, particularly once the Hays Production Code had been formally enforced in 1934, which restricted filmmakers in terms of the acts and situations they could portray on-screen.

When it comes to this use of jazz as signifier, it is perhaps instructive to look at a pre-1934 item rather than more obvious examples (such as in the gangster films of the 1930s or film noir and social problem dramas of the 1940s). I want to consider a short sequence from the 1921 Harold Lloyd comedy *Never Weaken* as an early instance of the on-screen binary opposition that would set jazz against classical music, even before the advent of sound. Blindfolded and near the top of a skyscraper, Lloyd attempts to shoot himself and mistakenly believes that he has arrived in heaven when he hears some harp music (in reality, a young woman in one of the neighboring apartments practicing a harp solo called "Angel Voices"). It is only when he hears the sound of a group of black jazz musicians far below at street level that he realizes he is still very much alive. Whether the jazz band is intended to represent a hellish noise as opposed to the divine sound of "Angel Voices," or a blast of earthiness that jolts Harold back to his senses, the clear implication is that jazz is the antithesis of sacred music and could not possibly be heard in heaven.

This contrast between classical music and jazz was a recurring theme, explicitly as well as implicitly, in the presentation and use of jazz in Hollywood films from the 1920s to the 1950s. *Never Weaken* is actually quite unusual in that the group it (briefly) portrays is African American: for much of the golden age of Hollywood production, white swing bands, then part of a mainstream culture, were the most visible. Jazz is heard in Hollywood films of the 1930s and '40s almost exclusively as diegetic source music—that is, music that has a visible and therefore justifiable on-screen presence; emanating from a jukebox perhaps or being performed by a band in a nightclub sequence—it is hardly ever associated with the privileged non-diegetic space. It is in this "invisible" realm of the non-diegetic score that characters often have their inner thoughts and unspoken desires, their psychological makeup, expressed musically. Not only was jazz absent from the non-diegetic score, but even in diegetic contexts it tended to be used as music that attacked a character's space and functioned as an aural threat.[4]

David Butler

That situation began to change in the early 1950s for several reasons, including the growing acceptance of jazz as an art music (especially after the advent of bebop), the increasing number of white musicians working in modern jazz styles, and the desperation of the Hollywood studios to find ways of combating the loss of film audiences in the 1950s, due largely to the rise of television. The 1950s, therefore, saw a wider acceptance of jazz as part of the film composer's palette and, following the success of Alex North's music for *A Streetcar Named Desire* (1951), a number of films featuring jazz-inflected scores began to appear. These scores still required a narrative or diegetic justification for the presence of jazz, so they tended to be attached to social problem films, urban crime dramas, and film noir; but now they held out the promise of financial benefits. Both *A Streetcar Named Desire* and Elmer Bernstein's score for the 1955 film *The Man with the Golden Arm* had successful tie-in record releases, which reassured producers and executives of the economic virtues of a jazz presence, although this remained within the provenance of white arrangers and performers.

While they were clearly jazz textured, there was little room for any actual improvisation in these scores, an absence due in part to prevailing film convention. By the 1950s a standardized approach to Hollywood film music had become established that worked in conjunction with the classical Hollywood narrative and editing procedures to ensure that the audience clearly understood character emotion and plot development.[5] As David Bordwell, Janet Staiger, and Kristin Thompson have asserted, classical Hollywood cinema was "excessively obvious" and the same is true of its film music,[6] which functioned to ensure continuity between shots and scenes and, above all, to reinforce spectator identification with the characters and narrative situations. Action, mood, and shifts in psychology tended to be reinforced through the music with pinpoint accuracy, an approach exemplified by composers such as Max Steiner, whose use of the click track enabled him to emphasize on-screen changes with remarkable precision in his scores.[7] Such a model was not seen as amenable to the incorporation of improvisation. In his discussion of Bernstein's score for *The Man with the Golden Arm,* film music scholar Roy Prendergast argues that improvisation is not really appropriate for the split-second timing required by film music if it is to be perfectly synchronized with the on-screen action and situations.[8] This is a restrictive view of the possibilities of the audio-visual relationship: Prendergast assumes a model of film music that is forced to parallel the visuals instead of being able to comment on or work in contrast to them. It also suggests a rather condescending attitude toward the abilities of improving musicians, implying that their playing is imprecise and that they are incapable of making rapid changes (the exact opposite of the musical sensibilities of the beboppers in particular).

Russell Lack has put forward a contrary view that jazz, "supposedly embodying freedom," has worked best in films as a "correlate of personal expression."[9] Rather than celebrating a score that follows the on-screen action at every turn, mimicking, say, a charge downstairs with a downward scalar run or the hero swinging across a crevasse with an expansive glissando, Lack notes the benefits of a more flexible relationship with the image, one in which music takes less notice of action and relates more to a film's or a character's mood and ethos. For Lack, the fluidity of jazz was perfectly suited to new filmmaking techniques and philosophies, such as the French new wave, and, not surprisingly, it was in France that improvisation first made its mark as part of the non-diegetic score.[10]

In the 1950s, several French filmmakers embraced the possibilities offered by jazz improvisation, with the music having a freer relationship to the image. This resulted, in the latter half of the decade, in a number of African American jazz musicians providing film scores that were not merely diegetic backdrops in nightclub scenes. In 1957, Miles Davis, who was touring in France at the time, improvised themes with his French quintet as they watched scenes from Louis Malle's thriller *Ascenseur pour l'echafaud*. Malle then used the resulting music in the film, though not necessarily in the scenes to which Davis and his musicians had originally improvised. In the same year, John Lewis was commissioned to compose the score for *Sait-on jamais* (aka *No Sun in Venice*), directed by Roger Vadim, and he offered in the process a perceptive summation of the way jazz was employed by Hollywood:

> Jazz is often thought to be limited in expression. It is used for "incidental" music or when a situation in a drama or film calls for jazz, but rarely in a more universal way apart from an explicit jazz context. Here it has to be able to run the whole gamut of emotions and carry the story from beginning to end.[11]

The situation in Hollywood remained much as Lewis had described it. The same year that Davis was working on an improvised score in France, the drummer and small-group leader Chico Hamilton was commissioned to provide music for the Alexander Mackendrick–directed film noir *Sweet Smell of Success* (1957). At this point, Hamilton's career was in the ascendancy: he had recently won the best drummer award in *Down Beat*'s annual poll and his quintet was

David Butler

gaining favorable reviews. According to *Down Beat*, Hamilton (along with his colleague, the white cellist Fred Katz) had been commissioned to provide the complete score for *Sweet Smell of Success*—a claim that was confirmed by Katz in a 1986 interview—but during the making of the film, their music was restricted to diegetic club sequences, and Elmer Bernstein was handed the non-diegetic scoring duties.[12] Bernstein employed a conventional approach to the use of jazz textures in his score, again linking it with disreputable activities such as crime and drug abuse, as he had in his earlier score for *The Man with the Golden Arm*.

Sweet Smell of Success is a caustic tale of a corrupt media baron whose sister is dating a modern jazz musician, a guitarist (dubbed by John Pisano) who leads a quintet that happens to feature Chico Hamilton and Fred Katz. The jazz guitarist is the only major character in the film with any sense of integrity (as *Down Beat* commented at the time, "what a blessed relief to see jazz musicians depicted as honest human beings!")[13] and with the courage to oppose the media mogul, J. J. Hunsecker, played by Burt Lancaster. Hunsecker attempts to destroy the musician and end the romance with his sister by printing stories about the musician's involvement with narcotics and the Communist Party. In terms of the narrative, these themes were standard justification for a jazz-inflected score: urban immorality, corruption, and psychological desperation. Yet Hamilton's presence in the film is an unusual one for an African American musician: in his few moments of screen time, his character is able to convey confidence, intellect, and a sense of detached cool. Similarly, Hamilton's band plays a music that had not been heard before from an African American musician in a major Hollywood film: with its mixed personnel of black and white musicians and unusual instrumentation—drums, bass, electric guitar, flute, and cello (the latter two being less typical of jazz)—the group's "chamber jazz" sensibility blurs the traditional distinction that Hollywood made between black jazz, usually portrayed as hot, rhythmic, and impulsive, and white classical music, often encoded as serious, intellectual, and thus culturally superior.

The same cannot be said for Bernstein's non-diegetic score. Although functionally effective, his music makes use of a familiar shorthand: big band textures and bluesy intonation are reserved for night-time shots of the city with its sleaze and corruption, whereas the white couple's romance is played out to the accompaniment of large-scale, legato string orchestration (which might seem odd given that one of the lovers is a jazz guitarist). Bernstein's swaggering big band motif for the corrupt city and its denizens (which is also the film's title music) is very much in the same idiom as his main theme for *The Man with the Golden Arm* and typifies the approach to jazz scoring that prevailed in Hollywood from the mid-'50s onward.

There were some more nuanced jazz-inflected scores during this time, such as Johnny Mandel's music for *I Want to Live!* (1958), but, as Bernstein acknowledged in an interview with Tony Thomas, the connotations that jazz had acquired in film music ("sleaziness, crime, juvenile delinquency, drug addiction") were not easy to resist:

> We're born into a society that has inherited all sorts of prejudices—racial, religious and even musical, and this one concerning jazz, like most prejudices, has its roots in truth or reality at some point. . . . It is a subtle prejudice and I find myself fighting it within myself. The times I've used jazz to color my music have been in films with sleazy atmospheres—*The Man with the Golden Arm* was about narcotics, *Sweet Smell of Success* dealt with some very unsavoury characters in New York, and *Walk on the Wild Side* was largely set in a New Orleans house of ill repute. So I'm guilty, although I don't think it's necessary to use jazz in this way. It's simply something that is very difficult to avoid.[14]

These 1950s scores, by Bernstein and others, tended to have a consistent sound, one which Philip Tagg has analyzed expertly in his article "Tritonal Crime and 'Music as Music.'"[15] For Tagg, the common denominators included the use of a minor mode, a significant amount of chromaticism, and the prominent use of tritones.[16] Many of these scores also revealed a strictly limited imagination in relation to the possibilities that jazz offered to film: often there was the merest allusion to jazz, achieved through particular instrumentation rather than improvisation—as Claudia Gorbman noted, a score might include no jazz other than the brief use of a saxophone to imply female sexuality.[17]

In 1959, however, John Lewis's music for *Odds Against Tomorrow* revealed a more sensitive and original approach to the possible uses of jazz in cinema. Lewis's score incorporates improvisation in a way previously unheard in a Hollywood film. It also avoids the standard jazz clichés, even though the film's genre and narrative—a film noir about a bank raid that goes wrong, focusing on crime and seduction—could easily have resulted in a conventional Hollywood treatment of jazz.

But *Odds Against Tomorrow* did not come from a mainstream Hollywood studio. It was an independent film made by Harry Belafonte's HarBel Productions with support from United Artists. By the late 1950s, Belafonte was established as an entertainer and musician—helping to launch the calypso craze in the process—but he was keen to pursue serious acting roles as well (interviewed in *Down Beat* in 1957, he had expressed a desire to "do a solid piece of contemporary drama dealing with life per se").[18] By setting up his own production company, Belafonte was able to secure creative control over the project and enlist the talents of those individuals that he wanted to work with. The source for the film was a 1957 book of the same name by William P. McGivern, and the on-screen credits for the screenplay listed the white screenwriter Nelson Gidding and the black novelist John O. Killens. Both names, however, were fronts—a smokescreen designed to cover the identity of the film's actual screenwriter, Abraham Polonsky, a victim of the anti-communist witch hunts. It was Belafonte who brought the blacklisted Polonsky aboard and arranged the John O. Killens cover story, as well as employing the director Robert Wise. And it was Belafonte who recommended that Wise bring in the talents of John Lewis.[19]

The liberal and progressive credentials of this team were impressive. Robert Wise had just finished work on the acclaimed social problem film, *I Want to Live!* (1958), which, as stated above, had made notable use of a modern jazz-based score by Johnny Mandel, with features for saxophonist Gerry Mulligan and trumpeter Art Farmer. Even in the 1951 sci-fi movie *The Day the Earth Stood Still*, Wise had revealed an ability to bring intelligence and a social conscience to what might otherwise have been a run-of-the-mill genre film. There were no such worries with *Odds Against Tomorrow*, even if the film appeared on the surface to be a typical noir-heist movie, drawing on such predecessors as *The Asphalt Jungle* (1950) and *White Heat* (1949). Belafonte had insisted at the time that the film was not explicitly about race. Interviewed in the *New York Times*, he observed:

> The character I play is not thrown in for a racial thesis, but because the bank robbers—played by Ed Begley and Robert Ryan—need a Negro who can enter the bank as a colored delivery man. While Robert Ryan hates the Negro, it is not merely a racial antagonism. He hates everybody, and the Negro is no stereotype of sweetness and light either. No brotherly love saves everyone here. Their hatred destroys them both.[20]

But, years later, he acknowledged that the film, although not specifically about race, did change the Hollywood landscape with its portrayal of African

American characters and the involvement of African American personnel at "the production end of the major film industry":

> Abe [Polonsky] took on the task of creating a black man's relationship to the world that had never been seen before. . . . When he [Belafonte's character] turns to the red neck who's giving him a hard time, they look at each other and you know there's no quarter here. There'll be no massa. Already the character's heroic and he hasn't done anything except just play his dignity and his strength as a person. . . . The audience's senses were being bombarded by the way this character moved through this part.[21]

(Indeed, the film was nominated for a 1960 Golden Globe award as a motion picture "promoting international understanding.")

Odds Against Tomorrow follows the efforts of an unlikely trio of criminals, led by former cop Burke (Ed Begley), to rob a bank. The antagonism between the other two members of the gang, Johnny Ingram, a jazz musician and chronic gambler (Belafonte), and a racist ex-con, Earle Slater (Robert Ryan), threatens to undermine the heist and results in an explosive shoot-out on top of a gas works that destroys both men. When the authorities pick through the ashen remains in a futile attempt to identify "which is which," they are told "take your pick," and the film closes with a shot of a sign saying "STOP! DEAD END" before panning down to a muddy puddle, mirroring the film's opening shot. Similarly, Lewis's score ends with exactly the same musical phrase that began the film (excluding the opening and closing credits): a two-note phrase for Jim Hall's electric guitar; a sparse, stripped-down orchestration that gives the film a cyclical quality and suggests that the same narrative pattern of hatred and mistrust will keep repeating.

If this ending (which was altered from Polonsky's more optimistic finale by Wise) seems heavy-handed social commentary, it nonetheless underlines the film's subtext about the need for racial harmony and the blurring of distinctions between black and white. The film makes no moral judgment between Ingram and Slater (and neither, significantly, does Lewis's score). Robert Ryan noted his distaste for the beliefs of his character and added that he only felt comfortable with the role when he realized that Slater was a misanthrope in general, and not just a racist. He also thought that the script established Belafonte's character as "the most dignified, intelligent and superior person in the drama."[22] Yet both men are depicted as flawed and, although Johnny may be the more likable

David Butler

character, the film does not demonize Slater as an obvious caricature of a bigot but presents him as a thwarted human being, unable to escape his prejudices and frustration. Interviewed by John Schultheiss in 1998, Belafonte asserted that:

> Slater is more than just a racist. He is a working class guy in America who gets trapped by the system . . . and has bought the story that it is race that is causing him to fail. He doesn't have a job, he's looking for a way out. He's in exactly the same stuff Ingram's in.[23]

Schultheiss argues that the film's script establishes the two men as perverse doubles of each other, in terms of their frustrated desires to escape from the circumstances in which they feel trapped (and, I would suggest, Lewis is equally aware of the parallels between Slater and Ingram in terms of the psychological and emotional functions that his score fulfills).[24] The film's opening credits highlight the subtext of racial oppositions being collapsed, contrasting a black background with white lettering, then a negative image of the same followed by shifting patterns of black, white, and gray as spots, veins, and blotches become blurred, overlapping and mixing into each other, foreshadowing the film's ending. This visual portrayal of the breakdown between black and white is further expressed through the film's striking cinematography (by Joseph Brun), which emphasizes shades of gray (a conscious strategy by Wise), particularly in the extensive location filming shot under a winter sun. Rather than the sharp distinctions between blacks and whites typical of noir cinematography, with its tendency toward low-key, high-contrast lighting, *Odds Against Tomorrow* carefully fosters a distinctive gray look.

These dissolutions of the white-black dualism found the perfect correlate in the choice of John Lewis to compose the film's score. His small group, the Modern Jazz Quartet (MJQ), was as well known for its emphasis on classical forms and influences, such as the fugue and baroque counterpoint, as for its expertise at improvisation. As Gary Kramer observed in his original sleeve notes to Lewis's recording of the *Sait-on jamais* score, compositions such as "The Golden Striker" and "Cortege," both composed by Lewis for the Vadim film, point up "a duality, European and American Negro, in the psychological roots and musical resources of the composer."[25] Lewis's music, with its combination of African American and European elements, contravened the usual Hollywood prejudice, which kept classical and jazz music in separate categories. (The tension inherent in the MJQ, between Lewis's finely structured compositions and the flowing, blues-inflected improvisations of vibraharpist Milt Jackson, perhaps functions as a metaphor for the film's narrative about disparate characters working together as they try to transcend their individual circumstances.)

The most remarkable example of this overlap between European and African American music in relation to Slater and Ingram takes place when the gang make their way to the town of Melton, where the bank raid will take place. By this stage in the film, Ingram has been established as a vibraharpist and jazz singer through a memorable nightclub sequence. The lead-in to the club sequence has Slater in close-up telling Burke that there's only one problem with the plan: "You didn't say nothing about the third man being a nigger." In a trademark piece of Wise editing, there is a sudden cut to a close-up of Johnny singing a blues at the vibraharp, with the first few words of the song heard over the preceding shot of Slater. Already, the two men's lives are overlapping, even though they have not actually met yet in the film (a textbook example of Eisensteinian collision). But Lewis's score goes even further during the journey to Melton, when Slater is testing the speed of the getaway car on the highway. As he puts his foot down on the accelerator and breaks into a smile, Lewis introduces a four-note rhythmic ostinato that gives Milt Jackson the opportunity to take an extended vibes solo for almost sixty seconds, until Slater's surge of elation is over.

What makes this sequence so striking is that Slater, a white racist, has his moment of emotional freedom accompanied by an improvised jazz solo played on the instrument diegetically associated with his colleague Johnny, the black jazz musician for whom he has nothing but contempt. Lewis underlines here, far more explicitly than anything in the script, the breakdown of the duality between Johnny and Slater. This point is of major significance—black jazz is employed to convey the innermost feelings of a white character. The composer Quincy Jones, who established his lengthy Hollywood film career in the 1960s, reported that Hollywood producers often assumed that, as a black musician, he would not be able to empathize with the white characters in a film. Interviewed in 1975, he explained how his reputation as a black composer and arranger in jazz had limited the range of film projects he was offered. According to Gene Lees:

When Quincy Jones was hired to write the score for one of his first movies, the producer had never met him. "And the cat . . . didn't know I was black until we came face to face. Then he became concerned whether I could relate to a love scene between Gregory Peck and Diane Baker. And I remember that producer said, 'I don't want any blues or Count Basie in this picture.' Y'know, as if I hadn't put in my time with Bartok and Brahms, like everybody else."[26]

David Butler

The use of African American improvisation as the "sound" that expresses a white character's psychology provides *Odds Against Tomorrow* with a genuinely subversive moment in terms of crossing the racial divide.

Scott DeVeaux has observed that the employment of black arrangers by the white swing bands of the 1930s helped to break down the unacknowledged racial barriers in musical repertory.[27] Similarly perhaps, Milt Jackson's vibes solo, in expressing a white character's feelings, functions as a moment of audio-visual miscegenation. The portrayal of mixed-race relationships was still a sensitive area for Hollywood productions at the time *Odds Against Tomorrow* was made, and miscegenation would remain a concern of the crumbling Production Code long after attitudes toward on-screen portrayals of, say, violence and narcotics were relaxing. (Two years after *Odds* was released, the makers of *Paris Blues* were forced to backtrack on their mixed-race romance plot, a decision that angered Duke Ellington, who had agreed to score the film on the understanding that it would remain faithful to the source novel's mixed-race romance). In this respect, John Lewis's score is several years in advance of Quincy Jones's groundbreaking score for *The Pawnbroker* (1965), which has rightly been acknowledged as an important breakthrough in musical miscegenation, not least because of its instrumentation. Jones was the first African American composer of a Hollywood score to employ the string section, long perceived as the preserve of the European symphony orchestra. Philip Brophy has celebrated this innovatory mixing:

> Reflecting a developing black consciousness that equally affected black and white America, the score for *The Pawnbroker* is among the first dark drops which would eventually allow film scores to sound overtly jazzy and funky. It is notable for its detailed combination of an urban black sensibility with a studied and perfected European-style mode of orchestration. Moments in *The Pawnbroker* deftly and cunningly slide between the two.[28]

Much the same can be said of Lewis's score for *Odds Against Tomorrow*, which also incorporates instruments not normally associated with jazz orchestration. Whereas he scored *Sait-on jamais* for the Modern Jazz Quartet, Lewis's music for *Odds* features a much larger orchestra yet creates, nonetheless, a cold, austere soundscape. Though still using his fellow members of the MJQ, Lewis expanded the group to a twenty-three-piece orchestra. There are prominent parts for harp and electric guitar (played by Jim Hall) as well as a second pianist (Bill Evans), with additional parts for celli and flutes. But the bulk of the orchestration centers on the brass (trombone, trumpet, tuba, and French horn): cold, hard, airy timbres. Indeed, the overall impression is of a chill, wintry sound that matches the crisp cinematography, desolate exteriors, and frequent harsh winds on the soundtrack. As Michelle Best outlines:

> The music for the film has a hard and lean sound. Lewis uses standard jazz harmonies and dissonant tones to create tension along with note bending and shifting rhythms. There are no love themes in the score because there is no real love for anyone in the picture.[29]

That is a rather reductive summary. There is a lot of dissonance to be sure, and Lewis expertly realizes the suggestions in Polonsky's script that the music be "in a modern, moody, sometimes progressive jazz vein, carrying an overtone of premonition, of tragedy—of people in trouble and doomed."[30] Yet there are playful, even exuberant, moments in the music, too. Slater's freedom when racing the car has already been discussed, and the Harry Belafonte character, Johnny Ingram, is introduced with a lyrical theme for the flute and vibes, which is all the more poignant for offering a respite from the score's general sense of foreboding. These lighter moods seldom last though, as Lewis seems only too aware of the underlying tensions and frustrations felt by the characters. An excellent example of the score's psychological astuteness is a scene where Ingram, Slater, and Burke are planning the bank heist that will ultimately result in their deaths. Ingram suggests how the heist can be pulled off and he and Burke share a brief moment of euphoria. A lone trumpet ascends a scale optimistically as Slater looks on, smiles, and then turns away almost immediately, the trumpet falling in a descending pattern as he does so. Slater cannot share in this moment of solidarity because of his racism, and he is unable to look at the two men celebrating. All three characters are in shot. Burke holds Ingram's face, then the camera pans right to focus on and isolate Slater spatially, removing the other men from the shot. The descending scale is a simple but effective means by which Lewis conveys the emotional repression within Slater. Rather than implying a negative moral judgment (perhaps through dissonance or an obviously malevolent phrase), Lewis chooses instead to convey the melancholia that dominates him; tellingly, his theme for the character is titled "No Happiness for Slater."

Lewis's choice of orchestration is significant for another reason: the absence of a saxophone section. The instrument's textural warmth is lost but so also are the associations that had been tethered to the saxophone within Hollywood film scoring. I have already referred to the standard Hollywood practice (quoting Claudia Gorbman) to "introduce its seductress on the screen by means of a sultry saxophone playing a Gershwinesque melody."[31] There is a seduction scene in *Odds Against Tomorrow* but Lewis scores it, in part, for the vibrapharp playing a chromatic phrase and sounding not unlike a celesta. The instrument evokes childhood (typically, a music box) and the chromatic blues phrasing lost innocence. This, too, reaffirms one of the underlying themes of the film, since all of the characters are seeking to escape the present and either secure an improbable future or return to a mythical past. In one telling scene, just after he has been beaten up by local gangsters, Johnny plays the vibrapharp in a drunken stupor at the club where his band is in residence. Though he takes his anger out on the vibes, it is not mindless chaos that he plays. Instead his music reverts to childhood and he bangs out simple chord progressions as if playing a child's toy piano. "That little boy's in big trouble," comments the female singer as Johnny tries to make musical sense of his world.

The seduction scene itself takes place between Slater and his neighbor Helen (Gloria Grahame), when she knocks on his apartment door. The pair have rowed earlier in the day over his refusal to baby-sit for (and flirt with) her. Now Slater invites Helen into the apartment and kisses her hand to make up. Lewis suggests the menace and transgression in this scene without resorting to any obvious "jazziness." The scene is initially scored for rolls of timpani, taut stutters of snare drum, and short phrases played in the lower register of the bowed bass, either a single sustained note or a two-note phrase ascending chromatically. The martial qualities of the snare drum also add to the sense of threat that is being musically generated at the outset of this scene; Helen is indeed playing a dangerous game, as once in the apartment she goads Slater and, as he correctly perceives, "dares him" to take advantage of her. The initial music is clearly non-diegetic but, once Helen accepts Slater's invitation of a drink, the score segues into what sounds like high-class cocktail party music: it then develops into an extended jazz piece for Lewis's piano, with bass and drums (the cue is titled "A Social Call" on the recording of themes from the film), and is centered around double-time phrasing. This piano trio jazz functions anempathetically in relation to the mind games Helen is playing with Slater in that it is not related to specific actions and dialogue.[32] The music continues, almost as if diegetically, even though there is no obvious on-screen source for it, irrespective of where Slater and Helen are heading and the somewhat perverse nature of their conversation. It is only when Helen's housecoat falls open, revealing her brassiere, and she closes it (with a "shameful sense of nakedness" as Polonsky's script describes it)[33] that the jazz stops and the score becomes clearly non-diegetic and cued to the action again. A descending harp phrase and piano runs are introduced, a musical "fall" cued to what is clearly now going to be a moral fall, then a sustained soft brass chord sounds as Slater goes to the apartment door and locks it, before returning, with music now absent, to Helen, who agrees to "just this once" as they kiss, ending the scene.

What is refreshing throughout this seduction scene is the avoidance of stereotypical jazz sounds and phrasing to imply sexual transgression. The piano solo that runs throughout the center of the scene is only introduced after the initial transgression has taken place and is replaced with a clearly arranged sequence the moment that Slater's actions make it clear that he intends to have sex with Helen. Similarly, much earlier in the film, Burke outlines the heist to Slater as the camera gives us their point of view of the street where the raid will take place. This scene, as the robbers discuss the crime, would be an obvious place for a stereotypical use of jazz. Again, Lewis rejects the hackneyed formula of "crime jazz": in sharp contrast, jazz is only introduced with the sudden cut to the next scene, where Johnny is singing in the nightclub. Writing about this crime scene, Martin Myrick comments that the music features a "medium jazz march-shuffle."[34] But there is actually no sense of jazz or swing at all. In fact, Lewis opts for something less jazz-like and more original. The score at this point is restricted to the timpani and emphatic snare drum, as if it is a military operation that is being planned.

Without the saxophone, Lewis's score is free of the most basic indicator of jazz and also of many of the corresponding themes that jazz was supposed to signify. In fact, his score is more in keeping with the ethos of what would soon become known as third stream music, a fusion of jazz and classical elements, with which he was closely associated. Another leading exponent of the third stream school, Gunther Schuller, conducted the score.[35] In his sleeve notes for the MJQ recording of themes from the film, Schuller demonstrated an awareness of the originality of Lewis's score, not just in musicological terms but also in terms of the characters, themes, and narrative that it accompanied. He noted that the music was not just a fully fledged cinematic score used for "dramatic situations *not* necessarily related to jazz," but that it could also "stand as absolute music apart from the film . . . [to] achieve a new dimension as pure jazz material in the repertory of one of the great chamber ensembles of our time."[36]

David Butler

Despite the praise that Lewis received for his work on the film (Robert Wise sent him a letter saying he was "damned glad we have you doing it"),[37] *Odds Against Tomorrow* did not result in a lengthy film career for the composer. Two albums of music relating to the film were released; one, the music as heard in the film, and the other, MJQ interpretations of six of the film's musical cues.[38] These pieces, particularly "Skating in Central Park" and "Odds Against Tomorrow," the film's elegiac title theme, would feature regularly in MJQ performances, even though "Skating in Central Park" was heard only briefly in the film (and as a piece of Tannoy Muzak at that, playing as children and families do indeed skate in Central Park). Following *Odds*, Lewis worked on another European production, *A Milanese Story* (1962), then came a lengthy gap until he wrote a series of scores in 1971 for Rod Serling's TV series *Night Gallery*.[39]

The dearth of opportunities available to Lewis in the wake of *Odds Against Tomorrow* is frustrating, to say the least, and a further example of the lack of imagination in the mainstream film industry. *Odds Against Tomorrow* is an outstanding score and not simply because it is one of the few by an African American composer for a major American film of the period. In its avoidance of jazz film cliché, its emphasis on character psychology, and its subversive use of improvisation, Lewis's music pointed the way to a significant change in film history. However, prevailing attitudes among Hollywood producers (as Quincy Jones put it, the assumption often being that he could only "do cop pictures")[40] ensured that jazz was rarely going to be allowed to "speak for itself" or demonstrate a wider emotional and thematic range than the urban crime setting. But given the freedom to be more original, John Lewis and his score for *Odds Against Tomorrow* at least provide a tantalizing glimpse of what might have been.

NOTES

1. Donald Bogle, *Toms, Coons, Mulattoes, Mammies, and Bucks: An Interpretive History of Blacks in American Films*, 3rd ed. (Oxford: Roundhouse, 1994).
2. For a more extensive discussion of the representation of jazz in American film and the ideological forces that shaped its use, see Krin Gabbard, *Jammin' at the Margins: Jazz and the American Cinema* (Chicago: University of Chicago Press, 1996); and David Butler, *Jazz Noir: Listening to Music from "Phantom Lady" to "The Last Seduction"* (Westport, CT: Praeger, 2002).

3. Charles Emge, "Little of Jazz Interest in 25 Years of Sound Films," *Down Beat*, 26 August 1953, 3; Willis Conover, "Jazz in the Media: A Personal View," *Jazz Forschung* 12.36 (1980): 36.

4. Examples of this use of jazz as an aural diegetic threat include *The Big Combo* (1955), where a bop drum solo on the radio is blasted into the ear of the protagonist as a torture device, and *D.O.A.* (1950), where the protagonist is disoriented during a frenzied sax solo by Illinois Jacquet and has his drink spiked with a lethal toxin in his confusion. See Butler, *Jazz Noir*, 68–71, 192–94.

5. For an overview of the development of film music convention, see Russell Lack, *Twenty Four Frames Under: A Buried History of Film Music* (London: Quartet Books, 1997), 112–48.

6. David Bordwell, Janet Staiger, and Kristin Thompson, *The Classical Hollywood Cinema: Film Style and Mode of Production to 1960* (New York: Columbia University Press, 1985).

7. Steiner was the most prolific composer during the classical studio era, and his score for *King Kong* (1933) did much to establish extensive non-diegetic music as a viable and even essential aspect of classical Hollywood filmmaking. His late-romantic orchestral scoring tended to emphasize action and emotion at every available point. See Claudia Gorbman, *Unheard Melodies: Narrative Film Music* (London: British Film Institute, 1987), 7.

8. Roy M. Prendergast, *Film Music: A Neglected Art*, 2nd ed. (New York: W. W. Norton, 1992), 117.

9. Lack, *Twenty Four Frames Under*, 201.

10. Ibid., 197.

11. Quoted in Gary Kramer, untitled CD insert notes to *No Sun in Venice* by the Modern Jazz Quartet (1957; reissue, Atlantic 1284, 1991), n.p.

12. See Don Gold, "Katz and the Fiddle," *Down Beat*, 3 October 1957, 27; and Leslie Zador, "Interview with Fred Katz," *The Cue Sheet: The Newsletter of the Society for the Preservation of Film Music* 3.2 (1986): 18.

13. Hal Holly, "Review of *Sweet Smell of Success*," *Down Beat*, 8 August 1957, 35.

14. Quoted in Tony Thomas, *Music for the Movies* (South Brunswick, NJ: A.S. Barnes, 1977), 190–91.

15. Philip Tagg, "Tritonal Crime and 'Music as Music.'" Philip Tagg Homepage, 19 December 2001. Available at http://www.mediamusicstudies.net/tagg/articles/xpdfs/morric70.pdf. Accessed 4 November 2004.

16. Ibid., 5.

17. Gorbman, *Unheard Melodies*, 3.

18. Dom Cerulli, "Belafonte: Where to From Here?" *Down Beat*, 4 April 1957, 17.

19. As Wise would later recollect: "The nature of the story *Odds Against Tomorrow* seemed to lend itself to jazz music which is why I chose it. I discussed this with Harry Belafonte who suggested that I use John Lewis . . . he made a fine contribution to the picture with his music. We had no problems at all in regard to employing a black musician or his group. It seems most artists respect other artists and admire their talents." Robert Wise, "Re: Quotes from Robert Wise," e-mail to the author, 14 January 2003.

20. Interview in the *New York Times*, cited by Jeff Stafford, "Odds Against Tomorrow," *Black History Month: The Black Experience in Cinema*, 22 October 2004. Available at www.turnerclassicmovies.com/ThisMonth/Article/ 0,,17688%7C17689%7C17736,00.html. Accessed 4 November 2004.

21. Quoted in John Schultheiss, "Critical Commentary—*Odds Against Tomorrow*: Film Noir Without Linguistic Irony," in *Odds Against Tomorrow: The Critical Edition*, ed. John Schultheiss (Northridge: Center for Telecommunication Studies, California State University, 1999), 250–52, 292.

22. Quoted in John Schultheiss, "Annotations to the Screenplay," in Schultheiss, *Odds Against Tomorrow*, 153.

23. Quoted in ibid., 151.

24. Ibid.

25. Kramer, CD insert notes, *No Sun in Venice*.

26. Quincy Jones, interviewed by Gene Lees, in Lees, "Adventures of a Black Composer in Hollywood," *New York Times*, 16 March 1975, sec. 2: 21.

27. Scott DeVeaux, *The Birth of Bebop: A Social and Musical History* (Berkeley: University of California Press, 1997), 123–24.

28. Philip Brophy, *100 Modern Soundtracks* (London: British Film Institute, 2004), 174.

29. Michelle Best, "John Lewis and the Film Score for *Odds Against Tomorrow*: II," in Schultheiss, *Odds Against Tomorrow*, 310.

30. Extract from Polonsky's screenplay, in Schultheiss, *Odds Against Tomorrow*, 14.

31. Gorbman, *Unheard Melodies*, 3.

32. Michel Chion defines anempathetic music as, "Indifferent music (which) has the effect not of freezing emotion but rather of intensifying it. The anempathetic impulse in the cinema produces those countless musical bits from player pianos, celestas, music boxes, and dance bands, whose studied frivolity and naïveté reinforce the individual emotion of the character and of the spectator, even as the music pretends not to notice them." Michel Chion, *Audio-Vision: Sound on Screen* (New York: Columbia University Press, 1994), 8.

33. Extract from Polonsky's screenplay, in Schultheiss, *Odds Against Tomorrow*, 89.

34. Martin C. Myrick, "John Lewis and the Film Score for *Odds Against Tomorrow*: I," in Schultheiss, *Odds Against Tomorrow*, 147.

35. It was Schuller who, in 1960, coined the term *third stream*.

36. Gunther Schuller, untitled CD insert notes to *Music from Odds Against Tomorrow* by the Modern Jazz Quartet (1959; reissue, Blue Note CDP 7 93415 2, 1990), n.p.

37. Letter from Robert Wise to John Lewis, quoted in Butler, *Jazz Noir*, 152.

38. The film score was released as John Lewis, *Odds Against Tomorrow* (1959; reissue, Sony AK 47487, 1991). For the MJQ release, see note 36.

39. A thorough assessment of these scores is, sadly, hampered by their current unavailability on CD or vinyl, although *Night Gallery* has recently been released on DVD.

40. Quoted in Lees, "Adventures of a Black Composer," 21.

WORKS CITED

Films

Anatomy of a Murder. Dir. Otto Preminger. Music, Duke Ellington and Billy Strayhorn. Columbia, 1959.

Ascenseur pour l'echafaud. Dir. Louis Malle. Music, Miles Davis. Lux Films, 1957.

I Want to Live! Dir. Robert Wise. Music, Johnny Mandel. United Artists, 1958.

The Man with the Golden Arm. Dir. Otto Preminger. Music, Elmer Bernstein. United Artists, 1955.

Never Weaken. Dir. Fred C. Newmeyer. Silent film. Pathé, 1921.

Odds Against Tomorrow. Dir. Robert Wise. Music, John Lewis. United Artists, 1959.

The Pawnbroker. Dir. Sidney Lumet. Music, Quincy Jones. American International Pictures, 1965.

Sait-on jamais. Dir. Roger Vadim. Music, John Lewis. Released in France in 1957; distributed in the United States by Kingsley-International Pictures, 1958.

A Streetcar Named Desire. Dir. Elia Kazan. Music, Alex North. Warner Bros., 1951.

Sweet Smell of Success. Dir. Alexander Mackendrick. Music, Elmer Bernstein, Chico Hamilton, Fred Katz. United Artists, 1957.

Recordings

Lewis, John. *Odds Against Tomorrow*. 1959. Reissue, Sony AK 47487, 1991.

Modern Jazz Quartet. *Music from Odds Against Tomorrow*. 1959. Reissue, Blue Note CDP 7 93415 2, 1990.

———. *No Sun in Venice*. 1957. Reissue, Atlantic 1284, 1991.

Texts

Best, Michelle. "John Lewis and the Film Score for *Odds Against Tomorrow*: II." In Schultheiss, *Odds Against Tomorrow*. 309–13.

Bogle, Donald. *Toms, Coons, Mulattoes, Mammies, and Bucks: An Interpretive History of Blacks in American Films*. 3rd ed. Oxford: Roundhouse, 1994.

Bordwell, David, Janet Staiger, and Kristin Thompson. *The Classical Hollywood Cinema: Film Style and Mode of Production to 1960*. New York: Columbia University Press, 1985.

Brophy, Philip. *100 Modern Soundtracks*. London: British Film Institute, 2004.

Butler, David. *Jazz Noir: Listening to Music from "Phantom Lady" to "The Last Seduction."* Westport, CT: Praeger, 2002.

Cerulli, Dom. "Belafonte: Where to From Here?" *Down Beat*, 4 April 1957, 17.

Chion, Michel. *Audio-Vision: Sound on Screen*. New York: Columbia University Press, 1994.

Conover, Willis. "Jazz in the Media: A Personal View." *Jazz Forschung* 12.36 (1980): 35–40.

DeVeaux, Scott. *The Birth of Bebop: A Social and Musical History*. Berkeley: University of California Press, 1997.

Emge, Charle. "Little of Jazz Interest in 25 Years of Sound Films." *Down Beat*,
26 August 1953, 3

Gabbard, Krin. *Jammin' at the Margins: Jazz and the American Cinema*. Chicago:
University of Chicago Press, 1996.

Gold, Don. "Katz and the Fiddle." *Down Beat*, 3 October 1957, 35.

Gorbman, Claudia. *Unheard Melodies: Narrative Film Music*. London: British
Film Institute, 1987.

Holly, Hal. "Review of *Sweet Smell of Success*." *Down Beat*, 8 August 1957, 27.

Kramer, Gary. Untitled CD insert notes. *No Sun in Venice*. By the Modern Jazz
Quartet. Atlantic 1284, 1991. N.p.

Lack, Russell. *Twenty Four Frames Under: A Buried History of Film Music*. London: Quartet Books, 1997.

Lees, Gene. "Adventures of a Black Composer in Hollywood." *New York Times*,
16 March 1975, sec 2: 21.

Myrick, Martin C. "John Lewis and the Film Score for *Odds Against Tomorrow*: I."
In Schultheiss, *Odds Against Tomorrow*. 299–307.

Prendergast, Roy M. *Film Music: A Neglected Art*. 2nd ed. New York:
W. W. Norton, 1992.

Schuller, Gunther. Untitled CD insert notes. *Music from "Odds Against Tomorrow."* By the Modern Jazz Quartet. Blue Note CDP 7 93415 2, 1990. N.p.

Schultheiss, John. "Critical Commentary—*Odds Against Tomorrow*: Film Noir
Without Linguistic Irony." In Schultheiss, *Odds Against Tomorrow*. 165–298.

———. "Annotation to the Screenplay." In Schultheiss, *Odds Against Tomorrow*.
137–64.

———, ed. *Odds Against Tomorrow: The Critical Edition*. Northridge: Center for
Telecommunication Studies, California State University, 1999.

Thomas, Tony. *Music for the Movies*. South Brunswick, NJ: A.S. Barnes, 1977.

Zador, Leslie. "Interview with Fred Katz." *The Cue Sheet: The Newsletter of the Society for the Preservation of Film Music* 3.2 (1986): 18–22.

Web Sites

Stafford, Jeff. "Odds Against Tomorrow." *Black History Month: The Black Experience in Cinema*. 22 October 2004. Available at www.turnerclassicmovies
.com/ThisMonth/Article/0,17688%7C17689%7C17736,00.html. Accessed
4 November 2004.

Tagg, Philip. "Tritonal Crime and 'Music as Music.'" Philip Tagg Homepage.
19 December 2001. Available at http://www.mediamusicstudies.net/tagg/
articles/xpdfs/morric70.pdf. Accessed 4 November 2004.

TWELVE

Anatomy of a Movie: Duke Ellington and 1950s Film Scoring

Mervyn Cooke

Music in pictures should say something without being obviously music, you know, and this was all new to me.

—Duke Ellington (1959)

Duke Ellington's and Billy Strayhorn's music for Otto Preminger's feature film *Anatomy of a Murder* (1959) came at the end of a watershed decade in the history of film music.[1] The diversification of musical styles and techniques in narrative cinema at this time had been partly caused by momentous changes in the film industry, although these musical developments coincided with what in any case seemed set to have been a period of enhanced experimentation on the part of both directors and composers. Several trends from the 1950s were to have a lasting impact on film music: the consolidation and expansion of existing orchestral scoring associated with the burgeoning of big-budget genres such as ancient and biblical epics; the growth of science fiction and fantasy, both of which by their very nature demanded imaginative music that was out of the ordinary; and an enhanced public awareness of how much an individual composer's contribution could add to the overall success of a film. This was also the decade in which title and theme song sales became an important source of additional revenue for film studios whose finances were ailing under the strain of competition from the massive boom in domestic television viewing. Not only did the latest popular music come to be featured in movies, but an emerging youth culture also began to shape the tastes and preoccupations of cinema both in America and across the globe.

Toward the end of the decade, conditions for composers and performers working in the film industry became somewhat unstable owing to litigation and industrial action relating to copyright and working-practice issues, and in 1958 strikes by musicians' unions in both the United States and Europe effectively killed off the concept of permanent studio orchestras that had formerly prevailed. As directors worked increasingly on independent productions, so musical provision for their films became of necessity more flexible and economical than it had ever been before. With the flouting and subsequent collapse of the draconian Production Code that had stunted the subject matter of Hollywood films for two decades, both the topics and style of narrative cinema became more hard-hitting in their often gritty realism. This departure prompted certain musically sensitive directors—notably Elia Kazan, Otto Preminger, and Nicholas Ray—to encourage composers to provide music in idioms far more adventurous than the overripe romanticism that had flavored so many golden-age Hollywood pictures with a sense of beckoning utopia.[2] With this new interest in musical modernism, most obviously heard in Leonard Rosenman's partly atonal orchestral music for the 1955 James Dean vehicles *East of Eden* (dir. Kazan) and *Rebel without a Cause* (dir. Ray), came a reappraisal of the creative possibilities of jazz in film soundtracks.

Much has been written about the clichéd manner in which jazz has often been used in narrative cinema, and the principal arguments concerning racial bias and cultural stereotyping are summarized by David Butler elsewhere in the present volume. My intention in this chapter is to offer a supplementary perspective on the motivation behind the inclusion of jazz and jazz elements in 1950s film scoring. In a volume such as this, concerned with the stimulating aesthetic territory of cultural criss-crossing, it seems appropriate to put in a modestly favorable word for the genuinely pioneering work of the composers who were responsible for foregrounding an updated "jazziness" in film music, since in jazz circles their work tends to be maligned for being both Eurocentric and condescending to the African American musical traditions from which it partly derived its inspiration. I do not wish to take issue with the perfectly sound arguments that have been advanced about the stereotypical applications of (mostly) blues-based jazz elements in certain specific filmic contexts, where explicit extra-musical factors make the music's narrative associations plain enough. My plea is rather that the wider musical and aesthetic value of the melding of jazz characteristics with classically oriented compositional techniques should not be undervalued because of an overly restrictive critical emphasis on cultural issues, nor by failing to take account of the important part such melding played in the context of the changing nature of film music throughout the decade as a whole.

On a technical level, the music track for *Anatomy of a Murder*, like much of the music produced by Duke Ellington's band in other contexts, utilizes pre-composition of a kind that invites direct comparison with procedures used by modern composers of concert music. I emphasize the technical level because comparisons between Ellington and classical music that do not specifically address the structural sophistication of his music on its own terms have always been in danger of falling into the trap of believing, as John Gennari puts it, "that jazz's creative breakthrough . . . required the legitimating, sanctifying influence of the elite European tradition before it could assume a place in the modernist canon."[3] If it is inappropriate on racial or cultural grounds to compare Ellington with composers such as Delius or Stravinsky—and I shall return to the specific case of the latter below—this should not blind us to the fact that Ellington openly admired the music of both, studied their scores (in the case of Delius, assiduously) and used harmonic and structural devices that owe a good deal to the modern concert music tradition. In its inimitable way, Ellington's work is not far removed from the structural procedures evident in various kinds of "symphonic" jazz that started life in the concert hall and then came to exert a direct influence on film music in the 1950s.[4] To be sure, Ellington's music was conceived and executed with far greater spontaneity and timbral expressiveness by musicians whose playing was deeply rooted in African American traditions; but complex compositional manipulation of musical raw material had always been a defining characteristic of his output, most obviously in those abstract pieces (such as *Diminuendo and Crescendo in Blue*, in its original 1937 version) that lack an extra-musical program or explicit mood associations. This was both part and parcel of Ellington's interest in twentieth-century concert music; to some extent, it was also an expression of the kind of modernism that in the 1950s came to affect both jazz and the cinema—and sometimes affected them both simultaneously.

To rigid critical sensibilities, Ellington's music for decades appeared to fall uncomfortably between two stools, exemplified by the early reactions to *Black, Brown and Beige*: his music may not have been esoteric enough to satisfy critics from the elitist classical camp, but neither was it jazzy enough to please those for whom the spontaneity of improvisation (about which Ellington's views were notoriously ambivalent) overrode all other musical considerations when it came to deciding what was "jazz" and what was not. When, years later, Max Harrison went so far as to dismiss one track on the original soundtrack album of *Anatomy of a Murder* as "stodgy non-jazz,"[5] one can reasonably wonder why Ellington was apparently being taken to task for not providing a particular kind of music that the critic had preconceived for him. In the light of put-downs

Mervyn Cooke

such as Harrison's, one can readily sympathize with Ellington's dislike of the term *jazz* because he felt it to be too limiting in its aesthetic implications: as Graham Lock has demonstrated, Ellington's various attempts to avoid or modify the concept were not motivated by any desire to achieve acceptance by classical critics, but as part of a reasonably concerted attempt to promote "an identification of jazz as original, modern, and—crucially—American."[6]

In understanding how film composers came to make use of up-to-date jazz elements in the 1950s, it is worth remembering that the initiative was more a question of updating an existing idiom of symphonic jazz rather than forging an entirely new one. The only jazz elements previously to have been heard in extra-diegetic film music had been those incorporated—and inevitably diluted—into a distinctive manner of orchestral scoring ultimately based on the dance band idiom popularized in the 1920s by white bandleaders such as Jean Goldkette and Paul Whiteman.[7] George Gershwin's further developments of this dance band style had been honed in Hollywood by experienced and highly proficient studio music directors and arrangers, many of whom had served their apprenticeships conducting shows on Broadway before the Wall Street crash: the best known were Max Steiner at RKO, Alfred Newman at Twentieth Century-Fox, and the impressive team responsible for MGM's celebrated series of film musicals. As a genre, the last were clearly a special case in the unique demands they placed on their musical provision, floating as it does in a never-never land poised somewhere between the diegetic and extra-diegetic; but the musical's jazzy brand of scoring also found specific applications in two other filmic contexts. First, lightweight symphonic jazz became a staple accompaniment to comedies, and this association has doggedly persisted: snappy syncopations enlivened early Cary Grant vehicles (several, such as *My Favorite Wife* [dir. Garson Kanin, 1940], scored by RKO's Roy Webb), much as easygoing mainstream jazz and pop continue to sweeten modern romantic comedies. Second, this early type of orchestral "jazz" served an additional function as locational music, becoming associated in America with the exciting bustle of the metropolis and being obligingly trotted out whenever a New York or Chicago skyscraper appeared on screen.

The appearance of more authentic jazz elements in 1950s extra-diegetic scoring seems to have been occasioned by an intriguing confluence of different motives. The most obvious was the nurturing by the motion picture industry of the already long-standing association between jazz and low life, present even in the silent era: a film entitled *Does the Jazz Lead to Destruction?* was made in Australia in 1919, just two years after the first recordings of the Original

Dixieland Jazz Band.[8] From the 1940s onward, jazz in film soundtracks habitually indicated the presence of alcoholism, drug addiction, crime, corruption, sleaze, and sexual promiscuity, often in urban settings; fusion and big band idioms, drawing on the pioneering work of Henry Mancini (*Peter Gunn*, 1958; the *Pink Panther* franchise, 1963–93) and Lalo Schifrin (*Mission Impossible*, 1966; *Bullitt*, 1968; *Starsky and Hutch*, 1975), have to this day remained standard modes of accompaniment to crime thrillers and TV detective series. The ease with which jazz elements initially fulfilled this function was partly the result of the extreme stylistic conservatism in film scoring during the 1930s and 1940s: in the prevailing context of easy-listening romanticism, even a dash of exotic musical color or mild dissonance seemed outside the norm, so the marked musical and cultural otherness of jazz as a projection of the darker side of human nature became quickly entrenched.

But unsalubrious settings, racial stereotyping, and sexual connotations, though they have been the most widely discussed, were by no means the only factor that propelled jazz into the movie limelight in the 1950s. Several composers viewed jazz as an ideal vehicle for American nationalism in music, and this sentiment resurfaced at a time when (as we have seen) modernism in film music was also on the increase. It is no accident that the film composers most active in adopting the surface characteristics of jazz in the 1950s—principally Elmer Bernstein, Alex North, David Raksin, and Leonard Rosenman—were those who were also in the vanguard of experimentation with modernist devices that had originated in the concert hall: atonality, athematicism, textural fragmentation, and (in exceptional cases) dodecaphonic serialism. Raksin, in particular, was one of the first film composers to combine the suggestive sonority of the saxophone with atonality, in his score for Abraham Polonsky's *Force of Evil* (1948). For film composers such as these, jazz-derived compositional material conveniently became an instrument of modernism, simultaneously satisfying both nationalistic and experimental creative urges.

Although novel in the cinema, this potent conjunction of jazz, nationalism, and modernism was far from new in American concert music. Back in the 1920s, Aaron Copland returned from his studies in Paris determined to build jazz elements into his compositions with the explicit intention of creating a new musical identity that other U.S. composers could emulate, expressing the hope that jazz would in time become "the substance not only of the American composer's fox trots and Charlestons, but also of his lullabies and nocturnes."[9] Copland's early symphonic jazz, best represented by *Music for the Theater* (1925) and the Piano Concerto (1926), was far bolder in conception than Gershwin's, but in the 1930s

Mervyn Cooke

Copland chose to abandon the marriage between jazz and concert music in favor of a more rarefied use of national folk materials that did not hail from African American traditions. When he came to score a clutch of acclaimed movies based on American literary classics (in 1939–40 and 1949), his work in the medium inspired younger film composers to adopt certain characteristics of his newly refined and jazz-less style, which proved particularly well suited to rural settings and significantly influenced the scoring of Hollywood westerns in the 1950s and 1960s. The development of symphonic jazz in the concert hall had meanwhile been spearheaded by Copland's protégé Leonard Bernstein, with works such as *Prelude, Fugue and Riffs* (written for Woody Herman) and the piano-and-percussion scherzo of his Second Symphony, *The Age of Anxiety*, both composed in 1949. As part of a spirited debate between Bernstein and Gene Krupa on the merits and demerits of symphonic jazz, published in the *Esquire Jazz Book* two years earlier, Bernstein declared that jazz had provided the "serious composer" with a solution to "the two problems of being original and of being American."[10] However, when Bernstein made his own solitary foray into film scoring, providing music for Kazan's *On the Waterfront* (1954), he followed Copland's example by avoiding extra-diegetic jazz elements in favor of an austere orchestral idiom—though his innate jazz impulses found a convenient release when he was asked to play diegetic jazz piano for a bar scene, a task for which he received a standard performer's payment of $39 in addition to his commission fee.[11]

Kazan was also responsible for what is generally considered to be the first narrative feature to employ sustained and explicit jazz elements in its extra-diegetic score: his adaptation of Tennessee Williams's play *A Streetcar Named Desire* (1951), with music by North, who evidently reveled in the insidious suggestiveness of jazz as an accompaniment to this sultry and humidly claustrophobic domestic drama.[12] Although the southern setting and proximity of the action to a diegetic jazz venue were obvious pretexts for using jazz as a locational signifier (as had Newman in his "culturally patronizing"[13] scoring of Kazan's southern-set *Pinky* two years earlier), North's primary motivation appears to have been nationalistic, for he declared that here was "an opportunity to make music talk, and talk very much in the American musical idiom of jazz, rather than to imitate the frequently overrated gods of music in Europe, whose influence too frequently tends to dominate and stultify American composers."[14] Modernism was clearly another germane impulse, North's score combining blues-tinged jazz melodies and harmonies with increased dissonance levels, melodic angularity, and economical chamber textures, thereby encapsulating four of the most prominent film-scoring trends that were increasingly to assert themselves throughout the 1950s. Given his stylistic leanings, it comes as no surprise to learn that North had in 1946 composed for Benny Goodman his *Revue* for clarinet and orchestra, premiered under the baton of Leonard Bernstein.

North's dissonant jazz idiom in *Streetcar* trod a designedly uncomfortable middle ground between populism and modernism, though his rawly expressionistic brand of what he termed "lowdown Basin Street blues" proved so potent in its sexual suggestiveness that, where it coincided with close-ups of Stanley (Marlon Brando) and Stella (Kim Hunter) in amorous mood, both visual images and music had to be significantly toned down and re-edited in accordance with the requirements of the Production Code. North was very much aware of the explicit link between jazziness and sensuality, annotating one passage in the manuscript of the *Streetcar* score with the label "sexy, virile"[15] and proceeding equally consciously to associate a jazz motif with prostitutes in his music for *The Rose Tattoo* (dir. Daniel Mann, 1955). The identification between jazz and the steaminess of Tennessee Williams and the Deep South left its mark on North's later scores for a trilogy of adaptations from William Faulkner's novels: *The Long Hot Summer* (dir. Martin Ritt, 1958), *The Sound and the Fury* (dir. Ritt, 1959), and *Sanctuary* (dir. Tony Richardson, 1961).

The value of North's achievement in forging a stylistic hybrid with jazz at the forefront has long been recognized by film music scholars, though *A Streetcar Named Desire* was—until the work of Butler—lucky to get even a passing mention in the jazz literature. (At least one leading jazz musician found something of value in it, however: in 1955, Miles Davis declared to *Down Beat* that North's score was "the best thing I've heard in a long time. . . . I'd recommend everyone hearing that music."[16]) The same is generally true of another groundbreaking 1950s film, Preminger's *The Man with the Golden Arm* (1955).[17] Notorious for its frank treatment of the subject of heroin addiction, for which its Production Code seal of approval was withheld, it was furnished with a jazz-based score by Elmer Bernstein that went significantly further than North's by adopting a hotter big band sound and utilizing the talents of West Coast jazzmen Shorty Rogers and Shelly Manne—both of whom appear in the film.[18] Like North, Bernstein was motivated by a combination of nationalism, modernism, and an awareness of the deep-seated emotive and associative power of jazz:

> The script had a Chicago slum street, heroin, hysteria, longing, frustration, despair and finally death. Whatever love one could feel in the script was the little, weak emotion left in a soul racked with heroin and guilt, a soul

consuming its strength in the struggle for the good life and losing pitifully. *There is something very American and contemporary about all the characters and their problems.* I wanted an element that could speak readily of hysteria and despair, an element that would localize these emotions to our country, to a large city if possible. Ergo,—jazz.[19]

The film's main title music—as in many seminal 1950s features, set against stark graphic designs by Saul Bass—commences with a simple bass riff, swung cymbal rhythm, and catchy head melody in hard-bop style; as the bass riffs mutate into a turbulently repetitive pattern, so the big band brass superimpose their own energetic riffs, both bass and upper strata of the texture repeatedly emphasizing the flattened blue fifth. This hot material is used throughout the film to represent the craving of the central character, would-be jazz drummer Frankie Machine (Frank Sinatra), for his next heroin fix; it climaxes in a number of frenetic, riff-based passages as each moment of injection approaches, whether explicitly shown on screen or implied by Frankie's visits to his pusher, and after each of these incidents the music relaxes. (Essentially the same idea had previously been used by Miklós Rózsa in his score for *The Lost Weekend*: instead of jazz, however, Rózsa relied on the disturbing electronic sound of the theremin to portray the protagonist's craving for his next shot of liquor.) Bernstein also included cues composed in a non-jazz style for scenes between Frankie and his neurotic and emotionally dependent wife, using chamber ensemble textures and, like his namesake, continuing to reveal the strong influence of Copland on this more classically oriented manner of scoring.

At a number of important points in the film, Bernstein deftly combines his jazz and non-jazz idioms. As the strings accompany an intimate domestic scene between Frankie and Zosh, for instance, the instruments subtly adopt jazz stylistic characteristics when Frankie talks about his addiction. Zosh, who is pretending to be wheelchair bound, later grows frustrated with Frankie and is about to blow her emergency whistle after he has left her: because she is succumbing to her own craving (in her case, a pathological cry for attention), Bernstein reintroduces his jazz riffs but now in far darker tonal and instrumental garb, the stark sonic gesture lapsing as soon as she thinks better of it and—much to the spectator's surprise—proceeds to get up and walk to the window. Less striking but equally deft is the entirely natural way in which Bernstein picks up the rhythmic energy of Manne's diegetic drumming at the end of the disastrous audition scene, the trembling Frankie's precipitate exit from the rehearsal room being caught by extra-diegetic music that seems to evolve naturally from the jazz idiom of Rogers's band. When Frankie's girlfriend Molly runs away from him, Bernstein combines extra-diegetic drumming from Manne with poundingly dissonant solo piano music and a frenetic pizzicato walking bass.

It is at moments such as these that the forward-thinking film composer's appreciation of jazz as a quintessentially modern music is most obvious: it is not just a mindless response to stereotyped cultural and dramatic situations, but a source of musical dynamism appropriate to the restlessness and angst of the modern age (the Age of Anxiety). This sentiment was shared by Ellington, who in 1944 declared that swing was the expression of "modern ideas" and "the kind of music that catches the rhythm of the way people feel and live today," commenting a year later, "Jazz is like the automobile and the airplane. It is modern and it is American."[20] Central to the workability of the crossover styles created by North and Elmer Bernstein is the essential similarity between applications of the riff in jazz and of the ostinato in much of the twentieth-century concert music in which their styles were rooted. As I have argued elsewhere,[21] the pre-serial music of Stravinsky—shot through with layered ostinato patterns, added-note harmonies, and energetic rhythmic displacements (some of which were intensified by the influence of jazz), and a colossal influence on many U.S. composers from Copland onward—may fruitfully be compared with that of Ellington, who possessed an equal command of a musical rhetoric so idiosyncratic that it is recognizable from almost every tiny detail, and relied on similar collage-like manipulation of instrumental timbres in blocks of shifting textures. The more abstract manipulation of jazz-inspired material evident in certain passages in film scores by North, Bernstein, and others is also to be encountered in film music by Ellington and other jazz musicians. As African American jazz musicians tried to avoid the situationally clichéd and "culturally patronizing" applications their music appeared to have suffered at the hands of other practitioners, so they too drew closer to a modernist aesthetic comparable to Ellington's "identification of jazz as original, modern, and—crucially—American."

The Ellington band recorded music for *Anatomy of a Murder* in Los Angeles on 29 May and 1–2 June 1959 for Columbia Records, and at a further session in early June for Columbia Pictures, selected tracks from these sessions subsequently being released on a Columbia long-playing album and as two singles; there appears to have been a reciprocal arrangement between the recording and film companies regarding selection of material for inclusion in the recordings and the film.[22] Ellington's own accounts of the circumstances of this, his first

Mervyn Cooke

feature-film commission, are unenlightening. He recalled attending the shooting of the film at Ishpeming, Michigan, and then pursuing a mildly hedonistic lifestyle in a spacious Sunset Boulevard apartment while waiting for his call to the recording studio. When the summons came, he suddenly realized he had left himself little time in which to bring off his allotted task: "I think we had about forty-eight hours. So then the writing really started. It turned out all right, too, because we won awards [including a Grammy Award] with it."[23] The composition and recording of the music was undertaken in a spirit of urgency because the film was due to be released just one month later, on 1 July. In the course of a conversation years later with Henry Whiston of the Canadian Broadcasting Company, Ellington revealed his view of the score:

> I never thought it would earn an academy award because it really hadn't an outstanding melody to hang on to, yet, it was a thing that was handled properly and with respect to the music—no, that's not a good way of saying it. What I mean is it wasn't done with the intention of trying to get a tune out of it, or a movie theme that would get an award.[24]

Walter van de Leur notes that both Ellington and Strayhorn visited the film set prior to their sojourn in Hollywood and that, as usual, the task of composition was divided between them.[25]

Only a modest quantity of both men's music was used as what van de Leur misleadingly calls the film's "soundtrack." His assertion that the "soundtrack," by which he more accurately means music track, was "barely audible"—directly echoing Krin Gabbard, who finds certain musical details in the film both "barely audible" and "virtually imperceptible"[26]—is an oversimplification. As is normal practice in narrative films, the music is summarily ducked in volume whenever it threatens to compete with dialogue or sound effects; but in many more strategically important places it is prominent and perfectly audible. According to the hyperbolic Irving Townsend, who produced the Columbia soundtrack album, Ellington apparently wrote enough music to "fill a picture twice its length" (i.e., in excess of five hours).[27] Martin Williams called for performances of "a full version of [Ellington's] exceptional score."[28] For the music's second release on CD as part of Sony's Ellington Centennial Edition in 1999, additional tracks (including snippets taped during rehearsal and interview material) were included to swell the running time from the thirty-four minutes of the LP album to in excess of seventy. More than a hint of canonization was evident in the sense given throughout the CD insert notes that this was not only a neglected masterpiece, but also that Ellington's musical intentions had been misrepresented in the film and that his music deserved to be heard on its own terms—even to the point of reducing the amount of reverberation present in the original recording and soundtrack, thereby preventing any newcomer to the music from hearing how it actually sounded in 1959.

Anatomy of a Murder is a curiously unsatisfying film, and furnishing it with effective extra-diegetic music would have posed a considerable challenge even for a film composer with far more experience in the medium than Ellington possessed at the time. Apart from its historical importance as one of the first films to be scored extra-diegetically by African American musicians, the film's sole claim to fame lies in the contemporaneous notoriety it achieved for its frank handling of sexual matters, including explicit references to penetration, climax, sperm, and women's underwear. In essence it is an overstretched (161-minute) courtroom drama in which a supposedly unorthodox but utterly typecast James Stewart doubles as amateur private investigator and defense attorney in the case of a man accused of murdering his wife's alleged rapist. The cinematography is drab and uninspiring, and the film's emotional tone insufficiently considered. Without Ellington's strongly characterized music and an endearingly eccentric performance by the judge (portrayed by real-life judge Joseph N. Welch), the film *succès* would undoubtedly have remained one solely *de scandale*.

In *The Man with the Golden Arm*, the jazz-inspired music had accompanied and colored specific dramatic actions portrayed on screen and central to the narrative. No such actions appear in *Anatomy of a Murder*, since they have all taken place prior to the beginning of the film and are only ever alluded to verbally: there is no use of flashback, for example, which traditionally elicits extra-diegetic music in narrative films. Unlike Elmer Bernstein's, at no point can Ellington's jazz score really be said to function in the time-honored fashion of promoting cultural or sexual overtones: it is difficult to agree with Gabbard that Johnny Hodges's refined saxophone tone is typical of the sleazy associations often carried by rawer reed timbres, and the harshly unsympathetic character of the defendant's wife, Laura Manion (Lee Remick), is far from the conventionally seductive.[29] Neither does Ellington's music establish specific kinds of dramatic atmosphere to compensate for the generally uninspiring visuals. Music is entirely and understandably absent from the protracted courtroom scenes at the heart of the story—as was to be the case in Bernstein's own (non-jazz) score for the far superior courtroom drama *To Kill a Mockingbird*

Mervyn Cooke

(dir. Robert Mulligan, 1962). Two questions inevitably arise: why then did Preminger employ Ellington for *Anatomy of a Murder*, and why does Ellington make a prominent personal appearance in the film?

A single and cynical answer to both questions would be commercial exploitation by the eternal triangle of film producer, record label, and contracted musician. The soundtrack album from Bernstein's score to the same director's *The Man with the Golden Arm* had been surprisingly successful, selling 100,000 copies on the strength of its main title music, which is essentially similar in conception to the hard-driving blues, powerfully steered by the low reeds, in Ellington's main title music to *Anatomy of a Murder*: the main titles of both films feature graphic animations designed by Bass, their abstract nature intensifying the audio-visual similarity between the sequences. Bernstein lamented that such "unheard-of" record sales quickly led to pop-oriented strategies in film music through which a film is scored "in such a way that it will make records that sell, rather than what [the music] does for the film. . . . This trend was, I think, absolutely ruinous for the art of film music."[30] Significantly, it was at around this time (c. 1958) that several Hollywood studios acquired subsidiary companies in the record business; independent record companies also routinely bid for the rights to issue soundtrack albums. That Preminger, who had been an independent producer as well as director since 1952 and fulfilled both functions in making *The Man with the Golden Arm*, had a keen eye toward the profitability of soundtrack and spinoff record sales is shown by his receipt in 1960 of $250,000 from RCA Victor for the rights to the music for his film *Exodus* (the score for which, by Ernest Gold, won an Academy Award).[31] Preminger co-produced *Anatomy of a Murder*, and both he and Columbia Records could expect an explicit film tie-in to guarantee significantly boosted sales of the film's soundtrack album, which prominently featured Bass's main title graphic design on its sleeve, and sales of the two spinoff singles (one seven-inch 33⅓ rpm in stereo and the other 45 rpm in mono). There seems no convincing reason for Ellington to have made a personal appearance in the film unless his visible presence on-screen was intended to draw attention to his role in providing the film's music track; as Gabbard points out, Preminger's timely exploitation of Ellington came when he was still very much in the public eye following his widely publicized comeback at the Newport Festival in 1956.[32] In spite of Ellington's own disingenuous comments quoted above, the *Anatomy* score did indeed include two memorable—and hence saleable—melodies, in the shape of the gently swinging "Flirtibird" (composed by Ellington, with a characteristically humorous title apparently in keeping with the sometimes flippant tone of the film noted above) and a lyrical theme (composed by Strayhorn) that appears in several different arrangements on the original album under the titles "Low Key Lightly," "Midnight Indigo," "Grace Valse," and "Haupê."

The pretext for jazz to figure prominently in the film's soundtrack is decidedly flimsy. Biegler (Stewart) has in the screenplay been turned into a jazz buff (which he is not in the novel by Robert Traver on which the film is based), and his status as a jazz aficionado is explicitly referred to in the script to signify unorthodoxy in his character. We are told that his record collection spans "from Dixieland to Brubeck" (not from Armstrong to Mingus, we note); and when he turns off a Dixieland record (specially recorded by a sextet of Ellingtonians), asking Laura why lawyers are not supposed to like music, she retorts, "Well, not *that* kind of music!" His gratuitous reply is: "Ah—I guess that settles it. I'm a funny kind of lawyer." (This equation of jazz with unorthodoxy was somewhat behind the times: when confronted with pretentious jazz talk in *Jailhouse Rock* [dir. Richard Thorpe, 1957], Elvis Presley flees from the scene in a passionate rebellion against what he perceives as an exclusive elitism.) Biegler plays solo jazz piano diegetically on two occasions, miming to pre-recorded tracks, the first neutral in tone and the second—in the recess before the verdict is pronounced—considerably more bluesy (on which occasion his sidekick, Parnell, moans, "Do you have to play that stuff?"). Ellington appears as jazz musician "Pie-Eye," playing diegetically with his roadhouse band as the locals dance to his music: Biegler joins him in a brief snatch of piano duet, and the two characters engage in lame dialogue.

Gabbard offers an insightful discussion of the film's music cues, and the ground he covers need not be reprised here.[33] In concentrating on cultural and sexual issues, however, and by referring to models of film music composition based on earlier industry practices much less applicable to late 1950s cinema (those which North would have described as perpetuating the influence of "the frequently overrated gods of music in Europe"), he undervalues a vital characteristic of the film's music track. Gabbard criticizes the music for sounding "randomly tacked on" because it was conceived "without knowing exactly how it would turn up in the film."[34] When compared with traditional notions of film music as something either integral with, or more often subservient to, the dictates of the narrative, this is inevitably judged to be a weakness, as it is in Harrison's opinion that "Instead merely of providing another set of miniature concertos for his famous sidemen, [Ellington] should have been more

Mervyn Cooke

concerned with enhancing the dramatic and visual specifics of Preminger's film."[35] But, as filmmakers were beginning to realize, more random conjunctions of music and image are a breath of fresh air when set alongside the stiltedly formulaic quality of many Hollywood scores, and a clear manifestation of modernist leanings in soundtrack design. Of the two solo piano cues "played" diegetically by Biegler, the earlier (non-bluesy) one is arguably the more valuable in allowing the spectator free interpretative reign in the absence of any putative cultural associations in the music. In this light, it seems unfair to criticize Ellington, as Gabbard does of another cue, for "vamping on the piano as if he had run out of ideas."[36] Similarly, the night-time car drive immediately before the first court scene is underscored with an extended cue in which the band's cool-style parallel harmonies and fully rounded trumpet theme appear to pursue an autonomous and concentrated musical structure, as in any number of Ellington's earlier small-scale compositions; only when the music's mood darkens in conjunction with an optical fade-out at the end of the scene does the cue appear to have been conceived specifically to accompany the images. As far as the musical challenges presented by the picture are concerned—to traditional narrative-dominated sensibilities, at least—Ellington's recording of his score without systematic advance spotting of the cues or reference to a rough cut meant that such obstacles were never met head-on.

There is thus a distinctly abstract quality in much of Ellington's music for *Anatomy of a Murder* that looks ahead to the autonomous and often culturally non-specific use of music in many 1960s French films. Independently minded directors of the French *nouvelle vague* took part of their tendency toward soundtrack experimentation from what Jean Cocteau termed *synchronisme accidentel* when describing his own abstract manipulations of music composed for his films by Georges Auric (e.g., in *La Belle et la Bête* in 1946). Miles Davis, in his innovative but slender score to Louis Malle's film *Ascenseur pour l'échafaud* (1957), turned such abstraction to his own creative advantage by exploring a modal manner of playing that would color his tonal language for years to come.[37] John Lewis's coolly detached music for Roger Vadim's *Sait-on jamais* (*No Sun in Venice*), dating from the same year, makes use of fugal techniques, regarded for centuries as among the most abstract of all structural strategies available to a composer. In a whole clutch of later French films, such as Jean-Luc Godard's *À bout de souffle* (*Breathless*, 1959), with its score by Martial Solal heavily based on a jazz lick reminiscent of Thelonious Monk, music came to be viewed as a more or less independent ingredient in the editorial mix—one that, in Godard's work in particular, might often be recorded in advance of the editing of the image track (and even composed without reference to the film's screenplay) and manipulated solely by directorial whim in the cutting room. European cinema was quick to capitalize on the film-scoring potential of emotionally neutral small-ensemble jazz that tended toward abstraction, as shown by the collaboration in Poland between Roman Polanski and pianist Krzysztof Komeda (e.g., on *Knife in the Water*, 1962).

Alan Williams commented of Godard's films that "if the sensory impact of recorded sounds and images is maintained by their textual differentiation and organization, so are the sociohistoric associations of the objects and events represented," noting that in essence this strategy derived from Brecht's concept of a separation of the elements that together make up a theatrical experience.[38] Brecht commented negatively on the Wagnerian concept of *Gesamtkunstwerk* (total work of art), a specious ideal under the heavy pretensions of which film music criticism has groaned and creaked since the days of silent film:

> So long as the arts are supposed to be "fused" together, the various elements will all be equally degraded, and each will act as a mere "feed" to the rest. The process of fusion extends to the spectator, who gets thrown into the melting pot too and becomes a passive (suffering) part of the total work of art. Witchcraft of this sort must of course be fought against. Whatever is intended to produce hypnosis, is likely to induce sordid intoxication, or creates fog, has got to be given up.
>
> Words, music, and setting must become more independent of one another.[39]

Such a separation of elements is identified by Royal S. Brown, a film music scholar well versed in French cinema, in Miles Davis's celebrated film score, which he feels "does not add substantially to our reading of *Ascenseur pour l'échafaud*, [and] it does tend to separate itself here and there, in a manner typical of French films of this period, as a parallel aesthetic component to the film's visual and narrative structures."[40] The same might be said of the music in *Anatomy of a Murder*. The film may not represent vintage Preminger or vintage Ellington—and the music can hardly be regarded as one of Ellington's "grandest accomplishments" (Stanley Crouch) or a "vernacular American symphony" (Tom Piazza),[41] let alone "an incredible work of art, one of the most important ever in jazz" (Wynton Marsalis)[42]—but, even so, the venture's sometimes

Mervyn Cooke

haphazard conjunction of music and drama is oddly compelling and thought provoking. As Saul Bass's end title card comes up on screen to the accompaniment of a stuttering high note from Cat Anderson's faltering trumpet, the spectator and would-be critic can at least temper any lingering sense of missed opportunity by appreciating the film's attempt, like many others at the time, to break away from the formulaic quality of so much film music in the previous decades.

NOTES

1. *Anatomy of a Murder*, dir. Otto Preminger, Columbia Pictures, 1959.
2. See Caryl Flinn, *Strains of Utopia: Gender, Nostalgia, and Hollywood Film Music* (Princeton, NJ: Princeton University Press, 1992).
3. John Gennari, "Jazz Criticism: Its Development and Ideologies," *Black American Literature Forum* 25 (1991): 468–69.
4. In adopting the overworked adjective *symphonic* to describe this kind of music, I mean merely "pre-composed orchestral"—though the term's inevitable implication of technical sophistication is not inappropriate when making parallels with Ellington's music. Until recently, film music literature was riddled with uncritical applications of vague terms such as *symphonic*, *organic development*, and *unity*, generally deployed in the entirely unnecessary attempt to prove that film music was as artistically accomplished as concert music.
5. Max Harrison, "Ellington's Music for *Anatomy of a Murder*," *Jazz Review*, 1959; revised version reprinted in *The Duke Ellington Reader*, ed. Mark Tucker (New York: Oxford University Press, 1993), 314.
6. Graham Lock, *Blutopia: Visions of the Future and Revisions of the Past in the Work of Sun Ra, Duke Ellington, and Anthony Braxton* (Durham, NC: Duke University Press, 1999), 129. For a detailed and fascinating assessment of Ellington's sometimes contradictory statements on "jazz" and related terminology, see ibid., 125–32.
7. Ellington was one of the few black jazz musicians to have anything complimentary to say about Whiteman's achievements, which he praised in fulsome terms: see Duke Ellington, *Music Is My Mistress* (Garden City, NY: Doubleday, 1973), 103; and Stuart Nicholson, *A Portrait of Duke Ellington: Reminiscing in Tempo* (London: Sidgwick and Jackson, 1999), 199–200. In 1938, Ellington contributed music to one of Whiteman's Experiment in Modern Music concerts.
8. Bruce Johnson, *The Oxford Companion to Australian Jazz* (Melbourne: Oxford University Press, 1987), 4. See also Bruce Johnson, "The Jazz

Diaspora," in *The Cambridge Companion to Jazz*, ed. Mervyn Cooke and David Horn (Cambridge: Cambridge University Press, 2002), 42.

9. Aaron Copland, "Jazz Structure and Influence," *Modern Music*, 1927, quoted in Aaron Copland and Vivian Perlis, *Copland: 1900 through 1942* (London: Faber and Faber, 1984), 119.

10. See Robert Gottlieb, ed., *Reading Jazz* (London: Bloomsbury, 1997), 774–84.

11. Humphrey Burton, *Leonard Bernstein* (London: Faber and Faber, 1994), 237.

12. *A Streetcar Named Desire*, dir. Elia Kazan, United Artists, 1951.

13. Krin Gabbard, *Jammin' at the Margins: Jazz and the American Cinema* (Chicago: University of Chicago Press, 1996), 134.

14. Quoted in Sanya Shoilevska Henderson, *Alex North, Film Composer* (Jefferson, NC: McFarland, 2003), 98.

15. David Butler, *Jazz Noir: Listening to Music from "Phantom Lady" to "The Last Seduction"* (Westport, CT: Praeger, 2002), 98.

16. Quoted in ibid., 103.

17. *The Man with the Golden Arm*, dir. Otto Preminger, Warner Brothers, 1955.

18. For selected musical transcriptions from Bernstein's score, see Roy M. Prendergast, *Film Music: A Neglected Art*, 2nd ed. (New York: W. W. Norton, 1992), 108–19.

19. Elmer Bernstein, "*The Man with the Golden Arm*," *Film Music Notes*, 1956, quoted in ibid., 109 (my italics).

20. Quoted in Lock, *Blutopia*, 129–30.

21. Mervyn Cooke, "Jazz among the Classics, and the Case of Duke Ellington," in Cooke and Horne, *Cambridge Companion to Jazz*, 153–73.

22. See Phil Schaap, "From the Soundtrack of the Motion Picture," CD insert notes to Duke Ellington, *Anatomy of a Murder* (Columbia Legacy CK65569, 1999), 24–27. The original 1959 soundtrack LP (Columbia CL 1360 mono; CS 8166 stereo) was later re-released on CD (COL 469137 2, n.d.), then remastered and reissued with the inclusion of additional material on Columbia Legacy CK65599 in 1999.

23. Ellington, *Music Is My Mistress*, 193–94.

24. *Jazz Journal*, 1967; quoted in Nicholson, *Portrait of Duke Ellington*, 320.

25. Walter van de Leur, *Something to Live For: The Music of Billy Strayhorn* (New York: Oxford University Press, 2002), 137.

26. Gabbard, *Jammin' at the Margins*, 190.

27. Irving Townsend, "When Duke Records," *Just Jazz 4*, 1960; reprinted in Tucker, *Duke Ellington Reader*, 321.

28. Martin Williams, "Form Beyond Form," *The Jazz Tradition*, 1970; revised 1993 and reprinted in Tucker, *Duke Ellington Reader*, 412.

29. Gabbard, *Jammin' at the Margins*, 188–89. According to David Raksin, Preminger had at one stage intended to use Ellington's "Sophisticated Lady" to typecast the eponymous role in *Laura*, though this was his second choice of jazz standard (the first was Gershwin's "Summertime," for which copyright clearance could not be obtained) and he ditched the idea after Raksin aired his view that the Ellington tune had "so many associations in the minds of people that it will arouse feelings that are outside of the frame of

this picture." Quoted in Kathryn Kalinak, *Settling the Score: Music and the Classical Hollywood Film* (Madison: University of Wisconsin Press, 1992), 167.

30. Quoted in Jeff Smith, *The Sounds of Commerce: Marketing Popular Film Music* (New York: Columbia University Press, 1998), 45. In making these comments, Bernstein probably had in mind the successful spinoff song spawned by the film (though not heard in it), which was based on his score and performed by Sammy Davis Jr.: see Butler, *Jazz Noir*, 146.

31. Smith, *Sounds of Commerce*, 46.

32. Gabbard, *Jammin' at the Margins*, 190.

33. Ibid., 185–92.

34. Ibid., 190.

35. Harrison, "Ellington's Music," 315.

36. Gabbard, *Jammin' at the Margins*, 190.

37. Although the apparently spontaneous improvisation in Davis's film score has been widely praised, it is intriguing to note the choice of wording in Davis's autobiographical account of the circumstances of the commission, in which he reports that Malle "wanted me to write the musical score. . . . I had never written a music score for a film before. I would look at the rushes of the film and get musical ideas to write down." Miles Davis and Quincy Troupe, *Miles: The Autobiography* (New York: Simon & Schuster, 1989), 207. This flatly contradicts Malle's recollection that the music was "completely improvised; I don't think Miles Davis had had time to prepare anything." In *Malle on Malle*, ed. Philip French (London: Faber and Faber, 1993), 19.

38. Alan Williams, "Godard's Use of Sound," in *Film Sound: Theory and Practice*, ed. Elisabeth Weis and John Belton (New York: Columbia University Press, 1985), 344.

39. Quoted in *Brecht on Theatre*, ed. John Willet (New York: Hill and Wang, 1964), 37–38.

40. Royal S. Brown, *Overtones and Undertones: Reading Film Music* (Berkeley: University of California Press, 1994), 186.

41. See Tucker, *Duke Ellington Reader*, 442.

42. Wynton Marsalis, "Music by Duke Ellington," CD insert notes to Ellington, *Anatomy*, 14.

WORKS CITED

Films

Anatomy of a Murder. Dir. Otto Preminger. Music, Duke Ellington and Billy Strayhorn. Columbia, 1959.

The Man with the Golden Arm. Dir. Otto Preminger. Music, Elmer Bernstein. United Artists, 1955.

A Streetcar Named Desire. Dir. Elia Kazan. Music, Alex North. Warner Bros., 1951.

Recordings

Ellington, Duke. *Anatomy of a Murder*. 1959. Columbia Legacy CK 65569, 1999.

Texts

Brown, Royal S. *Overtones and Undertones: Reading Film Music*. Berkeley: University of California Press, 1994.

Burton, Humphrey. *Leonard Bernstein*. London: Faber and Faber, 1994.

Butler, David. *Jazz Noir: Listening to Music from "Phantom Lady" to "The Last Seduction."* Westport, CT: Praeger, 2002.

Cooke, Mervyn. "Jazz among the Classics, and the Case of Duke Ellington." In Cooke and Horne, *Cambridge Companion to Jazz*. 153–73.

Cooke, Mervyn, and David Horn, eds. *The Cambridge Companion to Jazz*. Cambridge: Cambridge University Press, 2002.

Copland, Aaron, and Vivian Perlis. *Copland: 1900 through 1942*. London: Faber and Faber, 1984.

Davis, Miles, and Quincy Troupe. *Miles: The Autobiography*. New York: Simon & Schuster, 1989.

Ellington, Duke. *Music Is My Mistress*. Garden City, NY: Doubleday, 1973.

Flinn, Caryl. *Strains of Utopia: Gender, Nostalgia, and Hollywood Film Music*. Princeton, NJ: Princeton University Press, 1992.

French, Philip, ed. *Malle on Malle*. London: Faber and Faber, 1993.

Gabbard, Krin. *Jammin' at the Margins: Jazz and the American Cinema*. Chicago: University of Chicago Press, 1996.

Gennari, John. "Jazz Criticism: Its Development and Ideologies." *Black American Literature Forum* 25 (1991): 449–523.

Gottlieb, Robert, ed. *Reading Jazz*. London: Bloomsbury, 1997.

Harrison, Max. "Ellington's Music for *Anatomy of a Murder*." 1959/1991. In Tucker, *Duke Ellington Reader*, 313–15.

Henderson, Sanya Shoilevska. *Alex North, Film Composer*. Jefferson, NC: McFarland, 2003.

Johnson, Bruce. "The Jazz Diaspora." In Cooke and Horn, *Cambridge Companion to Jazz*. 33–54.

———. *The Oxford Companion to Australian Jazz*. Melbourne: Oxford University Press, 1987.

Kalinak, Kathryn. *Settling the Score: Music and the Classical Hollywood Film*. Madison: University of Wisconsin Press, 1992.

Lock, Graham. *Blutopia: Visions of the Future and Revisions of the Past in the Work of Sun Ra, Duke Ellington, and Anthony Braxton*. Durham, NC: Duke University Press, 1999.

Marsalis, Wynton. "Music by Duke Ellington." CD insert notes. Duke Ellington, *Anatomy of a Murder*. Columbia Legacy CK65569, 1999. 11–16.

Nicholson, Stuart. *A Portrait of Duke Ellington: Reminiscing in Tempo*. London: Sidgwick and Jackson, 1999.

Prendergast, Roy M. *Film Music: A Neglected Art*. 2nd ed. New York: W. W. Norton, 1992.

Schaap, Phil. "From the Soundtrack of the Motion Picture." CD insert notes. Duke Ellington, *Anatomy of a Murder*. Columbia Legacy CK65569, 1999. 19–27.

Smith, Jeff. *The Sounds of Commerce: Marketing Popular Film Music*. New York: Columbia University Press, 1998.

Townsend, Irving. "When Duke Records." 1960. In Tucker, *Duke Ellington Reader*. 319–24.

Tucker, Mark, ed. *The Duke Ellington Reader*. New York: Oxford University Press, 1993.

van de Leur, Walter. *Something to Live For: The Music of Billy Strayhorn*. New York: Oxford University Press, 2002.

Weis, Elisabeth, and John Belton, eds. *Film Sound: Theory and Practice*. New York: Columbia University Press, 1985.

Willet, John, ed. *Brecht on Theatre*. New York: Hill and Wang, 1964.

Williams, Martin. "Form Beyond Form." 1970/1993. In Tucker, *Duke Ellington Reader*. 400–412.

Criss Cross: Jazzisticologics

Jumping Tracks: The Path of Conduction

THIRTEEN

Michael Jarrett

> *To write is perhaps . . . to select the whispering voices, to gather the tribes and secret idioms from which I extract something I call my self.*
>
> —Deleuze and Guattari

I am interviewing a musician—Howlin' Wolf, for example. Or Count Basie. Make it Louis Armstrong. It does not matter that these musicians are dead. I want to make an observation about structured encounters between people who write about music and people who make music. Like dancers performing for a movie camera, the musician and the writer are obligated to hit their marks, to arrive at topics predetermined by a rhetorical situation with which they are familiar. Figures invented on the path to the marks might count as improvisation—and, more often than not, placed "off the record"—but musician and writer are duty bound to arrive at and, then, to pass through various commonplaces. I know and the musician knows that, sooner or later, we will have to touch upon the question of influence. We must visit this topic.

"Mr. Armstrong, what phenomena"—I am not sure if *phenomena* is the word I would use—"what sorts of stuff came prior to and led to your innovations?" Isn't this the basic question of influence? Namely, what brought you here? How did you find this place? How in the world did you arrive at your artistic conclusions? For a while, weary of the who-begat-whom question, I asked a simple variation. Interviewing drummer Bobby Previte in 1989, after he released *Claude's Late Morning*, I asked, "Outside the realm of music, what influences you?" He said:

> That's one of the most important questions that you can possibly ask someone. There's so much. Painting: I get a lot from painting. I get a lot of ideas about form from painting—not about color, just about form. Sometimes the specific time of year has a lot to do with how I write. Like I said on my album cover, I thanked the musicians for helping me "bring an early winter

daydream into the late spring light." All this was conceived in the dead of winter and recorded in spring. Now it's winter again, and it's coming out. It's kind of *a propos*. That very much influences me: physical surroundings. We live in an age of collage. My music is pretty much opposite that. That's another thing that influences me, only in another way. I don't really write my own music and try not to have it as a collage. But I think that the more of it that goes on, the farther away I get from it in my own music.[1]

Responding to pretty much the same question, record producer Craig Street said:

I draw heavily from architecture, from my past as a construction worker. I also draw really heavily from filmmakers. . . . I was just talking to somebody about the new Hole record [*Celebrity Skin*, 1998], Courtney Love's band. Michael Beinhorn produced it. Now I really like what Beinhorn does. I would never want to do what he does. But I like what he does. I like how his records sound. I like the Hole record. I like Courtney Love's voice. I always have. If you were to think about producers as directors, Beinhorn reminds me of Hitchcock or Kurosawa. He's anal. He's exacting. He takes a long time to do something. He knows precisely what he wants essentially at the beginning, or it appears that he does. And he goes through this elaborate, detailed process to get there. He changes things all the time. If he doesn't like the way the room is, he'll go to another room. If he doesn't like the drum kit, he'll go to another drum kit. He'll do all of these kind of things in the process of making a recording.

. . . [I]n an ideal sense, I would love to function more like Fellini. He's a director that I completely and totally identify with. There's a really wonderful book out called *Fellini on Fellini*, something done a long time ago. It's really wild. For example, Fellini hated rehearsals. He loved it when stuff would go wrong—a light bank would blow up. All of the cameramen were like, "We can't work like this!" He was like, "Hey man, it's a different kind of light. It's cool. Let's go for it." He never ever saw one of his films in the theater. When he was done in the editing room, that was it. He moved on to the next thing. He had an ensemble of actors that he worked with on a regular basis, but he also loved to grab characters who were there. I identify more with that, although I love Hitchcock. I love Kurosawa.[2]

However interesting these musicians' answers might be, the question potentially reinforces a basic misunderstanding. Influence implies that a variety of forces act upon a performer and lead directly to innovation or invention. But that line of reasoning is, at least conceivably, *post hoc*. For example, we decide that Armstrong's artistic accomplishments—analogous to the design we find so

Michael Jarrett

evident in nature—demand an intelligent, originating cause: that is, agents of influence. Influence becomes a type of metaphysics—art's version of creationism. Accomplishment—the appearance of intelligent design—summons or calls forth influence as cause. But influence can be understood, just as plausibly, as a result of accomplishment. We do not speculate about the influences of those who accomplish nothing. Influence is an effect that is retroactively read back as the cause or the source of accomplishment.

Michael Baxandall issues a corrective to the conventional notion of influence. At first glance, it looks like a naïve re-instatement of agency. It is not. Influence, Baxandall writes, arises when an artist acts upon the environment.[3] We might picture the environment from a Darwinian viewpoint. A bumblebee in a meadow darts from blossom to blossom. "The colors and shapes of the flowers," writes Frederick Turner, "are a precise record of what bees find attractive."[4] The artist is similarly arrested by and, thereby, selects (or, conversely, is selected by) elements to include in his or her aesthetic (work or practice). She or he is, in Althusser's term, "interpellated" by what she or he might later claim as influences. The flowers in the meadow employ the bee just as surely as the bee selects the flowers. But for the moment assume a fixed, stable perspective: the meadow does not grow prior to or without the bumblebee's dance. Through the process that Darwin called natural selection, the bee brings the meadow into being and prompts it to flower. Subjectivity and agency are unnecessary, or rather they are effects. (Only when subjectivity and agency and intention are introduced can a distinction between natural and artificial selection be created and sustained.) By extension, we might ask: without the inescapable accomplishments of Louis Armstrong, would Buddy Bolden, one of Armstrong's primary influences, even exist? This is not an ontological question. It is practical and historical. Were it not for Armstrong, would we think to look for Bolden? More important, could we locate him? Would there be any trace of the man? Or consider another, perhaps more significant, question, especially pertinent to the essays in this book. Were it not for a long line of painters, poets, novelists, photographers, and filmmakers claiming jazz and blues as a major influence on their art, what would "jazz" and "blues" mean? Again, I am not suggesting that, for example, the music of saxophonists Lester Young, Louis Jordan, and Roscoe Mitchell would not "exist" without the work of Sterling Brown, Romare Bearden, Roy DeCarava, or Jayne Cortez. That is, at some level, nonsense. But what makes the sounds of these very different musicians culturally audible or identifiable as "jazz" and "blues"? Answer: an artist assigning jazz and blues a position of influence on his or her art is one way that "jazz" and "blues" become terms that carry meaning (as well as a mechanism by which the artist's work and self come to have meaning). By analogy, this is how a meadow (the field of influence) appears and seems to "exist" prior to pollination by bees. Declaring that one is a jazz painter retroactively imbues disparate types of music with coherence—it establishes a unified set, a style, or genre—sufficient to define both painting and music. Connections between Young's, Jordan's, and Mitchell's approaches to the saxophone are far from obvious—certainly not inherent in the music they have made. Connections have to be conferred, and naming these saxophonists as an influence on one's painting or poetry would do just that: confer connections.

An even larger point needs to be emphasized. When influence is not conceptualized through arboreal metaphors that graph lineage as "family trees"—towering oaks instead of knotted rhizomes—it is understood as temporally ordered "routes of linkage."[5] To illustrate—or, better, to make audible—the routes of linkage that govern conventional notions of influence, I refer readers to what I suspect will be a generally unfamiliar piece of music. I came across it one Friday while listening to Monica's show on WFMU.[6] The selection Monica played is titled "Lunch Life." It is by Wang Changcun and can be found on *China: The Sonic Avant-Garde*, issued by the Post-Concrete label. "Lunch Life" features a steady-state rattle topped by a metal-sheering-metal drone that sings in chorus. It prompts a rush of recognition—a series of recollections, really. That is why I seized upon it. That is why I love it. It repeats an old song: the railroad refrain. It vibrates sympathetically—to railroad time. It situates listeners in a space that recalls an empty boxcar clipping along rails at a moderate speed. In short, just about anyone hearing the track would immediately notice that it sounds like a train; just about anyone would conclude that it was obviously influenced by the sound of trains. What Wang Changcun might actually think is irrelevant. (He's a bee in the meadow of music.) "Lunch Life" is irrefutably a train track.

"Thriving on a Riff (Criss Cross Mix)" is the name I have given another train track: my audio collage of jazz, blues, gospel, and R&B. It ought to remind readers that the railroad exerted a massive influence on African American music of all varieties. Or as Houston Baker puts it: "The dominant blues syntagm in America is an instrumental imitation of *train-wheels-over-track-junctures*." He continues:

> This sound is the "sign," as it were of the blues, and it combines an intriguing melange of phonics: rattling gondolas, clattering flatbeds, quilling whistles, clanging bells, rumbling boxcars, and other railroad sounds. A blues text may

thus announce itself by the onomatopoeia of the train's whistle sounded on the indrawn breath of a harmonica or a train's bell tinkled on the high keys of an upright piano. The blues stanzas may then roll through an extended meditative repertoire with a steady train-wheels-over-track-junctures guitar back beat as a traditional, syntagmatic complement. If desire and absence are driving conditions of blues performance, the amelioration of such conditions is implied by the onomatopoeic *training* of blues voice and instrument. Only a *trained* voice can sing the blues.[7]

Assembled for this chapter, my four-minute, twenty-six-second track is represented below and available for download at my Web site.[8] Upon hearing the barrage of train tunes sampled for this mix, some listeners have felt compelled to point out omissions. There are, of course, hundreds. Where is the hip-hop? Actually, I believe the piece is hip-hop, inspired in particular by Double Dee and Steinski's "Lessons."[9] But a more overt reference would have been helpful. "And what about . . . ?" For example, Walter van de Leur told me about a composition, "On the Wrong Side of the Rail Road Tracks," written by Billy Strayhorn but never recorded by the Ellington band.[10] Krin Gabbard reminded me of the closing scene to *Paris Blues*—set in a train station. It, too, features a theme written by Strayhorn. Paul Oliver detected that I had left out any example of stride and boogie-woogie piano. Corrections, it seems, resemble projections. I admitted that, in pursuit of brevity, tell-tale snippets by Meade Lux Lewis and Count Basie ended up in my computer's recycle bin. Thelonious Monk was tasked with referencing earlier piano styles. Every sample can be heard as synecdoche. I had reluctantly edited out recordings by Elizabeth Cotton, Leadbelly, Robert Johnson, Big Joe Turner, Al Green, and plenty more. Most egregious was my decision not to feature the opening to "Lucille."[11] While Little Richard takes full credit for inventing rock and roll, he is quick to credit the railroad, even more than the church, with influencing his piano sound. In the WGBH/BBC series *Rock & Roll*, Little Richard speaks of his childhood in Macon, Georgia. "The train would shake the house that was in front of the track," he says. "Everybody would get out of the bed 'cause the train shook the house, 'cause they couldn't sleep. And the train would say, 'Chocka chocka chocka, chocka chocka, chocka chocka chocka, chocka chocka.' To me it was a rhythm. To me it was just like a song, you know. It had this thing to it, to me."[12] I would like to borrow the title of Kip Hanrahan's record label and call "this thing," this railroad thing, American clave: one-two-three, one-two; one-two-three, one-two. "Chocka chocka chocka, if you get a notion."

The alignment of popular music and the railroad has been exceptionally generative. It has produced music for more than 150 years. In the next few pages, I want to work through the sorts of linkages understood by the music/railroad connection. More abstractly, I want to show the sorts of couplings referred to by influence as the term is conventionally used. If we understand influence not as a cause of innovation but as an effect that follows from what we make, then we can more easily use the concept of innovation generatively as a set of instructions for making art. We can learn how to make ourselves be influenced. There are three basic tracks of influence. They correspond directly to the three traditional modes of reasoning: abduction, deduction, and induction—and to three basic tropes of figurative language—metaphor, metonymy, and synecdoche.

To make the tracks of influence concrete, let's stick with the alignment of popular music and the railroad. If we declare that a song was influenced by the sound of the railroad, then presumably one of three tracks of logical inference have been taken:

1. I notice that a song *integrates* an essential quality of railroads into music; the song is an instance of a rule about the sound of trains, or, conversely, the sound of trains makes the song intelligible.

   Abduction/synecdoche: The thing prompts recollection of a rule or quality. "Hear that rattle and repetition—those overtones—in Chessie's 'At Grade'?[13] There is really only one likely explanation for such features. They are basic qualities of the railroad. Hence, the song was influenced by the railroad."

2. I notice that a song *represents* the sound of railroads; a rule about trains has been mapped onto a song, establishing the song as a case. The song "explains" the sound of trains.

   Deduction/metaphor: The rule is applied to—or better, represented by—a case. "If Little Richard's 'Lucille' is a train song, it will be heard as similar to the sound of trains—e.g., its syncopated momentum and repetitions as 'train like'—despite manifest differences between train sounds and songs."

3. I notice that a song *reduces* train sounds into music; certain songs can be tested against train sounds to see if they are train songs.

   Induction/metonymy: The case is compared to things; test case against things or reality. "This song epitomizes the rattles and drones of the train that runs behind my house." "Brian Eno's 'Chemin de Fer' (1976) refers to Pierre Schaeffer's *Étude aux Chemins de Fer* (1948), the first example of *musique concrète*, which alluded to Auguste and Louis Lumière's *L'Arrivé d'un train en gare de La Ciotat* (1895)."[14]

And so, if we want to make music influenced by trains, we might turn the above descriptions into instructions for inquiry:

1. The route of abduction/synecdoche: "Create music that integrates sounds of the railroad." "Make music that evokes essential qualities of nights spent riding the rails."
2. The route of deduction/metaphor: "Create music that represents sounds of the railroad." "Map or translate a rule about train sounds into the language of music."
3. The route of induction/metonymy: "Create music that reduces some aspect of train sounds." "Make a song that manifests some sonic feature of trains."

I do not doubt that influence can work in the above-described manner: that we can trace its motions following traditional routes of logic or inference; and that it tropes or transforms data through basic cognitive operations. I am, however, very skeptical that influence generally travels such orderly routes. Traditional ways of conceptualizing influence derive from a literate or logocentric paradigm—the step-by-step patterns of induction—institutionalized in universities, especially in English, philosophy, and comparative literature departments. Stated differently, we have known for a long time now that "logic" was a historical consequence—an effect—of the invention and institutionalization of "alphabetic writing." Like mathematics enabled by Arabic numerals, it was not done in the head. For example, deductive logic required physical support—the apparatus of writing (pencil and paper)—and associated institutions (the cultural support of church, school, and state).[15] "Concept formation," notes Gregory Ulmer, following Lord, Parry, Ellis, Ong, and other theorists, was "invented through literacy." It "allowed us to move beyond myths and storytelling into philosophy and analysis."[16] We should not be surprised when comparative approaches favored by literate analysis employ influence as a concept to explain the relationships between black music and other African American art forms (or, as I have done, the relationship between music and trains). And we should not be surprised when influence comes to resemble a logical process, when it follows preset tracks. The trick is how to unthink influence as a literate concept and rethink influence as a practice useful in electronic culture.

"We're now at a stage," claims Ulmer, "where we have equivalent support to move beyond the concept—now three thousand years old—and we're ready to develop a new dimension of reasoning that's a practice and not something that's in the brain."[17] More than any other contemporary theorist, Ulmer has conceptualized—tried to think through—the paradigm shift represented by electronic culture. He writes, "There is now equipment"—which we might picture metonymically as the computer—"which will support inferences that move directly from thing to thing." Instead of supporting step-by-step patterns, the "chains of reasoning" enabled by print culture, this equipment makes possible "inference patterns" that (from a literate perspective) seem improbable, irrelevant, and unexpected: a kind of "duction," then, that jumps tracks. Ulmer calls this newly emerging mode of inference "conduction."[18] It "puts into logic the aesthetic operations of images (word and picture)."[19] Its trope is catachresis—"the manifestly absurd Metaphor designed to inspire Ironic second thoughts about the nature of the thing characterized."[20] We need the syntax of conduction/catachresis, says Ulmer. We need to learn how to infer directly from thing to thing, how to make influence jump tracks.

Any incredulity I have had about conduction—about the logic (that is not a logic) operative within the paradigm Ulmer calls "electracy"—has been laid to rest by a fairly simple realization. This type of inference has long been the norm among African American musicians. Though he does not label it as such, Graham Lock explicates conduction in *Blutopia*, as he reveals the "sense" behind the perceived madness of Sun Ra and Anthony Braxton.[21] We discover that, more often than not, conduction describes (or names) how influence actually operates. Inferences are drawn directly from thing to thing. For example, graffiti ("bombing" subway trains), break dancing, and rap music connect—they fit or match up—and that fit yields hip-hop. Ulmer says as much when he writes: "The process by which Africans integrated their cultural practices with the materials of whatever place they found themselves offers a frame for understanding how literacy becomes electronic"[22] (Figure 13.1). We should note that this process of integration—of criss-crossing—is nothing less than another name for influence retooled and operating within electronic culture. It is not oedipal, not driven by anxiety.

A number of theorists have charted parallels between mainstream jazz musicians and the poets—the griots and bards—of oral cultures: both invent in

Michael Jarrett

the moment, collapsing (literate) distinctions between composition and performance. Both draw upon "licks"—preset formulas—sometimes borrowed—stitched together. Both ascribe to an aesthetic of virtuosity, the cult of the soloist. The list could continue. But once exhausted, it might only substantiate Ong's point that electronic culture is "secondary orality."[23] More pointedly, we might ask: why have African American artists proven remarkably adept at managing electronic culture? "Natural rhythm," said the traditional, racist answer, and its sting makes us avoid a difficult but still intriguing question. Clearly, the matter is grossly overdetermined. But while there may be no single reason for the disproportionately large success of African American artists, and musicians in particular, there is a useful explanation. Blocked from any meaningful involvement in literate culture, African Americans were allowed to participate in entertainment culture. Indeed, "allowed" is too weak a word. The cultural productions of black Americans were largely restricted to entertainment culture, which, beginning in the late nineteenth century, transformed into an early manifestation of electronic culture. As a group, black artists were practically force-marched into a newly emerging paradigm.

In 1966, Glenn Gould wrote: "We must be prepared to accept the fact that, for better or worse, recording will forever alter our notions about what is appropriate to the performance of music."[24] Gould seems transfixed by "the prospects of recording," and in particular by the invention of "a new kind of listener."[25] But to whom is he speaking? (The question is rhetorical; you already know the answer.) If his audience is the largely white audience for classical music, then Gould's oracular, almost apocalyptic tone makes perfect sense. The statement, and his larger essay, reads as manifesto. But just for kicks, imagine Gould directing his comments to Louis Armstrong, at that time enjoying immense fame but nearing the end of his life. (Gould and Armstrong both recorded for the same record label, Columbia.) Gould's future-tense world turns out to be the only world that Armstrong has known—for almost half a century. Gould's manifesto rates as old news. Or better, as Sun Ra put it, "We are in the future."[26]

In his autobiography, *Satchmo*, Armstrong recalls a rainy day in New Orleans spent with his first wife. He writes: "Daisy and I were in the front room listening to some new records I had just bought, new releases of the Original Dixieland Jazz Band [1917], which we were playing on an upright Victrola we were very proud of. The records were 'Livery Stable Blues' and 'Tiger Rag,' the first 'Tiger Rag' to be recorded. (Between you and me, it's still the best.)."[27]

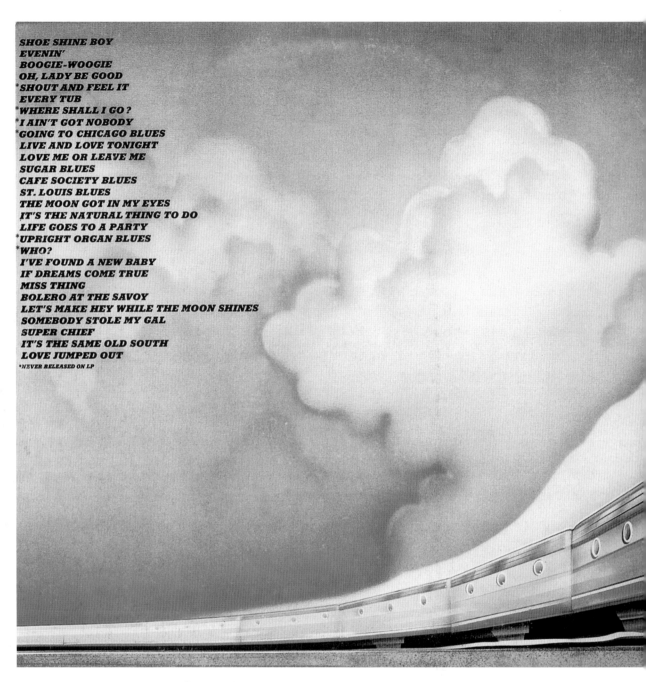

SHOE SHINE BOY
EVENIN'
BOOGIE-WOOGIE
OH, LADY BE GOOD
*SHOUT AND FEEL IT
EVERY TUB
*WHERE SHALL I GO?
*I AIN'T GOT NOBODY
*GOING TO CHICAGO BLUES
LIVE AND LOVE TONIGHT
LOVE ME OR LEAVE ME
SUGAR BLUES
CAFE SOCIETY BLUES
ST. LOUIS BLUES
THE MOON GOT IN MY EYES
IT'S THE NATURAL THING TO DO
LIFE GOES TO A PARTY
*UPRIGHT ORGAN BLUES
*WHO?
I'VE FOUND A NEW BABY
IF DREAMS COME TRUE
MISS THING
BOLERO AT THE SAVOY
LET'S MAKE HEY WHILE THE MOON SHINES
SOMEBODY STOLE MY GAL
SUPER CHIEF
IT'S THE SAME OLD SOUTH
LOVE JUMPED OUT
*NEVER RELEASED ON LP

Figure 13.1. Count Basie, *Super Chief.* LP cover design, John Berg; LP cover art, David Willardson. Columbia CG31224, 1972.

28 LEGENDARY PERFORMANCES BY BASIE AND/OR HIS SIDE MEN FEATURING
BILLIE HOLIDAY, MILDRED BAILEY, HELEN HUMES AND JIMMY RUSHING

COUNT BASIE
SUPER CHIEF

mbia
31224

ohn
mond
ection

Willardson

The point is not so much that the Victrola has replaced the hearth in this domestic scene. Or that, in reference to the newly emerging music (created by hometown boys), "song" has come to mean "record." It is to underscore that Armstrong arrived "prepared," his notions about what was appropriate to the performance of music already altered by the implications of recording technology. Armstrong seemed fashioned for (and by) recording. He was a perfect fit. The new technology seemed to summon him forth. As a young man in the 1920s, now living in Chicago, Armstrong fronted the Hot Five and the Hot Seven, groups created specifically for recording in a studio, and he responded to "the prospects of recording" with astonishing confidence, demonstrating in the process how recording had altered notions about appropriate performance. What was an option to Gould—whether to accommodate implications of a new paradigm—was a mandate to Armstrong.

If we want to study conduction/catachresis, we would do well to understand how influence has operated in African American music—within the realm of entertainment—for a full century. Entertainment provides us with good models for new patterns of thinking. In fact I should clearly state that popular music, of all sorts, has been electronic for a long time and is, therefore, a rich source—a tutor text—for operating within the new paradigm. Black music just makes a particularly good example of possibilities suggested by electronic culture. Obviously, the railroad did not influence black music alone. In an essay on the "man-machine interface," Peter Shapiro writes: "The rhythm of life in most of America was created by the railroad, and pre-war blues and Country records were often little more than imitations of the locomotive using jugs and guitars: listen to The Memphis Jug Band's 'K.C. Moan' from 1929; Darby & Tarlton's 'Freight Train Ramble,' also from 1929; or Bill Monroe's 1941 'Orange Blossom Special.'"[28]

The railroad undoubtedly meant different things to black Americans than it did to white Americans. Muddy Waters catches the train to sweet home Chicago and, forever, leaves behind his life on Stovall's Plantation. Elvis Presley covers Junior Parker's "Mystery Train" for Sun Records. Shortly thereafter, he takes a train to New York and a series of television appearances. It is a wonder Presley finds his way back home to Memphis. The earth has shifted on its axis. Focusing exclusively on the connection between black music and the railroad is, therefore, arbitrary—wholly a convenience.

But while particular manifestations of the railroad's influence vary from artist to artist, the type of connection between the railroad and music remains generally constant across electronic culture. It is "conduction." Conduction jumps the tracks of logic, aligning thing and thing. In electronic culture

Michael Jarrett

"influence" becomes a type of artistic inquiry—a practice. The train becomes a catachrestic vehicle, a means to invention, a way to make music.

Let me close with an example. On the day it was recorded, "Shhh/Peaceful," the Miles Davis composition that became side one of *In a Silent Way* (1969), was known as "Mornin' Fast Train from Memphis to Harlem." In all probability that was Davis's working title, not producer Teo Macero's. On the session sheet, an engineer labeled the tune simply "Choo-choo train."[29] Heard through this frame, the composition—in John Szwed's phrase a "slow-moving fog of sonority" over a shuffle beat—anticipates Kraftwerk's "Trans-Europe Express," Irmin Schmidt and Bruno Spoerri's "Rapido de Noir," Herbert Distel's *Die Reise*, the KLF's "Elvis on the Radio, Steel Guitar in My Soul," Banco de Gaia's "Last Train to Lhasa," the Chemical Brothers' "Star Guitar," and Out Hud's "The 'L' Train Is a Swell Train and I Don't Want to Hear You Indies Complain."[30]

Davis was notorious for communicating musical information to his sidemen through the most laconic sorts of code. Bob Belden, who produced *The Complete In a Silent Way Sessions*, told me: "As a musician, you go up to the bass player and say, 'F and C.' You go to the drummer, and you say 'Cold Sweat.' You go to the keyboard player, put your hands on the keys, and shape a sound. Like he [Davis] would say to Herbie, 'I don't want any Rachmaninov.' Nothing else would be said."[31] Given the caliber of musicians in the Davis band, these instructions were sufficient—as was the title, "Mornin' Fast Train from Memphis to Harlem." The musicians understood. (In fact, the ability to understand and to execute instructions identified them as a particular type and level of musician.) They came prepared, fully cognizant that recording had altered what was appropriate to the performance of music. Their job was to figure out a way to make improvised music and train sounds go together; to understand a "mornin' fast train from Memphis to Harlem" as catachresis, a precisely absurd line of inference leading to a set of instructions for improvising.

"The general theory that I'm working on," poet Kamau Brathwaite told me,

is that Shàngó [Yoruba god of electricity and thunder] comes over to the New World. One of his disguises or apotheoses is the locomotive engine. Wherever you turn, you have music which not only has "train" in the title but, of course, is using an imitation, a mimesis, of the train. In fact, I go on to say that nearly all black music is based on the concept in one way or another, either from the howl or the engine stutter or from the click of the track—and here you get a lot of drumming coming out of that—all of this is based on the train. Which I then go on to call Shàngó rather than simply locomotive engine.[32]

We know how influence works within a literate paradigm. We know how to think our way from railroad to music using abductive, deductive, and inductive logic. The problem posed by influence in electronic culture is how to work conductively, how to "reason" directly from thing to thing. Brathwaite suggests a model that recalls "possession" by spirits. Filled with Shàngó—locomotive breath—we get in a groove, form a human-machine conjunction that replicates and mutates. "Groove," writes Kodwo Eshun,

> is when overlapping patterns of rhythm interlock, when beats syncromesh until they generate an automotion effect, an inexorable, effortless sensation which pushes you along from behind until you're funky like a train. To get into the Groove is to lock into the polyrhythmotor, to be adapted by a fictionalized rhythm engine which draws you on its own momentum.[33]

On "Shhh/Peaceful" the Miles Davis band vibrates sympathetically to railroad time: "less a question of imitating than of occupying corresponding frequencies."[34] They are conductors, converting "locomotive energies" into music.[35] Through them, the railroad invents music. The railroad trains the band.

NOTES

1. Michael Jarrett, unpublished interview with Bobby Previte, 18 January 1989.
2. Michael Jarrett, unpublished portion of interview with Craig Street, 24 September 1998.
3. Michael Baxandall, *Patterns of Intention: On the Historical Explanation of Pictures* (New Haven: Yale University Press, 1992), 58–62.
4. Frederick Turner, quoted in Michael Pollan, *The Botany of Desire: A Plant's-Eye View of the World* (New York: Random House, 2001), 76.
5. Gregory L. Ulmer, *Heuretics: The Logic of Invention* (Baltimore: Johns Hopkins University Press, 1994), 194–95.
6. Monica Lynch, WFMU, 30 April 2004. Available at www.wfmu.org/playlists/ML.
7. Houston Baker, *Blues, Ideology, and Afro-American Literature: A Vernacular Theory* (Chicago: University of Chicago Press, 1984), 8.
8. Michael Jarrett, "Thriving on a Riff (Criss Cross Mix)," 18 June 2004. Available at www.yk.psu.edu/~jmj3/. This audio montage cobbles together bits and pieces from a number of recordings, roughly in the following order (for full discographical details, see Works Cited): James Brown, "Night Train"; Little Axe, "Crossroads"; Wynton Marsalis and the Lincoln Center Jazz

Orchestra, "All Aboard"; Delta Rhythm Boys, "Take the 'A' Train"; Henry "Ragtime Texas" Thomas, "Railroadin' Some"; James Cotton, "Mississippi Freight Train"; Lightnin' Slim, "Mean Ol' Lonesome Train"; The Neville Brothers, "Waiting at the Station"; The Impressions, "People Get Ready"; Rahsaan Roland Kirk, "Clickety Clack"; Quad City DJ's, "C'mon n' Ride It (The Train)"; Duke Ellington, "Daybreak Express"; Junior Parker, "Mystery Train"; Thelonious Monk, "Locomotive"; Blind Willie McTell, "Broke Down Engine"; Otis Rush, "So Many Roads, So Many Trains"; Sister Rosetta Tharpe, "This Train"; Golden Gate Quartet, "Golden Gate Gospel Train"; Little Eva, "The Loco-Motion"; Marion Williams, "The New Gospel Train"; Bo Diddley, "Down Home Special"; Lee Fields, "Steam Train"; The Equals, "Funky Like a Train"; Wilson Pickett, "Engine Number 9"; Rufus Thomas, "Memphis Train"; Chuck Berry, "Downbound Train"; Louis Jordan, "Choo Choo Ch'Boogie"; Howlin' Wolf, "Smokestack Lightnin'"; Tiny Bradshaw, "The Train Kept A-Rollin'"; The Coasters, "Keep on Rolling"; The O'Jays, "Love Train"; Gladys Knight and the Pips, "Midnight Train to Georgia"; T-Bone Walker, "Railroad Station Blues."

9. Double Dee and Steinski, "The Payoff Mix/Lesson Two/Lesson 3" (Tommy Boy, never released, 1985).

10. The Dutch Jazz Orchestra, "On the Wrong Side of the Tracks," *Something to Live For: The Music of Billy Strayhorn* (Challenge CHR 70092, 2002).

11. Little Richard, "Lucille," 1956, *The Georgia Peach* (Specialty 7012-2, 1991).

12. Little Richard, in *Rock & Roll*, senior prod. David Espar, executive prod. Elizabeth Deane and Hugh Thomson, WGBH/BBC, 1995.

13. Chessie, "At Grade," *Signal Series* (Drop Beat SPL05, 1997).

14. Brian Eno, "Chemin de Fer," 1976, *Enobox/Instrumental* (Virgin 7243, 1993); Pierre Schaeffer, "Étude aux Chemins de Fer," 1946, *Early Modulations Vintage Volts* (Caipirinha CAI-2027, 1999); *L'Arrivé d'un train en gare de La Ciotat*, prod. Bret Wood, dir. Auguste and Louis Lumière, 1895, on *The Lumière Brothers' First Films* (Kino, 1996).

15. Gregory L. Ulmer, "*Seulemonde*, Conversation with Gregory Ulmer," n.d. Available at http://www.cas.usf.edu/journal/ulmer/ulmer.html.

16. Quoted in Laurence Rickels, "I Was There: Talking with Michel Serres and Gregory Ulmer," Fall 1994. Available at http://proxy.arts.uci.edu/~nideffer/Tvc/interviews/21.Tvc.v9.intrvws.Ser_Ulm.html.

17. Ibid.

18. "*Seulemonde*, Conversation with Gregory Ulmer."

19. Gregory L. Ulmer, *Internet Invention: From Literacy to Electracy* (New York: Longman, 2003), 10.

20. Hayden White, *Metahistory: The Historical Imagination in Nineteenth-Century Europe* (Baltimore: Johns Hopkins University Press, 1973), 37.

21. Graham Lock, *Blutopia: Visions of the Future and Revisions of the Past in the Work of Sun Ra, Duke Ellington, and Anthony Braxton* (Durham, NC: Duke University Press, 1999).

22. Quoted in Rickels, "I Was There."

23. Walter J. Ong, *Orality and Literacy: The Technologizing of the Word* (New York: Methuen, 1982), 3.

24. Glenn Gould, "The Prospects of Recording," 1966, reprinted in *The Glen Gould Reader*, ed. Tim Page (New York: Random House, 1984), 337.

25. Ibid., 347.

26. Sun Ra, *We Are in the Future*, aka *The Futuristic Sounds of Sun Ra* (1961; reissue, Savoy SV-0213, 1993).

27. Louis Armstrong, *Satchmo: My Life in New Orleans* (1954; reprint, New York: Da Capo, 1986), 161.

28. Peter Shapiro, "Automating the Beat: The Robotics of Rhythm," in *Undercurrents: The Hidden Wiring of Modern Music*, ed. RobYoung (London: Continuum, 2002), 134.

29. John Szwed, *So What: The Life of Miles Davis* (New York: Simon & Schuster, 2002), 280.

30. Szwed, 281; Kraftwerk, "Trans-Europe Express," 1977, *Trans-Europe Express* (Cleopatra 58762, 1993); Irmin Schmidt and Bruno Spoerri, "Rapido de Noir," *Toy Planet*, (Spoon 011, 1990); Herbert Distel, *Die Reise* (created 1984–85; hat ART 6001, 1988); The KLF, "Elvis on the Radio, Steel Guitar in My Soul," *Chill Out* (Wax Trax 7155, 1990); Banco de Gaia, "Last Train to Lhasa," *Last Train to Lhasa* (Mammath/Planet Dog MR0115–2, 1995); The Chemical Brothers, "Star Guitar," *Come with Us* (Astralwerks 11682, 2002); Out Hud, "The 'L' Train Is a Swell Train and I Don't Want to Hear You Indies Complain," *Street Dad* (Kranky 057, 2002).

31. Michael Jarrett, unpublished interview with Bob Belden, 5 July 2001.

32. Michael Jarrett, unpublished interview with Kamau Brathwaite, 8 August 2001.

33. Kodwo Eshun, *More Brilliant Than the Sun: Adventures in Sonic Fiction* (London: Quartet, 1999), 82.

34. Gilles Deleuze and Félix Guattari, *A Thousand Plateaus: Capitalism and Schizophrenia*, trans. Brian Massumi (Minneapolis: University of Minnesota Press, 1987), 331.

35. Baker, *Blues, Ideology, and Afro-American Literature*, 11.

WORKS CITED

Recordings

Banco de Gaia. "Last Train to Lhasa." *Last Train to Lhasa*. Mammath/Planet Dog MR0115-2, 1995.

Basie, Count. *Super Chief*. Columbia CG31224, 1972.

Berry, Chuck. "Downbound Train." 1956. *The Chess Box*. MCA/Chess CHD3-80001, 1989.

Bradshaw, Tiny. "The Train Kept A-Rollin'." 1951. *Blues Masters, Volume 5: Jump Blues Classics*. Rhino R2-71125, 1992.

Brown, James. "Night Train." 1961. *Star Time: Disc 1—Mr. Dynamite*. Polydor 849-109-2, 1991.

Changcun, Wang. "Lunch Life." *China: The Sonic Avant-Garde*. Post-Concrete 005, 2003.

The Chemical Brothers. "Star Guitar." *Come with Us*. Astralwerks 11682, 2002.

Chessie. "At Grade." *Signal Series*. Drop Beat SPL05, 1997.

The Coasters. "Keep on Rolling." 1961. *50 Coastin' Classics*. Rhino/Atlantic R2 71090, 1992.

Cotton, James. "Mississippi Freight Train." *Living the Blues*. Gitanes/Polygram 3145212382, 1994.

Darby and Tarlton. "Freight Train Ramble." *Complete Recordings*. Bear Family BCD 15764, 1995.

Davis, Miles. "Shhh/Peaceful." 1969. *The Complete In a Silent Way Sessions*. Columbia/Legacy C3K65362, 2001.

Delta Rhythm Boys. "Take the 'A' Train." 1947. *Night Train: Classic Railroad Songs, Volume 3*. Rounder 1144, 1998.

Diddley, Bo. "Down Home Special." 1956. *The Chess Box*. MCA/Chess CHD2-19502, 1990.

Distel, Herbert. *Die Reise*. 1984–85. hat ART 6001, 1988.

Double Dee and Steinski. "The Payoff Mix/Lesson Two/Lesson 3." Tommy Boy (never released), 1985.

The Dutch Jazz Orchestra. "On the Wrong Side of the Tracks." *Something to Live For: The Music of Billy Strayhorn*. Challenge CHR 70092, 2002.

Ellington, Duke. "Daybreak Express." 1933. *The Duke Ellington Centennial Edition: The Complete RCA Victor Recordings*. RCA Victor 09026-63386-2, 1999.

Eno, Brian. "Chemin de Fer." 1976. *Enobox/Instrumental*. Virgin 7243, 1993.

The Equals. "Funky Like a Train." 1977. *Supa Funky II*. Universal International n.a., 2003.

Fields, Lee. "Steam Train." *Spike's Choice: The Desco Funk 45' Collection*. Desco DSCD 201, n.d.

Golden Gate Quartet. "Golden Gate Gospel Train." 1937. *Train 45: Railroad Songs of the Early 1900s*. Rounder 1143, 1998.

Hole. *Celebrity Skin*. Geffen DGCD25164, 1998.

The Impressions. "People Get Ready." 1965. *Definitive Impressions*. Kent 48–50, 1989.

Jordan, Louis. "Choo Choo Ch'Boogie." 1946. *The Best of Louis Jordan*. MCA 4079, 1975.

Kirk, Rahsaan Roland. "Clickety Clack." 1973 *Bright Moments*. Rhino/Atlantic R2 71409, 1993.

The KLF. "Elvis on the Radio, Steel Guitar in My Soul." *Chill Out*. Wax Trax 7155, 1990.

Knight, Gladys, and the Pips. "Midnight Train to Georgia." 1973. *Behind the Music*. Buddha/BMG 74465-99726-2, 2000.

Kraftwerk. "Trans-Europe Express." 1977. *Trans-Europe Express*. Cleopatra 58762, 1993.

Little Axe. "Crossroads." *The Wolf That House Built*. Okeh/Epic EK64254, 1994.

Little Eva. "The Loco-Motion." 1962. *The Best of the Girl Groups, Volume 2*. Rhino R2 70989, 1990.

Little Richard. "Lucille." 1956. *The Georgia Peach*. Specialty 7012-2, 1991.

Marsalis, Wynton, and the Lincoln Center Jazz Orchestra. "All Aboard." *Big Train*. Columbia CK 69860, 1999.

McTell, Blind Willie. "Broke Down Engine." 1931. *Between the Rails: America's Train Songs*. GNP Crescendo GNPD 2249, 1996.

Memphis Jug Band. "K.C. Moan." 1929. *The Best of the Memphis Jug Band*. Yazoo 2059, 2001.

Monk, Thelonious. "Locomotive." 1966. *Straight, No Chaser*. Columbia/Legacy CK 64886, 1996.

Monroe, Bill. "Orange Blossom Special." 1941. *The Essential Bill Monroe and the Monroe Brothers*. RCA 67450, 1997.

The Neville Brothers. "Waiting at the Station." 1962. *Treacherous: A History of the Neville Brothers*. Rhino R2 71494, 1990.

The O'Jays. "Love Train." 1972. *Back Stabbers*. Epic/Legacy ZK 66113, 1996.

Original Dixieland Jazz Band. "Livery Stable Blues" and "Tiger Rag." 1917. *The 75th Anniversary*. RCA Bluebird 61098-2, 1992.

Out Hud. "The 'L' Train Is a Swell Train and I Don't Want to Hear You Indies Complain." *Street Dad*. Kranky 057, 2002.

Parker, Junior. "Mystery Train." 1953. *The Blues*. Smithsonian/Sony RD101, 1993.

Pickett, Wilson. "Get Me Back on Time, Engine Number 9." 1970. *A Man and a Half: The Best of Wilson Pickett*. Rhino R2 70287, 1992.

Previte, Bobby. *Claude's Late Morning*. Gramavision 18-8811-2, 1988.

Quad City DJ's. "C'mon n' Ride It (The Train)." *Get on Up and Dance*. Atlantic/Big Beat 82905-2, 1996.

Rush, Otis. "So Many Roads, So Many Trains." 1960. *The Blues*. Smithsonian/Sony RD 101, 1993.

Schaeffer, Pierre. "Étude aux Chemins de Fer." 1946. *Early Modulations Vintage Volts*. Caipirinha CAI-2027, 1999.

Schmidt, Irmin, and Bruno Spoerri. "Rapido de Noir." *Toy Planet*. Spoon 011, 1990.

Slim, Lightnin'. "Mean Ol' Lonesome Train." 1956. *The Excello Story, Volume 2, 1955–1957*. Hip-O HIPD-40150, 1999.

Sun Ra. *The Futuristic Sounds of Sun Ra*. Aka *We Are in the Future*. 1961. Savoy SV-0213, 1993.

Tharpe, Sister Rosetta. "This Train." 1939. *The Original Soul Sister*. Properbox 51, 2002.

Thomas, Henry. "Ragtime Texas." "Railroadin' Some." 1929. *Night Train: Classic Railroad Songs, Volume 3*. Rounder 1144, 1998.

Thomas, Rufus. "Memphis Train." 1968. *The Complete Stax/Volt Singles: 1959–1968, Volume 9*. Atlantic 7-82218-2, 1991.

Walker, T-Bone. "Railroad Station Blues." 1953. *The Complete Imperial Recordings, 1950–1954*. EMI CDP-7-96737-2, 1991.

Williams, Marion. "The New Gospel Train." *Can't Keep It to Myself*. Spirit Feel/Shanachie 6007, 1993.

Wolf, Howlin'. "Smokestack Lightnin'." 1956. *The Chess Box*. Chess/MCA CHD3-9332, 1991.

Texts

Armstrong, Louis. *Satchmo: My Life in New Orleans*. 1954. Reprint, New York: Da Capo, 1986.

Baker, Houston. *Blues, Ideology, and Afro-American Literature: A Vernacular Theory*. Chicago: University of Chicago Press, 1984.

Baxandall, Michael. *Patterns of Intention: On the Historical Explanation of Pictures*. New Haven: Yale University Press, 1992.

Deleuze, Gilles, and Félix Guattari. *A Thousand Plateaus: Capitalism and Schizophrenia*. Trans. Brian Massumi. Minneapolis: University of Minnesota Press, 1987.

Eshun, Kodwo. *More Brilliant Than the Sun: Adventures in Sonic Fiction*. London: Quartet, 1999.

Gould, Glenn. "The Prospects of Recording." In *The Glenn Gould Reader*. Ed. Tim Page. New York: Random House, 1984. 331–53.

Lock, Graham. *Blutopia: Visions of the Future and Revisions of the Past in the Work of Sun Ra, Duke Ellington, and Anthony Braxton*. Durham, NC: Duke University Press, 1999.

Ong, Walter J. *Orality and Literacy: The Technologizing of the Word*. New York: Methuen, 1982.

Pollan, Michael. *The Botany of Desire: A Plant's-Eye View of the World*. New York: Random House, 2001.

Shapiro, Peter. "Automating the Beat: The Robotics of Rhythm." In *Undercurrents: The Hidden Wiring of Modern Music*. Ed. Rob Young. London: Continuum, 2002.132–39.

Szwed, John. *So What: The Life of Miles Davis*. New York: Simon & Schuster, 2002.

Ulmer, Gregory L. *Heuretics: The Logic of Invention*. Baltimore: Johns Hopkins University Press, 1994.

———. *Internet Invention: From Literacy to Electracy.* New York: Longman, 2003.

White, Hayden. *Metahistory: The Historical Imagination in Nineteenth-Century Europe*. Baltimore: Johns Hopkins University Press, 1972.

Videos

L'Arrivé d'un train en gare de La Ciotat. Prod. Bret Wood. Dir. Auguste and Louis Lumière, 1895. On *The Lumière Brothers' First Films*. Kino, 1996.

Rock & Roll. Senior prod. David Espar. Executive prod. Elizabeth Deane and Hugh Thomson. WGBH/BBC, 1995.

Web Sites

Jarrett, Michael. "Thriving on a Riff (Criss Cross Mix)." 18 June 2004. Available at www.yk.psu.edu/~jmj3/.

Lynch, Monica. WFMU. 30 April 2004. Available at www.wfmu.org/playlists/ML.

Rickels, Laurence. "I Was There: Talking with Michel Serres and Gregory Ulmer." Fall 1994. Available at http://proxy.arts.uci.edu/~nideffer/Tvc/interviews/21.Tvc.v9.intrvws.Ser_Ulm.html.

Ulmer, Gregory L. "*Seulemonde,* Conversation with Gregory Ulmer." Available at http://www.cas.usf.edu/journal/ulmer/ulmer.html.

Copyright Acknowledgments

Index